Two Years in the
French West Indies

Lost and Found Series

New editions of the best in travel writing—old and modern—from around the world

The Pilgrimage to Santiago by Edwin Mullins
Old Provence by Theodore Andrea Cook

Classic Travel
Writing

Two Years in the
French West Indies

Lafcadio Hearn

Interlink Books

An imprint of Interlink Publishing Group, Inc.
New York • Northampton

This edition first published in 2001 by

INTERLINK BOOKS
An imprint of Interlink Publishing Group, Inc.
46 Crosby Street, Northampton, Massachusetts 01060 and
99 Seventh Avenue, Brooklyn, New York 11215
www.interlinkbooks.com

First published 1890
Foreword © Raphaël Confiant, 2001

Library of Congress Cataloging-in-Publication Data
Hearn, Lafcadio, 1850-1904.
    Two years in the French West Indies / Lafcadio Hearn.
        p. cm. -- (Lost and found series)
Originally published: New York : Harper & Brothers, 1890.
Includes bibliographical references.
    ISBN 1-56656-370-4
  1. Martinique--Description and travel. 2. Hearn, Lafcadio,
1850-1904--Journeys--Martinique. I. Title II. Series.
    F2081 .H43 2001
    972.98'2--dc21   00-011340

Cover image: Paul Gauguin, *Coming and Going: Martinique,* courtesy
of the Carmen Thyssen-Bornemisza Collection, Madrid

Printed and bound in Canada

"La façon d'être du pays est si agréable, la température si bonne, et l'on y vit dans une liberté si honnête, que je n'aye pas vu un seul homme, ny une seule femme, qui en soient revenus, en qui je n'aye remarqué une grande passion d'y retourner."

The way of life in the country is so pleasant, the temperature so good, and one lives there in such a state of straightforward freedom, that I have never met one single man or woman of all those who came back therefrom in whom I have not remarked a most passionate desire to return thereunto.

Le Père Dutertre (1667)

À Mon Cher Ami

Léopold Arnoux

Notaire à Saint Pierre, Martinique

Souvenir de nos promenades,—de nos voyages,—de nos causeries,— des sympathies échangées,—de tout le charme d'une amitié inaltérable et inoubliable,—de tout ce qui parle à l'âme au doux Pays des Revenants.

A Martinique Métisse

Contents

Preface

DURING a trip to the Lesser Antilles in the summer of 1887, the writer of the following pages, landing at Martinique, fell under the influence of that singular spell which the island has always exercised upon strangers, and by which it has earned its poetic name,—*Le Pays des Revenants*. Even as many another before him, he left its charmed shores only to know himself haunted by that irresistible regret,—unlike any other,—which is the enchantment of the land upon all who wander away from it. So he returned, intending to remain some months; but the bewitchment prevailed, and he remained two years.

Some of the literary results of that sojourn form the bulk of the present volume. Several, or portions of several, papers have been published in *Harper's Magazine*; but the majority of the sketches now appear in print for the first time.

The introductory paper, entitled "A Midsummer Trip to the Tropics," consists for the most part of notes taken upon a voyage of nearly three thousand miles, accomplished in less than two months. During such hasty journeying it is scarcely possible for a writer to attempt anything more serious than a mere reflection of the personal experiences undergone; and, in spite of sundry justifiable departures from simple note-making, this paper is offered only as an effort to record the visual and emotional impressions of the moment.

My thanks are due to Mr. William Lawless, British Consul at St. Pierre, for several beautiful photographs, taken by himself, which have been used in the preparation of the illustrations.

Lafcadio Hearn
Philadelphia, 1889

Foreword

Lafcadio Hearn: The Magnificent Traveler

I shall not forget the day when I suddenly realized that Lafcadio Hearn was the first person to have truly understood—or more precisely, to have put into words—the reality of a tropical nightfall. An extraordinary achievement for the Anglo-Greek journalist-poet-folk researcher and diarist who visited my mother country Martinique at the end of the nineteenth century. Not only that, but his other great triumph was to have described this event in a way both precise and poetic. This revelation came to me at the end of an April day, during the dramatically short moment of time that we islanders generally hesitate to call "dusk". I was staring at the summit of Mont Pelée, that famous volcano which erupted in 1902 destroying the 30,000 inhabitants of St. Pierre, the former capital of Martinique. It was then that I noticed that the sky around it was extremely clear and bright. This aura had a charming gray-pink color—and even the flanks of the volcano were surrounded by a soft orange light that contrasted sharply with the massive folds of darkness that were settling over the land and the forest around me. In fact, the sky was still in daylight, whereas the earth had almost plunged into the mysterious arms of the tropical night.

At that moment, I remembered the strange lines I read three days before in Hearn's *Two Years in the French West Indies*. This was a book in which, pursuing my ecological interests, I had looked for the confirmation that in the nineteenth century the *courbaril* tree, a now rare and precious wood, was extremely common. I had never paid much attention to Hearn before, considering him as just one more European dandy in search of exotic charms and landscapes. I was making a big mistake. Let's listen to his description of Martinique's tropical night:

> In these tropic latitudes Night does not seem "to fall,"—to descend
> over the many-peaked land: it appears to rise up, like an exhalation,
> from the ground. The coast-lines darken first;—then the slopes and the
> lower hills and valleys become shadowed;—then, very swiftly, the
> gloom mounts to the heights, whose very loftiest peak may remain

glowing like a volcano at its tip for several minutes after the rest of the
island is veiled in blackness and all the stars are out...

After less than two years of living in Martinique, Lafcadio Hearn had
succeeded in penetrating one of the most jealously guarded secrets of our
ancient *quimboiseurs* (witch-doctors): that the secret spirits of the
countless thousands of Caribs and Africans who perished under
European colonization are still protecting us, the Creole people. These
spirits don't live in the skies like Christian ones, but remain asleep during
the day in the high branches of sacred trees such as the *fromager* (cotton-
silk tree). Only once the last rays of the sun begin to glimmer, do they
start roaming in the darkness that rapidly engulfs men, houses, animals
and fields. Lafcadio Hearn had the intuition of their presence and this is
why he paid so much attention to the Creole tales and legends that he
gathered from the mouths of old maids or venerable storytellers. This
magnificent traveler was sensitive to colors and sounds and the peculiar
way they shape our everyday lives in the Caribbean islands.

First the colors: he discovered that gray, blue, brown, violet and green
are not "cold colors" as classified by European artists. They do not express
sadness or melancholy in the tropical landscape, since they invent many
and multiform shades and hues at every hour (sometimes every minute) of
the day, giving you yellowish gray, bluish gray, reddish gray and so on. It
depends upon the trajectory of the sun and the wandering of the clouds. It
also depends upon where you are standing. From St. Pierre, for instance,
Mont Pelée may seem bluish green in the morning, whereas if you decide
to climb it at the very same moment and come closer to it, it seems to be
clad in a splendid velvet-green robe. And from the sea, it looks like a
gigantic blue pipe puffing lily-white clouds of smoke from time to time.

This is the way Lafcadio Hearn "painted" not only the volcano but
the markets, the streets, the sugar-cane plantations, the bays and, above
all, the women of Martinique. We are very far from that sort of
exoticism that insists on casting a foreign gaze upon the tropical world.
The famous French painter, Paul Gauguin, who spent a few months in
Martinique at around the same time as Hearn, did not escape this trap;
in his works, red and yellow, that is to say "hot colors" in the European
conception of landscape, are omnipresent, even if you rarely find them
in tropical nature. In fact, Hearn was a modern pagan (or pantheist), a
man who had an instinctive relationship with the various lands he
visited. He recognized the subtle links that unite the tropical
environment of Martinique and its Creole people.

Hearn also had an unusually fine ear for language and natural sounds. His unconscious mind had probably captured the Romany, Italian and Greek melodies his mother used to sing to him when a small child. He may have remembered, too, the Gaelic and English ballads his father, a military man, sang when he longed for his native land, although the young boy spent little time with his parents. His mixed origins had certainly prepared him to experience and confront the "diversity" of the world and its linguistic variety. This explains why Hearn immediately adored the Creole culture and language of New Orleans and, later, Martinique's French *patois* or Creole: a mixture of Carib, French and African languages. He wrote:

> *And the creole street-cries, uttered in a sonorous, far-reaching high key, interblend and produce random harmonies very pleasant to hear.*

Creoleness

What strikes me most in this third part of Hearn's life (the first part being his childhood in the small Greek island of Lefkas and later in Dublin and London; the second being his experience as a journalist in Cincinatti; the fourth and last part being his conversion to Japanese identity) is his ungovernable tendency to associate with black and mulatto people. Although he rapidly became one of the most brilliant and admired journalists of Cincinatti and later New Orleans, his first love was Mattie, a whimsical colored beauty whom he married at a time when interracial unions were banned. Moreover, he was fired from the Cincinatti newspaper, *The Enquirer*, when a group of individuals he used to attack mercilessly (Christian fundamentalists, politicians, etc.) discovered that he was living with such a "devil creature". He moved on to the capital of Louisiana, where he started to frequent the famous brothels of the "Vieux Carré", the French quarter, where black prostitutes abounded. Lafcadio Hearn had a tremendous appetite for what he himself defined as the "vital energy of the African race", its lack of hypocrisy, its glorification of the body and dancing. In his books about the West Indies, he never owns up to any relationship with a woman, but we may imagine that he did not remain untouched by the sensuality of the various phenotypes of mixed-race people he described so well:

> *A population fantastic, astonishing,—a population of the Arabian Nights. It is many-colored; but the general dominant tint is yellow, like that of the town itself—yellow in the interblending of all the hues characterizing*

mûlatresse, capresse, griffe, quarteronne, métisse, chabine,—a general effect of rich brownish yellow. You are among a people of half-breeds,— the finest mixed race of the West Indies.

Of course, Hearn was not totally free from the racial prejudices of his time (for example, he preferred mixed-race people to "pure" black ones) and was inevitably influenced by contemporary Eurocentric racial theorizing and discourse. Some of his observations are regrettably redolent of the conventional and banal racial attitudes in common currency. He also—quite erroneously—believed that most islanders were simple and naïve, but his actions, responses and his essentially loving descriptions were very often in contradiction with any such prejudice and racism.

A Multiple Identity

To end, I would like to insist upon the fact that Lafcadio Hearn, though largely ignored by historians of English and American literature, is one of the most modern writers of the second half of the nineteenth century. More than that, he displayed a visionary conception of personal identity since he was able, all through his short life (54 years), to draw upon his unusually mixed parental origins, but also to adopt, everywhere he went and temporarily settled, new ways of life as well as original conceptions of nature and God. Hearn invented what today we might call "multiple identity" or "creoleness"—that is to say the assumption in daily existence, throughout the most common of actions, of various cultural, racial, linguistic and religious components of oneself.

Hearn was very far from modern Anglo-Saxon "multiculturalism", which is often little more than just an agglomeration, a juxtaposition of different cultures (Chinatown, Little Italy, Black Ghetto, Wasp suburbs, Barrio Latino, etc.). This cultural model exists without real intermingling, without true synthesis and, above all, without questioning what each individual has inherited from family, neighborhood, city and country. Lafcadio Hearn, this magnificent traveler, taught us that identity is a changing, not a fixed or eternal reality, that it must mutate and embrace new influences and stimuli to remain alive. That humankind is capable of (re-)inventing itself day by day in the form of every individual on this planet.

Raphaël Confiant
Vauclin, Martinique, October 2000

A Midsummer Trip to the Tropics

I

... A LONG, narrow, graceful steel steamer, with two masts and an orange-yellow chimney,—taking on cargo at pier 49 East River. Through her yawning hatchways a mountainous piling up of barrels is visible below;—there is much rumbling and rattling of steam-winches, creaking of derrick-booms, groaning of pulleys as the freight is being lowered in. A breezeless July morning, and a dead heat,—87° already.

The saloon-deck gives one suggestion of past and of coming voyages. Under the white awnings long lounge-chairs sprawl here and there,—each with an occupant, smoking in silence, or dozing with head drooping to one side. A young man, awaking as I pass to my cabin, turns upon me a pair of peculiarly luminous black eyes,—creole eyes. Evidently a West Indian...

The morning is still gray, but the sun is dissolving the haze. Gradually the gray vanishes, and a beautiful, pale, vapory blue—a spiritualized Northern blue—colors water and sky. A cannon-shot suddenly shakes the heavy air: it is our farewell to the American shore;—we move. Back floats the wharf, and becomes vapory with a bluish tinge. Diaphanous mists seem to have caught the sky color; and even the great red storehouses take a faint blue tint as they recede. The horizon now has a greenish glow. Everywhere else the effect is that of looking through very light-blue glasses...

We steam under the colossal span of the mighty bridge; then for a little while Liberty towers above our passing,—seeming first to turn towards us, then to turn away from us, the solemn beauty of her passionless face of bronze. Tints brighten;—the heaven is growing a little bluer. A breeze springs up...

Then the water takes on another hue: pale-green lights play through it. It has begun to sound. Little waves lift up their heads as though to look at us,—patting the flanks of the vessel, and whispering to one another.

Far off the surface begins to show quick white flashes here and there, and the steamer begins to swing... We are nearing Atlantic waters. The sun is high up now, almost overhead: there are a few thin clouds in the tender-colored sky,—flossy, long-drawn-out, white things. The horizon has lost its greenish glow: it is a spectral blue. Masts, spars, rigging,—the white boats and the orange chimney,—the bright deck-lines, and the snowy rail,—cut against the colored light in almost dazzling relief. Though the sun shines hot the wind is cold: its strong irregular blowing fans one into drowsiness. Also the somnolent chant of the engines—*do-do, hey! do-do hey!*—lulls to sleep.

... Towards evening the glaucous sea-tint vanishes,—the water becomes blue. It is full of great flashes, as of seams opening and reclosing over a white surface. It spits spray in a ceaseless drizzle. Sometimes it reaches up and slaps the side of the steamer with a sound as of a great naked hand. The wind waxes boisterous. Swinging ends of cordage crack like whips. There is immense humming that drowns speech,—a humming made up of many sounds: whining of pulleys, whistling of riggings, flapping and fluttering of canvas, roar of nettings in the wind. And this sonorous medley, ever growing louder, has rhythm,—a *crescendo* and *diminuendo*, timed by the steamer's regular swinging: like a great Voice crying out, "Whoh-oh-oh! whoh-oh-oh!" We are nearing the life-centres of winds and currents. One can hardly walk on deck against the ever-increasing breath;—yet now the whole world is blue,—not the least cloud is visible; and the perfect transparency and voidness about us make the immense power of this invisible medium seem something ghostly and awful... The log, at every revolution, whines exactly like a little puppy;—one can hear it through all the roar fully forty feet away.

...It is nearly sunset. Across the whole circle of the Day we have been steaming south. Now the horizon is gold green. All about the falling sun, this gold-green light takes vast expansion... Right on the edge of the sea is a tall, gracious ship, sailing sunsetward. Catching the vapory fire, she seems to become a phantom,—a ship of gold mist: all her spars and sails are luminous, and look like things seen in dreams.

Crimsoning more and more, the sun drops to the sea. The phantom ship approaches him,—touches the curve of his glowing face, sails right athwart it! Oh, the spectral splendor of that vision! The whole great ship in full sail instantly makes an acute silhouette against the monstrous disk,—rests there in the very middle of the vermilion sun. His face crimsons high above her top-masts,—broadens far beyond helm and bowsprit. Against this weird magnificence, her whole shape changes color: hull, masts, and sails turn black—a greenish black.

Sun and ship vanish together in another minute. Violet the night comes; and the rigging of the foremast cuts a cross upon the face of the moon.

II

MORNING: the second day. The sea is an extraordinary blue,—looks to me something like violet ink. Close by the ship, where the foam-clouds are, it is beautifully mottled,—looks like blue marble with exquisite veinings and nebulosities... Tepid wind, and cottony white clouds,— cirri climbing up over the edge of the sea all around. The sky is still pale blue, and the horizon is full of a whitish haze.

...A nice old French gentleman from Guadeloupe presumes to say this is not blue water;—he declares it greenish (*verdâtre*). Because I cannot discern the green, he tells me I do not yet know what blue water is. *Attendez un peu!*...

...The sky-tone deepens as the sun ascends,—deepens deliciously. The warm wind proves soporific. I drop asleep with the blue light in my face,—the strong bright blue of the noonday sky. As I doze it seems to burn like a cold fire right through my eyelids. Waking up with a start, I fancy that everything is turning blue,—myself included. "Do you not call this the real tropical blue?" I cry to my French fellow-traveller. "*Mon Dieu! non,*" he exclaims, as in astonishment at the question;—"this is not blue!"... What can be *his* idea of blue, I wonder!

Clots of sargasso float by,—light-yellow sea-weed. We are nearing the Sargasso-sea,—entering the path of the trade-winds. There is a long ground-swell, the steamer rocks and rolls, and the tumbling water always seems to me growing bluer; but my friend from Guadeloupe says that this color "which I call blue" is only darkness—only the shadow of prodigious depth.

Nothing now but blue sky and what I persist in calling blue sea. The clouds have melted away in the bright glow. There is no sign of life in the azure gulf above, nor in the abyss beneath;—there are no wings or fins to be seen. Towards evening, under the slanting gold light, the color of the sea deepens into ultramarine; then the sun sinks down behind a bank of copper-colored cloud.

III

MORNING of the third day. Same mild, warm wind. Bright blue sky, with some very thin clouds in the horizon,—like puffs of steam. The glow of the sea-light through the open ports of my cabin makes them seem filled with thick blue glass... It is becoming too warm for New York clothing...

Certainly the sea has become much bluer. It gives one the idea of liquefied sky: the foam might be formed of cirrus clouds compressed,—so extravagantly white it looks today, like snow in the sun. Nevertheless, the old gentleman from Guadeloupe still maintains this is not the true blue of the tropics!

...The sky does not deepen its hue today: it brightens it;—the blue glows as if it were taking fire throughout. Perhaps the sea may deepen its hue;—I do not believe it can take more luminous color without being set aflame... I ask the ship's doctor whether it is really true that the West Indian waters are any bluer than these. He looks a moment at the sea, and replies, "*Oh* yes!" There is such a tone of surprise in his "oh" as might indicate that I had asked a very foolish question; and his look seems to express doubt whether I am quite in earnest... I think, nevertheless, that this water is extravagantly, nonsensically blue!

...I read for an hour or two; fall asleep in the chair; wake up suddenly; look at the sea,—and cry out! This sea is impossibly blue! The painter who should try to paint it would be denounced as a lunatic...Yet it is transparent; the foam-clouds, as they sink down, turn sky-blue,—a sky-blue which now looks white by contrast with the strange and violent splendor of the sea color. It seems as if one were looking into an immeasurable dyeing vat, or as though the whole ocean had been thickened with indigo. To say this is a mere reflection of the sky is nonsense!—the sky is too pale by a hundred shades for that! This must be the natural color of the water,—a blazing azure,—magnificent, impossible to describe.

The French passenger from Guadeloupe observes that the sea is "beginning to become blue."

IV

AND the fourth day. One awakens unspeakably lazy;—this must be the West Indian languor. Same sky with a few more bright clouds than yesterday;—always the warm wind blowing. There is a long swell. Under this trade-breeze, warm like a human breath, the ocean seems to pulse,—to rise and fall as with a vast inspiration and expiration. Alternately its blue circle lifts and falls before us and behind us;—we rise very high; we sink very low,—but always with a slow long motion.

Nevertheless the water *looks* smooth, perfectly smooth; the billowings which lift us cannot be seen;—it is because the summits of these swells are mile-broad,—too broad to he discerned from the level of our deck.

...Ten A.M.—Under the sun the sea is a flaming, dazzling lazulite. My French friend from Guadeloupe kindly confesses this is *almost* the color of tropical water...Weeds floating by, a little below the surface, are azured. But the Guadeloupe gentleman says he has seen water still more blue. I am sorry,—I cannot believe him.

Mid-day.—The splendor of the sky is weird! No clouds above—only blue fire! Up from the warm deep color of the sea-circle the edge of the heaven glows as if bathed in greenish flame. The swaying circle of the resplendent sea seems to flash its jewel-color to the zenith.

Clothing feels now almost too heavy to endure; and the warm wind brings a languor with it as of temptation... One feels an irresistible desire to drowse on deck;—the rushing speech of waves, the long rocking of the ship, the lukewarm caress of the wind, urge to slumber;—but the light is too vast to permit of sleep. Its blue power compels wakefulness. And the brain is wearied at last by this duplicated azure splendor of sky and sea. How gratefully comes the evening to us,—with violet glooms and promises of coolness!

All this sensuous blending of warmth and force in winds and waters more and more suggests an idea of the spiritualism of elements,—a sense of world-life. In all these soft sleepy swayings, these caresses of wind and sobbing of waters, Nature seems to confess some passional mood. Passengers converse of pleasant tempting things,—tropical fruits, tropical beverages, tropical mountain-breezes, tropical women... It is a time for dreams—those day-dreams that come gently as a mist, with ghostly realization of hopes, desires, ambitions... Men sailing to the mines of Guiana dream of gold.

The wind seems to grow continually warmer; the spray feels warm like blood. Awnings have to be clewed up, and wind-sails taken in;—still, there are no white-caps,—only the enormous swells, too broad to see, as the ocean falls and rises like a dreamer's breast...

The sunset comes with a great burning yellow glow, fading up through faint greens to lose itself in violet light;—there is no gloaming. The days have already become shorter... Through the open ports, as we lie down to sleep, comes a great whispering,—the whispering of the seas: sounds as of articulate speech under the breath, of women telling secrets...

V

FIFTH day out. Trade-winds from the south-east; a huge tumbling of mountain-purple waves;—the steamer careens under a full spread of canvas. There is a sense of spring in the wind today,—something that makes one think of the bourgeoning of Northern woods, when naked trees first cover themselves with a mist of tender green,—something that recalls the first bird-songs, the first climbings of sap to sun, and gives a sense of vital plenitude.

...Evening fills the west with aureate woolly clouds,—the wool of the Fleece of Gold. Then Hesperus beams like another moon, and the stars burn very brightly. Still the ship bends under the even pressure of the warm wind in her sails; and her wake becomes a trail of fire. Large sparks dash up through it continuously like an effervescence of flame;—and queer broad clouds of pale fire swirl by. Far out, where the water is black as pitch, there are no lights: it seems as if the steamer were only grinding out sparks with her keel, striking fire with her propeller.

VI

SIXTH day out. Wind tepid and still stronger, but sky very clear. An indigo sea, with beautiful white-caps. The ocean color is deepening: it is very rich now, but I think less wonderful than before;—it is an opulent pansy hue. Close by the ship it looks black-blue,—the color that bewitches in certain Celtic eyes.

There is a feverishness in the air;—the heat is growing heavy; the least exertion provokes perspiration; below-decks the air is like the air of an oven. Above-deck, however, the effect of all this light and heat is not altogether disagreeable;—one feels that vast elemental powers are near at hand, and that the blood is already aware of their approach.

All day the pure sky, the deepening of sea-color, the lukewarm wind. Then comes a superb sunset! There is a painting in the west wrought of cloud-colors,—a dream of high carmine cliffs and rocks outlying in a green sea, which lashes their bases with a foam of gold...

Even after dark the touch of the wind has the warmth of flesh. There is no moon; the sea-circle is black as Acheron; and our phosphor wake reappears quivering across it,—seeming to reach back to the very horizon. It is brighter tonight,—looks like another *Via Lactea*,—with points breaking through it like stars in a nebula. From our prow ripples rimmed with fire keep fleeing away to right and left into the night,—brightening as they run, then vanishing suddenly as if they had passed over a precipice. Crests of swells seem to burst into showers of sparks, and great patches of spume catch flame, smoulder through, and disappear... The Southern Cross is visible,—sloping backward and sidewise, as if propped against the vault of the sky: it is not readily discovered by the unfamiliarized eye; it is only after it has been well pointed out to you that you discern its position. Then you find it is only the *suggestion* of a cross—four stars set almost quadrangularly, some brighter than others.

For two days there has been little conversation on board. It may be due in part to the somnolent influence of the warm wind,—in part to the ceaseless booming of waters and roar of rigging, which drown men's voices; but I fancy it is much more due to the impressions of space and depth and vastness,—the impressions of sea and sky, which compel something akin to awe.

VII

MORNING over the Caribbean Sea,—a calm, extremely dark-blue sea. There are lands in sight,—high lands, with sharp, peaked, unfamiliar outlines.

We passed other lands in the darkness: they no doubt resembled the shapes towering up around us now; for these are evidently volcanic creations,—jagged, coned, truncated, eccentric. Far off they first looked a very pale gray; now, as the light increases, they change hue a little,—showing misty greens and smoky blues. They rise very sharply from the sea to great heights,—the highest point always with a cloud upon it;—they thrust out singular long spurs, push up mountain shapes that have an odd scooped-out look. Some, extremely far away, seem, as they catch the sun, to be made of gold vapor; others have a madderish tone: these are colors of cloud. The closer we approach them, the more do tints of green make themselves visible. Purplish or bluish masses of coast slowly develop green surfaces; folds and wrinkles of land turn brightly verdant. Still, the color gleams as through a thin fog.

...The first tropical visitor has just boarded our ship: a wonderful fly, shaped like a common fly, but at least five times larger. His body is a beautiful shining black; his wings seem ribbed and jointed with silver, his head is jewel-green, with exquisitely cut emeralds for eyes.

Islands pass and disappear behind us. The sun has now risen well; the sky is a rich blue, and the tardy moon still hangs in it. Lilac tones show through the water. In the south there are a few straggling small white clouds,—like a long flight of birds. A great gray mountain shape looms up before us. We are steaming on Santa Cruz.

The island has a true volcanic outline, sharp and high: the cliffs sheer down almost perpendicularly. The shape is still vapory, varying in coloring from purplish to bright gray; but wherever peaks and spurs fully catch the sun they edge themselves with a beautiful green glow, while interlying ravines seem filled with foggy blue.

As we approach, sunlighted surfaces come out still more luminously green. Glens and sheltered valleys still hold blues and grays; but points fairly illuminated by the solar glow show just such a fiery green as burns in the plumage of certain humming-birds. And just as the lustrous colors of these birds shift according to changes of light, so the island shifts colors here and there,—from emerald to blue, and blue to gray… But now we are near: it shows us a lovely heaping of high bright hills in front,—with a further coast-line very low and long and verdant, fringed with a white beach, and tufted with spidery palm-crests. Immediately opposite, other palms are poised; their trunks look like pillars of unpolished silver, their leaves shimmer like bronze.

…The water of the harbor is transparent and pale green. One can see many fish, and some small sharks. White butterflies are fluttering about us in the blue air. Naked black boys are bathing on the beach;—they swim well, but will not venture out far because of the sharks. A boat puts off to bring colored girls on board. They are tall, and not uncomely, although very dark;—they coax us, with all sorts of endearing words, to purchase bay rum, fruits, Florida water… We go ashore in boats. The water of the harbor has a slightly fetid odor.

VIII

VIEWED from the bay, under the green shadow of the hills overlooking it, Frederiksted has the appearance of a beautiful Spanish town, with its Romanesque piazzas, churches, many arched buildings peeping through breaks in a line of mahogany, bread-fruit, mango, tamarind, and palm trees,—an irregular mass of at least fifty different tints, from a fiery emerald to a sombre bluish-green. But on entering the streets the illusion of beauty passes: you find yourself in a crumbling, decaying town, with buildings only two stories high. The lower part, of arched Spanish design, is usually of lava rock or of brick painted a light, warm yellow; the upper stories are most commonly left unpainted, and are rudely constructed of light timber. There are many heavy arcades and courts opening on the streets with large archways. Lava blocks have been used in paving as well as in building; and more than one of the narrow streets, as it slopes up the hill through the great light, is seen to cut its way through craggy masses of volcanic stone.

But all the buildings look dilapidated; the stucco and paint is falling or peeling everywhere; there are fissures in the walls, crumbling façades, tumbling roofs. The first stories, built with solidity worthy of an earthquake region, seem extravagantly heavy by contrast with the frail wooden superstructures. One reason may be that the city was burned and sacked during a negro revolt in 1878;—the Spanish basements resisted the fire well, and it was found necessary to rebuild only the second stories of the buildings; but the work was done cheaply and flimsily, not massively and enduringly, as by the first colonial builders.

There is great wealth of verdure. Cabbage and cocoa palms overlook all the streets, bending above almost every structure, whether hut or public building;—everywhere you see the splitted green of banana leaves. In the court-yards you may occasionally catch sight of some splendid palm with silver-gray stem so barred as to look jointed, like the body of an annelid

In the market-place—a broad paved square, crossed by two rows of tamarind-trees, and bounded on one side by a Spanish piazza—you can study a spectacle of savage picturesqueness. There are no benches, no stalls, no booths; the dealers stand, sit, or squat upon the ground under the sun, or upon the steps of the neighbouring arcade. Their wares are piled up at their feet, for the most part. Some few have little tables, but as a rule the eatables are simply laid on the dusty ground or heaped upon the steps of the piazza—reddish-yellow mangoes, that look like great apples squeezed out of shape, bunches of bananas, pyramids of bright-green cocoanuts, immense golden-green oranges, and various other fruits and vegetables totally unfamiliar to Northern eyes... It is no use to ask questions—the black dealers speak no dialect comprehensible outside of the Antilles: it is a negro-English that sounds like some African tongue,—a rolling current of vowels and consonants, pouring so rapidly that the inexperienced ear cannot detach one intelligible word.

A friendly white coming up enabled me to learn one phrase: "Massa, youwancocknerfoobuy?" (Master, do you want to buy a cocoanut?)

The market is quite crowded,—full of bright color under the tremendous noon light. Buyers and dealers are generally black;—very few yellow or brown people are visible in the gathering. The greater number present are women; they are very simply, almost savagely, garbed—only a skirt or petticoat, over which is worn a sort of calico short dress, which scarcely descends two inches below the hips, and is confined about the waist with a belt or a string. The skirt bells out like the skirt of a dancer, leaving the feet and bare legs well exposed; and the head is covered with a white handkerchief, twisted so as to look like a turban. Multitudes of these bare-legged black women are walking past us,—carrying bundles or baskets upon their heads, and smoking very long cigars.

They are generally short and thick-set, and walk with surprising erectness, and with long, firm steps, carrying the bosom well forward. Their limbs are strong and finely rounded. Whether walking or standing, their poise is admirable,—might be called graceful, were it not for the absence of real grace of form in such compact, powerful little figures. All wear brightly colored cottonade stuffs, and the general effect of the costume in a large gathering is very agreeable, the dominant hues being pink, white, and blue. Half the women are smoking. All chatter loudly, speaking their English jargon with a pitch of voice totally unlike the English timbre: it sometimes sounds as if they were trying to pronounce English rapidly according to French pronunciation and pitch of voice.

These green oranges have a delicious scent and amazing juiciness. Peeling one of them is sufficient to perfume the skin of the hands for the rest of the day, however often one may use soap and water... We smoke Porto Rico cigars, and drink West Indian lemonades strongly flavored with rum. The tobacco has a rich, sweet taste; the rum is velvety, sugary, with a pleasant, soothing effect: both have a rich aroma. There is a wholesome originality about the flavor of these products, a uniqueness which certifies to their naif purity: something as opulent and frank as the juices and odors of tropical fruits and flowers.

The streets leading from the plaza glare violently in the strong sunlight;—the ground, almost dead-white, dazzles the eyes... There are few comely faces visible,—in the streets all are black who pass. But through open shop-doors one occasionally catches glimpses of a pretty quadroon face,—with immense black eyes,—a face yellow like a ripe banana.

...It is now after mid-day. Looking up to the hills, or along sloping streets towards the shore, wonderful variations of foliage-color meet the eye: gold-greens, sap-greens, bluish and metallic greens of many tints, reddish-greens, yellowish-greens. The cane-fields are broad sheets of beautiful gold-green; and nearly as bright are the masses of *pomme-cannelle* frondescence, the groves of lemon and orange; while tamarind and mahoganies are heavily sombre. Everywhere palm-crests soar above the wood-lines, and tremble with a metallic shimmering in the blue light. Up through a ponderous thickness of tamarind rises the spire of the church; a skeleton of open stone-work, without glasses or lattices or shutters of any sort for its naked apertures: it is all open to the winds of heaven; it seems to be gasping with all its granite mouths for breath—panting in this azure heat. In the bay the water looks greener than ever: it is so clear that the light passes under every boat and ship to the very bottom; the vessels only cast very thin green shadows,—so transparent that fish can be distinctly seen passing through from sunlight to sunlight.

The sunset offers a splendid spectacle of pure color; there is only an immense yellow glow in the west,—a lemon-colored blaze; but when it melts into the blue there is an exquisite green light... We leave tomorrow.

...Morning: the green hills are looming in a bluish vapor: the long faint-yellow slope of beach to the left of the town, under the mangoes and tamarinds, is already thronged with bathers,—all men or boys, and all naked: black, brown, yellow, and white. The white bathers are Danish soldiers from the barracks; the Northern brightness of their skins forms an almost startling contrast with the deep colors of the nature about them, and with the dark complexions of the natives. Some very slender, graceful brown lads are bathing with them,—lightly built as deer: these are probably creoles. Some of the black bathers are clumsy-looking, and have astonishingly long legs... Then little boys come down, leading horses;—they strip, leap naked on the animals' backs, and ride into the sea,—yelling, screaming, splashing, in the morning light. Some are a fine brown color, like old bronze. Nothing could be more statuesque than the unconscious attitudes of these bronze bodies in leaping, wrestling, running, pitching shells. Their simple grace is in admirable harmony with that of Nature's green creations about them,—rhymes faultlessly with the perfect self-balance of the palms that poise along the shore...

Boom! and a thunder-rolling of echoes. We move slowly out of the harbor, then swiftly towards the south-east... The island seems to turn slowly half round; then to retreat from us. Across our way appears a long band of green light, reaching over the sea like a thin protraction of color from the extended spur of verdure in which the western end of the island terminates. That is a sunken reef, and a dangerous one. Lying high upon it, in very sharp relief against the blue light, is a wrecked vessel on her beam-ends,—the carcass of a brig. Her decks have been broken in; the roofs of her cabins are gone; her masts are splintered off short; her empty hold yawns naked to the sun; all her upper parts have taken a yellowish-white color,—the color of sun-bleached bone.

Behind us the mountains still float back. Their shining green has changed to a less vivid hue; they are taking bluish tones here and there; but their outlines are still sharp, and along their high soft slopes there are white specklings, which are villages and towns. These white specks diminish swiftly,—dwindle to the dimensions of salt-grains,—finally vanish. Then the island grows uniformly bluish; it becomes cloudy, vague as a dream of mountains;—it turns at last gray as smoke, and then melts into the horizon-light like a mirage.

Another yellow sunset, made weird by extraordinary black, dense, fantastic shapes of cloud. Night darkens, and again the Southern Cross glimmers before our prow, and then the two Milky Ways reveal themselves,—that of the Cosmos and that ghostlier one which stretches over the black deep behind us. This alternately broadens and narrows at regular intervals, concomitantly with the rhythmical swing of the steamer. Before us the bows spout fire; behind us there is a flaming and roaring as of Phlegethon; and the voices of wind and sea become so loud that we cannot talk to one another,—cannot make our words heard even by shouting.

IX

EARLY morning: the eighth day. Moored in another blue harbor,—a great semicircular basin, bounded by a high billowing of hills all green from the fringe of yellow beach up to their loftiest clouded summit. The land has that up-tossed look which tells a volcanic origin. There are curiously scalloped heights, which, though emerald from base to crest, still retain all the physiognomy of volcanoes: their ribbed sides must be lava under that verdure. Out of sight westward—in successions of bright green, pale green, bluish-green, and vapory gray—stretches a long chain of crater shapes. Truncated, jagged, or rounded, all these elevations are interunited by their curving hollows of land or by filaments,—very low valleys. And as they grade away in varying color through distance, these hill-chains take a curious segmented, jointed appearance, like insect forms, enormous ant-bodies... This is St. Kitt's.

We row ashore over a tossing dark-blue water, and leaving the long wharf, pass under a great arch and over a sort of bridge into the town of Basse-Terre, through a concourse of brown and black people.

It is very tropical-looking; but more sombre than Frederiksted. There are palms everywhere,—cocoa, fan, and cabbage palms; many bread-fruit trees, tamarinds, bananas, Indian fig-trees, mangoes and unfamiliar things the negroes call by incomprehensible names,—"sap-saps," "dhool-dhools." But there is less color, less reflection of light than in Santa Cruz; there is less quaintness; no Spanish buildings, no canary-colored arcades. All the narrow streets are gray or neutral-tinted; the ground has a dark ashen tone. Most of the dwellings are timber, resting on brick props, or elevated upon blocks of lava rock. It seems almost as if some breath from the enormous and always clouded mountain overlooking the town had begrimed everything, darkening even the colors of vegetation.

The population is not picturesque. The costumes are commonplace; the tints of the women's attire are dull. Browns and sombre blues and grays are commoner than pinks, yellows, and violets. Occasionally you observe a fine half-breed type—some tall brown girl walking by with a swaying grace like that of a sloop at sea;—but such spectacles are not frequent. Most of those you meet are black or a blackish brown. Many stores are kept by yellow men with intensely black hair and eyes,—men who do not smile. These are Portuguese. There are some few fine buildings; but the most pleasing sight the little town can offer the visitor is the pretty Botanical Garden, with its banyans and its palms, its monstrous lilies and extraordinary fruit-trees, and its beautiful little fountains. From some of these trees a peculiar tillandsia streams down, much like our Spanish moss,—but it is black!

...As we move away southwardly, the receding outlines of the island look more and more volcanic. A chain of hills and cones, all very green, and connected by strips of valley-land so low that the edge of the sea-circle on the other side of the island can be seen through the gaps. We steam past truncated hills, past heights that have the look of the stumps of peaks cut half down,—ancient fire-mouths choked by tropical verdure.

Southward, above and beyond the deep-green chain, tower other volcanic forms,—very far away, and so pale-gray as to seem like clouds.

Those are the heights of Nevis,—another creation of the subterranean fires.

It draws nearer, floats steadily into definition: a great mountain flanked by two small ones; three summits; the loftiest, with clouds packed high upon it, still seems to smoke;—the second highest displays the most symmetrical crater-form I have yet seen. All are still grayish-blue or gray. Gradually through the blues break long high gleams of green.

As we steam closer, the island becomes all verdant from flood to sky; the great dead crater shows its immense wreath of perennial green. On the lower slopes little settlements are sprinkled in white, red, and brown: houses, windmills, sugar-factories, high chimneys are distinguishable;—cane-plantations unfold gold-green surfaces.

We pass away. The island does not seem to sink behind us, but to become a ghost. All its outlines grow shadowy. For a little while it continues green;—but it is a hazy, spectral green, as of colored vapor. The sea today looks almost black: the south-west wind has filled the day with luminous mist; and the phantom of Nevis melts in the vast glow, dissolves utterly... Once more we are out of sight of land,—in the centre of a blue-black circle of sea. The water-line cuts blackly against the immense light of the horizon,—a huge white glory that flames up very high before it fades and melts into the eternal blue.

X

THEN a high white shape like a cloud appears before us,—on the purplish-dark edge of the sea. The cloud-shape enlarges, heightens without changing contour. It is not a cloud, but an island! Its outlines begin to sharpen,—with faintest pencillings of color. Shadowy valleys appear, spectral hollows, phantom slopes of pallid blue or green. The apparition is so like a mirage that it is difficult to persuade oneself one is looking at real land,—that it is not a dream. It seems to have shaped itself all suddenly out of the glowing haze. We pass many miles beyond it; and it vanishes into mist again.

...Another and a larger ghost; but we steam straight upon it until it materializes,—Montserrat. It bears a family likeness to the islands we have already passed—one dominant height, with massing of bright crater shapes about it, and ranges of green hills linked together by low valleys. About its highest summit also hovers a flock of clouds. At the foot of the vast hill nestles the little white and red town of Plymouth. The single salute of our gun is answered by a stupendous broadside of echoes.

Plymouth is more than half hidden in the rich foliage that fringes the wonderfully wrinkled green of the hills at their base;—it has a curtain of palms before it. Approaching, you discern only one or two façades above the sea-wall, and the long wharf projecting through an opening in the masonry, over which young palms stand thick as canes on a sugar plantation. But on reaching the street that descends towards the heavily bowldered shore you find yourself in a delightfully drowsy little burgh,—a miniature tropical town,—with very narrow paved ways,—steep, irregular, full of odd curves and angles,—and likewise of tiny courts everywhere sending up jets of palm-plumes, or displaying above their stone enclosures great candelabra-shapes of cacti. All is old-fashioned and quiet and queer and small. Even the palms are diminutive,—slim and delicate; there is a something in their poise and slenderness like the charm of young girls who have not yet ceased to be children, though soon to become women...

There is a glorious sunset,—a fervid orange splendor, shading starward into delicate roses and greens. Then black boatmen come astern and quarrel furiously for the privilege of carrying one passenger ashore; and as they scream and gesticulate, half naked, their silhouettes against the sunset seem forms of great black apes.

...Under steam and sail we are making south again, a warm wind blowing south-east,—a wind very moist, powerful, and soporific. Facing it, one feels almost cool; but the moment one is sheltered from it profuse perspiration bursts out. The ship rocks over immense swells; night falls very blackly; and there are surprising displays of phosphorescence.

XI

...MORNING. A gold sunrise over an indigo sea. The wind is a great warm caress; the sky a spotless blue. We are steaming on Dominica,—the loftiest of the lesser Antilles. While the silhouette is yet all violet in distance, nothing more solemnly beautiful can well be imagined: a vast cathedral shape, whose spires are mountain peaks, towering in the horizon, sheer up from the sea.

We stay at Roseau only long enough to land the mails, and wonder at the loveliness of the island. A beautifully wrinkled mass of green and blue and gray;—a strangely abrupt peaking and heaping of the land.

Behind the green heights loom the blues; behind these the grays—all pinnacled against the sky-glow—thrusting up through gaps or behind promontories. Indescribably exquisite the foldings and hollowings of the emerald coast. In glen and vale the color of cane-fields shines like a pooling of fluid bronze, as if the luminous essence of the hill tints had been dripping down and clarifying there. Far to our left, a bright green spur pierces into the now turquoise sea; and beyond it, a beautiful mountain form, blue and curved like a hip, slopes seaward, showing lighted wrinkles here and there, of green. And from the foreground, against the blue of the softly outlined shape, cocoa-palms are curving,—all sharp and shining in the sun.

…Another hour; and Martinique looms before us. At first it appears all gray, a vapory gray; then it becomes bluish-gray; then all green.

It is another of the beautiful volcanic family: it owns the same hill shapes with which we have already become acquainted; its uppermost height is hooded with the familiar cloud; we see the same gold-yellow plains, the same wonderful varieties of verdancy, the same long green spurs reaching out into the sea,—doubtless formed by old lava torrents. But all this is now repeated for us more imposingly, more grandiosely;—it is wrought upon a larger scale than anything we have yet seen. The semicircular sweep of the harbor, dominated by the eternally veiled summit of the Montagne Pelée (misnamed, since it is green to the very clouds), from which the land slopes down on either hand to the sea by gigantic undulations, is one of the fairest sights that human eye can gaze upon. Thus viewed, the whole island shape is a mass of green, with purplish streaks and shadowings here and there: glooms of forest-hollows, or moving umbrages of cloud. The city of St. Pierre, on the edge of the land, looks as if it had slided down the hill behind it, so strangely do the streets come tumbling to the port in cascades of masonry,—with a red billowing of tiled roofs over all, and enormous palms poking up through it,—higher even than the creamy white twin towers of its cathedral.

We anchor in limpid blue water; the cannon-shot is answered by a prolonged thunder-clapping of mountain echo.

Then from the shore a curious flotilla bears down upon us. There is one boat, two or three canoes; but the bulk of the craft are simply wooden frames,—flat-bottomed structures, made from shipping-cases or lard-boxes, with triangular ends. In these sit naked boys,—boys between ten and fourteen years of age,—varying in color from a fine clear yellow to a deep reddish-brown or chocolate tint. They row with two little square, flat pieces of wood for paddles, clutched in each hand; and these lid-shaped things are dipped into the water on either side with absolute precision, in perfect time,—all the pairs of little naked arms seeming moved by a single impulse. There is much unconscious grace in this paddling, as well as skill. Then all about the ship these ridiculous little boats begin to describe circles,—crossing and inter-crossing so closely as almost to bring them into collision, yet never touching. The boys have simply come out to dive for coins they expect passengers to fling to them. All are chattering creole, laughing and screaming shrilly; every eye, quick and bright as a bird's, watches the faces of the passengers on deck. "'Tention-là!" shriek a dozen soprani. Some passenger's fingers have entered his vest-pocket, and the boys are on the alert. Through the air, twirling and glittering, tumbles an English shilling, and drops into the deep water beyond the little fleet. Instantly all the lads leap, scramble, topple head-foremost out of their little tubs, and dive in pursuit. In the blue water their lithe figures look perfectly red,—all but the soles of their upturned feet, which show nearly white. Almost immediately they all rise again: one holds up at arm's-length above the water the recovered coin, and then puts it into his mouth for safe-keeping. Coin after coin is thrown in, and as speedily brought up; a shower of small silver follows, and not a piece is lost. These lads move through the water without apparent effort, with the suppleness of fishes. Most are decidedly fine-looking boys, with admirably rounded limbs, delicately formed extremities. The best diver and swiftest swimmer, however, is a red lad;—his face is rather commonplace, but his slim body has the grace of an antique bronze.

...We are ashore in St. Pierre, the quaintest, queerest, and the prettiest withal, among West Indian cities: all stone-built and stone-flagged, with very narrow streets, wooden or zinc awnings, and peaked roofs of red tile, pierced by gabled dormers. Most of the buildings are painted in a clear yellow tone, which contrasts delightfully with the burning blue ribbon of tropical sky above; and no street is absolutely level; nearly all of them climb hills, descend into hollows, curve, twist, describe sudden angles. There is everywhere a loud murmur of running water,—pouring through the deep gutters contrived between the paved thoroughfare and the absurd little sidewalks, varying in width from one to three feet. The architecture is quite old: it is seventeenth century, probably; and it reminds one a great deal of that characterizing the

La Place Bertin (The Sugar Landing), St. Pierre, Martinique

antiquated French quarter of New Orleans. All the tints, the forms, the vistas, would seem to have been especially selected or designed for aquarelle studies,—just to please the whim of some extravagant artist. The windows are frameless openings without glass; some have iron bars; all have heavy wooden shutters with movable slats, through which light and air can enter as through Venetian blinds. These are usually painted green or bright bluish-gray.

So steep are the streets descending to the harbor,—by flights of old mossy stone steps,—that looking down them to the azure water you have the sensation of gazing from a cliff. From certain openings in the main street—the Rue Victor Hugo—you can get something like a bird's-eye view of the harbor with its shipping. The roofs of the street below are under your feet, and other streets are rising behind you to meet the mountain roads. They climb at a very steep angle, occasionally breaking into stairs of lava rock, all grass-tufted and moss-lined.

The town has an aspect of great solidity: it is a creation of crag—looks almost as if it had been hewn out of one mountain fragment, instead of having been constructed stone by stone. Although commonly consisting of two stories and an attic only, the dwellings have walls three feet in thickness;—on one street, facing the sea, they are even heavier, and slope outward like ramparts, so that the perpendicular recesses of windows and doors have the appearance of being opened between buttresses. It may have been partly as a precaution against earthquakes, and partly for the sake of coolness, that the early colonial architects built thus;—giving the city a physiognomy so well worthy of its name,—the name of the Saint of the Rock.

And everywhere rushes mountain water,—cool and crystal clear, washing the streets;—from time to time you come to some public fountain flinging a silvery column to the sun, or showering bright spray over a group of black bronze tritons or bronze swans. The Tritons on the Place Bertin you will not readily forget;—their curving torsos might have been modelled from the forms of those ebon men who toil there tirelessly all day in the great heat, rolling hogsheads of sugar or casks of rum. And often you will note, in the course of a walk, little drinking-fountains contrived at the angle of a building, or in the thick walls bordering the bulwarks or enclosing public squares: glittering threads of water spurting through lion-lips of stone. Some mountain torrent, skilfully directed and divided, is thus perpetually refreshing the city,—supplying its fountains and cooling its courts... This is called the Gouyave water: it is not the same stream which sweeps and purifies the streets.

Picturesqueness and color: these are the particular and the unrivalled charms of St. Pierre. As you pursue the Grande Rue, or Rue Victor Hugo,—which traverses the town through all its length, undulating over hill-slopes and into hollows and over a bridge,—you become more and more enchanted by the contrast of the yellow-glowing walls to right and left with the jagged strip of gentian-blue sky overhead. Charming also it is to watch the cross-streets climbing up to the fiery green of the mountains behind the town. On the lower side of the main thoroughfare other streets open in wonderful bursts of blue—warm blue of horizon and sea. The steps by which these ways descend towards the bay are black with age, and slightly mossed close to the wall on either side: they have an alarming steepness,—one might easily stumble from the upper into the lower street. Looking towards the water through these openings from the Grande Rue, you will notice that the sea-line cuts across the blue space just at the level of the upper story of the house on the lower street-corner. Sometimes, a hundred feet below, you see a ship resting in the azure aperture,—seemingly suspended there in sky-color, floating in blue light. And everywhere and always, through sunshine or shadow, comes to you the scent of the city,—the characteristic odor of St. Pierre;—a compound odor suggesting the intermingling of sugar and garlic in those strange tropical dishes which creoles love...

XII

A POPULATION fantastic, astonishing,—a population of the Arabian Nights. It is many-colored; but the general dominant tint is yellow, like that of the town itself—yellow in the interblending of all the hues characterizing *mulâtresse, capresse, griffe, quarteronne, métisse, chabine,*— a general effect of rich brownish yellow. You are among a people of half-breeds,—the finest mixed race of the West Indies.

Straight as palms, and supple and tall, these colored women and men impress one powerfully by their dignified carriage and easy elegance of movement. They walk without swinging of the shoulders;—the perfectly set torso seems to remain rigid; yet the step is a long full stride, and the whole weight is springily poised on the very tip of the bare foot. All, or nearly all, are without shoes: the treading of many naked feet over the heated pavement makes a continuous whispering sound.

...Perhaps the most novel impression of all is that produced by the singularity and brilliancy of certain of women's costumes. These were developed, at least a hundred years ago, by some curious sumptuary law regulating the dress of slaves and colored people of free condition,—a law which allowed considerable liberty as to material and tint, prescribing chiefly form. But some of these fashions suggest the Orient: they offer beautiful audacities of color contrast; and the full-dress coiffure, above all, is so strikingly Eastern that one might be tempted to believe it was first introduced into the colony by some Mohammedan slave. It is merely an immense Madras handkerchief, which is folded about the head with admirable art, like a turban;—one bright end pushed through at the top in front, being left sticking up like a plume. Then this turban, always full of bright canary-color, is fastened with golden brooches,—one in front and one at either side. As for the remainder of the dress, it is simple enough: an embroidered, low-cut chemise with sleeves; a skirt or *jupe*, very long behind, but caught up and fastened in front below the breasts so as to bring the hem everywhere to a level with the end of the long chemise; and finally a *foulard*, or silken kerchief, thrown over the shoulders. These *jupes* and *foulards*, however, are exquisite in pattern and color: bright crimson, bright yellow, bright blue, bright green,—lilac, violet, rose,—sometimes mingled in plaidings or checkerings or stripings: black with orange, sky-blue with purple. And whatever be the colors of the costume, which vary astonishingly, the coiffure must be yellow— brilliant, flashing yellow: the turban is certain to have yellow stripes or yellow squares. To this display add the effect of costly and curious jewellery: immense ear-rings, each pendant being formed of five gold cylinders joined together (cylinders sometimes two inches long, and an inch at least in circumference);—a necklace of double, triple, quadruple, or quintuple rows of large hollow gold beads (sometimes smooth, but generally graven)—the wonderful *collier-choux*. Now, this glowing jewellery is not a mere imitation of pure metal: the ear-rings are worth one hundred and seventy-five francs a pair; the necklace of a Martinique quadroon may cost five hundred or even one thousand francs... It may be the gift of her lover, her *doudoux*; but such articles are usually purchased either on time by small payments, or bead by bead singly until the requisite number is made up.

But few are thus richly attired: the greater number of the women carrying burdens on their heads,—peddling vegetables, cakes, fruit, ready-cooked food, from door to door,—are very simply dressed in a single plain robe of vivid colors (*douillette*) reaching from neck to feet, and made with a train, but generally girded well up so as to sit close to the figure and leave the lower limbs partly bare and perfectly free. These women can walk all day long up and down hill in the hot sun, without shoes, carrying loads of from one hundred to one hundred and fifty pounds on their heads; and if their little stock sometimes fails to come up to the accustomed weight stones are added to make it heavy enough. Doubtless the habit of carrying everything in this way from childhood has much to do with the remarkable vigor and erectness of the population... I have seen a grand piano carried on the heads of four men. With the women the load is very seldom steadied with the hand after having been once placed in position. The head remains almost motionless; but the black, quick, piercing eyes flash into every window and door-way to watch for a customer's signal. And the creole street-cries, uttered in a sonorous, far-reaching high key, interblend and produce random harmonies very pleasant to hear.

...*" 'Çé moune-là, ça qui lè bel mango?"* Her basket of mangoes certainly weighs as much as herself... *"Ça qui lè bel avocat?"* The alligator-pear—cuts and tastes like beautiful green cheese... *"Ça qui lè escargot?"* Call her, if you like snails... *"Ça qui lè titiri?"* Minuscule fish, of which a thousand would scarcely fill a tea-cup;—one of the most delicate of Martinique dishes... "*Ça qui lè cannà?—Ça qui lè charbon?— Ça qui lè di pain aubè?*" (Who wants ducks, charcoal, or pretty little loaves shaped like cucumbers.)... "*Ça qui lè pain-mi?*" A sweet maize cake in the form of a tiny sugar-loaf, wrapped in a piece of banana leaf... "*Ça qui lè fromassé*" (*pharmacie*) "*lapotécai créole?*" She deals in creole roots and herbs, and all the leaves that make *tisanes* or poultices or medicines: *matriquin, feuill-corossol, balai-doux, manioc-chapelle, Marie-Perrine, graine-enba-feuill, bois-d'lhomme, zhèbe-gras, bonnet-carré, zhèbe-codeinne, zhèbe-à-femme, zhèbe-à-chatte, canne-dleau, poque, fleu-papillon, lateigne,* and a score of others you never saw or heard of before... "*Ça qui lè dicaments?*" (overalls for laboring-men)... "*Çé moune-là, si ou pa lè acheté canari-à dans lanmain moin, moin ké crazé y.*" The vender of red clay cooking-pots;—she has only one left, if you do not buy it she will break it!

"*Hé! zenfants-là!—en dehò!*" Run out to meet her, little children, if you like the sweet rice-cakes... "*Hé! gens pa' enho', gens pa' enbas, gens di galtas, moin ni bel gououôs poisson!*" Ho! people upstairs, people downstairs, and all ye good folks who dwell in the attics,—know that she has very big and very beautiful fish to sell!... "*Hé! ça qui lè mangé yonne?*"— those are "akras,"—flat yellow-brown cakes, made of pounded codfish, or beans, or both, seasoned with pepper and fried in butter... And then comes the pastry-seller, black as ebony, but dressed all in white, and white-aproned and white-capped like a French cook, and chanting half in French, half in creole, with a voice like a clarinet:

"*C'est louvouier de la pâtisserie qui passe,*
Qui té ka veillé pou' gagner son existence,
Toujours content,
Toujours joyeux.
Oh, qu'ils sont bons!—
Oh, qu'ils sont doux!"

It is the pastryman passing by, who has been up all night to gain his livelihood,—always content,—always happy... Oh, how good they are (the pies)!—Oh, how sweet they are!

The quaint stores bordering both sides of the street bear no names and no signs over their huge arched doors;—you must look well inside to know what business is being done. Even then you will scarcely be able to satisfy yourself as to the nature of the commerce;—for they are selling gridirons and frying-pans in the dry goods stores, holy images and

Itinerant Pastry-Seller — "Toujours content, toujours joyeux"

rosaries in the notion stores, sweet-cakes and confectionery in the crockery stores, coffee and stationery in the millinery stores, cigars and tobacco in the china stores, cravats and laces and ribbons in the jewellery stores, sugar and guava jelly in the tobacco stores! But of all the objects exposed for sale the most attractive, because the most exotic, is a doll,—the Martinique *poupée*. There are two kinds,—the *poupée-capresse*, of which the body is covered with smooth reddish-brown leather, to imitate the tint of the *capresse* race; and the *poupée-négresse*, covered with black leather. When dressed, these dolls range in price from eleven to thirty-five francs,—some, dressed to order, may cost even more; and a good *poupée-capresse* is a delightful curiosity. Both varieties of dolls are attired in the costume of the people; but the *négresse* is usually dressed the more simply. Each doll has a broidered chemise, a tastefully arranged *jupe* of bright hues, a silk *foulard*, a *collier-choux*, ear-rings of five cylinders (*zanneaux-à-clous*), and a charming little yellow-banded Madras turban. Such a doll is a perfect costume-model,—a perfect miniature of Martinique fashions, to the smallest details of material and color: it is almost too artistic for a toy.

These old costume-colors of Martinique—always relieved by brilliant yellow stripings or checkerings, except in the special violet dresses worn on certain religious occasions—have an indescribable luminosity,—a wonderful power of bringing out the fine warm tints of this tropical flesh. Such are the hues of those rich costumes Nature gives to her nearest of kin and her dearest,—her honey-lovers—her insects: these are wasp-colors. I do not know whether the fact ever occurred to the childish fancy of this strange race; but there is a creole expression which first suggested it to me;—in the patois, *pouend guêpe*, "to catch a wasp," signifies making love to a pretty colored girl... And the more one observes these costumes, the more one feels that only Nature could have taught such rare comprehension of powers and harmonies among colors,—such knowledge of chromatic witchcrafts and chromatic laws.

This evening, as I write, La Pelée is more heavily coiffed than is her wont. Of purple and lilac cloud the coiffure is,—a magnificent Madras, yellow-banded by the sinking sun. La Pelée is in *costume de fête*, like a *capresse* attired for a baptism or a ball; and in her phantom turban one great star glimmers for a brooch.

XIII

FOLLOWING the Rue Victor Hugo in the direction of the Fort,—crossing the Rivière Roxelane, or Rivière des Blanchisseuses, whose rocky bed is white with unsoaped linen far as the eye can each,—you descend through some tortuous narrow streets into the principal marketplace.[1] A square—well paved and well shaded—with a fountain in the midst. Here the dealers are seated in rows;—one half of the market is devoted to fruits and vegetables; the other to the sale of fresh fish and meats. On first entering you are confused by the press and deafened by the storm of creole chatter;—then you begin to discern some order in this chaos, and to observe curious things.

In the middle of the paved square, about the market fountain, are lying boats filled with fish, which have been carried up from the water upon men's shoulders,—or, if very heavy, conveyed on rollers... Such fish!—blue, rosy, green, lilac, scarlet, gold: no spectral tints these, but luminous and strong like fire. Here also you see heaps of long thin fish looking like piled bars of silver,—absolutely dazzling,—of almost equal thickness from head to tail;—near by are heaps of flat pink creatures;— beyond these, again, a mass of azure backs and golden bellies. Among the stalls you can study the monsters,—twelve or fifteen feet long,—the shark, the *vierge*, the sword-fish, the *tonne*;—or the eccentricities. Some are very thin round disks, with long, brilliant, wormy feelers in lieu of fins, flickering in all directions like a moving pendent silver fringe;— others bristle with spines;—others, serpent-bodied, are so speckled as to resemble shapes of red polished granite. These are *moringues*. The *balaou, couliou, macriau, tazard, tcha-tcha, bonnique,* and *zorphi* severally represent almost all possible tints of blue and violet. The *souri* is rose-color and yellow; the *cirurgien* is black, with yellow and red stripes; the *patate*, black and yellow; the *gros-zié* is vermilion; the *couronné*, red and black. Their names are not less unfamiliar than their shapes and tints;—the *aiguille-de-mer*, or sea-needle, long and thin as a pencil;—the *Bon-Dié-manié-moin* ("the Good-God handled me"), which has something like finger-marks upon it;—the *lambi*, a huge sea-snail;—the *pisquette*, the *laline* (the Moon);—the *crapaud-de-mer*, or sea-toad, with a dangerous dorsal fin;—the *vermeil*, the *jacquot*, the *chaponne*, and fifty others... As the sun gets higher, banana or balisier leaves are laid over the fish.

Even more puzzling, perhaps, are the astonishing varieties of green, yellow, and parti-colored vegetables, and fruits of all hues and forms,— out of which display you retain only a confused general memory of sweet smells and luscious colors. But there are some oddities which impress the recollection in a particular way. One is a great cylindrical ivory-colored thing, shaped like an elephant's tusk, except that it is not curved: this is the head of the cabbage-palm, or palmiste,—the brain of one of the noblest trees in the tropics, which must be totally destroyed to obtain it. Raw or cooked, it is eaten in a great variety of ways,—in salads, stews, fritters, or *akras*. Soon after this compact cylinder of young germinating leaves has been removed, large worms begin to appear in the hollow of the dead tree,—the *vers-palmiste*. You may see these for sale in the market, crawling about in bowls or cans: they are said, when fried alive, to taste like almonds, and are esteemed as a great luxury.

...Then you begin to look about you at the faces of the black, brown, and yellow people who are watching you curiously from beneath their Madras turbans, or from under the shade of mushroom-shaped hats as large as umbrellas. And as you observe the bare backs, bare shoulders, bare legs and arms and feet, you will find that the colors of flesh are even more varied and surprising than the colors of fruit. Nevertheless, it is only with fruit-colors that many of these skin-tints can be correctly compared: the only terms of comparison used by the colored people themselves being terms of this kind,—such as *peau-chapotille*, "sapota-skin." The *sapota* or *sapotille* is a juicy brown fruit with a rind satiny like a human cuticle, and just the color, when flushed and ripe, of certain half-breed skins. But among the brighter half-breeds, the colors, I think, are much more fruit-like;—there are banana-tints, lemon-tones, orange-hues, with sometimes such a mingling of ruddiness as in the pink ripening of a mango. Agreeable to the eye the darker skins certainly are, and often very remarkable—all clear tones of bronze being represented; but the brighter tints are absolutely beautiful. Standing perfectly naked at door-ways, or playing naked in the sun, astonishing children may sometimes be seen,— banana-colored or orange babies. There is one rare race-type, totally un-like the rest: the skin has a perfect gold-tone, an exquisite metallic yellow; the eyes are long, and have long silky lashes;—the hair is a mass of thick, rich, glossy curls that show blue lights in the sun. What mingling of races produced this beautiful type?—there is some strange blood in the blending,—not of coolie, nor of African, nor of Chinese, although there are Chinese types here of indubitable beauty.[2]

...All this population is vigorous, graceful, healthy: all you see passing by are well made—there are no sickly faces, no scrawny limbs. If by some rare chance you encounter a person who has lost an arm or a leg, you can be almost certain you are looking at a victim of the fer-de-lance,—the serpent whose venom putrefies living tissue... Without fear of exaggerating facts, I can venture to say that the muscular development of the workingmen here is something which must be seen in order to be believed;—to study fine displays of it, one should watch the blacks and half-breeds working naked to the waist,—on the landings, in the gas-houses and slaughter-houses, or on the nearest plantations. They are not generally large men, perhaps not extraordinarily powerful; but they have the aspect of sculptural or even of anatomical models; they seem absolutely devoid of adipose tissue; their muscles stand out with a saliency that astonishes the eye. At a tanning-yard, while I was watching a dozen blacks at work, a young mulatto with the mischievous face of a faun walked by, wearing nothing but a clout (*lantcho*) about his loins; and never, not even in bronze, did I see so beautiful a play of muscles. A demonstrator of anatomy could have used him for a class-model;—a sculptor wishing to shape a fine Mercury would have been satisfied to take a cast of such a body without thinking of making one modification from neck to heel. "Frugal diet is the cause of this physical condition," a young French professor assures me; "all these men, he says, "live upon salt codfish and fruit." But frugal living alone could never produce such symmetry and saliency of muscles: race-crossing, climate, perpetual exercise, healthy labor—many conditions must have combined to cause it. Also it is certain that this tropical sun has a tendency to dissolve spare flesh, to melt away all superfluous tissue, leaving the muscular fibre dense and solid as mahogany.

At the *mouillage*, below a green *morne*, is the bathing-place. A rocky beach rounding away under heights of tropical wood;—palms curving out above the sand, or bending half-way across it. Ships at anchor in blue water, against golden-yellow horizon. A vast blue glow. Water clear as diamond, and lukewarm.

It is about one hour after sunrise; and the higher parts of Montagne Pelée are still misty blue. Under the palms and among the lava rocks, and also in little cabins farther up the slope, bathers are dressing or undressing: the water is also dotted with heads of swimmers. Women and girls enter it very well robed from feet to shoulders;—men go in very sparsely clad;—there are lads wearing nothing. Young boys—yellow and brown little fellows—run in naked, and swim out to pointed rocks that jut up black above the bright water. They climb up one at a time to dive down. Poised for the leap upon the black lava crag, and against the blue light of the sky, each lithe figure, gilded by the morning sun, has a statuesqueness and a luminosity impossible to paint in words. These bodies seem to radiate color; and the azure light intensifies the hue: it is idyllic, incredible;—Coomans used paler colors in his Pompeiian studies, and his figures were never so symmetrical. This flesh does not look like flesh, but like fruit-pulp...

XIV

...EVERYWHERE crosses, little shrines, way-side chapels, statues of saints. You will see crucifixes and statuettes even in the forks or hollows of trees shadowing the high-roads. As you ascend these towards the interior you will see, every mile or half-mile, some chapel, or a cross erected upon a pedestal of masonry, or some little niche contrived in a wall, closed by a wire grating, through which the image of a Christ or a Madonna is visible. Lamps are kept burning all night before these figures. But the village of Morne Rouge,—some two thousand feet above the sea, and about an hour's drive from St. Pierre—is chiefly remarkable for such displays: it is a place of pilgrimage as well as a health resort. Above the village, upon the steep slope of a higher morne, one may note a singular succession of little edifices ascending to the summit,—fourteen little tabernacles, each containing a *relievo* representing some incident of Christ's Passion. This is called *Le Calvaire*: it requires more than a feeble piety to perform the religious exercise of climbing the height, and saying a prayer before each little shrine on the way. From the porch of the crowning structure the village of Morne Rouge appears so far below that it makes one almost dizzy to look at it; but even for the profane one ascent is well worth making, for the sake of the beautiful view. On all the neighboring heights around are votive chapels or great crucifixes.

St. Pierre is less peopled with images than Morne Rouge; but it has several colossal ones, which may be seen from any part of the harbor. On the heights above the middle quarter, or *Centre*; a gigantic Christ overlooks the bay; and from the Morne d'Orange, which bounds the city on the south, a great white Virgin—Notre Dame de la Garde, patron of mariners—watches above the ships at anchor in the mouillage.

...Thrice daily, from the towers of the white cathedral, a superb chime of bells rolls its *carillon* through the town. On great holidays the bells are wonderfully rung;—the ringers are African, and something of African feeling is observable in their impressive but incantatory manner of ringing. The *bourdon* must have cost a fortune. When it is made to speak, the effect is startling: all the city vibrates to a weird sound difficult to describe,—an abysmal, quivering moan, producing unfamiliar harmonies as the voices of the smaller bells are seized and interblended by it... One will not easily forget the ringing of a *bel-midi.*

...Behind the cathedral, above the peaked city roofs, and at the foot of the wood-clad Morne d'Orange, is the *Cimetière du Mouillage...* It is full of beauty,—this strange tropical cemetery. Most of the low tombs are covered with small square black and white tiles, set exactly after the fashion of the squares on a chess-board; at the foot of each grave stands a black cross, bearing at its centre a little white plaque, on which the name is graven in delicate and tasteful lettering. So pretty these tombs are, that you might almost believe yourself in a toy cemetery. Here and there, again, are miniature marble chapels built over the dead,—containing white Madonnas and Christs and little angels,—while flower-creepers climb and twine about the pillars. Death seems so luminous here that one thinks of it unconsciously as a soft rising from this soft green earth,—like a vapor invisible,—to melt into the prodigious day. Everything is bright and neat and beautiful; the air is sleepy with jasmine scent and odor of white lilies; and the palm—emblem of immortality—lifts its head a hundred feet into the blue light. There are rows of these majestic and symbolic trees;—two enormous ones guard the entrance;—the others rise from among the tombs,—white-stemmed, out-spreading their huge parasols of verdure higher than the cathedral towers.

Behind all this, the dumb green life of the morne seems striving to descend, to invade the rest of the dead. It thrusts green hands over the wall,—pushes strong roots underneath;—it attacks every joint of the stonework, patiently, imperceptibly, yet almost irresistibly.

...Some day there may be a great change in the little city of St. Pierre;—there may be less money and less zeal and less remembrance of the lost. Then from the morne, over the bulwark, the green host will move down unopposed;—creepers will prepare the way, dislocating the pretty tombs, pulling away the checkered tiling;—then will come the giants, rooting deeper,—feeling for the dust of hearts, groping among the bones;—and all that love has hidden away shall be restored to Nature,—

In the Cimetière du Mouillage, St. Pierre

absorbed into the rich juices of her verdure,—revitalized in her bursts of color,—resurrected in her upliftings of emerald and gold to the great sun...

XV

SEEN from the bay, the little red-white-and-yellow city forms but one multicolored streak against the burning green of the lofty island. There is no naked soil, no bare rock: the chains of the mountains, rising by successive ridges towards the interior, are still covered with forests;—tropical woods ascend the peaks to the height of four and five thousand feet. To describe the beauty of these woods—even of those covering the mornes in the immediate vicinity of St. Pierre—seems to me almost impossible;—there are forms and colors which appear to demand the creation of new words to express. Especially is this true in regard to hue;—the green of a tropical forest is something which one familiar only with the tones of Northern vegetation can form no just conception of: it is a color that conveys the idea of green fire.

You have only to follow the high-road leading out of St. Pierre by way of the Savane du Fort to find yourself, after twenty minutes' walk, in front of the Morne Parnasse, and before the verge of a high wood,—remnant of the enormous growth once covering all the island. What a tropical forest is, as seen from without, you will then begin to feel, with a sort of awe, while you watch that beautiful upclimbing of green shapes to the height of perhaps a thousand feet overhead. It presents one seemingly solid surface of vivid color,—rugose like a cliff. You do not readily distinguish whole trees in the mass;—you only perceive suggestions, dreams of trees, Doresqueries. Shapes that seem to be staggering under weight of creepers rise a hundred feet above you;—others, equally huge, are towering above these;—and still higher, a legion of monstrosities are nodding, bending, tossing up green arms, pushing out great knees, projecting curves as of backs and shoulders, intertwining mockeries of limbs. No distinct head appears except where some palm pushes up its crest in the general fight for sun. All else looks as if under a veil,—hidden and smothered by heavy drooping things. Blazing green vines cover every branch and stem;—they form draperies and tapestries and curtains and motionless cascades—pouring down over all projections like a thick silent flood: an amazing inundation of parasitic life... It is a weird and awful beauty that you gaze upon; and yet the spectacle is imperfect. These woods have been decimated;—the finest trees have been cut down: you see only a ruin of what was. To see the true primeval forest, you must ride well into the interior.

The absolutism of green does not, however, always prevail in these woods. During a brief season, corresponding to some of our winter months, the forests suddenly break into a very conflagration of color, caused by blossoming of the lianas—crimson, canary-yellow, blue and white. There are other flowerings, indeed; but that of the lianas alone has chromatic force enough to change the aspect of a landscape.

XVI

...IF it is possible for a West Indian forest to be described at all, it could not be described more powerfully than it has been by Dr. E. Rufz, a creole of Martinique, from one of whose works I venture to translate the following remarkable pages:

..."The sea, the sea alone, because it is the most colossal of earthly spectacles,—only the sea can afford us any term of comparison for the attempt to describe a *grand-bois*;—but even then one must imagine the sea on a day of storm, suddenly immobilized in the expression of its mightiest fury. For the summits of these vast woods repeat all the inequalities of the land they cover; and these inequalities are mountains from 4,200 to 4,800 feet in height, and valleys of corresponding profundity. All this is hidden, blended together, smoothed over by verdure, in soft and enormous undulations,—in immense billowings of foliage. Only, instead of a blue line at the horizon, you have a green line; instead of flashings of blue, you have flashings of green,—and in all the tints, in all the combinations of which green is capable: deep green, light green, yellow-green, black-green.

"When your eyes grow weary—if it indeed be possible for them to weary—of contemplating the exterior of these tremendous woods, try to penetrate a little into their interior. What an inextricable chaos it is! The sands of a sea are not more closely pressed together than the trees are here; some straight, some curved, some upright, some toppling,—fallen, or leaning against one another, or heaped high upon each other. Climbing lianas, which cross from one tree to the other, like ropes passing from mast to mast, help to fill up all the gaps in this treillage; and parasites—not timid parasites like ivy or like moss, but parasites which are trees self-grafted upon trees—dominate the primitive trunks, overwhelm them, usurp the place of their foliage, and fall back to the ground, forming factitious weeping-willows. You do not find here, as in the great forests of the North, the eternal monotony of birch and fir: this is the kingdom of infinite variety;—species the most diverse elbow each other, interlace, strangle and devour each other: all ranks and orders are confounded, as in a human mob. The soft and tender *balisier* opens its parasol of leaves beside the *gommier*, which is the cedar of the colonies;— you see the *acomat*, the *courbaril*, the mahogany, the *tendre-à-caillou*, the iron-wood… but as well enumerate by name all the soldiers of an army! Our oak, the balata, forces the palm to lengthen itself prodigiously in order to get a few thin beams of sunlight; for it is as difficult for the poor trees to obtain one glance from this King of the world, as for us, subjects of a monarchy, to obtain one look from our monarch. As for the soil, it is needless to think of looking at it: it lies as far below us probably as the bottom of the sea;—it disappeared, ever so long ago, under the heaping of débris,—under a sort of manure that has been accumulating there since the creation: you sink into it as into slime; you walk upon putrefied trunks, in a dust that has no name! Here indeed it is that one can get some comprehension of what vegetable antiquity signifies;—a lurid light (*lurida lux*), greenish, as wan at noon as the light of the moon at midnight, confuses forms and lends them a vague and fantastic aspect; a mephitic humidity exhales from all parts; an odor of death prevails; and a calm which is not silence (for the ear fancies it can hear the great movement of composition and of decomposition perpetually going on) tends to inspire you with that old mysterious horror which the ancients felt in the primitive forests of Germany and of Gaul:

"Arboribus suus horror inest" [3]

XVII

But the sense of awe inspired by a tropic forest is certainly greater than the mystic fear which any wooded wilderness of the North could ever have created. The brilliancy of colors that seem almost preternatural; the vastness of the ocean of frondage, and the violet blackness of rare gaps, revealing its inconceived profundity; and the million mysterious sounds which make up its perpetual murmur,—compel the idea of a creative force that almost terrifies. Man feels here like an insect,—fears like an insect on the alert for merciless enemies; and the fear is not unfounded. To enter these green abysses without a guide were folly: even with the best of guides there is peril. Nature is dangerous here: the powers that build are also the powers that putrefy; here life and death are perpetually interchanging office in the never-ceasing transformation of forces,—melting down and reshaping living substance simultaneously within the same vast crucible. There are trees distilling venom, there are plants that have fangs, there are perfumes that affect the brain, there are cold green creepers whose touch blisters flesh like fire; while in all the recesses and the shadows is a swarming of unfamiliar life, beautiful or hideous,—insect, reptile, bird,— interwarring, devouring, preying... But the great peril of the forest—the danger which deters even the naturalist—is the presence of the terrible *fer-de-lance* (*trigonocephalus lanceolatus,—bothrops lanceolatus,— craspodecephalus*),—deadliest of the Occidental thanatophidia, and probably one of the deadliest serpents of the known world.

...There are no less than eight varieties of it,—the most common being the dark gray, speckled with black—precisely the color that enables the creature to hide itself among the protruding roots of the trees, by simply coiling about them, and concealing its triangular head. Sometimes the snake is a clear bright yellow: then it is difficult to distinguish it from the bunch of bananas among which it conceals itself. Or the creature may be a dark yellow,—or a yellowish brown,—or the color of wine-lees, speckled pink and black,—or dead black with a yellow belly,—or black with a pink belly: all hues of tropical forest-mould, of old bark, of decomposing trees.

...The iris of the eye is orange,—with red flashes: it glows at night like burning charcoal.

And the fer-de-lance reigns absolute king over the mountains and the ravines; he is lord of the forest and the solitudes by day, and by night he extends his dominion over the public roads, the familiar paths, the parks, the pleasure resorts. People must remain at home after dark, unless they dwell in the city itself: if you happen to be out visiting after sunset, only a mile from town, your friends will caution you anxiously not to follow the boulevard as you go back, and to keep as closely as possible to the very centre of the path. Even in the brightest noon you cannot venture to enter the woods without an experienced escort; you cannot trust your eyes to detect danger: at any moment a seeming branch, a knot of lianas, a pink or gray root, a clump of pendent yellow fruit may suddenly take life, writhe, stretch, spring, strike... Then you will need aid indeed, and most quickly; for within the span of a few heart-beats the wounded flesh chills, tumefies, softens. Soon it changes color, and begins to spot violaceously; while an icy coldness creeps through all the blood. If the *panseur* or the physician arrives in time, and no vein has been pierced, there is hope; but it more often happens that the blow is received directly on a vein of the foot or ankle,—in which case nothing can save the victim. Even when life is saved the danger is not over. Necrosis of the tissues is likely to set in: the flesh corrupts, falls from the bone sometimes in tatters; and the colors of its putrefaction simulate the hues of vegetable decay,—the ghastly grays and pinks and yellows of trunks rotting down into the soil which gave them birth. The human victim moulders as the trees moulder,—crumbles and dissolves as crumbles the substance of the dead palms and balatas: the Death-of-the-Woods is upon him.

Today a fer-de-lance is seldom found exceeding six feet in length; but the dimensions of the reptile, at least, would seem to have been decreased considerably by man's warring upon it since the time of Père Labat, who mentions having seen a fer-de-lance nine feet long and five inches in diameter. He also speaks of a *couresse*—a beautiful and harmless serpent said to kill the fer-de-lance—over ten feet long and thick as a man's leg; but a large couresse is now seldom seen. The negro woodsmen kill both creatures indiscriminately; and as the older reptiles are the least likely to escape observation, the chances for the survival of extraordinary individuals lessen with the yearly decrease of forest-area.

...But it may be doubted whether the number of deadly snakes has been greatly lessened since the early colonial period. Each female produces viviparously from forty to sixty young at a birth. The favorite haunts of the fer-de-lance are to a large extent either inaccessible or unexplored, and its multiplication is prodigious. It is really only the surplus of its swarming that overpours into the cane-fields, and makes the public roads dangerous after dark;—yet more than three hundred snakes have been killed in twelve months on a single plantation. The introduction of the Indian mongoos, or *mangouste* (ichneumon), proved futile as a means of repressing the evil. The mangouste kills the fer-de-lance when it has a chance; but it also kills fowls and sucks their eggs, which condemns it irrevocably with the country negroes, who live to a considerable extent by raising and selling chickens.

...Domestic animals are generally able to discern the presence of their deadly enemy long before a human eye can perceive it. If your horse rears and plunges in the darkness, trembles and sweats, do not try to ride on until you are assured the way is clear. Or your dog may come running back, whining, shivering: you will do well to accept his warning. The animals kept about country residences usually try to fight for their lives; the hen battles for her chickens; the bull endeavors to gore and stamp his supple enemy; the pig gives more successful combat; but the creature who fears the

In the Jardin des Plantes, St. Pierre

monster least is the brave cat. Seeing a snake, she at once carries her kittens to a place of safety, then boldly advances to the encounter. She will walk to the very limit of the serpent's striking range, and begin to feint,—teasing him, startling him, trying to draw his blow. How the emerald and the topazine eyes glow then!—they are flames! A moment more and the triangular head, hissing from the coil, flashes swift as if moved by wings. But swifter still the stroke of the armed paw that dashes the horror aside, flinging it mangled in the dust. Nevertheless, pussy does not dare yet to spring;—the enemy, still active, has almost instantly reformed his coil;—but she is again in front of him, watching,—vertical pupil against vertical pupil. Again the lashing stroke; again the beautiful countering;—again the living death is hurled aside; and now the scaled skin is deeply torn,—one eye socket has ceased to flame. Once more the stroke of the serpent; once more the light, quick, cutting blow. But the trigonocephalus is blind, is stupefied;—before he can attempt to coil pussy has leaped upon him,—nailing the horrible flat head fast to the ground with her two sinewy paws. Now let him lash, writhe, twine, strive to strangle her!—in vain! he will never lift his head: an instant more, and he lies still:—the keen white teeth of the cat have severed the vertebra just behind the triangular skull!...

XVIII

The Jardin des Plantes is not absolutely secure from the visits of the serpent; for the trigonocephalus goes everywhere,—mounting to the very summits of the cocoa-palms, swimming rivers, ascending walls, hiding in palm-thatched roofs, breeding in bagasse heaps. But, despite what has been printed to the contrary, this reptile fears man and hates light: it rarely shows itself voluntarily during the day. Therefore, if you desire to obtain some conception of the magnificence of Martinique vegetation, without incurring the risk of entering the high woods, you can do so by visiting the Jardin des Plantes,—only taking care to use your eyes well while climbing over fallen trees, or picking your way through dead branches. The garden is less than a mile from the city, on the slopes of the Morne Parnasse; and the primitive forest itself has been utilized in the formation of it,—so that the greater part of the garden is a primitive growth. Nature has accomplished here infinitely more than art of man (though such art has done much to lend the place its charm),—and until within a very recent time the result might have been deemed, without exaggeration, one of the wonders of the world.

A moment after passing the gate you are in twilight,—though the sun may be blinding on the white road without. All about you is a green gloaming, up through which you see immense trunks rising. Follow the first path that slopes up on your left as you proceed, if you wish to obtain the best general view of the place in the shortest possible time. As you proceed, the garden on your right deepens more and more into a sort of ravine;—on your left rises a sort of foliage-shrouded cliff; and all this in a beautiful crepuscular dimness, made by the foliage of great trees meeting overhead. Palms rooted a hundred feet below you hold their heads a hundred feet above you; yet they can barely reach the light... Farther on the ravine widens to frame in two tiny lakes, dotted with artificial islands, which are miniatures of Martinique, Guadeloupe, and Dominica: these are covered with tropical plants, many of which are total strangers even here: they are natives of India, Senegambia, Algeria, and the most eastern East. Arborescent ferns of unfamiliar elegance curve up from path-verge or lake-brink; and the great *arbre-du-voyageur* outspreads its colossal fan. Giant lianas droop down over the way in loops and festoons; tapering green cords, which are creepers descending to take root, hang everywhere; and parasites with stems thick as cables coil about the trees like boas. Trunks shooting up out of sight, into the green wilderness above, display no bark; you cannot guess what sort of trees they are; they are so thickly wrapped in creepers as to seem pillars of leaves. Between you and the sky, where everything is fighting for sun, there is an almost unbroken vault of leaves, a cloudy green confusion in which nothing particular is distinguishable.

You come to breaks now and then in the green steep to your left,— openings created for cascades pouring down from one mossed basin of brown stone to another,—or gaps occupied by flights of stone steps, green with mosses, and chocolate-colored by age. These steps lead to loftier paths; and all the stone-work,—the grottos, basins, terraces, steps,—are darkened by time and velveted with mossy things... It is of another century, this garden: special ordinances were passed concerning it during the French Revolution (*An.II.*);—it is very quaint; it suggests an art spirit as old as Versailles, or older; but it is indescribably beautiful even now.

...At last you near the end, to hear the roar of falling water;—there is a break in the vault of green above the bed of a river below you; and at a sudden turn you come in sight of the cascade. Before you is the Morne itself; and against the burst of descending light you discern a precipice-verge. Over it, down one green furrow in its brow, tumbles the rolling foam of a cataract, like falling smoke, to be caught below in a succession of moss-covered basins. The first clear leap of the water is nearly seventy feet... Did Josephine ever rest upon that shadowed bench near by?... She knew all these paths by heart: surely they must have haunted her dreams in the after-time!

Returning by another path, you may have a view of other cascades—though none so imposing. But they are beautiful; and you will not soon forget the effect of one,—flanked at its summit by white-stemmed palms which lift their leaves so high into the light that the loftiness of them gives the sensation of vertigo... Dizzy also the magnificence of the great colonnade of palmistes and angelins, two hundred feet high, through which you pass if you follow the river-path from the cascade,—the famed *Allée des duels*...

The vast height, the pillared solemnity of the ancient trees in the green dimness, the solitude, the strangeness of shapes but half seen,—suggesting fancies of silent aspiration, or triumph, or despair,—all combine to produce a singular impression of awe... You are alone; you hear no human voice,—no sounds but the rushing of the river over its volcanic rocks, and the creeping of millions of lizards and tree-frogs and little toads. You see no human face; but you see all around you the labor of man being gnawed and devoured by nature,—broken bridges, sliding steps, fallen arches, strangled fountains with empty basins;—and everywhere arises the pungent odor of decay. This omnipresent odor affects one unpleasantly;—it never ceases to remind you that where Nature is most puissant to charm, there also is she mightiest to destroy.

The beautiful garden is now little more than a wreck of what it once was: since the fall of the Empire it has been shamefully abused and neglected. Some *agronome* sent out to take charge of it by the Republic, began its destruction by cutting down acres of enormous and magnificent trees,—including a superb alley of palms,—for the purpose of experimenting with roses. But the rose-trees would not be cultivated there; and the serpents avenged the demolition by making the experimental garden unsafe to enter;—they always swarm into underbush and shrubbery after forest trees have been cleared away... Subsequently the garden was greatly damaged by storms and torrential rains; the mountain river overflowed, carrying bridges away and demolishing stone-work. No attempt was made to repair these destructions; but neglect alone would not have ruined the loveliness of the place;—barbarism was necessary! Under the present negro-radical régime orders have been given for the

Cascade in the Jardin des Plantes

wanton destruction of trees older than the colony itself;—and marvels that could not be replaced in a hundred generations were cut down and converted into charcoal for the use of public institutions.

XIX

...HOW gray seem the words of poets in the presence of this Nature!... The enormous silent poem of color and light—(you who know only the North do not know color, do not know light!)—of sea and sky, of the woods and the peaks, so far surpasses imagination as to paralyze it— mocking the language of admiration, defying all power of expression. That is before you which never can be painted or chanted, because there is no cunning art or speech able to reflect it. Nature realizes your most hopeless ideals of beauty, even as one gives toys to a child. And the sight of this supreme terrestrial expression of creative magic numbs thought. In the great centres of civilization we admire and study only the results of mind,—the products of human endeavor: here one views only the work of Nature,—but Nature in all her primeval power, as in the legendary frostless morning of creation. Man here seems to bear scarcely more relation to the green life about him than the insect; and the results of human effort seem impotent by comparison with the operation of those vast blind forces which clothe the peaks and crown the dead craters with impenetrable forest. The air itself seems inimical to thought,—soporific, and yet pregnant with activities of dissolution so powerful that the mightiest tree begins to melt like wax from the moment it has ceased to live. For man merely to exist is an effort; and doubtless in the perpetual struggle of the blood to preserve itself from fermentation, there is such an expenditure of vital energy as leaves little surplus for mental exertion.

...Scarcely less than poet or philosopher, the artist, I fancy, would feel his helplessness. In the city he may find wonderful picturesqueness to invite his pencil, but when he stands face to face alone with Nature he will discover that he has no colors! The luminosities of tropic foliage could only be imitated in fire. He who desires to paint a West Indian forest,—a West Indian landscape,—must take his view from some great height, through which the colors come to his eye softened and subdued by distance,—toned with blues or purples by the astonishing atmosphere.

...It is sunset as I write these lines, and there are witchcrafts of color. Looking down the narrow, steep street opening to the bay, I see the motionless silhouette of the steamer on a perfectly green sea,—under a lilac sky,—against a prodigious orange light.

XX

IN these tropic latitudes Night does not seem "to fall,"—to descend over the many-peaked land: it appears to rise up, like an exhalation, from the ground. The coast-lines darken first;—then the slopes and the lower hills and valleys become shadowed;—then, very swiftly, the gloom mounts to the heights, whose very loftiest peak may remain glowing like a volcano at its tip for several minutes after the rest of the island is veiled in blackness and all the stars are out...

...Tropical nights have a splendor that seems strange to northern eyes. The sky does not look so high—so far away as in the North; but the stars are larger, and luminously greater.

With the rising of the moon all the violet of the sky flushes;—there is almost such a rose-color as heralds northern dawn.

Then moon appears over the mornes, very large, very bright,—brighter certainly than many a befogged sun one sees in northern Novembers; and it seems to have a weird magnetism—this tropical moon. Night-birds, insects, frogs,—everything that can sing,—all sing very low on the nights of great moons. Tropical wood-life begins with dark: in the immense white light of a full moon this nocturnal life seems afraid to cry out as usual. Also, this moon has a singular effect on the nerves. It is very difficult to sleep on such bright nights: you feel such a vague uneasiness as the coming of a great storm gives...

XXI

YOU reach Fort-de-France, the capital of Martinique, by steamer from St. Pierre, in about an hour and a half... There is an overland route—*La Trace*; but it is a twenty-five-mile ride, and a weary one in such a climate, notwithstanding the indescribable beauty of the landscapes which the lofty road commands.

...Rebuilt in wood after the almost total destruction by an earthquake of its once picturesque streets of stone, Fort-de-France (formally Fort-Royal) has little of outward interest by comparison with St. Pierre. It lies in a low, moist plain, and has few remarkable buildings:

Departure of Steamer for Fort-de-France

you can walk all over the little town in about half an hour. But the Savane,—the great green public square, with its grand tamarinds and *sabliers*,—would be worth the visit alone, even were it not made romantic by the marble memory of Josephine.

I went to look at the white dream of her there, a creation of master-sculptors... It seemed to me absolutely lovely.

Sea winds have bitten it; tropical rains have streaked it: some microscopic growth has darkened the exquisite hollow of the throat. And yet such is the human charm of the figure that you almost fancy you are gazing at a living presence... Perhaps the profile is less artistically real,—statuesque to the point of betraying the chisel; but when you look straight up into the sweet creole face, you can believe she lives: all the wonderful West Indian charm of the woman is there.

She is standing just in the centre of the Savane, robed in the fashion of the First Empire, with gracious arms and shoulders bare: one hand leans upon a medallion bearing the eagle profile of Napoleon... Seven tall palms stand in a circle around her, lifting their comely heads into the blue glory of the tropic day. Within their enchanted circle you feel that you tread holy ground,—the sacred soil of artist and poet;—here the recollections of memoir-writers vanish away; the gossip of history is hushed for you; you no longer care to know how rumor has it that she spoke or smiled or wept: only the bewitchment of her lives under the

Statue of Josephine

thin, soft, swaying shadows of those feminine palms... Over violet space of summer sea, through the vast splendor of azure light, she is looking back to the place of her birth, back to beautiful drowsy Trois-Islets,—and always with the same half-dreaming, half-plaintive smile,—unutterably touching...

XXII

ONE leaves Martinique with regret, even after so brief a stay: the old colonial life itself, not less than the revelation of tropic nature, having in this island a quality of uniqueness, a special charm, unlike anything previously seen... We steam directly for Barbadoes; the vessel will touch at the intervening islands only on her homeward route.

...Against a hot wind south,—under a sky always deepening in beauty. Towards evening dark clouds begin to rise before us; and by nightfall they spread into one pitch-blackness over all the sky. Then comes a wind in immense sweeps, lifting the water,—but a wind that is still strangely warm. The ship rolls heavily in the dark for an hour or more;—then torrents of tepid rain make the sea smooth again; the clouds pass, and the violet transparency of tropical night reappears,—ablaze with stars.

At early morning a long low land appears on the horizon,—totally unlike the others we have seen; it has no visible volcanic forms. That is Barbadoes,—a level burning coral coast,—a streak of green, white-edged, on the verge of the sea. But hours pass before the green line begins to show outlines of foliage.

...As we approach the harbor an overhanging black cloud suddenly bursts down in illuminated rain,—through which the shapes of moored ships seem magnified as through a golden fog. It ceases as suddenly as it began; the cloud vanishes utterly; and the azure is revealed unflecked, dazzling, wondrous... It is a sight worth the whole journey,—the splendor of this noon sky at Barbadoes;—the horizon glow is almost blinding, the sea-line sharp as a razor-edge; and motionless upon the sapphire water nearly a hundred ships lie,—masts, spars, booms, cordage, cutting against the amazing magnificence of blue... Meanwhile the island coast has clearly brought out all its beauties: first you note the long white winding thread-line of beach—coral and bright sand;—then the deep green fringe of vegetation through which roofs and spires project here and there, and quivering feathery heads of palms with white trunks. The general tone of this verdure is sombre green, though it is full of lustre: there is a glimmer in it as of metal. Beyond all this coast-front long undulations of misty pale green are visible,—far slopes of low hill and plain; the highest curving line, the ridge of the island, bears a row of cocoa palms. They are so far that their stems diminish almost to invisibility: only the crests are clearly distinguishable,—like spiders hanging between land and sky. But there are no forests: the land is a naked unshadowed green far as the eye can reach beyond the coastline. There is no waste space in Barbadoes: it is perhaps one of the most densely-peopled places on the globe—(one thousand and thirty-five inhabitants to the square mile);—and it sends black laborers by thousands to the other British colonies every year,— the surplus of its population.

The city of Bridgetown disappoints the stranger who expects to find any exotic features of architecture or custom,—disappoints more, perhaps, than any other tropical port in this respect. Its principal streets give you the impression of walking through an English town,—not an old-time town, but a new one, plain almost to commonplaceness, in spite of Nelson's monument. Even the palms are powerless to lend the place a really tropical look;—the streets are narrow without being picturesque, white as lime roads and full of glare;—the manners, the costumes, the style of living, the system of business are thoroughly English;—the population lacks visible originality; and its extraordinary activity, so odd-

Inner Basin, Bridgetown, Barbadoes

ly at variance with the quiet indolence of other West Indian peoples, seems almost unnatural. Pressure of numbers has largely contributed to this characteristic; but Barbadoes would be in any event, by reason of position alone, a busy colony. As the most windward of the West Indies it has naturally become not only the chief port, but also the chief emporium of the Antilles. It has railroads, telephones, street-cars, fire and life insurance, good hotels, libraries and reading-rooms and excellent public schools. Its annual export trade figures for nearly $6,000,000.

The fact which seems most curious to the stranger, on his first acquaintance with the city, is that most of this business activity is represented by black men—black merchants, shopkeepers, clerks. Indeed, the Barbadian population, as a mass, strikes one as the darkest in the West Indies. Black regiments march through the street to the sound of English music,—uniformed as Zouaves; black police in white helmets and white duck uniforms, maintain order; black postmen distribute the mails; black cabmen wait for customers at a shilling an hour. It is by no means an attractive population, physically,—rather the reverse, and frankly brutal as well—different as possible from the colored race of Martinique; but it has immense energy and speaks excellent English. One almost startled on hearing Barbadian negroes speaking English with a strong Old Country accent. Without seeing the speaker, you could scarcely believe such English uttered by black lips; and the commonest negro laborer about the port pronounces as well as a Londoner. The purity of Barbadian English is partly due, no doubt, to the fact that unlike most of the other islands, Barbadoes has always remained in the possession of Great Britain. Even as far back as 1676 Barbadoes was in a very different condition of prosperity from that of other colonies, and offered a totally different social aspect—having a white population of 50,000. At that time the island could muster 20,000 infantry and 3,000 horse; there were 80,000 slaves; there were 1,500 houses in Bridgetown and an immense number of shops; and not less than two hundred ships were required to export the annual sugar crop alone.

But Barbadoes differs also from most of the Antilles geologically; and there can be no question that the nature of its soil has considerably influenced the physical character of its inhabitants. Although Barbadoes is now known to be also of volcanic origin,—a fact which its low undulating surface could enable no unscientific observer to suppose,—it is superficially a calcareous formation; and the remarkable effect of limestone soil upon the bodily development of a people is not less marked in this latitude than elsewhere. In most of the Antilles the white race degenerates and dwarfs under the influence of climate and environment; but the Barbadian creole—tall, muscular, large of bone—preserves and perpetuates in the tropics the strength and sturdiness of his English forefathers.

XXIII

...NIGHT: steaming for British Guiana;—we shall touch at no port before reaching Demerara. A strong warm gale, that compels the taking in of every awning and wind-sail. Driving tepid rain; and an intense darkness, broken only by the phosphorescence of the sea, which tonight displays extraordinary radiance.

The steamer's wake is a great broad, seething river of fire,—white like strong moonshine: the glow is bright enough to read by. At its centre the trail is brightest;—towards either edge it pales off cloudily,— curling like smoke of phosphorus. Great sharp lights burst up momentarily through it like meteors. Weirder than this strange wake are the long slow fires that keep burning about us at a distance, out in the dark. Nebulous incandescences mount up from the depths, change form, and

Trafalgar Square, Bridgetown, Barbadoes

pass;—serpentine flames wriggle by;—there are long billowing crests of fire. These seem to be formed of millions of tiny sparks, that light up all at the same time, glow for a while, disappear, reappear, and swirl in a prolonged smouldering.

There are warm gales and heavy rain each night,—it is the hurricane season;—and it seems these become more violent the farther south we sail. But we are nearing those equinoctial regions where the calm of nature is never disturbed by storms.

…Morning: still steaming south, through a vast blue day. The azure of the heaven always seems to be growing deeper. There is a bluish-white glow in the horizon,—almost too bright to look at. An indigo sea… There are no clouds; and the splendor endures until sunset.

Then another night, very luminous and calm. The southern constellations burn whitely… We are nearing the great shallows of the South American coast.

XXIV

…It is the morning of the third day since we left Barbadoes, and for the first time since entering tropic waters all things seem changed. The atmosphere is heavy with strange mists; and the light of an orange-colored sun, immensely magnified by vapors, illuminates a greenish-yellow sea,—foul and opaque, as if stagnant… I remember just such a sunrise over the Louisiana gulf-coast.

We are in the shallows, moving very slowly. The line-caster keeps calling, at regular intervals: "Quarter less five, sir!" "And a half four, sir!"… There is little variation in his soundings—a quarter of a fathom or half a fathom difference. The warm air has a sickly heaviness, like the air of a swamp; the water shows olive and ochreous tones alternately;—the foam is yellow in our wake. These might be the colors of a fresh-water inundation…

A fellow-traveller tells me, as we lean over the rail, that this same viscous, glaucous sea washes the great penal colony of Cayenne—which he visited. When a convict dies there, the corpse, sewn up in a sack, is borne to the water, and a great bell tolled. Then the still surface is suddenly broken by fins innumerable,—black fins of sharks rushing to the hideous funeral: they know the Bell!…

There is land in sight—very low land,—a thin dark line suggesting marshiness; and the nauseous color of the water always deepens.

As the land draws near, it reveals a beautiful tropical appearance. The sombre green line brightens color, sharpens into a splendid fringe of fantastic evergreen fronds, bristling with palm crests. Then a mossy seawall comes into sight—dull gray stone-work, green-lined at all its joints. There is a fort. The steamer's whistle is exactly mocked by a queer echo, and the cannon-shot once reverberated—only once: there are no mountains here to multiply a sound. And all the while the water becomes a thicker and more turbid green; the wake looks more and more ochreous, the foam ropier and yellower. Vessels becalmed everywhere speck the glass-level of the sea, like insects sticking upon a mirror. It begins, all of a sudden, to rain torrentially; and through the white storm of falling drops nothing is discernible.

XXV

AT Georgetown, steamers entering the river can lie close to the wharf;—we can enter the Government warehouses without getting wet. In fifteen minutes the shower ceases; and we leave the warehouses to find ourselves in a broad, palm-bordered street illuminated by the most prodigious day that yet shone upon our voyage. The rain has cleared the air and

Street in Georgetown, Demerara

dissolved the mists; and the light is wondrous.

My own memory of Demerara will always be a memory of enormous light. The radiance has an indescribable dazzling force that conveys the idea of electric fire; the horizon blinds like a motionless sheet of lightning; and you dare not look at the zenith... The brightest summer-day in the North is a gloaming to this. Men walk only under umbrellas, or with their eyes down; and the pavements, already dry, flare almost unbearably.

...Georgetown has an exotic aspect peculiar to itself,—different from that of any West Indian city we have seen; and this is chiefly due to the presence of palm-trees. For the edifices, the plan, the general idea of the town, are modern; the white streets, laid out very broad to the sweep of the sea-breeze, and drained by canals running through their centres, with bridges at cross-streets, display the value of nineteenth-century knowledge regarding house-building with a view to coolness as well as to beauty. The architecture might be described as a tropicalized Swiss style—Swiss eaves are developed into veranda roofs, and Swiss porches prolonged and lengthened into beautiful piazzas and balconies. The men who devised these large cool halls, these admirably ventilated rooms, these latticed windows opening to the ceiling, may have lived in India; but the physiognomy of the town also reveals a fine sense of beauty in the designers: all that is strange and beautiful in the vegetation of the tropics has had a place contrived for it, a home prepared for it. Each dwelling has its garden; each garden blazes with singular and lovely color; but everywhere and always tower the palms. There are colonnades of palms, clumps of palms, groves of palms—sago and cabbage and cocoa and fan palms. You can see that the palm is cherished here, is loved for its beauty, like a woman. Everywhere you find palms, in all stages of development, from the first sheaf of tender green plumes rising above the soil to the wonderful colossus that holds its head a hundred feet above the roofs; palms border the garden walks in colonnades; they are grouped in exquisite poise about the basins of fountains; they stand like magnificent pillars at either side of gates; they look into the highest windows of public buildings and hotels.

...For miles and miles and miles we drive along avenues of palms—avenues leading to opulent cane-fields, traversing queer coolie villages. Rising on either side of the road to the same level, the palms present the vista of a long unbroken double colonnade of dead-silver trunks, shining tall pillars with deep green plume-tufted summits, almost touching, almost forming something like the dream of an interminable Moresque

Avenue in Georgetown, Demerara

arcade. Sometimes for a full mile the trees are only about thirty or forty feet high; then, turning into an older alley, we drive for half a league between giants nearly a hundred feet in altitude. The double perspective lines of their crests, meeting before us and behind us in a bronze-green darkness, betray only at long intervals any variation of color, where some dead leaf droops like an immense yellow feather.

XXVI

IN the marvellous light, which brings out all the rings of their bark, these palms sometimes produce a singular impression of subtle, fleshy, sentient life,—seem to move with a slowly stealthy motion as you ride or drive past them. The longer you watch them, the stronger this idea becomes,—the more they seem alive,—the more their long silver-gray articulated bodies seem to poise, undulate, stretch… Certainly the palms of a Demerara country-road evoke no such real emotion as that produced by the stupendous palms of the Jardin des Plantes in Martinique. That beautiful, solemn, silent life up-reaching through tropical forest to the sun for warmth, for color, for power,—filled me, I remember, with a sensation of awe different from anything which I had ever experienced... But even here in Guiana, standing alone under the sky, the palm still seems a creature rather than a tree,—gives you the idea of personality;—you almost believe each lithe shape animated by a thinking force,—believe that all are watching you with such passionless calm as legend lends to beings supernatural... And I wonder if some kindred fancy might not have inspired the name given by the French colonists to the male palmiste,—*angelin*...

Very wonderful is the botanical garden here. It is new; there are no groves, no heavy timber, no shade; finely laid-out grounds,— alternations of lawn and flower-bed,—offer everywhere surprising sights. You observe curious orange-colored shrubs; plants speckled with four different colors; plants that look like wigs of green hair; plants with enormous broad leaves that seem made of colored crystal; plants that do not look like natural growths, but like idealizations of plants,—those beautiful fantasticalities imagined by sculptors. All these we see in glimpses from a carriage-window,—yellow, indigo black, and crimson plants... We draw rein only to observe in the ponds the green navies of the Victoria Regia,—the monster among water-lilies. It covers all the ponds and many of the canals. Close to shore the leaves are not extraordinarily large; but they increase in breadth as they float farther out, as if gaining bulk proportionately to the depth of water. A few yards off, they are large as soup-plates; farther out, they are broad as dinner-trays; in the centre of the pond or canal they have surface large as tea-tables. And all have an upturned edge, a perpendicular rim. Here and there you see the imperial flower,—towering above the leaves... Perhaps, if your hired driver be a good guide, he will show you the snake-nut,— the fruit of an extraordinary tree native to the Guiana forests. This swart nut—shaped almost like a clam-shell, and halving in the same way along its sharp edges—encloses something almost incredible. There is a pale envelope about the kernel; remove it, and you find between your fingers a little viper, triangular-headed, coiled thrice upon itself, perfect in every detail of form from head to tail. Was this marvellous mockery evolved for a protective end? It is no eccentricity: in every nut the serpent-kernel lies coiled the same.

...Yet in spite of a hundred such novel impressions, what a delight it is to turn again cityward through the avenues of palms, and to feel once more the sensation of being watched, without love or hate, by all those lithe, tall, silent, gracious shapes!

XXVII

HINDOOS; coolies; men, women, and children—standing, walking, or sitting in the sun, under the shadowing of the palms. Men squatting, with hands clasped over their black knees, are watching us from under their white turbans—very steadily, with a slight scowl. All these Indian faces have the same set, stern expression, the same knitting of the brows; and the keen gaze is not altogether pleasant. It borders upon hostility; it is the look of measurement—measurement physical and moral. In the mighty swarming of India these have learned the full meaning and force of life's law as we Occidentals rarely learn it. Under the dark fixed frown the eye glitters like a serpent's.

Nearly all wear the same Indian dress; the thickly folded turban, usually white, white drawers reaching but half-way down the thigh, leaving the knees and the legs bare, and white jacket. A few don long blue robes, and colored head-dress: these are babagees—priests. Most of the men look tall; they are slender and small-boned, but the limbs are well turned. They are grave—talk in low tones, and seldom smile. Those you see with heavy black beards are probably Mussulmans: I am told they have their mosques here, and that the muezzin's call to prayer is chanted three times daily on many plantations. Others shave, but the Mohammedans allow all the beard to grow… Very comely some of the women are in their close-clinging soft brief robes and tantalizing veils—a costume leaving shoulders, arms, and ankles bare. The dark arm is always tapered and rounded; the silver-circled ankle always elegantly knit to the light straight foot. Many slim girls, whether standing or walking or in repose, offer remarkable studies of grace; their attitude when erect always suggests lightness and suppleness, like the poise of a dancer.

…A coolie mother passes, carrying at her hip a very naked baby. It has exquisite delicacy of limb: its tiny ankles are circled by thin bright silver rings; it looks like a little bronze statuette, a statuette of Kama, the Indian Eros. The mother's arms are covered from elbow to wrist with silver bracelets,—some flat and decorated; others coarse, round, smooth, with ends hammered into the form of viper-heads. She has large flowers of gold in her ears, a small gold flower in her very delicate little nose. This nose ornament does not seem absurd; on these dark skins the effect is almost as pleasing as it is bizarre. This jewellery is pure metal;—it is

Victoria Regia in the Canal at Georgetown

thus the coolies carry their savings,—melting down silver or gold coin, and recasting it into bracelets, ear-rings, and nose ornaments.

…Evening is brief: all this time the days have been growing shorter: it will be black at 6 P.M. One does not regret it;—the glory of such a tropical day as this is almost too much to endure for twelve hours. The sun is already low, and yellow with a tinge of orange: as he falls between the palms his stare colors the world with a strange hue—such a phantasmal light as might be given by a nearly burnt-out sun. The air is full of unfamiliar odors. We pass a flame-colored bush; and an extraordinary perfume—strange, rich, sweet—envelops us like a caress: the soul of a red jasmine…

…What a tropical sunset is this—within two days' steam-journey of the equator! Almost to the zenith the sky flames up from the sea,—one tremendous orange incandescence, rapidly deepening to vermilion as the sun dips. The indescribable intensity of this mighty burning makes one totally unprepared for the spectacle of its sudden passing: a seeming drawing down behind the sea of the whole vast flare of light… Instantly the world becomes indigo. The air grows humid, weighty with vapor; frogs commence to make a queer bubbling noise; and some unknown creature begins in the trees a singular music, not trilling, like the note of our cricket, but one continuous shrill tone, high, keen, as of a thin jet of steam leaking through a valve. Strong vegetal scents, aromatic and novel, rise up. Under the trees of our hotel I hear a continuous dripping sound; the drops fall heavily, like bodies of clumsy insects. But it is not dew, nor insects; it is a thick, transparent jelly—a fleshy liquor that falls

Demerara Coolie Girl

in immense drops... The night grows chill with dews, with vegetable breath; and we sleep with windows nearly closed.

XXVIII

...ANOTHER sunset like the conflagration of a world, as we steam away from Guiana;—another unclouded night; and morning brings back to us that bright blue in the sea-water which we missed for the first time on our approach to the mainland. There is a long swell all day, and tepid winds. But towards evening the water once more shifts its hue—takes olive tint—the mighty flood of the Orinoco is near.

Over the rim of the sea rise shapes faint pink, faint gray—misty shapes that grow and lengthen as we advance. We are nearing Trinidad.

It first takes definite form as a prolonged, undulating, pale gray mountain chain,—the outline of a sierra. Approaching nearer, we discern other hill summits rounding up and shouldering away behind the chain itself. Then the nearest heights begin to turn faint green— very slowly. Right before the outermost spur of cliff, fantastic shapes of rock are rising sheer from the water: partly green, partly reddish-gray where the surface remains unclothed by creepers and shrubs. Between them the sea leaps and whitens.

And we begin to steam along a magnificent tropical coast,—before a billowing of hills wrapped in forest from sea to summit,—astonishing forest, dense, sombre, impervious to sun—every gap a blackness as of ink. Giant palms here and there overtop the denser foliage; and queer monster trees rise above the forest-level against the blue,—spreading out huge flat crests from which masses of lianas stream down. This forest-front has the apparent solidity of a wall, and forty-five miles of it undulate uninterruptedly by us—rising by terraces, or projecting like turret-lines, or shooting up into semblance of cathedral forms or suggestions of castellated architecture... But the secrets of these woods have not been unexplored;—one of the noblest writers of our time has so beautifully and fully written of them as to leave little for any one else to say. He who knows Charles Kingsley's "At Last" probably knows the woods of Trinidad far better than many who pass them daily.

Even as observed from the steamer's deck, the mountains and forests of Trinidad have an aspect very different from those of the other Antilles. The heights are less lofty,—less jagged and abrupt,— with rounded summits; the peaks of Martinique or Dominica rise fully two thousand feet higher. The land itself is a totally different formation,—anciently being a portion of the continent; and its flora and fauna are of South America.

…There comes a great cool whiff of wind,—another and another;—then a mighty breath begins to blow steadily upon us,—the breath of the Orinoco… It grows dark before we pass through the Ape's Mouth, to anchor in one of the calmest harbors in the world,—never disturbed by hurricanes. Over unruffled water the lights of Port-of-Spain shoot long still yellow beams… The night grows chill;—the air is made frigid by the breath of the enormous river and the vapors of the great woods.

XXIX

…SUNRISE: a morning of supernal beauty,—the sky of a fairy tale,—the sea of a love-poem.

Under a heaven of exquisitely tender blue, the whole smooth sea has a perfect luminous dove-color,—the horizon being filled to a great height with greenish-golden haze,—a mist of unspeakably sweet tint, a hue that, imitated in any aquarelle, would be cried out against as an impossibility. As yet the hills are nearly all gray, the forests also inwrapping them are gray and ghostly, for the sun has but just risen above them, and vapors hang like a veil between. Then, over the glassy level of the flood, bands of purple and violet and pale blue and fluid gold begin to shoot and quiver and broaden; these are the currents of the morning, catching varying color with the deepening of the day and the lifting of the tide.

Then, as the sun rises higher, green masses begin to glimmer among the grays; the outlines of the forest summits commence to define themselves through the vapory height, to left and right of the great glow. Only the city still remains invisible; it lies exactly between us and the downpour of solar splendor, and the mists there have caught such radiance that the place seems hidden by a fog of fire. Gradually the gold-green of the horizon changes to a pure yellow; the hills take soft, rich, sensuous colors. One of the more remote has turned a marvellous tone—a seemingly diaphanous aureate color, the very ghost of gold. But at last all of them sharpen bluely, show bright folds and ribbings of green through their haze. The valleys remain awhile clouded, as if filled with something like blue smoke; but the projecting masses of cliff and slope swiftly change their misty green to a warmer hue. All these tints and colors have a spectral charm, a preternatural loveliness; everything seems subdued, softened, semi-vaporized,—the only very sharply defined silhouettes being those of the little becalmed ships sprinkling the western water, all spreading wings to catch the morning breeze.

The more the sun ascends, the more rapid the development of the landscape out of vapory blue; the hills all become green-faced, reveal the details of frondage. The wind fills the waiting sails—white, red, yellow,—ripples the water, and turns it green. Little fish begin to leap; they spring and fall in glittering showers like opalescent blown spray. And at last, through the fading vapor, dew-glittering red-tiled roofs reveal themselves: the city is unveiled—a city full of color, somewhat quaint, somewhat Spanish-looking—a little like St. Pierre, a little like New Orleans in the old quarter; everywhere fine tall palms.

XXX

ASHORE, through a black swarming and a great hum of creole chatter... Warm yellow narrow streets under a burning blue day;—a confused impression of long vistas, of low pretty houses and cottages, more or less quaint, bathed in sun and yellow-wash,—and avenues of shade-trees,—and low garden-walls overtopped by waving banana leaves and fronds of palms... A general sensation of drowsy warmth and vast light and exotic

St. James Avenue, Port-of-Spain, Trinidad

vegetation,—coupled with some vague disappointment at the absence of that picturesque humanity that delighted us in the streets of St. Pierre, Martinique. The bright costumes of the French colonies are not visible here: there is nothing like them in any of the English islands. Nevertheless, this wonderful Trinidad is as unique ethnologically as it is otherwise remarkable among all the other Antilles. It has three distinct creole populations,—English, Spanish, and French,—besides its German and Madeiran settlers. There is also a special black or half-breed element, corresponding to each creole race, and speaking the language of each; there are fifty thousand Hindoo coolies, and a numerous body of Chinese. Still, this extraordinary diversity of race elements does not make itself at once apparent to the stranger. Your first impressions, as you pass through the black crowd upon the wharf, is that of being among a population as nearly African as that of Barbadoes; and indeed the black element dominates to such an extent that upon the streets white faces look strange by contrast. When a white face does appear, it is usually under the shadow of an Indian helmet, and heavily bearded, and austere: the physiognomy of one used to command. Against the fantastic ethnic background of all this colonial life; this bearded English visage takes something of heroic relief;—one feels, in a totally novel way, the dignity of a white skin.

...I hire a carriage to take me to the nearest coolie village;—a delightful drive... Sometimes the smooth white road curves round the slope of a forest-covered mountain;—sometimes overlooks a valley shining with twenty different shades of surface green; sometimes traverses marvellous natural arcades formed by the interweaving and intercrossing of bamboos fifty feet high. Rising in vast clumps, and spreading out sheafwise from the soil towards the sky, the curves of their beautiful jointed steams meet at such perfect angles above the way, and on either side of it, as to imitate almost exactly the elaborate Gothic arch-work of old abbey cloisters. Above the road, shadowing the slopes of lofty hills, forests beetle in dizzy precipices of verdure. They are green—burning, flashing green—covered with parasitic green creepers and vines; they show enormous forms, or rather dreams of form, fetichistic and startling. Banana leaves flicker and flutter along the way-side; palms shoot up to vast altitudes, like pillars of white metal; and there is a perpetual shifting of foliage color, from yellow-green to orange, from reddish-green to purple, from emerald-green to black-green. But the background color, the dominant tone, is like the plumage of a green parrot.

Coolies of Trinidad

…We drive into the coolie village, along a narrower way, lined with plantain-trees, bananas, flamboyants, and similar shrubs with large broad leaves. Here and there are cocoa-palms. Beyond the little ditches on either side, occupying openings in the natural hedge, are dwellings—wooden cabins, widely separated from each other. The narrow lanes that enter the road are also lined with habitations, half hidden by banana-trees. There is a prodigious glare, an intense heat. Around, above the trees and the roofs, rise the far hill shapes, some brightly verdant, some cloudy blue, some gray. The road and the lanes are almost deserted; there is little shade; only at intervals some slender brown girl or naked baby appears at a door-way. The carriage halts before a shed built against a wall—a simple roof of palm thatch supported upon jointed posts of bamboo.

It is a little coolie temple. A few weary Indian laborers slumber in its shadow; pretty naked children, with silver rings round their ankles, are playing there with a white dog. Painted over the wall surface, in red, yellow, brown, blue, and green designs upon a white ground, are extraordinary figures of gods and goddesses. They have several pairs of arms, brandishing mysterious things,—they seem to dance, gesticulate, threaten; but they are all very *naïf*,—remind one of the first efforts of a child with the first box of paints. While I am looking at these things, one coolie after another wakes up (these men sleep lightly) and begins to observe me almost as curiously, and I fear much less kindly, than I have been observing the gods. "Where is your babagee?" I inquire. No one seems to comprehend my question; the gravity of each dark face remains unrelaxed. Yet I would have liked to make an offering unto Siva.

…Outside the Indian goldsmith's cabin, palm shadows are crawling slowly to and fro in the white glare, like shapes of tarantulas. Inside, the heat is augmented by the tiny charcoal furnace which glows beside a ridiculous little anvil set into a wooden block buried level with the soil. Through a rear door come odors of unknown flowers and the cool brilliant green of banana leaves… A minute of waiting in the hot silence;—then, noiselessly as a phantom, the nude-limbed smith enters by a rear door,—squats down, without a word, on his little mat beside his little anvil,—and turns towards me inquiringly, a face half veiled by a black beard,—a turbaned Indian face, sharp, severe, and slightly unpleasant in expression. "*Vlé béras!*" explains my creole pointing to his client. The smith opens his lips to utter in the tone of a call the single syllable "*Ra!*" then folds his arms.

Almost immediately a young Hindoo woman enters, squats down on the earthen floor at the end of the bench which forms the only furniture of the shop, and turns upon me a pair of the finest black eyes I have seen,—like the eyes of a fawn. She is very simply clad in a coolie robe leaving arms and ankles bare, and clinging about the figure in gracious folds; her color is a clear bright brown—new bronze; her face a fine oval, and charmingly aquiline. I perceive a little silver ring, in the form of a twisted snake, upon the slender second toe of each bare foot; upon each arm she has at least ten heavy silver rings; there are also silver rings about her ankles; a gold flower is fixed by a little hook in one nostril, and two immense silver circles, shaped like new moons, shimmer in her ears. The smith mutters something to her in his Indian tongue. She rises, and seating herself on the bench beside me, in an attitude of perfect grace, holds out one beautiful brown arm to me that I may choose a ring.

The arm is much more worthy of attention than the rings: it has the tint, the smoothness, the symmetry, of a fine statuary's work in metal;— the upper arm, tattooed with a bluish circle of arabesques, is otherwise unadorned; all the bracelets are on the fore-arm. Very clumsy and coarse they prove to be on closer examination: it was the fine dark skin which by color contrast made them look so pretty. I choose the outer one, a round ring with terminations shaped like viper heads;—the smith inserts a pair of tongs between these ends, presses outward slowly and strongly, and the ring is off.

It has a faint musky odor, not unpleasant, the perfume, of the tropical flesh it clung to. I would have taken it thus; but the smith snatches it from me, heats it red in his little charcoal furnace, hammers it into a nearly perfect circle again, slakes it, and burnishes it.

Then I ask for children's *béras,* or bracelets; and the young mother brings in her own baby girl,—a little darling just able to walk. She has extraordinary eyes;—the mother's eyes magnified (the father's are small and fierce). I bargain for the single pair of thin rings on her little wrists;—while the smith is taking them off, the child keeps her wonderful gaze fixed on my face. Then I observe that the peculiarity of the eye is the size of the iris rather than the size of the ball. These eyes are not soft like the mother's, after all; they are ungentle, beautiful as they are; they have the dark and splendid flame of the eyes of a great bird—a bird of prey.

…She will grow up, this little maid, into a slender, graceful woman, very

Coolie Servant

beautiful, no doubt; perhaps a little dangerous. She will marry, of course: probably she is betrothed even now, according to Indian custom,— pledged to some brown boy, the son of a friend. It will not be so many years before the day of their noisy wedding: girls shoot up under this sun with as swift a growth as those broad-leaved beautiful shapes which fill the open door-way with quivering emerald. And she will know the witchcraft of those eyes, will feel the temptation to use them,—perhaps to smile one of those smiles which have power over life and death.

And then the old coolie story! One day, in the yellowing cane-fields, among the swarm of veiled and turbaned workers, a word is overheard, a side glance intercepted;—there is the swirling flash of a cutlass blade; a shrieking gathering of women about a headless corpse in the sun; and passing cityward, between armed and helmeted men, the vision of an Indian prisoner, blood-crimsoned, walking very steadily, very erect, with the solemnity of a judge, the dry bright gaze of an idol...

XXXI

...WE steam very slowly into the harbor of St. George, Grenada, in dead silence. No cannon-signal allowed here... Some one suggests that the violence of the echoes in this harbor renders the firing of cannon dangerous; somebody else says the town is in so ruinous a condition that the report of a gun would shake it down.

...There are heavy damp smells in the warm air as of mould, or of wet clay freshly upturned.

This harbor is a deep clear basin, surrounded and shadowed by immense volcanic hills, all green. The opening by which we entered is cut off from sight by a promontory, and hill shapes beyond the promontory;—we seem to be in the innermost ring of a double crater. There is a continuous shimmering and plashing of leaping fish in the shadow of the loftiest height, which reaches half across the water.

As it climbs up the base of the huge hill at a precipitous angle, the city can be seen from the steamer's deck almost as in a bird's-eye view. A senescent city; mostly antiquated Spanish architecture,—ponderous archways and earthquake-proof walls. The yellow buildings fronting us beyond the wharf seem half decayed; they are strangely streaked with green, look as if they had been long under water. We row ashore, land in a crowd of lazy-looking, silent blacks.

What a quaint, dawdling, sleepy place it is! All these narrow streets are falling into ruin; everywhere the same green stains upon the walls, as of slime left by a flood; everywhere disjointed brickwork, crumbling roofs, pungent odors of mould. Yet this Spanish architecture was built to endure; those yellow, blue, or green walls were constructed with the solidity of fortress-work; the very stairs are stone; the balustrades and the railings were made of good wrought iron. In a Northern clime such edifices would resist the wear and tear of five hundred years. But here the powers of disintegration are extraordinary, and the very air would seem to have the devouring force of an acid. All surfaces and angles are yielding to the attacks of time, weather, and microscopic organisms; paint peels, stucco falls, tiles tumble, stones slip out of place, and in every chink tiny green things nestle, propagating themselves through the jointures and dislocating the masonry. There is an appalling mouldiness, an exaggerated mossiness—the mystery and the melancholy of a city deserted. Old warehouses without signs, huge and void, are opened regularly every day for so many hours; yet the business of the aged merchants within seems to be a problem;—you might fancy those gray men were always waiting for ships that sailed away a generation ago, and will never return. You see no customers entering the stores, but only a black mendicant from time to time. And high above all this, overlooking streets too steep for any vehicle, slope the red walls of the mouldering fort, patched with the viridescence of ruin.

By a road leading up beyond the city, you reach the cemetery. The staggering iron gates by which you enter it are almost rusted from their hinges, and the low wall enclosing it is nearly all verdant. Within, you see a wilderness of strange weeds, vines, creepers, fantastic shrubs run mad, with a few palms mounting above the green confusion;—only here and there a gleam of slabs with inscriptions half erased. Such as you can read are epitaphs of seamen, dating back to the years 1800, 1802, 1812. Over these lizards are running; undulations in the weeds warn you to beware of snakes; toads leap away as you proceed; and you observe everywhere crickets perched—grass-colored creatures with two ruby specks for eyes. They make a sound shrill as the scream of machinery bevelling marble. At the farther end of the cemetery is a heavy ruin that would seem to have once been part of a church: it is so covered with creeping weeds now that you only distinguish the masonry on close approach, and high trees are growing within it.

There is something in tropical ruin peculiarly and terribly impressive: this luxuriant, evergreen, ever-splendid Nature consumes the results of human endeavor so swiftly, buries memories so profoundly, distorts the

Coolie Merchant

labors of generations so grotesquely, that one feels here, as nowhere else, how ephemeral man is, how intense and how tireless the effort necessary to preserve his frail creations even a little while from the vast unconscious forces antagonistic to all stability, to all factitious equilibrium.

...A gloomy road winds high around one cliff overlooking the hollow of the bay. Following it, you pass under extraordinarily dark shadows of foliage, and over a blackish soil strewn with pretty bright green fruit that has fallen from above. Do not touch them even with the tip of your finger! Those are manchineel apples; with their milky juice the old Caribs were wont to poison the barbs of their parrot-feathered arrows. Over the mould, swarming among the venomous fruit, innumerable crabs make a sound almost like the murmuring of water. Some are very large, with

Church Street, St. George, Grenada

prodigious stalked eyes, and claws white as ivory, and a red cuirass; others, very small and very swift in their movements, are raspberry-colored; others, again, are apple-green, with queer mottlings of black and white. There is an unpleasant odor of decay in the air—vegetable decay.

Emerging from the shadow of the manchineel-trees, you may follow the road up, up, up, under beetling cliffs of plutonian rock that seem about to topple down upon the path-way. The rock is naked and black near the road; higher, it is veiled by a heavy green drapery of lianas, curling creepers, unfamiliar vines. All around you are sounds of crawling, dull echoes of dropping; the thick growths far up waver in the breathless air as if something were moving sinuously through them. And always the odor of humid decomposition. Farther on, the road looks wilder, sloping between black rocks, through strange vaultings of foliage and night-black shadows. Its lonesomeness oppresses; one returns without regret, by rusting gate-ways and tottering walls, back to the old West Indian city rotting in the sun.

Yet Grenada, despite the dilapidation of her capital and the seeming desolation of its environs, is not the least prosperous of the Antilles. Other islands have been less fortunate: the era of depression has almost passed for Grenada; through the rapid development of her secondary cultures—coffee and cocoa—she hopes with good reason to repair some of the vast losses involved by the decay of the sugar industry.

Still, in this silence of mouldering streets, this melancholy of abandoned dwellings, this invasion of vegetation, there is a suggestion of what any West Indian port might become when the resources of the island had been exhausted, and its commerce ruined. After all persons of means and energy enough to seek other fields of industry and enterprise had taken their departure, and the plantations had been abandoned, and the warehouses closed up forever, and the voiceless wharves left to rot down into the green water, Nature would soon so veil the place as to obliterate every outward visible sign of the past. In scarcely more than a generation from the time that the last merchant steamer had taken her departure some traveller might look for the once populous and busy mart in vain: vegetation would have devoured it.

...In the mixed English and creole speech of the black population one can discern evidence of a linguistic transition. The original French *patois* is being rapidly forgotten or transformed irrecognizably.

Now, in almost every island the negro idiom is different. So often have some of the Antilles changed owners, moreover, that in them the negro has never been able to form a true *patois*. He had scarcely acquired some idea of the language of his first masters, when other rulers and another tongue were thrust upon him,—and this may have occurred three or four times! The result is a totally incoherent agglomeration of speech-forms—a *baragouin* fantastic and unintelligible beyond the power of any one to imagine who has not heard it...

XXXII

...A BEAUTIFUL fantastic shape floats to us through the morning light; first cloudy gold like the horizon, then pearly gray, then varying blue, with growing green lights;—Saint Lucia. Most strangely formed of all this volcanic family—everywhere mountainings sharp as broken crystals. Far off the Pitons—twin peaks of the high coast—show softer contours, like two black breasts pointing against the sky...

...As we enter the harbor of Castries, the lines of the land seem no less exquisitely odd, in spite of their rich verdure, than when viewed afar off;—they have a particular pitch of angle... Other of these islands show more or less family resemblance;—you might readily mistake one silhouette for another as seen at a distance, even after several West Indian journeys. But Saint Lucia at once impresses you by its eccentricity.

Castries, drowsing under palm leaves at the edge of its curving harbor,—perhaps an ancient crater,—seems more of a village than a town: streets of low cottages and little tropic gardens. It has a handsome half-breed population: the old French colonial manners have been less changed here by English influence than in Saint Kitt's and elsewhere;—the creole *patois* is still spoken, though the costumes have changed... A more beautiful situation could scarcely be imagined,—even in this tropic world. In the massing of green heights about the little town are gaps showing groves of palm beyond; but the peak summits catch the clouds. Behind us the harbor mouth seems spanned by steel-blue bars: these are lines of currents. Away, on either hand, volcanic hills are billowing to vapory distance; and in their nearer hollows are beautiful deepenings of color: ponded shades of diaphanous blue or purplish tone... I first remarked this extraordinary coloring of shadows in Martinique, where it exists to a degree that tempts one to believe the island has a special atmosphere of its own... A friend tells me the phenomenon is probably due to inorganic substances floating in the air,—each substance in diffusion having its own index of refraction. Substances so held in suspension by vapors would vary according to the nature of soil in different islands, and might thus produce special local effects of atmospheric tinting.

...We remain but half an hour at Castries; then steam along the coast to take in freight at another port. Always the same delicious color-effects as we proceed, with new and surprising visions of hills. The near slopes descending to the sea are a radiant green, with streaks and specklings of darker verdure;—the farther-rising hills faint blue, with green saliencies catching the sun;—and beyond these are upheavals of luminous gray—pearl-gray—sharpened in the silver glow of the horizon... The general impression of the whole landscape is one of motion suddenly petrified,—of an earthquake surging and tossing suddenly arrested and fixed: a raging of cones and peaks and monstrous truncated shapes.

...We approach the Pitons.

Seen afar off, they first appeared twin mammiform peaks—naked and dark against the sky; but now they begin to brighten a little and show color,—also change form. They take a lilaceous hue, broken by gray and green lights; and as we draw yet nearer they prove dissimilar both in shape and tint... Now they separate before us, throwing long pyramidal shadows across the steamer's path. Then, as they open to our coming, between them a sea bay is revealed—a very lovely curving bay, bounded by hollow cliffs of fiery green. At either side of the gap the Pitons rise like

Castries, St. Lucia

monster pylones. And a charming little settlement, a beautiful sugar-plantation, is nestling there between them, on the very edge of the bay.

Out of a bright sea of verdure, speckled with oases of darker foliage, these Pitons from the land side tower in sombre vegetation. Very high up, on the nearer one, amid the wooded slopes, you can see houses perched; and there are bright breaks in the color there—tiny mountain pastures that look like patches of green silk velvet.

...We pass the Pitons, and enter another little craterine harbor, to cast anchor before the village of Choiseul. It lies on a ledge above the beach and under high hills: we land through a surf, running the boat high up on soft yellowish sand. A delicious saline scent of seaweed.

It is disappointing, the village: it is merely one cross of brief streets, lined with blackening wooden dwellings; there are no buildings worth looking at, except the queer old French church, steep-roofed and bristling with points that look like extinguishers. Over broad reaches of lava rock a shallow river flows by the village to the sea, gurgling under shadows of tamarind foliage. It passes beside the market-place—a market-place without stalls, benches, sheds, or pavements: meats, fruits, and vegetables are simply fastened to the trees. Women are washing and naked children bathing in the stream; they are bronze-skinned, a fine dark color with a faint tint of red in it.

...There is little else to look at: steep wooded hills cut off the view towards the interior.

But over the verge of the sea there is something strange growing visible, looming up like a beautiful yellow cloud. It is an island, so lofty, so luminous, so phantom-like, that it seems a vision of the Island of the Seven Cities. It is only the form of St. Vincent, bathed in vapory gold by the sun.

...Evening at La Soufrière: still another semicircular bay in a hollow of green hills. Glens hold bluish shadows. The color of the heights is very tender; but there are long streaks and patches of dark green, marking watercourses and very abrupt surfaces. From the western side immense shadows are pitched brokenly across the valley and over half the roofs of the palmy town. There is a little river flowing down to the bay on the left; and west of it a walled cemetery is visible, out of which one monumental palm rises to a sublime height: its crest still bathes in the sun, above the invading shadow. Night approaches; the shade of the hills inundates all the landscape, rises even over the palm-crest. Then, black-towering into the golden glow of sunset, the land loses all its color, all its charm; forms of frondage, variations of tint, become invisible. Saint Lucia is only a monstrous silhouette; all its billowing hills, its volcanic bays, its amphitheatrical valleys, turn black as ebony.

And you behold before you a geological dream, a vision of the primeval sea: the apparition of the land as first brought forth, all peak-tossed and fissured and naked and grim, in the tremendous birth of an archipelago.

XXXIII

HOMEWARD bound.

Again the enormous poem of azure and emerald unrolls before us, but in order inverse; again is the island-Litany of the Saints repeated for us, but now backward. All the bright familiar harbors once more open to receive us;—each lovely Shape floats to us again, first golden yellow, then vapory gray, then ghostly blue, but always sharply radiant at last, symmetrically exquisite, as if chiselled out of amethyst and emerald and sapphire. We review the same wondrous wrinkling of volcanic hills, the cities that sit in extinct craters, the woods that tower to heaven, the peaks perpetually wearing that luminous cloud which seems the breathing of each island-life,—its vital manifestation...

Only now do the long succession of exotic and unfamiliar impressions received begin to group and blend, to form homogeneous results,—general ideas or convictions. Strongest among these is the belief that the white race is disappearing from these islands, acquired and held at so vast a cost of blood and treasure. Reasons almost beyond enumeration have been advanced—economical, climatic, ethnical, political,—all of which contain truth, yet no single one of which can wholly explain the fact. Already the white West Indian populations are diminishing at a rate that almost staggers credibility. In the island paradise of Martinique in 1848 there were 12,000 whites; now, against more than 160,000 blacks and half-breeds, there are perhaps 5000 whites left to maintain the ethnic struggle, and the number of these latter is annually growing less. Many of the British islands have been almost deserted by their former cultivators: St. Vincent is becoming desolate; Tobago is a ruin; St. Martin lies half abandoned; St. Christopher is crumbling; Grenada has lost more than half her whites; St. Thomas, once the most prosperous; the most active, the most cosmopolitan of West Indian ports, is in full decadence. And while the white element is disappearing, the dark races are multiplying as never before;—the increase of the negro and half-breed populations has been everywhere one of the startling results of emancipation. The general belief among the creole whites of the Lesser Antilles would seem to confirm the old prediction that the slave races of the past must become the masters of the future. Here and there the struggle may be greatly prolonged, but everywhere the ultimate result must be the same, unless the present conditions of commerce and production become marvellously changed. The exterminated Indian peoples of the Antilles have already been replaced by populations equally fitted to cope with the forces of the nature about them,—that splendid and terrible Nature of the tropics which consumes the energies of the races of the North, which devours all that has been accomplished by their heroism or their crimes,—effacing their cities, rejecting their civilization. To those peoples physiologically in harmony with this Nature belong all the chances of victory in the contest—already begun—for racial supremacy.

But with the disappearance of the white populations the ethnical problem would be still unsettled. Between the black and mixed peoples prevail hatreds more enduring and more intense than any race prejudices between whites and freedmen in the past;—a new struggle for supremacy could not fail to begin, with the perpetual augmentation of numbers, the ever-increasing competition for existence. And the true black element, more numerically powerful, more fertile, more cunning, better adapted to pyrogenic climate and tropical environment, would surely win. All these mixed races, all these beautiful fruit-colored populations, seem doomed to extinction: the future tendency must be to universal blackness, if existing conditions continue—perhaps to universal savagery. Everywhere the sins of the past have borne the same fruit, have furnished the colonies with social enigmas that mock the wisdom of legislators,—a dragon-crop of problems that no modern political sense has yet proved competent to deal with. Can it even be hoped that future sociologists will be able to answer them, after Nature—who never forgives—shall have exacted the utmost possible retribution for all the crimes and follies of three hundred years?

NOTES

1. Since this was written the market has been removed to the Savane,—to allow of the erection of a large new market-building on the old site; and the beautiful trees have been cut down.

2. I subsequently learned the mystery of this very strange and beautiful mixed race,—many fine specimens of which may also be seen in Trinidad. Three widely diverse elements have combined to form it: European, negro, and Indian,—but, strange to say, it is the most savage of these three bloods which creates the peculiar charm... I cannot speak of this comely and extraordinary type without translating a passage from Dr. J. J. J. Cornilliac, an eminent Martinique physician, who recently published a most valuable series of studies upon the ethnology, climatology, and history of the Antilles. In these he writes:

..."When, among the populations of the Antilles, we first notice those remarkable *métis* whose olive skins, elegant and slender figures, fine straight profiles, and regular features remind us of the inhabitants of Madras or Pondicherry, we ask ourselves in wonder, while looking at their long eyes, full of a strange and gentle melancholy (especially among the women), and at the black, rich, silky-gleaming hair curling in abundance over the temples and falling in profusion over the neck,—to what human race can belong this singular variety,—in which there is a dominant characteristic that seems indelible, and always shows more and more strongly in proportion as the type is further removed from the African element. It is the Carib blood,—blended with blood of Europeans and of blacks,—which in spite of all subsequent crossings, and in spite of the fact that it has not been renewed for more than two hundred years, still conserves as markedly as at the time of the first inter-blending, the race-characteristic that invariably reveals its presence in the blood of every being through whose veins it flows."—"Recherches chronologiques et historiques sur l'Origine et la Propagation de la Fièvre Jaune aux Antilles." Par J. J. J. Cornilliac. Fort-de-France: Imprimerie du Gouvernement. 1886.

But I do not think the term "olive" always indicates the color of these skins, which seemed to me exactly the tint of gold; and the hair flashes with bluish lights, like the plumage of certain black birds.

3. "Enquête sur le Serpent de la Martinique (Vipère Fer-de-Lance, Bothrops Lancéolé, etc.)." Par le Docteur E.Rufz. 2 ed. 1859. Paris: Germer-Ballière. pp. 55-57 (note).

Martinique Sketches

I. Les Porteuses

I

WHEN you find yourself for the first time, upon some shadowed day, in the delightful West Indian city of St. Pierre,—supposing that you own the sense of poetry, the recollections of a student,—there is apt to steal upon your fancy an impression of having seen it all before, ever so long ago,—you cannot tell where. The sensation of some happy dream you cannot wholly recall might be compared to this feeling. In the simplicity and solidity of the quaint architecture,—in the eccentricity of bright narrow streets, all aglow with warm coloring,—in the tints of roof and wall, antiquated by streakings and patchings of mould greens and grays,—in the startling absence of window-sashes, glass, gas lamps, and chimneys,—in the blossom-tenderness of the blue heaven, the splendor of tropic light, and the warmth of the tropic wind,—you find less the impression of a scene of today than the sensation of something that was and is not. Slowly this feeling strengthens with your pleasure in the colorific radiance of costume,—the semi-nudity of passing figures,—the puissant shapeliness of torsos ruddily swart like statue metal,—the rounded outline of limbs yellow as tropic fruit,—the grace of attitudes,—the unconscious harmony of groupings,—the gathering and folding and falling of light robes that os-cillate with swaying of free hips,—the sculptural symmetry of unshod feet. You look up and down the lemon-tinted streets,—down to the dazzling azure brightness of meeting sky and sea; up to the perpetual verdure of mountain woods—wondering at the mellowness of tones, the sharpness of lines in the light, the diaphaneity of colored shadows; always asking memory: "When?... where did I see all this... long ago?"...

Then, perhaps, your gaze is suddenly riveted by the vast and solemn beauty of the verdant violet-shaded mass of the dead Volcano,—high-towering above the town, visible from all its ways, and umbraged, maybe, with thinnest curlings of cloud,—like spectres of its ancient smoking to heaven. And all at once the secret of your dream is revealed, with the rising of many a luminous memory,—dreams of the Idyllists, flowers of old Sicilian song, fancies limned upon Pompeiian walls. For a moment the illusion is delicious: you comprehend as never before the charm of a vanished world,—the antique life, the story of terra-cottas and graven stones and gracious things exhumed: even the sun is not of today, but of twenty centuries gone;—thus, and under such a light, walked the women of the elder world. You know the fancy absurd;—that the power of the orb has visibly abated nothing in all the eras of man,—that millions are the ages of his almighty glory; but for one instant of reverie he seemeth larger,—even that sun impossible who coloreth the words, coloreth the works of artist-lovers of the past, with the gold light of dreams.

Too soon the hallucination is broken by modern sounds, dissipated by modern sights,—rough trolling of sailors descending to their boats,—the heavy boom of a packet's signal-gun,—the passing of an American buggy. Instantly you become aware that the melodious tongue spoken by the passing throng is neither Hellenic nor Roman: only the beautiful childish speech of French slaves.

II

BUT what slaves were the fathers of this free generation? Your anthropologists, your ethnologists, seem at fault here: the African traits have become transformed; the African characteristics have been so modified within little more than two hundred years—by inter-blending of blood, by habit, by soil and sun and all those natural powers which shape the mould of races,—that you may look in vain for verification of ethnological assertions... No: the heel does *not* protrude;—the foot is *not* flat, but finely arched;—the extremities are not large;—all the limbs taper, all the muscles are developed; and prognathism has become so rare that months of research may not yield a single striking case of it... No: this is a special race, peculiar to the island as are the shapes of its peaks,—a mountain race; and mountain races are comely... Compare it with the population of black Barbadoes, where the apish grossness of African coast types has been perpetuated unchanged;—and the contrast may well astonish!...

III

THE erect carriage and steady swift walk of the women who bear burdens is especially likely to impress the artistic observer: it is the sight of such passers-by which gives, above all, the antique tone and color to his first sensations;—and the larger part of the female population of mixed race are practised carriers. Nearly all the transportation of light merchandise, as well as of meats, fruits, vegetables, and food stuffs,—to and from the interior,—is effected upon human heads. At some of the ports the regular local packets are loaded and unloaded by women and girls,—able to carry any trunk or box to its destination. At Fort-de-France the great steamers of the Compagnie Générale Transatlantique are entirely coaled by women, who carry the coal on their heads, singing as they come and go in processions of hundreds; and the work is done with incredible rapidity. Now, the creole *porteuse*, or female carrier, is certainly one of the most remarkable physical types in the world; and whatever artistic enthusiasm her graceful port, lithe walk, or half-savage beauty may inspire you with, you can form no idea, if a total stranger, what a really wonderful being she is... Let me tell you something about that highest type of professional female carrier, which is to the *charbonnière*, or coaling-girl, what the thoroughbred racer is to the draught-horse,—the type of porteuse selected for swiftness and endurance to distribute goods in the interior parishes, or to sell on commission at long distances. To the same class naturally belong those country carriers able to act as porteuses of plantation produce, fruits, or vegetables,—between the nearer ports and their own interior parishes... Those who believe that great physical endurance and physical energy cannot exist in the tropics do not know the creole carrier-girl.

IV

AT a very early age—perhaps at five years—she learns to carry small articles upon her head,—a bowl of rice,—a *dobanne*, or red earthen decanter, full of water,—even an orange on a plate; and before long she is able to balance these perfectly without using her hands to steady them. (I have often seen children actually run with cans of water upon their heads, and never spill a drop.) At nine or ten she is able to carry thus a tolerably heavy basket, or a *trait* (a wooden tray with deep outward sloping sides) containing a weight of from twenty to thirty pounds; and is able to accompany her mother, sister, or cousin on long peddling journeys,—walking barefoot twelve and fifteen miles a day. At sixteen or seventeen she is a tall robust girl,—lithe, vigorous, tough,—all tendon and hard flesh;—she carries a tray or a basket of the largest size, and a burden of one hundred and twenty to one hundred and fifty pounds weight;—she can now earn about thirty francs (about six dollars) a month, by *walking fifty miles a day*, as an itinerant seller.

Among her class there are figures to make you dream of Atalanta;— and all, whether ugly or attractive as to feature, are finely shapen as to body and limb. Brought into existence by extraordinary necessities of environment, the type is a peculiarly local one,—a type of human thoroughbred representing the true secret of grace: economy of force. There are no corpulent porteuses for the long interior routes; all are built lightly and firmly as racers. There are no old porteuses;—to do the work even at forty signifies a constitution of astounding solidity. After the full force of youth and health is spent, the poor carrier must seek lighter labor;—she can no longer compete with the girls. For in this calling the young body is taxed to its utmost capacity of strength, endurance, and rapid motion.

As a general rule, the weight is such that no well-freighted porteuse can, unassisted, either "load" or "unload" (*châgé* or *déchâgé*, in creole phrase); the effort to do so would burst a blood-vessel, wrench a nerve, rupture a muscle. She cannot even sit down under her burden without risk of breaking her neck: absolute perfection of the balance is necessary for self-preservation. A case came under my own observation of a woman rupturing a muscle in her arm through careless haste in the mere act of aiding another to unload.

And no one not a brute will ever refuse to aid a woman to lift or to relieve herself of her burden;—you may see the wealthiest merchant, the proudest planter, gladly do it;—the meanness of refusing, or of making any conditions for the performance of this little kindness has only been imagined in those strange Stories of Devils wherewith the oral and uncollected literature of the creole abounds.[1]

V

PREPARING for her journey, the young *màchanne* (marchande) puts on the poorest and briefest chemise in her possession, and the most worn of her light calico robes. These are all she wears. The robe is drawn upward and forward, so as to reach a little below the knee, and is confined thus by a waist-string, or a long kerchief bound tightly round the loins. Instead of a Madras or painted turban-kerchief, she binds a plain *mouchoir* neatly and closely about her head; and if her hair be long, it is combed back and gathered into a loop behind. Then, with a second mouchoir of coarser

'Ti Marie (On the route from St. Pierre to Basse-Pointe)

quality she makes a pad, or, as she calls it, *tòche,* by winding the kerchief round her fingers as you would coil up a piece of string;—and the soft mass, flattened with a patting of the hand, is placed upon her head, over the coiffure. On this the great loaded trait is poised.

She wears no shoes! To wear shoes and do her work swiftly and well in such a land of mountains would be impossible. She must climb thousands and descend thousands of feet every day,—march up and down slopes so steep that the horses of the country all break down after a few years of similar journeying. The girl invariably outlasts the horse,—though carrying an equal weight. Shoes, unless extraordinarily well made, would shift place a little with every change from ascent to descent, or the reverse, during the march,—would yield and loosen with the ever-varying strain,—would compress the toes,—produce corns, bunions, raw places by rubbing, and soon cripple the porteuse. Remember, she has to walk perhaps fifty miles between dawn and dark, under a sun to which a single hour's exposure, without the protection of an umbrella, is perilous to any European or American—the terrible sun of the tropics! Sandals are the only conceivable foot-gear suited to such a calling as hers; but she needs no sandals: the soles of her feet are toughened so as to feel no asperities, and present to sharp pebbles a surface at once yielding and resisting, like a cushion of solid caoutchouc.

Besides her load, she carries only a canvas purse tied to her girdle on the right side, and on the left a very small bottle of rum, or white *tafia,*—usually the latter, because it is so cheap… For she may not always find the Gouyave Water to drink,—the cold clear pure stream conveyed to the fountains of St. Pierre from the highest mountains by a beautiful and marvellous plan of hydraulic engineering: she will have to drink betimes the common spring-water of the bamboo-fountains on the remoter high-roads; and this may cause dysentery if swallowed without a spoonful of spirits. Therefore she never travels without a little liquor.

VI

…So!—She is ready: "*Châgé moin, souplè, chè!*" She bends to lift the end of the heavy trait: some one takes the other,—*yon!—dè!—toua!*—it is on her head. Perhaps she winces an instant;—the weight is not perfectly balanced; she settles it with her hands,—gets it in the exact place. Then, all steady,—lithe, light, half naked,—away she moves with a long springy step. So even her walk that the burden never sways; yet so rapid her motion that however good a walker you may fancy yourself to be you will tire out after a sustained effort of fifteen minutes to follow her uphill. Fifteen minutes!—and she can keep up that pace without slackening—save for a minute to eat and drink at midday, for at least twelve hours and fifty-six minutes, the extreme length of a West Indian day. She starts before dawn; tries to reach her resting-place by sunset: after dark, like all her people, she is afraid of meeting *zombis*.

Let me give you some idea of her average speed under an average weight of one hundred and twenty-five pounds,—estimates based partly upon my own observations, partly upon the declarations of the trustworthy merchants who employ her, and partly on the assertion of habitants of the burghs or cities named—all of which statements perfectly agree. From St. Pierre to Basse-Pointe, by the national road, the distance is a trifle less than twenty-seven kilometres and three-quarters. She makes the transit easily in three hours and a half; and returns in the afternoon, after an absence of scarcely more than eight hours. From St. Pierre to Morne Rouge—two thousand feet up in the mountains (an ascent so abrupt that no one able to pay carriage-fare dreams of attempting to walk it)—the distance is seven kilometres and three-quarters. She makes it in little more than an hour. But this represents only the beginning of her journey. She passes on to Grande Anse, twenty-one and three-quarter kilometres away. But she does not rest there: she returns at the same pace, and reaches St. Pierre before dark. From St. Pierre to Gros-Morne the distance to be twice traversed by her is more than thirty-two kilometres. A journey of sixty-four kilometres,—daily, perhaps,—forty miles! And there are many màchannes who make yet longer trips,—trips of three or four days' duration;—these rest at villages upon their route.

VII

SUCH travel in such a country would be impossible but for the excellent national roads,—limestone highways, solid, broad, faultlessly graded,—that wind from town to town, from hamlet to hamlet, over mountains, over ravines; ascending by zigzags to heights of twenty-five hundred feet; traversing the primeval forests of the interior; now skirting the dizziest precipices, now descending into the loveliest valleys. There are thirty-one of these magnificent routes, with a total length of 488,052 metres (more than 303 miles), whereof the construction required engineering talent of the highest order,—the building of bridges beyond counting, and devices the most ingenious to provide against dangers of storms, floods, and land-slips. Most have drinking-fountains along their course at almost regular intervals,—generally made by the negroes, who have a simple but excellent plan for turning the water of a spring through bamboo pipes to the road-way. Each road is also furnished with mile-stones, or rather kilometre-stones; and the drainage is perfect enough to assure of the highway becoming dry within fifteen minutes after the heaviest rain, so long as the surface is maintained in tolerably good condition. Well-kept embankments of earth (usually covered with a rich growth of mosses, vines, and ferns), or even solid walls of masonry, line the side that overhangs a dangerous depth. And all these highways pass through landscapes of amazing beauty,—visions of mountains so many-tinted and so singular of outline that they would almost seem to have been created for the express purpose of compelling astonishment. This tropic Nature appears to call into being nothing ordinary: the shapes which she evokes are always either gracious or odd,—and her eccentricities, her extravagances, have a fantastic charm, a grotesqueness as of artistic whim. Even where the landscape-view is cut off by high woods the forms of ancient trees—the infinite interwreathing of vine growths all on fire with violence of blossom-color,—the enormous green outbursts of balisiers, with leaves ten to thirteen feet long,—the columnar solemnity of great palmistes,—the pliant quivering exquisiteness of bamboo,—the furious splendor of roses run mad—more than atone for the loss of the horizon. Sometimes you approach a steep covered with a growth of what, at first glance, looks precisely like fine green fur: it is a first-growth of young bamboo. Or you see a hill-side covered with huge green feathers, all shelving down and overlapping as in the tail of some unutterable bird: these are baby ferns. And where the road leaps some deep ravine with a double or triple bridge of white stone, note well what delicious shapes spring up into sunshine from the black profundity on either hand! Palmiform you might hastily term them,—but no palm was ever so gracile; no palm ever bore so dainty a head of green plumes light as lace! These likewise are ferns (rare survivors, maybe, of that period of monstrous vegetation which preceded the apparition of man), beautiful tree-ferns, whose every young plume, unrolling in a spiral from the bud, at first assumes the shape of a crozier,—a crozier of emerald! Therefore are some of this species called "archbishop-trees," no doubt… But one might write for a hundred years of the sights to be seen upon such a mountain road.

VIII

IN every season, in almost every weather, the porteuse makes her journey,—never heeding rain;—her goods being protected by double and triple water-proof coverings well bound down over her trait. Yet these tropical rains, coming suddenly with a cold wind upon her heated and almost naked body, are to be feared. To any European or unacclimated white such a wetting, while the pores are all open during a profuse perspiration, would probably prove fatal: even for white natives the result is always a serious and protracted illness. But the porteuse seldom suffers in consequences: she seems proof against fevers, rheumatisms, and ordinary colds. When she does break down, however, the malady is a frightful one,—a pneumonia that carries off the victim within forty-eight hours. Happily, among her class, these fatalities are very rare.

And scarcely less rare than such sudden deaths are instances of failure to appear on time. In one case, the employer, a St. Pierre shopkeeper, on finding his *marchande* more than an hour late, felt so certain something very extraordinary must have happened that he sent out messengers in all directions to make inquiries. It was found that the woman had become a mother when only half-way upon her journey home…The child lived and thrived;—she is now a pretty chocolate-colored girl of eight, who

Fort-de-France, Martinique (Formerly Fort Royal)

follows her mother every day from their mountain ajoupa down to the city, and back again,—bearing a little trait upon her head.

Murder for purposes of robbery is not an unknown crime in Martinique; but I am told the porteuses are never molested. And yet some of these girls carry merchandise to the value of hundreds of francs; and all carry money,—the money received for goods sold, often a considerable sum. This immunity may be partly owing to the fact that they travel during the greater part of the year only by day,—and usually in company. A very pretty girl is seldom suffered to journey unprotected: she has either a male escort or several experienced and powerful women with her. In the cacao season—when carriers start from Grande Anse as early as two o'clock in the morning, so as to reach St. Pierre by dawn—they travel in strong companies of twenty or twenty-five, singing on the way. As a general rule the younger girls at all times go two together,—keeping step perfectly as a pair of blooded fillies; only the veterans, or women selected for special work by reason of extraordinary physical capabilities, go alone. To the latter class belong certain girls employed by the great bakeries of Fort-de-France and St. Pierre: these are veritable caryatides. They are probably the heaviest-laden of all, carrying baskets of astounding size far up into the mountains before daylight, so as to furnish country families with fresh bread at an early hour; and for this labor they receive about four dollars (twenty francs) a month and one loaf of bread per diem... While stopping at a friend's house among the hills, some two miles from Fort-de-France, I saw the local bread-carrier halt before our porch one morning, and a finer type of the race it would be difficult for a sculptor to imagine. Six feet tall,—strength and grace united throughout her whole figure from neck to heel; with that clear black skin which is beautiful to any but ignorant or prejudiced eyes; and the smooth, pleasing, solemn features of a sphinx,—she looked to me, as she towered there in the gold light, a symbolic statue of Africa. Seeing me smoking one of those long thin Martinique cigars called *bouts*, she begged one; and, not happening to have another, I gave her the price of a bunch of twenty,—ten sous. She took it without a smile, and went her way. About an hour and a half later she came back and asked for me,—to present me with the finest and largest mango I had ever seen, a monster mango. She said she wanted to see me eat it, and sat down on the ground to look on. While eating it, I learned that she had walked a whole mile out of her way under that sky of fire, just to bring her little gift of gratitude.

IX

FORTY to fifty miles a day, always under a weight of more than a hundred pounds,—for when the trait has been emptied she puts in stones for ballast;—carrying her employer's merchandise and money over the mountain ranges, beyond the peaks, across the ravines, through the tropical forest, sometimes through by-ways haunted by the fer-de-lance,—and this in summer or winter, the season of rains or the season of heat, the time of fevers or the time of hurricanes, at a franc a day!... How does she live upon it?

There are twenty sous to the franc. The girl leaves St. Pierre with her load at early morning. At the second village, Morne Rouge, she halts to buy one, two, or three biscuits at a sou apiece; and reaching Ajoupa-Bouillon later in the forenoon, she may buy another biscuit or two. Altogether she may be expected to eat five sous of biscuit or bread before reaching Grande Anse, where she probably has a meal waiting for her. This ought to cost her ten sous,—especially if there be meat in her ragoût: which represents a total expense of fifteen sous for eatables. Then there is the additional cost of the cheap liquor, which she must mix with her drinking-water, as it would be more than dangerous to swallow pure cold water in her heated condition; two or three sous more. This almost makes the franc. But such a hasty and really erroneous estimate does not include expenses of lodging and clothing;—she may sleep on the bare floor sometimes, and twenty francs a year may keep her in clothes; but she must rent the floor and pay for the clothes out of that franc. As a matter of fact she not only does all this upon her twenty sous a day, but can even economize something which will enable her, when her youth and force decline, to start in business for herself. And her economy will not seem so wonderful when I assure you that thousands of men here—huge men muscled like bulls and lions—live upon an average expenditure of five sous a day. One sou of bread, two sous of manioc flour, one sou of dried codfish, one son of tafia: such is their meal.

There are women carriers who earn more than a franc a day,—women with a particular talent for selling, who are paid on commission—from ten to fifteen per cent. These eventually make themselves independent in many instances;—they continue to sell and bargain in person, but hire a young girl to carry the goods.

X

…"*Ou 'lè màchanne!*" rings out a rich alto, resonant as the tone of a gong, from behind the balisiers that shut in our garden. There are two of them—no, three—Maiyotte, Chéchelle, and Rina. Maiyotte and Chéchelle have just arrived from St. Pierre;—Rina comes from Gros-Morne with fruits and vegetables. Suppose we call them all in, and see what they have got. Maiyotte and Chéchelle sell on commission; Rina sells for her mother, who has a little garden at Gros-Morne.

…"*Bonjou', Maiyotte,—bonjou', Chéchelle! coument ou kallé, Rina, chè!*"
…Throw open the folding-doors to let the great trays pass… Now all three are unloaded by old Théréza and by young Adou;—all the packs are on the floor, and the water-proof wrappings are being uncorded, while Ah-Manmzell, the adopted child, brings the rum and water for the tall walkers.

…"Oh, what a medley, Maiyotte!"… Inkstands and wooden cows; purses and paper dogs and cats; dolls and cosmetics; pins and needles and soap and toothbrushes; candied fruits and smoking-caps; *pelotes* of thread, and tapes, and ribbons, and laces, and Madeira wine; cuffs, and collars, and dancing-shoes, and tobacco *sachets*… But what is in that little flat bundle? Presents for your *guêpe*, if you have one… *Jesis-Maïa!*—the pretty foulards! Azure and yellow in checkerings; orange and crimson in stripes; rose and scarlet in plaidings; and bronze tints, and beetle-tints of black and green.

"Chéchelle, what a *bloucoutoum* if you should ever let that tray fall—*aïe yaïe yaïe!*" Here is a whole shop of crockeries and porcelains;—plates, dishes, cups,—earthen-ware *canaris* and *dobannes*; and gift-mugs and cups bearing creole girls' names,—all names that end in *ine*:

"Micheline", "Honorine," "Prospérine" [you will never sell that, Chéchelle: there is not a Prospérine this side of St. Pierre], "Azaline," "Leontine," "Zéphyrine," "Albertine," "Chrysaline," "Florine," "Coralline," "Alexandrine." … And knives and forks, and cheap spoons, and tin coffee-pots, and tin rattles for babies, and tin flutes for horrid little boys,—and pencils and note-paper and envelopes!…

"Oh, Rina, what superb oranges!—fully twelve inches round!… and these, which look something like our mandarins, what do you call them?" "Zorange-macaque!" (monkey-oranges). And here are avocados—beauties!—guavas of three different kinds,—tropical cherries (which have four seeds instead of one),—tropical raspberries, whereof the entire eatable portion comes off in one elastic piece, lined with something like white silk... Here are fresh nutmegs: the thick green case splits in equal halves at a touch; and see the beautiful heart within,—deep dark glossy red, all wrapped in a bright net-work of flat blood-colored fibre, spun over like branching veins... This big heavy red-and-yellow thing is a *pomme-cythère*: the smooth cuticle, bitter as gall, covers a sweet juicy pulp, interwoven with something that seems like cotton thread... Here is a *pomme-cannelle:* inside its scaly covering is the most delicious yellow custard conceivable, with little black seeds floating in it. This larger *corossol* has almost as delicate an interior, only the custard is white instead of yellow... Here are *christophines,*—great pear-shaped things, white and green, according to kind, with a peel prickly and knobby as the skin of a horned toad; but they stew exquisitely. And *mélongènes,* or egg-plants; and palmiste-pith, and *chadèques,* and *pommes-d'Haïti,*—and roots that at first sight look all alike, but they are not: there are *camanioc,* and *couscous,* and *choux-caraïbes,* and *zignames,* and various kinds of *patates* among them. Old Théréza's magic will transform these shapeless muddy things, before evening, into pyramids of smoking gold,—into odorous porridges that will look like messes of molten amber and liquid pearl;—for Rina makes a good sale.

Then Chéchelle manages to dispose of a tin coffee-pot and a big canari... And Maiyotte makes the best sale of all; for the sight of a funny *biscuit* doll has made Ah-Manmzell cry and smile so at the same time that I should feel unhappy for the rest of my life if I did not buy it for her. I know I ought to get some change out of that six francs;—and Maiyotte, who is black but comely as the tents of Kedar, as the curtains of Solomon, seems to be aware of the fact.

Oh, Maiyotte, how plaintive that pretty sphinx face of yours, now turned in profile;—as if you knew you looked beautiful thus,—with the great gold circlets of your ears glittering and swaying as you bend! And why are you so long, so long untying that poor little canvas purse?— fumbling and fingering it?—is it because you want me to think of the weight of that trait and the sixty kilometres you must walk, and the heat, and the dust, and all the disappointments? Ah, you are cunning, Maiyotte! No, I do not want the change!

XI

TRAVELLING together, the porteuses often walk in silence for hours at a time;—this is when they feel weary. Sometimes they sing,—most often when approaching their destination;—and when they chat, it is in a key so high-pitched that their voices can be heard to a great distance in this land of echoes and elevations.

But she who travels alone is rarely silent: she talks to herself or to inanimate things;—you may hear her talking to the trees, to the flowers,—talking to the high clouds and the far peaks of changing color,—talking to the setting sun!

Over the miles of the morning she sees, perchance, the mighty Piton Gélé, a cone of amethyst in the light; and she talks to it: "*Ou jojoll, oui!—moin ni envie monté assou ou, pou moin ouè bien, bien!*" (Thou art pretty, pretty, aye—I would I might climb thee, to see far, far off!)

By a great grove of palms she passes;—so thickly mustered they are that against the sun their intermingled heads form one unbroken awning of green. Many rise straight as masts; some bend at beautiful angles, seeming to intercross their long pale single limbs in a fantastic dance; others curve like bows: there is one that undulates from foot to crest, like a monster serpent poised upon its tail. She loves to look at that one,—*joli pié-bois-là!*—talks to it as she goes by,—bids it good-day.

Or, looking back as she ascends, she sees the huge blue dream of the sea,—the eternal haunter, that ever becomes larger as she mounts the road; and she talks to it: "*Mi lanmé ka gadé moin!*" (There is the great sea looking at me!) "*Màché toujou deïë moin, lanmé!*" (Walk after me, O Sea!)

Or she views the clouds of Pelée, spreading gray from the invisible summit, to shadow against the sun; and she fears the rain, and she talks to it: "*Pas mouillé moin, laplie-à! Quitté moin rivé avant mouillé moin!*" (Do not wet me, O Rain! Let me get there before thou wettest me!)

Sometimes a dog barks at her, menaces her bare limbs; and she talks to the dog: "*Chien-a, pas mòdé moin, chien—anh! Moin pa fé ou arien, chien, pou ou mòdé moin!*" (Do not bite me, O Dog! Never did I anything to thee that thou shouldst bite me, O Dog! Do not bite me, dear! Do not bite me, *doudoux!*)

Sometimes she meets a laden sister travelling the opposite way… "*Coument ou yé, chè?*" she cries. (How art thou, dear?) And the other makes answer, "*Toutt douce, ché—et ou?*" (All sweetly, dear,—and thou?) And each passes on without pausing: they have no time!

It is perhaps the last human voice she will hear for many a mile. After that only the whisper of the grasses—*graïe-gras, graïe-gras!*—and the gossip of the canes—*chououa, chououa!*—and the husky speech of the *pois-Angole, ka babillé conm yon vié fenme,*—that babbles like an old woman;—and the murmur of the *filao*-trees, like the murmur of the River of the Washerwomen.

XII

...SUNDOWN approaches: the light has turned a rich yellow;—long black shapes lie across the curving road, shadows of balisier and palm, shadows of tamarind and Indian-reed, shadows of ceiba and giant-fern. And the porteuses are coming down through the lights and darknesses of the way from far Grande Anse, to halt a moment in this little village. They are going to sit down on the road-side here, before the house of the baker; and there is his great black workman, Jean-Marie, looking for them from the door-way, waiting to relieve them of their loads... Jean-Marie is the strongest man in all the Champ-Flore: see what a torso,—as he stands there naked to the waist!... His day's work is done; but he likes to wait for the girls, though he is old now, and has sons as tall as himself. It is a habit: some say that he had a daughter once,—a porteuse like those coming, and used to wait for her thus at that very door-way until one evening that she failed to appear, and never returned till he carried her home in his arms dead,—stricken by a serpent in some mountain path where there was none to aid... The roads were not as good then as now.

Here they come, the girls—yellow, red, black. See the flash of the yellow feet where they touch the light! And what impossible tint the red limbs take in the changing glow!... Finotte, Pauline, Médelle,—all together, as usual,—with Ti-Clé trotting behind, very tired... Never mind, Ti-Clé!—you will outwalk your cousins when you are a few years older,—pretty Ti-Clé... Here come Cyrillia and Zabette, and Féfé and Dodotte and Fevriette. And behind them are coming the two *chabines*,— golden girls: the twin-sisters who sell silks and threads and foulards; always together, always wearing robes and kerchiefs of similar color,—so that you can never tell which is Lorrainie and which is Édoualise.

And all smile to see Jean-Marie waiting for them, and to hear his deep kind voice calling, "*Coument ou yé chè? coument ou kallé?*" (How art thou, dear?—How goes it with thee?)

And they mostly make answer, "*Toutt douce, chè,—et ou?*" (All sweetly, dear,—and thou?) But some weary, cry to him, "*Ah! déchâgé moin vite, chè! Moin lasse, lasse!*" (Unload me quickly, dear; for I am very weary.) Then he takes off their burdens, and fetches bread for them, and says foolish little things to make them laugh. And they are pleased, and laugh, just like children, as they sit right down on the road, there to munch their dry bread.

…So often have I watched that scene!… Let me but close my eyes one moment, and it will come to me,—through all the thousand miles,—over the graves of the days…

Again I see the mountain road in the yellow glow, banded with umbrages of palm. Again I watch the light feet coming,—now in shadow, now in sun,—soundlessly as falling leaves. Still I can hear the voices crying, "*Ah! déchâgé moin vite, chè!—moin lasse!* "—and see the mighty arms outreach to take the burdens away.

…Only, there is a change,—I know not what!… All vapory the road is, and the fronds, and the comely coming feet of the bearers, and even this light of sunset,—sunset that is ever larger and nearer to us than dawn, even as death than birth. And the weird way appeareth a way whose dust is the dust of generations;—and the Shape that waits is never Jean-Marie, but one darker and stronger;—and these are surely voices of tired souls who cry to Thee, thou dear black Giver of the perpetual rest, "*Ah! déchâgé moin vite, chè—moin lasse!* "

NOTES

1. Extract from the "Story of Marie," as written from dictation:

> …*Manman-à té ni yôn gouôs jà à caïe-li. Jà-la té touôp lou'de pou Marie. Cé té li menm manman là qui té kallé pouend dileau. Yon jou y pouend jà-la pou y té allé pouend dileau. Lhè manman-à rivé bò la fontaine, y pa trouvé pésonne pou châgé y. Y rété; y ka crié, "Toutt bon Chritien, vini châgé moin!"*
>
> …*Lhé manman rété y ouè pa té ni piess bon Chritien pou châgé y. Y rété; y crié: "Puoloss, si pa ni bon Chritien, ni mauvais Chritien! Toutt mauvais Chritien vini châgé moin!"*
>
> *Lhé y fini di ça, y oué yon diabe qui ka vini, ka di conm ça, "Pou moin châgé ou, ça ou ké baill moin?" Manman-là di,—y réponne, "Moin pa ni arien!" Diabe-la réponne y, "Y fau ba moin Marie pou moin pé châgé ou."*

…This mamma had a great jar in her house. The jar was too heavy for Marie. It was this mamma herself who used to go for water. One day she took that jar to go for water. When this mamma had got to the fountain, she could not find any one to load her. She stood there, crying out, "Any good Christian, come load me!"

…As the mamma stood there she saw there was not a single good Christian to help her load. She stood there, and cried out: "Well, then, if there are no good Christians, there are bad Christians. Any bad Christian, come and load me!"

The moment she said that, she saw a devil coming, who said to her, "If I load you, what will you give me?" This mamma answered, and said, "I have nothing!" The devil answered her, "Must give me Marie if you want me to load you."

II. La Grande Anse

I

WHILE at the village of Morne Rouge, I was frequently impressed by the singular beauty of young girls from the north-east coast—all porteuses, who passed almost daily, on their way from Grande Anse to St. Pierre and back again,—a total trip of thirty-five miles... I knew they were from Grande Anse, because the village baker, at whose shop they were wont to make brief halts, told me a good deal about them: he knew each one by name. Whenever a remarkably attractive girl appeared, and I would inquire whence she came, the invariable reply (generally preceded by that peculiarly intoned French "Ah!" signifying, "Why, you certainly ought to know!") was "Grande Anse." ...*Ah! c'est de Grande Anse, ça!* And if any commonplace, uninteresting type showed itself, it would be signalled as from somewhere else—Gros-Morne, Capote, Marigot, perhaps,—but never from Grande Anse. The Grande Anse girls were distinguishable by their clear yellow or brown skins, lithe light figures, and a particular grace in their way of dressing. Their short robes were always of bright and pleasing colors, perfectly contrasting with the ripe fruit-tint of nude limbs and faces: I could discern a partiality for white stuffs with apricot-yellow stripes, for plaidings of blue and violet, and various patterns of pink and mauve. They had a graceful way of walking under their trays, with hands clasped behind their heads, and arms uplifted in the manner of caryatides. An artist would been wild with delight for the chance to sketch some of them... On the whole, they conveyed the impression that they belonged to a particular race, very different from that of the chief city or its environs.

"Are they all banana-colored at Grande Anse?" I asked,—"and all as pretty as these?"

"I was never at Grande Anse," the little baker answered, "although I have been forty years in Martinique; but I know there is a fine class of young there: *il y a une belle jeunesse là, mon cher!*"

Then I wondered why the youth of Grande Anse should be any finer than the youth of other places; and it seemed to me that the baker's own statement of his never having been there might possibly furnish a clew...

Out of the thirty-five thousand inhabitants of St. Pierre and its suburbs, there are at least twenty thousand who never have been there, and most probably never will be. Few dwellers of the west coast visit the east coast: in fact, except among the white creoles, who represent but a small percentage of the total population, there are few persons to be met with who are familiar with all part their native island. It is so mountainous, and travelling is so wearisome, that populations may live and die in adjacent valleys without climbing the intervening ranges to look at one another. Grande Anse is only about twenty miles from the principal city; but it requires some considerable inducement to make the journey on horseback; and only the professional carrier-girls, plantation messengers, and colored people of peculiarly tough constitution attempt it on foot. Except for the transportation of sugar and rum, there is practically no communication by sea between the west and the north-east coast—the sea is too dangerous— and thus the populations on either side of the island are more or less isolated from each other, besides being further subdivided and segregated by the lesser mountain chains crossing their respective territories... In view of all these things I wondered whether a community so secluded might not assume special characteristics within two hundred years—might not develop into a population of some yellow, red, or brown type, according to the predominant element of the original race-crossing.

II

I HAD long been anxious to see the city of the Porteuses, when the opportunity afforded itself to make the trip with a friend obliged to go thither on some important business;—I do not think I should have ever felt resigned to undertake it alone. With a level road the distance might be covered very quickly, but over mountains the journey is slow and wearisome in the perpetual tropic heat. Whether made on horseback or in a carriage, it takes between four and five hours to go from St. Pierre to Grande Anse, and it requires a longer time to return, as the road is then nearly all uphill. The young porteuse travels almost as rapidly; and the barefooted black postman, who carries the mails in a square box at the end of a pole, is timed on leaving Morne Rouge at 4 A.M. to reach Ajoupa-Bouillon a little after six, and leaving Ajoupa-Bouillon at half-past six to reach Grande Anse at half-past eight, including many stoppages and delays on the way.

Going to Grande Anse from the chief city, one can either hire a horse or carriage at St. Pierre, or ascend to Morne Rouge by the public conveyance, and there procure a vehicle or animal, which latter is the cheaper and easier plan. About a mile beyond Morne Rouge, where the old Calebasse road enters the public highway, you reach the highest point of the journey,—the top of the enormous ridge dividing the north-east from the western coast, and cutting off the trade-winds from sultry St. Pierre. By climbing the little hill, with a tall stone cross on its summit, overlooking the Champ-Flore just here, you can perceive the sea on both sides of the island at once—*lapis lazuli* blue. From this elevation the road descends by a hundred windings and lessening undulations to the eastern shore. It sinks between mornes wooded to their summits,—bridges a host of torrents and ravines,—passes gorges from whence colossal trees tower far overhead, through heavy streaming of lianas, to mingle their green crowns in magnificent gloom. Now and then you hear a low long sweet sound like the deepest tone of a silver flute,—a bird-call, the cry of the *siffleur-de-montagne*; then all is stillness. You are not likely to see a white face again for hours, but at intervals a porteuse passes, walking very swiftly, or a field-hand heavily laden; and these salute you either by speech or a lifting of the hand to the head... And it is very pleasant to hear the greetings and to see the smiles of those who thus pass,—the fine brown girls bearing trays, the dark laborers bowed under great burdens of bamboo-grass,—*Bonjou',Missie!* Then you should reply, if the speaker be a woman and pretty, "Good-day, dear" *(bonjou', chè)*, or, "Good-day, my daughter" *(mafi)* even if she be old; while if the passer-by be a man, your proper reply is, "Good-day, my son" *(monfi)*...They are less often uttered now than in other years, these kindly greetings, but they still form part of the good and true creole manners.

The feathery beauty of the tree-ferns shadowing each brook, the grace of bamboo and arborescent grasses, seem to decrease as the road descends,—but the palms grow taller. Often the way skirts a precipice dominating some marvellous valley prospect; again it is walled in by high green banks or shrubby slopes which cut off the view; and always it serpentines so that you cannot see more than a few hundred feet of the white track before you.

About the fifteenth kilometre a glorious landscape opens to the right, reaching to the Atlantic;—the road still winds very high; forests are billowing hundreds of yards below it, and rising miles away up the slopes of mornes, beyond which, here and there, loom strange shapes of mountain,—shading off from misty green to violet and faintest gray. And through one grand opening in this multicolored surging of hills and

A Creole Capre in Working Garb

peaks you perceive the gold-yellow of cane-fields touching the sky-colored sea. Grande Anse lies somewhere in that direction... At the eighteenth kilometre you pass a cluster of little country cottages, a church, and one or two large buildings framed in shade-trees—the hamlet of Ajoupa-Bouillon. Yet a little farther, and you find you have left all the woods behind you. But the road continues its bewildering curves around and between low mornes covered with cane or cocoa plants: it dips down very low, rises again, dips once more;—and you perceive the soil is changing color; it is taking a red tint like that of the land of the American cotton-belt. Then you pass the Rivière Falaise (marked *Filasse* upon old maps),—with its shallow crystal torrent flowing through a very deep and rocky channel—and the Capote and other streams; and over the yellow rim of cane-hills the long blue bar of the sea appears, edged landward with a dazzling fringe of foam. The heights you have passed are no longer verdant, but purplish or gray,—with Pelée's cloud-wrapped enormity overtopping all. A very strong warm wind is blowing upon you—the trade-wind, always driving the clouds west: this is the sunny side of Martinique, where gray heavy rains are less frequent. Once or twice more the sea disappears and reappears, always over canes; and then, after passing a bridge and turning a last curve, the road suddenly drops down to the shore and into the burgh of Grande Anse.

III

LEAVING Morne Rouge at about eight in the morning, my friend and I reached Grande Anse at half-past eleven. Everything had been arranged to make us comfortable. I was delighted with the airy corner room, commanding at once a view of the main street and of the sea—a very high room, all open to the trade-winds—which had been prepared to receive me. But after a long carriage ride in the heat of a tropical June day, one always feels the necessity of a little physical exercise. I lingered only a minute or two in the house, and went out to look at the little town and its surroundings.

As seen from the high-road, the burgh of Grande Anse makes a long patch of darkness between the green of the coast and the azure of the water: it is almost wholly black and gray—suited to inspire an etching. High slopes of cane and meadow rise behind it and on either side, undulating up and away to purple and gray tips of mountain ranges. North and south, to left and right, the land reaches out in two high promontories, mostly green, and about a mile apart—the Pointe du Rochet and the Pointe de Séguinau, or Croche-Mort, which latter name preserves the legend of an insurgent slave, a man of color, shot dead upon the cliff. These promontories form the semicircular bay of Grande Anse. All this Grande Anse, or "Great Creek," valley is an immense basin of basalt; and narrow as it is, no less than five streams water it, including the Rivière de la Grande Anse.

There are only three short streets in the town. The principal, or Grande Rue, is simply a continuation of the national road; there is a narrower one below, which used to be called the Rue de la Paille, because the cottages lining it were formerly all thatched with cane straw; and there is one above it, edging the cane-fields that billow away to the meeting of morne and sky. There is nothing of architectural interest, and all is sombre,—walls and roofs and pavements. But after you pass through the city and follow the southern route that ascends the Séguinau promontory, you can obtain some lovely landscape views,—a grand surging of rounded mornes, with farther violet peaks, truncated or horned, pushing up their heads in the horizon above the highest flutterings of cane; and looking back above the town, you may see Pelée all unclouded,—not as you see it from the other coast, but an enormous ghostly silhouette, with steep sides and almost square summit, so pale as to seem transparent. Then if you cross the promontory southward, the same road will lead you into another very beautiful valley, watered by a broad rocky torrent,—the Valley of the Rivière du Lorrain. This clear stream rushes to the sea through a lofty opening in the hills; and looking westward between them, you will be charmed by the exquisite vista of green shapes piling and pushing up one behind another to reach a blue ridge which forms the background—a vision of tooth-shaped and fantastical mountains,— part of the great central chain running south and north through nearly the whole island. It is over those blue summits that the wonderful road called *La Trace* winds between primeval forest walls.

But the more you become familiar with the face of the little town itself, the more you are impressed by the strange swarthy tone it preserves in all this splendid expanse of radiant tinting. There are only two points of visible color in it,—the church and hospital, built of stone, which have been painted yellow: as a mass in the landscape, lying between the dead-gold of the cane-clad hills and the delicious azure of the sea, it remains almost black under the prodigious blaze of light. The foundations of volcanic rock, three or four feet high, on which the frames of the wooden dwellings rest, are black; and the sea-wind appears to have the power of blackening all timber-work here through any coat of paint. Roofs and façades look as if they had been long exposed to coal-smoke, although probably no one in Grande Anse ever saw coal; and the pavements of pebbles and cement are of a deep ash-color, full of micaceous scintillation, and so hard as to feel disagreeable even to feet protected by good thick shoes. By-and-by you notice walls of black stone, bridges of black stone, and perceive that black forms an element of all the landscape about you. On the roads leading from the town you note from time to time masses of jagged rock or great bowlders protruding through the green of the slopes, and dark as ink. These black surfaces also sparkle. The beds of all the neighboring rivers are filled with dark gray stones; and many of these, broken by those violent floods which dash rocks together,—deluging the valleys, and strewing the soil of the bottom-lands *(fonds)* with dead serpents,—display black cores. Bare crags projecting from the green cliffs here and there are soot-colored, and the outlying rocks of the coast offer a similar aspect. And the sand of the beach is funereally black—looks almost like powdered charcoal; and as you walk over it, sinking three or four inches every step, you are amazed by the multitude and brilliancy of minute flashes in it, like a subtle silver effervescence.

This extraordinary sand contains ninety per cent of natural steel, and efforts have been made to utilize it industrially. Some years ago a company was formed, and a machine invented to separate the metal from the pure sand,—an immense revolving magnet, which, being set in motion under a sand shower, caught the ore upon it. When the covering thus formed by the adhesion of the steel became of a certain thickness, the simple interruption of an electric current precipitated the metal into appropriate receptacles. Fine bars were made from this volcanic steel, and excellent cutting tools manufactured from it: French metallurgists pronounced the product of peculiar excellence, and nevertheless the project of the company was abandoned. Political disorganization consequent upon the establishment of universal suffrage frightened capitalists who might have aided the undertaking under a better condition of affairs; and the lack of large means, coupled with the cost of freight to remote markets, ultimately baffled this creditable attempt to found a native industry.

Sometimes after great storms bright brown sand is up from the sea-depths; but the heavy black sand always reappears again to make the universal color of the beach.

IV

BEHIND the roomy wooden house in which I occupied an apartment there was a small garden-plot surrounded with a hedge strengthened by bamboo fencing, and radiant with flowers of the *loseille-bois*,—the creole name for a sort of begonia, whose closed bud exactly resembles a pink and white dainty bivalve shell, and whose open blossom imitates the form of a butterfly. Here and there, on the grass, were nets drying, and *nasses*—curious fish-traps made of split bamboos interwoven and held in with *mibi* stalks (the mibi is a liana heavy and tough as copper wire); and immediately behind the garden hedge appeared the white flashing of the surf. The most vivid recollection connected with my trip to Grande Anse is that of the first time that I went to the end of that garden, opened the little bamboo gate, and found myself overlooking the beach—an immense breadth of soot-black sand, with pale green patches and stripings here and there upon it—refuse of cane thatch, decomposing rubbish spread out by old tides. The one solitary boat owned in the community lay there before me, high and dry. It was the hot period of the afternoon; the town slept; there was no living creature in sight; and the booming of the surf drowned all other sounds; the scent of the warm strong sea-wind annihilated all other odors. Then, very suddenly, there came to me a sensation absolutely weird, while watching the strange wild sea roaring over its beach of black sand,—the sensation of seeing something unreal, looking at something that had no more tangible existence than a memory! Whether suggested by the first white vision of the surf over the bamboo hedge,—or by those old green tide-lines on the desolation of the black beach,—or by some tone of the speaking of the sea,—or something indefinable in the living touch of the wind,—or by all of these, I cannot say;—but slowly there became defined within me the thought of having beheld just such a coast very long ago, I could not tell where,—in those child-years of which the recollections gradually become indistinguishable from dreams.

Soon as darkness comes upon Grande Anse the face of the clock in the church-tower is always lighted: you see it suddenly burst into yellow glow above the roofs and the cocoa-palms,—just like a pharos. In my room I could not keep the candle lighted because of the sea-wind; but it never occurred to me to close the shutters of the great broad windows,—sashless, of course, like all the glassless windows of Martinique;—the breeze was too delicious. It seemed full of something vitalizing that made one's blood warmer, and rendered one full of contentment—full of eagerness to believe life all sweetness. Likewise, I found it soporific—this pure, dry, warm wind. And I thought there could be no greater delight in existence than to lie down at night, with all the windows open,—and the Cross of the South visible from my pillow,—and the sea-wind pouring over the bed,—and the tumultuous whispering and muttering of the surf in one's ears,—to dream of that strange sapphire sea white-bursting over its beach of black sand.

V

CONSIDERING that Grande Anse lies almost opposite to St. Pierre, at a distance of less than twenty miles even by the complicated windings of the national road, the differences existing in the natural conditions of both places are remarkable enough. Nobody in St. Pierre sees the sun rise, because the mountains immediately behind the city continue to shadow its roofs long after the eastern coast is deluged with light and heat. At Grande Anse, on the other hand, those tremendous sunsets which delight west coast dwellers are not visible at all; and during the briefer West Indian days Grande Anse is all wrapped in darkness as early as half-past four,—or nearly an hour before the orange light has ceased to flare up the streets of St. Pierre from the sea;—since the great mountain range topped by Pelée cuts off all the slanting light from the east valleys. And early as folks rise in St. Pierre, they rise still earlier at Grande Anse—before the sun emerges from the rim of the Atlantic: about half-past four, doors are being opened and coffee is ready. At St. Pierre one can enjoy a sea bath till seven or half-past seven o'clock, even during the time of the sun's earliest rising, because the shadow of the mornes still reaches out upon the bay;—but bathers leave the black beach of Grande Anse by six o'clock; for once the sun's face is up, the light, levelled straight at the eyes, becomes blinding. Again, at St. Pierre it rains almost every twenty-four hours for a brief while, during at least the greater part of the year; at Grande Anse it rains more moderately and less often. The atmosphere at St. Pierre is always more or less impregnated with vapor, and usually an enervating heat prevails, which makes exertion unpleasant; at Grande Anse the warm wind keeps the skin comparatively dry, in spite of considerable exercise. It is quite rare to see a heavy surf at St. Pierre, but it is much rarer not to see it at Grande Anse... A curious fact concerning custom is that few white creoles care to bathe in front of the town, notwithstanding the superb beach and magnificent surf, both so inviting to one accustomed to the deep still water and rough pebbly shore of St. Pierre. The creoles really prefer their rivers as bathing-places; and when willing to take a sea bath, they will walk up and down hill for kilometres in order to reach some river mouth, so as to wash off in the fresh-water afterwards. They say that the effect of sea-salt upon the skin gives *boutons-chauds* (what we call "prickly heat"). Friends took me all the way to the mouth of the Lorrain one morning that I might have the experience of such a double bath; but after leaving the tepid sea, I must confess the plunge into the river was something terrible—an icy shock which cured me of all further desire for river baths. My willingness to let the sea-water dry upon me was regarded as an eccentricity.

VI

IT may be said that on all this coast the ocean, perpetually moved by the blowing of the trade-winds, never rests—never hushes its roar. Even in the streets of Grande Anse, one must in breezy weather lift one's voice above the natural pitch to be heard; and then the breakers come in lines more than a mile long, between the Pointe du Rochet and the Pointe de Séguinau,—every unfurling a thunder-clap. There is no travelling by sea. All large vessels keep well away from the dangerous coast. There is scarcely any fishing; and although the sea is thick with fish, fresh fish at Grande Anse is a rare luxury. Communication with St. Pierre is chiefly by way of the national road, winding over mountain ridges two thousand feet high; and the larger portion of merchandise is transported from the chief city on the heads of young women. The steepness of the route soon kills draught-horses and ruins the toughest mules. At one time the managers of a large estate at Grande Anse attempted the experiment of sending their sugar to St. Pierre in iron carts, drawn by five mules; but the animals could not endure the work. Cocoa can be carried to St. Pierre by the porteuses, but sugar and rum must go by sea, or not at all; and the risks and difficulties of shipping these seriously affect the prosperity of all the north and north-east coast. Planters have actually been ruined by inability to send their products to market during a protracted spell of rough weather. A railroad has been proposed and planned: in a more prosperous era it might be constructed, with the result of greatly developing all the Atlantic side of the island, and converting obscure villages into thriving towns.

Sugar is very difficult to ship; rum and tafia can be handled with less risk. It is nothing less than exciting to watch a shipment of tafia from Grande Anse to St. Pierre.

A little vessel approaches the coast with extreme caution, and anchors in the bay some hundred yards beyond the breakers. She is what they call a *pirogue* here, but not at all what is called a pirogue in the United States: she has a long narrow hull, two masts, no deck; she has usually a crew of five, and can carry thirty barrels of tafia. One of the pirogue men puts a great shell to his lips and sounds a call, very mellow and deep, that can be heard over the roar of the waves far up among the hills. The shell is one of those great spiral shells, weighing seven or eight pounds—rolled like a scroll, fluted and scalloped about the edges, and pink-pearled inside,—such as are sold in America for mantle-piece ornaments,—the shell of a *lambi*. Here you can often see the lambi crawling about with its nacreous house upon its back: an enormous sea-snail with a yellowish back and rose-colored belly, with big horns and eyes in the tip of each horn—very pretty eyes, having a golden iris. This creature is a common article of food; but its thick white flesh is almost compact as cartilage, and must be pounded before being cooked.[1]

At the sound of the blowing of the lambi-shell, wagons descend to the beach, accompanied by young colored men running beside the mules. Each wagon discharges a certain number of barrels of tafia, and simultaneously the young men strip. They are slight, well built, and generally well muscled. Each man takes a barrel of tafia, pushes it before him into the surf, and then begins to swim to the pirogue,—impelling the barrel before him. I have never seen a swimmer attempt to convey more than one barrel at a time; but I am told there are experts who manage as many as three barrels together,—pushing them forward in line, with the head of one against the bottom of the next. It really requires much dexterity and practice to handle even one barrel or cask. As the swimmer advances he keeps close as possible to his charge,—so as to be able to push it forward with all his force against each breaker in succession,—making it dive through. If it once glide well out of his reach while he is in the breakers, it becomes an enemy, and he must take care to keep out of its way,—for if a wave throws it at him, or rolls it over him, he may be seriously injured; but the expert seldom abandons a barrel. Under the most favorable conditions, man and barrel will both disappear a score of times before the clear swells are reached, after which the rest of the journey is not difficult. Men lower ropes from the pirogue, the swimmer passes them under his barrel, and it is hoisted aboard.

…Wonderful surf-swimmers these men are;—they will go far out for mere sport in the roughest kind of a sea, when the waves, abnormally swollen by the peculiar conformation of the bay, come rolling in thirty and forty feet high. Sometimes, with the swift impulse of ascending a swell, the swimmer seems suspended in air as it passes beneath him, before he plunges into the trough beyond. The best swimmer is a young capre who cannot weigh more than a hundred and twenty pounds. Few of the Grande Anse men are heavily built; they do not compare for stature and thew with those longshoremen at St. Pierre who can be seen any busy afternoon on the landing, lifting heavy barrels at almost the full reach of their swarthy arms.

…There is but one boat owned in the whole parish of Grande Anse,—a fact due to the continual roughness of the sea. It has a little mast and sail, and can hold only three men. When the water is somewhat less angry than usual, a colored crew take it out for a fishing expedition. There is always much interest in this event; a crowd gathers on the beach; and the professional swimmers help to bring the little craft beyond the breakers. When the boat returns after a disappearance of several hours, everybody runs down from the village to meet it. Young colored women twist their robes up about their hips, and wade out to welcome it: there is a display of limbs of all colors on such occasions, which is not without grace, that untaught grace which tempts an artistic pencil. Every *bonne* and every house-keeper struggles for first chance to buy the fish;—young girls and children dance in the water for delight, all screaming, "*Rhalé bois-canot!*"… Then as the boat is pulled through the surf and hauled up on the sand, the pushing and screaming and crying become irritating and deafening; the fishermen lose patience and say terrible things. But nobody heeds them in the general clamoring and haggling and furious bidding for the *pouèsson-ououge*, the *dorades*, the *volants* (beautiful purple-backed flying-fish with silver bellies, and fins all transparent, like the wings of dragon-flies). There is great bargaining even for a young shark,—which makes very nice eating cooked after the creole fashion. So seldom can the fishermen venture out that each trip makes a memorable event for the village.

The St. Pierre fishermen very seldom approach the bay, but they do much fishing a few miles beyond it, almost in front of the Pointe du

Rochet and the Roche à Bourgaut. There the best flying-fish are caught,—and besides edible creatures, many queer things are often brought up by the nets: monstrosities such as the *coffre*-fish, shaped almost like a box, of which the lid is represented by an extraordinary conformation of the jaws;—and the *barrique-de-vin* ("wine cask"), with round boneless body, secreting in a curious vesicle a liquor precisely resembling wine lees;—and the "needle-fish" (*aiguille de mer*), less thick than a Faber lead-pencil, hut more than twice as long;—and huge cuttle-fish and prodigious eels. One conger secured off this coast measured over twenty feet in length, and weighed two hundred and fifty pounds—a veritable sea-serpent ... But even the fresh-water inhabitants of Grande Anse are amazing. I have seen crawfish by actual measurement fifty centimetres long, but these were not considered remarkable. Many are said to much exceed two feet from the tail to the tip of the claws and horns. They are of an iron-black color, and have formidable pincers with serrated edges and tip-points inwardly converging, which cannot crush like the weapons of a lobster, but which will cut the flesh and make a small ugly wound. At first sight one not familiar with the crawfish of these regions can hardly believe he is not viewing some variety of gigantic lobster instead of the common fresh-water crawfish of the east coast. When the head, tail, legs, and cuirass have all been removed, after boiling, the curved trunk has still the size and weight of a large pork sausage.

These creatures are trapped by lantern-light. Pieces of manioc root tied fast to large bowlders sunk in the river are the only bait;—the crawfish will flock to eat it upon any dark night, and then they are caught with scoop-nets and dropped into covered baskets.

VII

ONE whose ideas of the people of Grande Anse had been formed only by observing the young porteuses of the region on their way to the other side of the island, might expect on reaching this little town to find its population yellow as that of a Chinese city. But the dominant hue is much darker, although the mixed element is everywhere visible; and I was at first surprised by the scarcity of those clear bright skins I supposed to be so numerous. Some pretty children—notably a pair of twin-sisters, and perhaps a dozen school-girls from eight to ten years of age—displayed the same characteristics I have noted in the adult porteuses of

Grande Anse; but within the town itself this brighter element is in the minority. The predominating race element of the whole commune is certainly colored (Grande Anse is even memorable because of the revolt of its *hommes de couleur* some fifty years ago)—but the colored population is not concentrated in the town; it belongs rather to the valleys and the heights surrounding the *chef-lieu.* Most of the porteuses are country girls, and I found that even those living in the village are seldom visible on the streets except when departing upon a trip or returning from one. An artist wishing to study the type might, however, pass a day at the bridge of the Rivière Falaise to advantage, as all the carrier-girls pass it at certain hours of the morning and evening.

But the best possible occasion on which to observe what my friend the baker called *la belle jeunesse,* is a confirmation day,—when the bishop drives to Grande Anse over the mountains, and all the population turns out in holiday garb, and the bells are tapped like tamtams, and triumphal arches—most awry to behold!—span the road-way, bearing in clumsiest lettering the welcome, *Vive Monseigneur.* On that event, the long procession of young girls to be confirmed—all in white robes, white veils, and white satin slippers—is a numerical surprise. It is a moral surprise also,—to the stranger at least; for it reveals the struggle of a poverty extraordinary with the self-imposed obligations of a costly ceremonialism.

A Confirmation Procession]

No white children ever appear in these processions: there are not half a dozen white families in the whole urban population of about seven thousand souls; and those send their sons and daughters to St. Pierre or Morne Rouge for their religious training and education. But many of the colored children look very charming in their costume of confirmation;—you could not easily recognize one of them as the same little *bonne* who brings your morning cup of coffee, or another as the daughter of a plantation *commandeur* (overseer's assistant),—a brown slip of a girl who will probably never wear shoes again. And many of those white shoes and white veils have been obtained only by the hardest physical labor and self-denial of poor parents and relatives: fathers, brothers, and mothers working with cutlass and hoe in the snake-swarming cane-fields;—sisters walking barefooted every day to St. Pierre and back to earn a few francs a month.

...While watching such a procession it seemed to me that I could discern in the features and figures of the young confirmants something of a prevailing type and tint, and I asked an old planter beside me if he thought my impression correct.

"Partly," he answered; "there is certainly a tendency towards an attractive physical type here, but the tendency itself is less stable than you imagine; it has been changed during the last twenty years within my own recollection. In different parts of the island particular types appear and disappear with a generation. There is a sort of race-fermentation going on, which gives no fixed result of a positive sort for any great length of time. It is true that certain elements continue to dominate in certain communes, but the particular characteristics come and vanish in the most mysterious way. As to color, I doubt if any correct classification can be made, especially by a stranger. Your eyes give you general ideas about a red type, a yellow type, a brown type; but to the more experienced eyes of a creole, accustomed to live in the country districts, every individual of mixed race appears to have a particular color of his own. Take, for instance, the so-called capre type, which furnishes the finest physical examples of all,—you, a stranger, are at once impressed by the general red tint of the variety; but you do not notice the differences of that tint in different persons, which are more difficult to observe than shade-differences of yellow or brown. Now, to me, every capre or capresse has an individual color; and I do not believe that in all Martinique there are two half-breeds—not having had the same father and mother—in whom the tint is precisely the same."

VIII

I THOUGHT Grande Anse the most sleepy place I had ever visited. I suspect it is one of the sleepiest in the whole world. The wind, which tans even a creole of St. Pierre to an unnatural brown within forty-eight hours of his sojourn in the village, has also a peculiarly somnolent effect. The moment one has nothing particular to do, and ventures to sit down idly with the breeze in one's face, slumber comes; and everybody who can spare the time takes a long nap in the afternoon, and little naps from hour to hour. For all that, the heat of the east coast is not enervating, like that of St. Pierre; one can take a great deal of exercise in the sun without feeling much the worse. Hunting excursions, river fishing parties, surf-bathing, and visits to neighboring plantations are the only amusements; but these are enough to make existence very pleasant at Grande Anse. The most interesting of my own experiences were those of a day passed by invitation at one of the old colonial estates on the hills near the village.

It is not easy to describe the charm of a creole interior, whether in the city or the country. The cool shadowy court, with its wonderful plants and fountain of sparkling mountain water, or the lawn, with its ancestral trees,—the delicious welcome of the host, whose fraternal easy manner immediately makes you feel at home,—the coming of the children to greet you, each holding up a velvety brown cheek to be kissed, after the old-time custom,—the romance of the unconventional chat, over a cool drink, under the palms and the ceibas,—the visible earnestness of all to please the guest, to inwrap him in a very atmosphere of quiet happiness,—combine to make a memory which you will never forget. And maybe you enjoy all this upon some exquisite site, some volcanic summit, overlooking slopes of a hundred greens,—mountains far winding in blue and pearly shadowing,—rivers singing seaward behind curtains of arborescent reeds and bamboos,—and, perhaps, Pelée, in the horizon, dreaming violet dreams under her foulard of vapors,—and, encircling all, the still sweep of the ocean's azure bending to the verge of day.

My host showed or explained to me all that he thought might interest a stranger. He had brought to me a nest of the *carouge*, a bird which suspends its home, hammock-fashion, under the leaves of the banana-tree;—showed me a little fer-de-lance, freshly killed by one of his field hands; and a field lizard (*zanoli tè* in creole), not green like the lizards which haunt the roofs of St. Pierre, but of a beautiful brown bronze, with shifting tints; and eggs of the *zanoli*, little soft oval things from which the young lizards will perhaps run out alive as fast as you open the shells; and the *matoutou-falaise*, or spider of the cliffs, of two varieties, red or almost black when adult, and bluish silvery tint when young,—less in size than the tarantula, but equally hairy and venomous; and the *crabe-c'est-ma-faute* (the "Through-my-fault Crab"), having one very small and one very large claw, which latter it carries folded up against its body, so as to have suggested the idea of a penitent striking his bosom, and uttering the sacramental words of the Catholic confession, "Through my fault, through my fault, through my most grievous fault."... Indeed I cannot recollect one half of the queer birds, queer insects, queer reptiles, and queer plants to which my attention was called. But speaking of plants, I was impressed by the profusion of the *zhèbe-moin-misé*—a little sensitive-plant I had rarely observed on the west coast. On the hill-sides of Grande Anse it prevails to such an extent as to give certain slopes its own peculiar greenish-brown color. It has many-branching leaves, only one inch and a half to two inches long, but which recall the form of certain common ferns; these lie almost flat upon the ground. They fold together upward from the central stem at the least touch, and the plant thus makes itself almost imperceptible;—it seems to live so, that you feel guilty of murder if you break off a leaf. It is called *zhèbe-moin-misé*, or "Plant-did-I-amuse-myself," because it is supposed to tell naughty little children who play truant, or who delay much longer than is necessary in delivering a message, whether they deserve a whipping or not. The guilty child touches the plant, and asks, "*Ess moin amisé moin?*" (Did I amuse myself?); and if the plant instantly shuts its leaves up, that means, "Yes, you did!" Of course the leaves invariably close; but I suspect they invariably tell the truth, for all colored children, in Grande Anse at least, are much more inclined to play than work.

The kind old planter likewise conducted me over the estate. He took me through the sugar-mill, and showed me, among other more recent inventions, some machinery devised nearly two centuries ago by the ingenious and terrible Père Labat, and still quite serviceable, in spite of all modern improvements in sugar-making;—took me through the *rhummerie*, or distillery, and made me taste some colorless rum which had the aroma and something of the taste of the most delicate gin;—and finally took me into the *cases-à-vent*, or "wind-houses,"—built as places of refuge during hurricanes. Hurricanes are rare, and more rare in this century by far than during the previous one; but this part of the island is particularly exposed to such visitations, and almost every old plantation used to have one or two cases-à-vent. They were always built in a hollow, either natural or artificial, below the land-level,—with walls of rock several feet thick, and very strong doors, but no windows. My host told me about the experiences of his family in some cases-à-vent during a hurricane which he recollected. It was found necessary to secure the door within by means of strong ropes; and the mere task of holding it taxed the strength of a dozen powerful men: it would bulge in under the pressure of the awful wind,—swelling like the side of a barrel; and had not its planks been made of a wood tough as hickory, they would have been blown into splinters.

I had long desired to examine a plantation drum, and see it played upon under conditions more favorable than the excitement of a holiday *caleinda* in the villages, where the amusement is too often terminated by a *voum* (general row) or a *goumage* (a serious fight);—and when I mentioned this wish to the planter he at once sent word to his commandeur, the best drummer in the settlement, to come up to the house and bring his instrument with him. I was thus enabled to make the observations necessary, and also to take an instantaneous photograph of the drummer in the very act of playing.

The old African dances, the *caleinda* and the *bélé* (which latter is accompanied by chanted improvisation) are danced on Sundays to the sound of the drum on almost every plantation in the island. The drum, indeed, is an instrument to which the country-folk are so much attached that they swear by it,—*Tambou!* being the oath uttered upon all ordinary occasions of surprise or vexation. But the instrument is quite as often called *ka*, because made out of a quarter-barrel, or *quart*,—in the patois "ka." Both ends of the barrel having been removed, a wet hide, well wrapped about a couple of hoops, is driven on, and in drying the stretched skin obtains still further tension. The other end of the ka is always left open. Across the face of the skin a string is tightly stretched, to which are attached, at intervals of about an inch apart, very short thin fragments of bamboo or cut feather stems. These lend a certain vibration to the tones.

In the time of Père Labat the negro drums had a somewhat different form. There were then two kinds of drums—a big tamtam and a little one, which used to be played together. Both consisted of skins tightly stretched over one end of a wooden cylinder, or a section of hollow tree trunk. The larger was from three to four feet long with a diameter of fifteen to sixteen inches; the smaller, called *baboula*,[2] was of the same length, but only eight

Manner of Playing the Ka

or nine inches in diameter. Père Labat also speaks, in his West Indian travels, of another musical instrument, very popular among the Martinique slaves of his time—"a sort of guitar" made out of a half-calabash or *couï*, covered with some kind of skin. It had four strings of silk or catgut, and a very long neck. The tradition of this African instrument is said to survive in the modern "*banza*" (*banza nèg Guinée*).

The skilful player (*bel tambouyé*) straddles his ka stripped to the waist, and plays upon it with the finger-tips of both bands simultaneously,—taking care that the vibrating string occupies a horizontal position. Occasionally the heel of the naked foot is pressed lightly or vigorously against the skin, so as to produce changes of tone. This is called "giving heel" to the drum—*baill y talon*. Meanwhile a boy keeps striking the drum at the uncovered end with a stick, so as to produce a dry clattering accompaniment. The sound of the drum itself, well played, has a wild power that makes and masters all the excitement of the dance—a complicated double roll, with a peculiar billowy rising and falling. The creole onomatopes, *b'lip-b'lib-b'lib-b'lip*, do not fully render the roll;—for each *b'lip* or *b'lib* stands really for a series of sounds too rapidly filliped out to be imitated by articulate speech. The tapping of a ka can be heard at surprising distances; and experienced players often play for hours at a time without exhibiting wearisomeness, or in the least diminishing the volume of sound produced.

It seems there are many ways of playing—different measures familiar to all these colored people, but not easily distinguished by anybody else; and there are great matches sometimes between celebrated *tambouyé*. The same *commandè* whose portrait I took while playing told me that he once figured in a contest of this kind, his rival being a drummer from the neighboring burgh of Marigot… "*Aïe, aïe, yaïe! mon chè!—y fai tambou-à pàlé*" said the commandè, describing the execution of his antagonist;—"my dear, he just made that drum talk! I thought I was going to be beaten for sure; I was trembling all the time—*aïe, yaïe-yaïe!* Then he got off that ka. I mounted it; I thought a moment; then I struck up the 'River-of-the-Lizard,'—*mais, mon chè, yon larivie-Léza toutt pi!*—such a River-of-the-Lizard, ah! just perfectly pure! I gave heel to that ka; I worried that ka;—I made it mad;—I made it crazy;—I made it talk;—I won!"

During some dances a sort of chant accompanies the music—a long sonorous cry, uttered at intervals of seven or eight seconds, which perfectly times a particular measure in the drum roll. It may be the burden of a song, or a mere improvisation:

"*Oh! yoïe-yoïe!*"

　　　　　　　　　　　(Drum roll)

"*Oh! missié-à!*"

　　　　　　　　　　　(Drum roll)

"*Y bel tambouyé!*"

　　　　　　　　　　　(Drum roll)

"*Aie, ya, yaie!*"

　　　　　　　　　　　(Drum roll)

"*Joli tambouyé!*"

　　　　　　　　　　　(Drum roll)

"*Chauffé tambou-à*"

　　　　　　　　　　　(Drum roll)

"*Géné tambou-à!*"

　　　　　　　　　　　(Drum roll)

"*Crazé tambou-à*" etc., etc.

...The *crieur*, or chanter, is also the leader of the dance. The caleinda is danced by men only, all stripped to the waist, and twirling heavy sticks in a mock fight. Sometimes, however—especially at the great village gatherings, when the blood becomes overheated by tafia—the mock fight may become a real one; and then even cutlasses are brought into play.

But in the old days, those improvisations which gave one form of dance its name, *bélé* (from the French *bel air*), were often remarkable rhymeless poems, uttered with natural simple emotion, and full of picturesque imagery. I cite part of one, taken down from the dictation of a common field-hand near Fort-de-France. I offer a few lines of the creole first, to indicate the form of the improvisation. There is a dancing pause at the end of each line during the performance:

Toutt fois lanmou vini lacase moin
Pou pàlé moin, moin ka reponne:
"Khé moin deja placé."
Moin ka crié, "Sécou! les voisinages!"
Moin ka crié, "Sécou! la gàde royale!"
Moin ka crié, "Sécou! la gendàmerie!
Lanmou pouend yon poignâ pou poignadé moin!"

The best part of the composition, which is quite long, might be rendered as follows:

Each time that Love comes to my cabin
To speak to me of love, I make answer,
"My heart is already placed."
I cry out, "Help, neighbors! help!"
I cry out, "Help, la Garde Royale! *"*
I cry out, "Help, help, gendarmes!
Love takes a poniard to stab me;
How can Love have a heart so hard
To thus rub me of my health!"
When the officer of police comes to me
To hear me tell him the truth,
To have him arrest my Love;—
When I see the Garde Royale
Coming to arrest my sweet heart,
I fall down at the feet of the Garde Royale,—
I pray for mercy and forgiveness.
"Arrest me instead, but let my dear Love go!"
How, alas! with this tender heart of mine,

Can I bear to see such an arrest made!
No, no! I would rather die!
Dost not remember, when our pillows lay close together,
How we told each to the other all that our hearts thought?...etc.

The stars were all out when I bid my host good-bye;—he sent his black servant along with me to carry a lantern and keep a sharp watch for snakes along the mountain road.

IX

...ASSUREDLY the city of St. Pierre never could have seemed more quaintly beautiful than as I saw it on the evening of my return, while the shadows were reaching their longest, and sea and sky were turning lilac. Palm-heads were trembling and masts swaying slowly against an enormous orange sunset,—yet the beauty of the sight did not touch me! The deep level and luminous flood of the bay seemed to me for the first time a dead water;—I found myself wondering whether it could form a part of that living tide by which I had been dwelling, full of foam-lightnings and perpetual thunder. I wondered whether the air about me—heavy and hot and full of faint leafy smells—could ever have been touched by the vast pure sweet breath of the wind from the sunrising. And I became conscious of a profound, unreasoning, absurd regret for the somnolent little black village of that bare east coast,—where there are no woods, no ships, no sunsets,... only the ocean roaring forever over its beach of black sand.

NOTES

1. *Y batt li conm lambi*—"he beat him like a lambi"—is an expression that may often be beard in a creole court from witnesses testifying in a case of assault and battery. One must have seen a lambi pounded to appreciate the terrible picturesqueness of the phrase.

2. Moreau de Saint-Méry writes, describing the drums of the negroes of Saint Domingue: "Le plus court de ces tambours est nommé *Bamboula,* attendu qu'il est formé quelquefois d'un très-gros bambou."—"Description de la partie française de Saint Domingue," vol. i., p.44.

III. Un Revenant

I

HE who first gave to Martinique its poetical name, *Le Pays de Revenants*, thought of his wonderful island only as "The Country of Comers-back," where Nature's unspeakable spell bewitches wandering souls like the caress of a Circe,—never as the Land of Ghosts. Yet either translation of the name holds equal truth: a land of ghosts it is, this marvellous Martinique! Almost every plantation has its familiar spirits,—its phantoms: some may be unknown beyond the particular district in which fancy first gave them being;—but some belong to popular song and story,—to the imaginative life of the whole people. Almost every promontory and peak, every village and valley along the coast, has its special folk-lore, its particular tradition. The legend of Thomasseau of Perinnelle, whose body was taken out of the coffin and carried away by the devil through a certain window of the plantation-house, which cannot be closed up by human power;—the Demarche legend of the spectral horseman who rides up the hill on bright hot days to seek a friend buried more than a hundred years ago;—the legend of the *Habitation Dillon,* whose proprietor was one night mysteriously summoned from a banquet to disappear forever;—the legend of l'Abbé Piot, who cursed the sea with the curse of perpetual unrest;—the legend of Aimée Derivry of Robert, captured by Barbary pirates, and sold to become a Sultana-Validé—(she never existed, though you can find an alleged portrait in M. Sidney Daney's history of Martinique): these and many similar tales might be told to you even on a journey from St. Pierre to Fort-de-France, or from Lamentin to La Trinité, according as a rising of some peak into view, or the sudden opening of an *anse* before the vessel's approach, recalls them to a creole companion.

And new legends are even now being made; for in this remote colony, to which white immigration has long ceased,—a country so mountainous that people are born and buried in the same valley without ever seeing towns but a few hours' journey beyond their native hills, and that distinct racial types are forming within three leagues of each other,—the memory of an event or of a name which has had influence enough to send one echo through all the forty-nine miles of peaks and craters is apt to create legend within a single generation. Nowhere in the world, perhaps, is popular imagination more oddly naïve and superstitious; nowhere are facts more readily exaggerated or distorted into unrecognizability; and the forms of any legend thus originated become furthermore specialized in each separate locality where it obtains a habitat. On tracing back such a legend or tradition to its primal source, one feels amazed at the variety of the metamorphoses which the simplest fact may rapidly assume in the childish fancy of this people.

I was first incited to make an effort in this direction by hearing the remarkable story of "Missié Bon." No legendary expression is more wide-spread throughout the country than *temps coudvent Missié Bon* (in the time of the big wind of Monsieur Bon). Whenever a hurricane threatens, you will hear colored folks expressing the hope that it may not be like the *coudvent Missié Bon*. And some years ago, in all the creole police-courts, old colored witnesses who could not tell their age would invariably try to give the magistrate some idea of it by referring to the never-to-be-forgotten *temps coudvent Missié Bon*.

… "*Temps coudvent Missié Bon, moin té ka tété encò*" (I was a child at the breast in the time of the big wind of Missié Bon); or "*Temps coudvent Missié Bon, moin té toutt piti manmaille,—moin ka souvini y pouend caïe manman moin pòté allé*" (I was a very, very little child in the time of the big wind of Missié Bon,—but I remember it blew mamma's cabin away.) The magistrates of those days knew the exact date of the *coudvent*.

But all I could learn about Missié Bon among the country-folk was this: Missié Bon used to be a great slave-owner and a cruel master. He was a very wicked man. And he treated his slaves so terribly that at last the Good-God (*Bon-Diè*) one day sent a great wind which blew away Missié Bon and Missié Bon's house and everybody in it, so that nothing was ever heard of them again.

It was not without considerable research that I succeeded at last in finding some one able to give me the true facts in the case of Monsieur Bon. My informant was a charming old gentleman, who represents a New York company in the city of St. Pierre, and who takes more interest in the history of his native island than creoles usually do. He laughed at the legend I had found, but informed me that I could trace it, with slight variations, through nearly every canton of Martinique.

"And now," he continued, "I can tell you the real history of 'Missié Bon,'—for he was an old friend of my grandfather; and my grandfather related it to me.

"It may have been in 1809—I can give you the exact date by reference to some old papers if necessary—Monsieur Bon was Collector of Customs at St. Pierre: and my grandfather was doing business in the Grande Rue. A certain captain, whose vessel had been consigned to my grandfather, invited him and the collector to breakfast in his cabin. My grandfather was so busy he could not accept the invitation;—but Monsieur Bon went with the captain on board the bark.

… "It was a morning like this; the sea was just as blue and the sky as clear. All of a sudden, while they were at breakfast, the sea began to break heavily without a wind, and clouds came up, with every sign of a hurricane. The captain was obliged to sacrifice his anchor; there was no time to land his guest: he hoisted a little jib and top-gallant, and made for open water, taking Monsieur Bon with him. Then the hurricane came; and from that day to this nothing has ever been heard of the bark nor of the captain nor of Monsieur Bon."[1]

"But did Monsieur Bon ever do anything to deserve the reputation he has left among the people?" I asked.

"*Ah! le pauvre vieux corps!*… A kind old soul who never uttered a harsh word to human being;—timid,—good-natured,—old-fashioned even for those old-fashioned days… Never had a slave in his life!"

II

THE legend of "Missié Bon" had prepared me to hear without surprise the details of a still more singular tradition,—that of Father Labat… I was returning from a mountain ramble with my guide, by way of the Ajoupa-Bouillon road;—the sun had gone down; there remained only a blood-red glow in the west, against which the silhouettes of the hills took a velvety blackness indescribably soft; and stars were beginning to twinkle out everywhere through the violet. Suddenly I noticed on the flank of a neighboring morne—which I remembered by day as an apparently uninhabitable wilderness of bamboos, tree-ferns, and balisiers—a swiftly moving point of yellow light. My guide had observed it simultaneously;—he crossed himself and exclaimed: "*Moin ka couè c'est fanal Pè Labatt!*" (I believe it is the lantern of Père Labat.)

"Does he live there?" I innocently inquired.

"Live there?—why he has been dead hundreds of years!... *Ouill!* you never heard of Pè Labatt?"...

"Not the same who wrote a book about Martinique?"

"Yes,—himself... They say he comes back at night. Ask mother about him;—she knows."...

...I questioned old Théréza as soon as we reached home; and she told me all she knew about "Pè Labatt." I found that the father had left a reputation far more wide-spread than the recollection of "Missié Bon,"—that his memory had created, in fact, the most impressive legend in all Martinique folk-lore.

"Whether you really saw Pè Labatt's lantern," said old Théréza, "I do not know;—there are a great many queer lights to be seen after nightfall among these mornes. Some are zombi-fires; and some are lanterns carried by living men; and some are lights burning in ajoupas so high up that you can only see a gleam coming through the trees now and then. It is not everybody who sees the lantern of Pè Labatt; and it is not good-luck to see it.

"Pè Labatt was a priest who lived here hundreds of years ago; and he wrote a book about what he saw. He was the first person to introduce slavery into Martinique; and it is thought that is why he comes back at night. It is his penance for having established slavery here.

"They used to say, before 1848, that when slavery should be abolished, Pè Labatt's light would not be seen any more. But I can remember very well when slavery was abolished; and I saw the light many a time after. It used to move up the Morne d'Orange every clear night;—I could see it very well from my window when I lived in St. Pierre. You knew it was Pè Labatt, because the light passed up places where no man could walk. But since the statue of Notre Dame de la Garde was placed on the Morne d'Orange, people tell me that the light is not seen there any more.

"But it is seen elsewhere; and it is not good-luck to see it. Everybody is afraid of seeing it... And mothers tell their children, when the little ones are naughty: '*Mi! moin ké fai Pè Labatt vini pouend ou,—oui!* (I will make Pè Labatt come and take you away.)"...

What old Théréza stated regarding the establishment of slavery in Martinique by Père Labat, I knew required no investigation,—inasmuch as slavery was a flourishing institution in the time of Père Du Tertre, another Dominican missionary and historian, who wrote his book,—a queer book in old French,[2]—before Labat was born. But it did not take me long to find out that such was the general belief about Père Labat's sin and penance, and to ascertain that his name is indeed used to frighten naughty children. *Eh! ti manmaille-là, moin ké fai Pè Labatt vini pouend ou!*—is an exclamation often heard in the vicinity of ajoupas just about the hour when all good little children ought to be in bed and asleep.

The first variation of the legend I heard was on a plantation in the neighborhood of Ajoupa-Bouillon. There I was informed that Père Labat had come to his death by the bite of a snake,—the hugest snake that ever was seen in Martinique. Père Labat had believed it possible to exterminate the fer-de-lance, and had adopted extraordinary measures for its destruction. On receiving his death-wound he exclaimed, "*C'est pè toutt sépent qui té ka mòdé moin*" (It is the Father of all Snakes that has bitten me); and he vowed that he would come back to destroy the brood, and would haunt the island until there should be not one snake left. And the light that moves about the peaks at night is the lantern of Père Labat still hunting for snakes.

"*Ou pa pè suive ti limié-là piess!*" continued my informant. "You cannot follow that little light at all;—when you first see it, it is perhaps only a kilometre away; the next moment it is two, three, or four kilometres away."

I was also told that the light is frequently seen near Grande Anse, on the other side of the island,—and on the heights of La Caravelle, the long fantastic promontory that reaches three leagues into the sea south of the harbor of La Trinité.[3] And on my return to St. Pierre I found a totally different version of the legend;—my informant being one Manm-Robert, a kind old soul who kept a little *boutique-lapacotte* (a little booth where cooked food is sold) near the precipitous Street of the Friendships.

…"*Ah! Pè Labatt, oui!*" she exclaimed, at my first question,—" Pè Labatt was a good priest who lived here very long ago. And they did him a great wrong here;—they gave him a wicked *coup d'langue* (tongue wound); and the hurt given by an evil tongue is worse than a serpent's bite. They lied about him; they slandered him until they got him sent away from the country. But before the Government 'embarked' him, when he got to that quay, he took off his shoe and he shook the dust of his shoe upon that quay, and he said: 'I curse you, O Martinique—I curse you! There will be food for nothing, and your people will not even be able to buy it! There will be clothing material for nothing, and your people will not be able to get so much as one dress! And the children will beat their mothers!… You banish me;—but I will come back again.'"[4]

"And then what happened, Manm-Robert?"

"*Eh! fouinq! chè*, all that Pè Labatt said has come true. There is food for almost nothing, and people are starving here in St. Pierre; there is clothing for almost nothing, and poor girls cannot earn enough to buy a dress. The pretty printed calicoes (*indiennes*) that used to be two francs and a half the metre, now sell at twelve sous the metre; but nobody has any money. And if you read our papers,—*Les Colonies, La Défense Coloniale*,—you will find that there are sons wicked enough to beat their mothers: *oui! yche ka batt manman!* It is the malediction of Pè Labatt."

This was all that Manm-Robert could tell me. Who had related the story to her? Her mother. Whence had her mother obtained it? From her grandmother... Subsequently I found many persons to confirm the tradition of the curse,—precisely as Manm-Robert had related it.

Only a brief while after this little interview I was invited to pass an afternoon at the home of a gentleman residing upon the Morne d'Orange,—the locality supposed to be especially haunted by Père Labat. The house of Monsieur M—stands on the side of the hill, fully five hundred feet up, and in a grove of trees: an antiquated dwelling, with foundations massive as the walls of a fortress, and huge broad balconies of stone. From one of these balconies there is a view of the city, the harbor, and Pelée, which I believe even those who have seen Naples would confess to be one of the fairest sights in the world... Towards evening I obtained a chance to ask my kind host some questions about the legend of his neighborhood.

"Ever since I was a child," observed Monsieur M—, "I heard it said that Père Labat haunted this mountain, and I often saw what was alleged to be his light. It looked very much like a lantern swinging in the hand of some one climbing the hill. A queer fact was that it used to come from the direction of Carbet, skirt the Morne d'Orange a few hundred feet above the road, and then move up the face of what seemed a sheer precipice. Of course somebody carried that light,—probably a negro; and perhaps the cliff is not so inaccessible as it looks: still, we could never discover who the individual was, nor could we imagine what his purpose might have been... But the light has not been seen here now for years."

III

AND who was Père Labat,—this strange priest whose memory, weirdly disguised by legend, thus lingers in the oral literature of the colored people? Various encyclopaedias answer the question, but far less fully and less interestingly than Dr. Rufz, the Martinique historian, whose article upon him in the *Études Statistiques et Historiques* has that charm of sympathetic comprehension by which a master-biographer sometimes reveals himself a sort of necromancer,—making us feel a vanished personality with the power of a living presence. Yet even the colorless data given by dictionaries of biography should suffice to convince most readers that Jean-Baptiste Labat must be ranked among the extraordinary men of his century.

Nearly two hundred years ago—24th August 1693—a traveller wearing the white habit of the Dominican order, partly covered by a black camlet overcoat, entered the city of Rochelle. He was very tall and robust, with one of those faces, at once grave and keen, which bespeak great energy and quick discernment. This was the Père Labat, a native of Paris, then in his thirtieth year. Half priest, half layman, one might have been tempted to surmise from his attire; and such a judgment would not have been unjust. Labat's character was too large for his calling,—expanded naturally beyond the fixed limits of the ecclesiastical life; and throughout the whole active part of his strange career we find in him this dual character of layman and monk. He had come to Rochelle to take passage for Martinique. Previously he had been professor of philosophy and mathematics at Nancy. While watching a sunset one evening from the window of his study, some one placed in his hands a circular issued by the Dominicans of the French West Indies, calling for volunteers. Death had made many wide gaps in their ranks; and various misfortunes had reduced their finances to such an extent that ruin threatened all their West Indian establishments. Labat, with the quick decision of a mind suffering from the restraints of a life too narrow for it, had at once resigned his professorship, and engaged himself for the missions.

In those days, communication with the West Indies was slow, irregular, and difficult. Labat had to wait at Rochelle six whole months for a ship. In the convent at Rochelle, where he stayed, there were others waiting for the same chance,—including several Jesuits and Capuchins as well as Dominicans. These unanimously elected him their leader,—a significant fact considering the mutual jealousy of the various religious orders of that period. There was something in the energy and frankness of Labat's character which seems to have naturally gained him the confidence and ready submission of others.

They sailed in November; and Labat still found himself in the position of a chief on board. His account of the voyage is amusing;—in almost everything except practical navigation, he would appear to have regulated the life of passengers and crew. He taught the captain mathematics; and invented amusements of all kinds to relieve the monotony of a two months' voyage.

...As the ship approached Martinique from the north, Labat first beheld the very grimmest part of the lofty coast,—the region of Macouba; and the impression it made upon him was not pleasing. "The island," he writes, "appeared to me all one frightful mountain, broken everywhere by precipices: nothing about it pleased me except the verdure which everywhere met the eye, and which seemed to me both novel and agreeable, considering the time of the year."

Almost immediately after his arrival he was sent by the Superior of the convent to Macouba, for acclimation; Macouba then being considered the healthiest part of the island. Whoever makes the journey on horseback thither from St. Pierre today can testify to the exactitude of Labat's delightful narrative of the trip. So little has that part of the island changed since two centuries that scarcely a line of the father's description would need correction to adopt it bodily for an account of a ride to Macouba in 1889.

At Macouba everybody welcomes him, pets him,—finally becomes enthusiastic about him. He fascinates and dominates the little community almost at first sight. "There is an inexpressible charm," says Rufz,—commenting upon this portion of Labat's narrative,—"in the novelty of relations between men: no one has yet been offended, no envy has yet been excited;—it is scarcely possible even to guess whence that ill-will you must sooner or later provoke is going to come from;—there are no rivals;—there are no enemies. You are everybody's friend; and many are hoping you will continue to be only theirs."... Labat knew how to take legitimate advantage of this good-will;—he persuaded his admirers to rebuild the church at Macouba, according to designs made by himself.

At Macouba, however, he was not permitted to sojourn as long as the good people of the little burgh would have deemed even reasonable: he had shown certain aptitudes which made his presence more than desirable at Saint-Jacques, the great plantation of the order on the Capesterre, or Windward coast. It was in debt for 700,000 pounds of sugar,—an appalling condition in those days,—and seemed doomed to get more heavily in debt every successive season. Labat inspected everything, and set to work for the plantation, not merely as general director, but as engineer, architect, machinist, inventor. He did really wonderful things. You can see them for yourself if you ever go to Martinique; for the old Dominican plantation—now Government property, and leased at an annual rent of 50,000 francs—remains one of the most valuable in the colonies because of Labat's work upon it. The watercourses directed by him still excite the admiration of modern professors of hydraulics; the mills he built or invented are still good;—the treatise he wrote on sugar-making remained for a hundred and fifty years the best of its kind, and the manual of French planters. In less than two years Labat had not only rescued the plantation from bankruptcy, but had made it rich; and if the monks deemed him veritably inspired, the test of time throws no ridicule on their astonishment at the capacities of the man.

...Even now the advice he formulated as far back as 1720—about secondary cultures,—about manufactories to establish,—about imports, exports, and special commercial methods—has lost little of its value.

Such talents could not fail to excite wide-spread admiration,—nor to win for him a reputation in the colonies beyond precedent. He was wanted everywhere... Auger, the Governor of Guadeloupe, sent for him to help the colonists in fortifying and defending the island against the English; and we find the missionary quite as much at home in this new role—building bastions, scarps, counterscarps, ravelins, etc.—as he seemed to be upon the plantation of Saint-Jacques. We find him even taking part in an engagement;—himself conducting an artillery duel,— loading, pointing, and firing no less than twelve times after the other French gunners had been killed or driven from their posts. After a tremendous English volley, one of the enemy cries out to him in French: "White Father, have they told?" (*Père Blanc, ont-ils porté?*) He replies only after returning the fire with a better-directed aim, and then repeats the mocking question: "Have they told?" "Yes, they have," confesses the Englishman, in surprised dismay; "but we will pay you back for that!"

...Returning to Martinique with new titles to distinction, Labat was made Superior of the order in that island, and likewise Vicar-Apostolic. After building the Convent of the Mouillage, at St. Pierre, and many other edifices, he undertook that series of voyages in the interests of the Dominicans whereof the narration fills six ample volumes. As a traveller Père Labat has had few rivals in his own field;—no one, indeed, seems to have been able to repeat some of his feats. All the French and several of the English colonies were not merely visited by him, but were studied in their every geographical detail. Travel in the West Indies is difficult to a degree of which strangers have little idea; but in the time of Père Labat there were few roads,—and a far greater variety of obstacles. I do not believe there are half a dozen whites in Martinique who thoroughly know their own island,—who have even travelled upon all its roads; but Labat knew it as he knew the palm of his hand, and travelled where roads had never been made. Equally well he knew Guadeloupe and other islands; and he learned all that it was possible to learn in those years about the productions and resources of the other colonies.

He travelled with the fearlessness and examined with the thoroughness of a Humboldt,—so far as his limited science permitted: had he possessed the knowledge of modern naturalists and geologists he would probably have left little for others to discover after him. Even at the present time West Indian travellers are glad to consult him for information.

These duties involved prodigious physical and mental exertion, in a climate deadly to Europeans. They also involved much voyaging in waters haunted by filibusters and buccaneers. But nothing appears to daunt Labat. As for the filibusters, he becomes their comrade and personal friend;—he even becomes their chaplain, and does not scruple to make excursions with them. He figures in several sea-fights;—on one occasion he aids in the capture of two English vessels,—and then occupies himself in making the prisoners, among whom are several ladies, enjoy the event like a holiday. On another voyage Labat's vessel is captured by a Spanish ship. At one moment sabres are raised above his head, and loaded muskets levelled at his breast;—the next, every Spaniard is on his knees, appalled by a cross that Labat holds before the eyes of the captors,—the cross worn by officers of the Inquisition,—the terrible symbol of the Holy Office. "It did not belong to me," he says, "but to one of our brethren who had left it by accident among my effects." He seems always prepared in some way to meet any possible emergency. No humble and timid monk this: he has the frame and temper of those mediaeval abbots who could don with equal indifference the helmet or the cowl. He is apparently even more of a soldier than a priest. When English corsairs attempt a descent on the Martinique coast at Sainte-Marie they find Père Labat waiting for them with all the negroes of the Saint-Jacques plantation, to drive them back to their ships.

For other dangers he exhibits absolute unconcern. He studies the phenomena of hurricanes with almost pleasurable interest, while his comrades on the ship abandon hope. When seized with yellow-fever, then known as the Siamese Sickness (*mal de Siam*), he refuses to stay in bed the prescribed time, and rises to say his mass. He faints at the altar; yet a few days later we hear of him on horseback again, travelling over the mountains in the worst and hottest season of the year.

Labat was thirty years old when he went to the Antilles;—he was only forty-two when his work was done. In less than twelve years he made his order the most powerful and wealthy of any in the West Indies,—lifted their property out of bankruptcy to rebuild it upon a foundation of extraordinary prosperity. As Rufz observes without exaggeration, the career of Père Labat in the Antilles seems to more than realize the antique legend of the labors of Hercules. Whithersoever he went,—except in the English colonies,—his passage was memorialized by the rising of churches, convents, and schools,—as well as mills, forts, and refineries. Even cities claim him as their founder. The solidity of his architectural creations is no less remarkable than their excellence of design;—much of what he erected still remains; what has vanished was removed by human agency, and not by decay; and when the old Dominican church at St. Pierre had to be pulled down to make room for a larger edifice, the workmen complained that the stones could not he separated,—that the walls seemed single masses of rock. There can be no doubt, moreover, that he largely influenced the life of the colonies during those years, and expanded their industrial and commercial capacities.

He was sent on a mission to Rome after these things had been done, and never returned from Europe. There he travelled more or less in after-years; but finally settled at Paris, where he prepared and published the voluminous narrative of his own voyages, and other curious books;— manifesting as a writer the same tireless energy he had shown in so many other capacities. He does not, however, appear to have been happy. Again and again he prayed to be sent back to his beloved Antilles, and for some unknown cause the prayer was always refused. To such a character, the restraint of the cloister must have proved a slow agony; but he had to endure it for many long years. He died at Paris in 1738, aged seventy-five.

…It was inevitable that such a man should make bitter enemies: his preferences, his position, his activity, his business shrewdness, his necessary self-assertion, must have created secret hate and jealousy even when open malevolence might not dare to show itself. And to these natural results of personal antagonism or opposition were afterwards superadded various resentments—irrational, perhaps, but extremely violent,—caused by the father's cynical frankness as a writer. He spoke freely about the family origin and personal failings of various colonists considered high personages in their own small world; and to this day his book has an evil reputation undeserved in those old creole communities, where any public mention of a family scandal is never forgiven or forgotten... But probably even before his work appeared it had been secretly resolved that he should never be permitted to return to Martinique or Guadeloupe after his European mission. The exact purpose of the Government in this policy remains a mystery,—whatever ingenious writers may have alleged to the contrary. We only know that M. Adrien Dessalles,—the trustworthy historian of Martinique,—while searching among the old *Archives de la Marine*, found there a ministerial letter to the Intendant de Vaucresson in which this statement occurs:— "Le Père Labat shall never be suffered to return to the colonies, whatever efforts he may make to obtain permission."

IV

ONE rises from the perusal of the "Nouveau Voyage aux Isles de l'Amérique" with a feeling approaching regret; for although the six pursy little volumes composing it—full of quaint drawings, plans, and odd attempts at topographical maps—reveal a prolix writer, Père Labat is always able to interest. He reminds you of one of those slow, precise, old-fashioned conversationalists who measure the weight of every word and never leave anything to the imagination of the audience, yet who invariably reward the patience of their listeners sooner or later by reflections of surprising profundity or theories of a totally novel description. But what particularly impresses the reader of these volumes is not so much the recital of singular incidents and facts as the revelation of the author's personality. Reading him, you divine a character of enormous force,—gifted but unevenly balanced; singularly shrewd in worldly affairs, and surprisingly credulous in other respects; superstitious and yet cynical; unsympathetic by his positivism, but agreeable through natural desire to give pleasure; just by nature, yet capable of merciless severity; profoundly devout, but withal tolerant for his calling and his time. He is sufficiently free from petty bigotry to make fun of the scruples of his brethren in the matter of employing heretics; and his account of the manner in which he secured the services of a first-class refiner for the Martinique plantation at the Fond Saint-Jacques is not the least amusing page in the book. He writes: "The religious who had been appointed Superior in Guadeloupe wrote me that he would find it difficult to employ this refiner because the man was a Lutheran. This scruple gave me pleasure, as I had long wanted to have him upon our plantation in the Fond Saint-Jacques, but did not know how I would be able to manage it. I wrote to the Superior at once that all he had to do was to send the man to me, because it was a matter of indifference to me whether the sugar he might make were Catholic or Lutheran sugar, provided it were very white."[5] He displays equal frankness in confessing an error or a discomfiture. He acknowledges that while Professor of Mathematics and Philosophy, he used to teach that there were no tides in the tropics; and in a discussion as to whether the *diablotin* (a now almost extinct species of West Indian nocturnal bird) were fish or flesh, and might or might not be eaten in Lent, he tells us that he was fairly worsted,— (although he could cite the celebrated myth of the "barnacle-geese" as a "fact" in justification of one's right to doubt the nature of diablotins).

One has reason to suspect that Père Labat, notwithstanding his references to the decision of the Church that diablotins were not birds, felt quite well assured within himself that they were. There is a sly humor in his story of these controversies, which would appear to imply that while well pleased at the decision referred to, he knew all about diablotins. Moreover, the father betrays certain tendencies to gormandize not altogether in harmony with the profession of an ascetic... There were parrots in nearly all of the French Antilles in those days; [6] and Père Labat does not attempt to conceal his fondness for—cooked parrots. (He does not appear to have cared much for them as pets: if they could not talk well, he condemned them forthwith to the pot.) "They all live upon fruits and seeds," he writes, "and their flesh contracts the odor and color of that particular fruit or seed they feed upon. They become exceedingly fat in the season when the guavas are ripe; and when they eat the seeds of the *Bois d'Inde* they have an odor of nutmeg and cloves which is delightful (*une odeur de muscade et de girofle qui fait plaisir*)." He recommends four superior ways of preparing them, as well as other fowls, for the table, of which the first and the best way is "to pluck them alive, then to make then swallow vinegar, and then to strangle them while they have the vinegar still in their throats by twisting their necks"; and the fourth way is "to skin them alive" (*de les écorcher tout en vie*)... "It is certain," he continues, "that these ways are excellent, and that fowls that have to be cooked in a hurry thereby obtain an admirable tenderness (*une tendreté admirable*)." Then he makes a brief apology to his readers, not for the inhumanity of his recipes, but for a display of culinary knowledge scarcely becoming a monk, and acquired only through those peculiar necessities which colonial life in the tropics imposed upon all alike. The touch of cruelty here revealed produces an impression which there is little in the entire work capable of modifying. Labat seems to have possessed but a very small quantity of altruism; his cynicism on the subject of animal suffering is not offset by any visible sympathy with human pain;—he never compassionates: you may seek in vain through all his pages for one gleam of the goodness of gentle Père Du Tertre, who, filled with intense pity for the condition of the blacks, prays masters to be merciful and just to their slaves for the love of God. Labat suggests, on the other hand, that slavery is a good means of redeeming negroes from superstition and saving their souls from hell: he selects and purchases them himself for the Saint-Jacques plantation, never makes a mistake or a bad bargain, and never appears to feel a particle of commiseration for their lot. In fact, the emotional feeling displayed by Père Du Tertre (whom he mocks slyly betimes) must have seemed to him rather condemnable than praiseworthy; for Labat regarded the negro as a natural child of the devil,—a born sorcerer,—an evil being wielding occult power.

Perhaps the chapters on negro sorcery are the most astonishing in the book, displaying on the part of this otherwise hard and practical nature a credulity almost without limit. After having related how he had a certain negro sent out of the country "who predicted the arrival of vessels and other things to come,—in so far, at least, as the devil himself was able to know and reveal these matters to him," he plainly states his own belief in magic as follows:—

"I know there are many people who consider as pure imagination, and as silly stories, or positive falsehoods, all that is related about sorcerers and their compacts with the devil. I was myself for a long time of this opinion. Moreover, I am aware that what is said on this subject is frequently exaggerated; but I am now convinced it must be acknowledged that all which has been related is not entirely false, although perhaps it may not be entirely true."…

Therewith he begins to relate stories upon what may have seemed unimpeachable authority in those days. The first incident narrated took place, he assures us, in the Martinique Dominican convent, shortly before his arrival in the colony. One of the fathers, Père Fraise, had had brought to Martinique, "from the kingdom of Juda (?) in Guinea," a little negro about nine or ten years old. Not long afterwards there was a serious drought, and the monks prayed vainly for rain. Then the negro child, who had begun to understand and speak a little French, told his masters that he was a Rain-maker, that he could obtain them all the rain they wanted. "This proposition," says Père Labat, "greatly astonished the fathers: they consulted together, and at last, curiosity overcoming reason, they gave their consent that this unbaptized child should make some rain fall on their garden." The unbaptized child asked them if they wanted "a big or a little rain"; they answered that a moderate rain would satisfy them. Thereupon the little negro got three oranges, and placed them on the ground in a line at a short distance from one another, and bowed down before each of them in turn, muttering words in an unknown tongue. Then he got three small orange-branches, stuck a branch in each orange, and repeated his prostrations and mutterings;—after which he took one of the branches, stood up, and watched the horizon. A small cloud appeared, and he pointed the branch at it. It approached swiftly, rested above the garden, and sent down a copious shower of rain. Then the boy made a hole in the ground, and buried the oranges and the branches. The fathers were amazed to find that not a single drop of rain had fallen outside their garden. They asked the boy who had taught him this sorcery, and he answered them that among the blacks on board the slave-ship which had brought him over there were some Rain-makers who had taught him. Père Labat declares there is no question as to the truth of the occurrence: he cites the names of Père Fraise, Père Rosié, Père Temple, and Père Bournot,—all members of his own order,—as trustworthy witnesses of this incident.

Père Labat displays equal credulity in his recital of a still more extravagant story told him by Madame la Comtesse du Gênes. M. le Comte du Gênes, husband of the lady in question, and commander of a French squadron, captured the English fort of Gorea in 1696, and made prisoners of all the English slaves in the service of the factory there established. But the vessel on which these were embarked was unable to leave the coast, in spite of a good breeze: she seemed bewitched. Some of the slaves finally told the captain there was a negress on board who had enchanted the ship, and who had the power to "dry up the hearts" of all who refused to obey her. A number of deaths taking place among the blacks, the captain ordered autopsies made, and it was found that the hearts of the dead negroes were desiccated. The negress was taken on deck, tied to a gun and whipped, but uttered no cry;—the ship's surgeon, angered at her stoicism, took a hand in the punishment, and flogged her "with all his force." Thereupon she told him that inasmuch as he had abused her without reason, his heart also should be "dried up." He died next day; and his heart was found in the condition predicted. All this time the ship could not be made to move in any direction; and the negress told the captain that until he should put her and her companions on shore he would never be able to sail. To convince him of her power she further asked him to place three fresh melons in a chest, to lock the chest and put a guard over it; when she should tell him to unlock it, there would be no melons there. The captain made the experiment. When the chest was opened, the melons appeared to be there; but on touching them it was found that only the outer rind remained: the interior had been dried up,—like the surgeon's heart. Thereupon the captain put the witch and her friends ashore, and sailed away without further trouble.

Another story of African sorcery for the truth of which Père Labat earnestly vouches is the following:—

A negro was sentenced to be burned alive for witchcraft at St. Thomas in 1701: his principal crime was "having made a little figure of baked clay to speak." A certain creole, meeting the negro on his way to the place of execution, jeeringly observed, "Well, you cannot make your little figure talk any more now;—it has been broken." "If the gentleman allow me," replied the prisoner, "I will make the cane he carries in his hand speak." The creole's curiosity was strongly aroused: he prevailed upon the guards to halt a few minutes, and permit the prisoner to make the experiment. The negro then took the cane, stuck it into the ground in the middle of the road, whispered something to it, and asked the gentleman what he wished to know. "I would like to know," answered the latter, "whether the ship — — has yet sailed from Europe, and when she will arrive." "Put your ear to the head of the cane," said the negro. On doing so the creole distinctly heard a thin voice which informed him that the vessel in question had left a certain French port on such a date; that she would reach St. Thomas within three days; that she had been delayed on her voyage by a storm which had carried away her foretop and her mizzen sail; that she had such and such passengers on board (mentioning the names), all in good health... After this incident the negro was burned alive; but within three days the vessel arrived in port, and the prediction or divination was found to have been absolutely correct in every particular.

Père Labat in no way disapproves the atrocious sentence inflicted upon the wretched negro: in his opinion such predictions were made by the power and with the personal aid of the devil; and for those who knowingly maintained relations with the devil, he could not have regarded any punishment too severe. That he could be harsh enough himself is amply shown in various accounts of his own personal experience with alleged sorcerers, and especially in the narration of his dealings with one—apparently a sort of African doctor—who was a slave on a neighboring plantation, but used to visit the Saint-Jacques quarters by stealth to practise his art. One of the slaves of the order, a negress, falling very sick, the wizard was sent for; and he came with all his paraphernalia—little earthen pots and fetiches, etc.—during the night. He began to practise his incantations, without the least suspicion that Père Labat was watching him through a chink; and, after having consulted his fetiches, he told the sick woman she would die within four days. At this juncture the priest suddenly burst in the door and entered, followed by several powerful slaves. He dashed to pieces the soothsayer's articles, and attempted to reassure the frightened negress, by declaring the prediction a lie inspired by the devil. Then he had the sorcerer stripped and flogged in his presence.

"I had him given," he calmly observes, "about (*environ*) three hundred lashes, which flayed him (*l'écorchait*) from his shoulders to his knees. He screamed like a madman. All the negroes trembled, and assured me that the devil would cause my death... Then I had the wizard put in irons, after having had him well washed with a *pimentade*;—that is to say, with brine in which pimentos and small lemons have been crushed. This causes a horrible pain to those skinned by the whip; but it is a certain remedy against gangrene."...

And then he sent the poor wretch back to his master with a note requesting the latter to repeat the punishment,—a demand that seems to have been approved, as the owner of the negro was "a man who feared God." Yet Père Labat is obliged to confess that in spite of all his efforts, the sick negress died on the fourth day,—as the sorcerer had predicted. This fact must have strongly confirmed his belief that the devil was at the bottom of the whole affair, and caused him to doubt whether even a flogging of *about* three hundred lashes, followed by a pimentade, were sufficient chastisement for the miserable black. Perhaps the tradition of this frightful whipping may have had something to do with the terror which still attaches to the name of the Dominican in Martinique. The legal extreme punishment was twenty-nine lashes.

Père Labat also avers that in his time the negroes were in the habit of carrying sticks which had the power of imparting to any portion of the human body touched by them a most severe chronic pain. He at first believed, he says, that these pains were merely rheumatic; but after all known remedies for rheumatism had been fruitlessly applied, he became convinced there was something occult and diabolical in the manner of using and preparing these sticks... A fact worthy of note is that this belief is still prevalent in Martinique!

One hardly ever meets in the country a negro who does not carry either a stick or a cutlass, or both. The cutlass is indispensable to those who work in the woods or upon plantations; the stick is carried both as a protection against snakes and as a weapon of offence and defence in village quarrels, for unless a negro be extraordinarily drunk he will not strike his fellow with a cutlass. The sticks are usually made of a strong dense wood: those most sought after of a material termed *moudongue*[7] almost as tough, but much lighter than, our hickory. On inquiring whether any of the sticks thus carried were held to possess magic powers, I was assured by many country people that there were men who knew a peculiar method of "arranging" sticks so that to touch any person with them even lightly, *and through any thickness of clothing*, would produce terrible and continuous pain.

Believing in these things, and withal unable to decide whether the sun revolved about the earth, or the earth about the sun,[8]—Père Labat was, nevertheless, no more credulous and no more ignorant than the average missionary of his time: it is only by contrast with his practical perspicacity in other matters, his worldly rationalism and executive shrewdness, that this superstitious naïveté impresses one as odd. And how singular sometimes is the irony of Time! All the wonderful work the Dominican accomplished has been forgotten by the people; while all the witchcrafts that he warred against survive and flourish openly; and his very name is seldom uttered but in connection with superstitions,—has been, in fact, preserved among the blacks by the power of superstition alone, by the belief in zombis and goblins... *"Mi! ti manmaille-là, moin ké fai Pè Labatt vini pouend ou!"*...

V

FEW habitants of St. Pierre now remember that the beautiful park behind the cathedral used to he called the Savanna of the White Fathers,—and the long shadowed meadow beside the Roxelane, the Savanna of the Black Fathers: the Jesuits. All the great religious orders have long since disappeared from the colony: their edifices have been either converted to other uses or demolished; their estates have passed into other hands... Were their labors, then, productive of merely ephemeral results?—was the colossal work of a Père Labat all in vain, so far as the future is concerned? The question is not easily answered; but it is worth considering.

Of course the material prosperity which such men toiled to obtain for their order represented nothing more, even to their eyes, than the means of self-maintenance, and the accumulation of force necessary for the future missionary labors of the monastic community. The real ultimate purpose was, not the acquisition of power for the order, but for the Church, of which the orders represented only a portion of the force militant; and this purpose did not fail of accomplishment. The orders passed away only when their labors had been completed,—when Martinique had become (exteriorly, at least) more Catholic than Rome itself,—after the missionaries had done all that religious zeal could do in moulding and remoulding the human material under their control. These men could scarcely have anticipated those social and political changes which the future reserved for the colonies, and which no ecclesiastical sagacity could, in any event, have provided against. It is in the existing religious condition of these communities that one may observe and estimate the character and the probable duration of the real work accomplished by the missions.

...Even after a prolonged residence in Martinique, its visible religious condition continues to impress one as something phenomenal. A stranger, who has no opportunity to penetrate into the home life of the people, will not, perhaps, discern the full extent of the religious sentiment; but, nevertheless, however brief his stay, he will observe enough of the extravagant symbolism of the cult to fill him with surprise. Wherever he may choose to ride or to walk, he is certain to encounter shrines, statues of saints, or immense crucifixes. Should he climb up to the clouds of the peaks, he will find them all along the way,—he will perceive them waiting for him, looming through the mists of the heights; and passing through the loveliest ravines, he will see niches hollowed out in the volcanic rocks, above and below him, or contrived in the trunks of trees bending over precipices, often in places so difficult of access that he wonders how the work could have been accomplished. All this has been done by the various property-owners throughout the country: it is the traditional custom to do it—it brings good-luck! After a longer stay in the island, one discovers also that in almost every room of every dwelling—stone residence, wooden cottage, or palm-thatched ajoupa—there is a *chapelle*: that is, a sort of large bracket fastened to the wall, on which crosses or images are placed, with vases of flowers, and lamps or wax-tapers to be burned at night. Sometimes, moreover, statues are placed in windows, or above doorways;—and all passers-by take off their hats to these. Over the porch of the cottage in a mountain village, where I lived for some weeks, there was an absurd little window contrived,—a sort of purely ornamental dormer,—and in this a Virgin about five inches high had been placed. At a little distance it looked like a toy,—a child's doll forgotten there; and a doll I always supposed it to be, until one day that I saw a long procession of black laborers passing before the house, every one of whom took off his hat to it... My bedchamber in the same cottage resembled a religious museum. On the chapelle there were no less than eight Virgins, varying in height from one to sixteen inches,—a St. Joseph,—a St. John,—a crucifix,—and a host of little objects in the shape of hearts or crosses, each having some special religious significance;—while the walls were covered with framed certificates of baptism, "first-communion," confirmation, and other documents commemorating the whole church life of the family for two generations.

...Certainly the first impression created by this perpetual display of crosses, statues, and miniature chapels is not pleasing,—particularly as the work is often inartistic to a degree bordering upon the grotesque, and nothing resembling art is anywhere visible. Millions of francs must have been consumed in these creations, which have the rudeness of mediaevalism without its emotional sincerity, and which—amid the loveliness of tropic nature, the grace of palms, the many-colored fire of liana blossoms—jar on the aesthetic sense with an almost brutal violence. Yet there is a veiled poetry in these silent populations of plaster and wood and stone. They represent something older than the Middle Ages, older than Christianity,—something strangely distorted and transformed, it is true, but recognizably conserved by the Latin race from those antique years when every home had its beloved ghosts, when every wood or hill or spring had its gracious divinity, and the boundaries of all fields were marked and guarded by statues of gods.

Instances of iconoclasm are of course highly rare in a country of which no native—rich or poor, white or half-breed—fails to doff his hat before every shrine, cross, or image he may happen to pass. Those merchants of St. Pierre or of Fort-de-France living only a few miles out of the city must certainly perform a vast number of reverences on their way

A Wayside Shrine or Chapelle

to or from business;—I saw one old gentleman uncover his white head about twenty times in the course of a fifteen minutes' walk. I never heard of but one image-breaker in Martinique; and his act was the result of superstition, not of any hostility to popular faith or custom: it was prompted by the same childish feeling which moves Italian fishermen sometimes to curse St. Antony or to give his image a ducking in bad weather. This Martinique iconoclast was a negro cattle-driver who one day, feeling badly in need of a glass of tafia, perhaps, left the animals entrusted to him in care of a plaster image of the Virgin, with this menace (the phrase is on record):—

"*Moin ka quitté bef-là ba ou pou gàdé ba moin. Quand moin vini, si moin pa trouvé compte-moin, moin ké fouté ou vingt-nèf coudfouètt!*" (I leave these cattle with you to take care of for me. When I come back, if I don't find them all here, I'll give you twenty-nine lashes.)

Returning about half an hour later, he was greatly enraged to find his animals scattered in every direction;—and, rushing at the statue, he broke it from the pedestal, flung it upon the ground, and gave it twenty-nine lashes with his bull-whip. For this he was arrested, tried, and sentenced to imprisonment, with hard labor, for life! In those days there were no colored magistrates;—the judges were all *békés*.

"Rather a severe sentence," I remarked to my informant, a planter who conducted me to the scene of the alleged sacrilege.

"Severe, yes," he answered;—"and I suppose the act would seem to you more idiotic than criminal. But here, in Martinique, there were large questions involved by such an offence. Relying, as we have always done to some extent, upon religious influence as a factor in the maintenance of social order, the negro's act seemed a dangerous example."…

That the Church remains still rich and prosperous in Martinique there can be no question; but whether it continues to wield any powerful influence in the maintenance of social order is more than doubtful. A Polynesian laxity of morals among the black and colored population, and the history of race-hatreds and revolutions inspired by race-hate, would indicate that neither in ethics nor in politics does it possess any preponderant authority. By expelling various religious orders;—by establishing lay schools, lycées, and other educational institutions where the teaching is largely characterized by aggressive antagonism to Catholic ideas;—by the removal of crucifixes and images from public buildings, French Radicalism did not inflict any great blow upon Church interests.

So far as the white, and, one may say, the wealthy, population is concerned, the Church triumphs in her hostility to the Government schools; and to the same extent she holds an educational monopoly. No white creole would dream of sending his children to a lay school or a lycée—notwithstanding the unquestionable superiority of the educational system in the latter institutions;—and, although obliged, as the chief tax-paying class, to bear the burden of maintaining these establishments, the whites hold them in such horror that the Government professors are socially ostracized. No doubt the prejudice or pride which abhors mixed schools aids the Church in this respect; she herself recognizes race-feeling, keeps her schools unmixed, and even in her convents, it is said, obliges the colored nuns to serve the white! For more than two centuries every white generation has been religiously moulded in the seminaries and convents; and among the native whites one never hears an overt declaration of free-thought opinion. Except among the colored men educated in the Government schools, or their foreign professors, there are no avowed free-thinkers;—and this, not because the creole whites, many of whom have been educated in Paris, are naturally narrow-minded, or incapable of sympathy with the mental expansion of the age, but because the religious question at Martinique has become so intimately complicated with the social and political one, concerning which there can be no compromise whatever, that to divorce the former from the latter is impossible. Roman Catholicism is an element of the cement which holds creole society together; and it is noteworthy that other creeds are not represented. I knew only of one Episcopalian and one Methodist in the island,—and heard a sort of legend about a solitary Jew whose whereabouts I never could discover;—but these were strangers.

It was only through the establishment of universal suffrage, which placed the white population at the mercy of its former slaves, that the Roman Church sustained any serious injury. All local positions are filled by blacks or men of color; no white creole can obtain a public office or take part in legislation; and the whole power of the black vote is ungenerously used against the interests of the class thus politically disinherited. The Church suffers in consequence: her power depended upon her intimate union with the wealthy and dominant class; and she will never be forgiven by those now in power for her sympathetic support of that class in other years. Politics yearly intensify this hostility; and as the only hope for the restoration of the whites to power, and of the Church to its old position, lies in the possibility of another empire or a revival of the monarchy, the white creoles and their Church are forced into hostility against republicanism and the republic. And political newspapers continually attack Roman Catholicism,—mock its tenets and teachings,—ridicule its dogmas and ceremonies,—satirize its priests.

In the cities and towns the Church indeed appears to retain a large place in the affection of the poorer classes; her ceremonies are always well attended; money pours into her coffers; and one can still witness the curious annual procession of the "converted,"—aged women of color and negresses going to communion for the first time, all wearing snow-white turbans in honor of the event. But among the country people, where the dangerous forces of revolution exist, Christian feeling is almost stifled by ghastly beliefs of African origin;—the images and crucifixes still command respect, but this respect is inspired by a feeling purely fetichistic. With the political dispossession of the whites, certain dark powers, previously concealed or repressed, have obtained formidable development. The old enemy of Père Labat, the wizard (the *quimboiseur*), already wields more authority than the priest, exercises more terror than the magistrate, commands more confidence than the physician. The educated mulatto class may affect to despise him;—but he is preparing their overthrow in the dark. Astonishing is the persistence with which the African has clung to these beliefs and practices, so zealously warred upon by the Church and so mercilessly punished by the courts for centuries. He still goes to mass, and sends his children to the priest; but he goes more often to the quimboiseur and the "*magnetise.*" He finds use for both beliefs, but gives large preference to the savage one,—just as he prefers the pattering of his tamtam to the music of the military band at the *Savane du Fort...* And should it come to pass that Martinique be ever totally abandoned by its white population,—an event by no means improbable in the present order of things,—the fate of the ecclesiastical fabric so toilsomely reared by the monastic orders is not difficult to surmise.

VI

FROM my window in the old Rue du Bois-Morin,—which climbs the foot of Morne Labelle by successions of high stone steps,—all the southern end of the city is visible as in a bird's-eye view. Under me is a long peaking of red-scaled roofs,—gables and dormer-windows,—with clouds of bright green here and there,—foliage of tamarind and corossolier;—westward purples and flames the great circle of the

Caribbean Sea;—east and south, towering to the violet sky, curve the volcanic hills, green-clad from base to summit;—and right before me the beautiful Morne d'Orange, all palm-plumed and wood-wrapped, trends seaward and southward. And every night, after the stars come out, I see moving lights there,—lantern fires guiding the mountain-dwellers home; but I look in vain for the light of Père Labat.

And nevertheless,—although no believer in ghosts,—I see thee very plainly sometimes, thou quaint White Father, moving through winter-mists in the narrower Paris of another century; musing upon the churches that arose at thy bidding under tropic skies; dreaming of the primeval valleys changed by thy will to green-gold seas of cane,—and the strong mill that will bear thy name for two hundred years (it stands solid unto this day),—and the habitations made for thy brethren in pleasant palmy places,—and the luminous peace of thy Martinique con-vent,—and odor of roasting parrots fattened upon *grains de bois d'Inde* and guavas,—"*l'odeur de muscade et de girofle qui fait plaisir.*"

Eh, Père Labat!—what changes there have been since thy day! The White Fathers have no place here now; and the Black Fathers, too, have been driven from the land, leaving only as a memory of them the perfect and ponderous architecture of the Perinnelle plantation-buildings, and the appellation of the river still known as the Rivière des Pères. Also the Ursulines are gone, leaving only their name on the corner of a crumbling street. And there are no more slaves; and there are new races of colors thou wouldst deem scandalous though beautiful; and there are no more parrots; and there are no more diablotins. And the grand woods thou sawest in their primitive and inviolate beauty, as if fresh from the Creator's touch in the morning of the world, are passing away; the secular trees are being converted into charcoal, or sawn into timber for the boat-builders: thou shouldst see two hundred men pulling some forest giant down to the sea upon the two-wheeled screaming thing they call a "devil" (*yon diabe*),—cric-crac!—cric-crac!—all chanting together:—

> "*Soh-soh!—yaïe-yah!*
> *Rhâlé bois-canot!*"

And all that ephemeral man has had power to change has been changed,—ideas, morals, beliefs, the whole social fabric. But the eternal summer remains,—and the Hesperian magnificence of azure sky and violet sea,—and the jewel-colors of the perpetual hills;—the same tepid winds that rippled thy cane-fields two hundred years ago still blow over Sainte-Marie;—the same purple shadows lengthen and dwindle and turn with the wheeling of the sun. God's witchery still fills this land; and the heart of the stranger is even yet snared by the beauty of it; and the dreams of him that forsakes it will surely be haunted—even as were thine own, Père Labat—by memories of its Eden-summer: the sudden leap of the light over a thousand peaks in the glory of tropic dawn,—the perfumed peace of enormous azure noons,—and shapes of palm wind-rocked in the burning of colossal sunsets,—and the silent flickering of the great fire-flies through the lukewarm darkness, when mothers call their children home... "*Mi fanal Pè Labatt!—mi Pè Labatt ka vini pouend ou!*"

NOTES

1. What is known in the West Indies as a hurricane is happily rare; it blows with the force of a cyclone, but not always circularly; it may come from one direction, and strengthen gradually for days until its highest velocity and destructive force are reached. One in the time of Père Labat blew away the walls of a fort;—that of 1780 destroyed the lives of twenty-two thousand people in four islands: Martinique, Saint Lucia, St. Vincent, and Barbadoes.

Before the approach of such a visitation animals manifest the same signs of terror they display prior to an earthquake. Cattle assemble together, stamp, and roar; sea-birds fly to the interior; fowl seek the nearest crevice they can hide in. Then, while the sky is yet clear, begins the breaking of the sea; then darkness comes, and after it the wind.

2. "Histoire Générale das Antilles...habitées par les Français" Par le R.P. Du Tertre, de l'Ordre des Frères Prescheurs. Paris: 1661-71. 4 vols. (with illustrations).

3. One of the lights seen on the Caravelle was certainly carried by a cattle-thief,—a colossal negro who had the reputation of being a sorcerer,—a *quimboiseur.* The greater part of the mountainous land forming La Caravelle promontory was at that time the property of a Monsieur Eustache, who used it merely for cattle-raising purposes. He allowed his animals to run wild in the hills; they multiplied exceedingly, and became very savage. Notwithstanding their ferocity, however, large numbers of them were driven away at night, and secretly slaughtered or sold, by somebody who used to practise the art of cattle-stealing with a lantern, and evidently without aid. A watch was set, and the thief arrested. Before the magistrate he displayed extraordinary assurance, asserting that he had never stolen from a poor man—he had stolen only from M. Eustache who could not count his own cattle—*yon richard, mon chè!* "How many cows did you steal from him?" asked the magistrate. "*Ess moin pè save?—moin té pouend yon savane toutt pleine*" replied the prisoner. (How can I tell?—I took a whole savanna-full.)... Condemned on the strength of his own confession, he was taken to jail. "*Moin*

pa ké rété la geôle," he observed. (I shall not remain in prison.) They put him in irons, but on the following morning the irons were found lying on the floor of the cell, and the prisoner was gone. He was never seen in Martinique again.

4. Y sucoué souyé y assous quai-là;—y ka di: "Moin ka maudi ou, Lanmatinique!—moin ka maudie ou!... Ké ni mangé pou engnien: ou pa ké pè menm acheté y! Ké ni touèle pou engnien: ou pa ké pè menm achéte yon robe! Epi yche ké batt manman... Ou banni moin!—moin ké vini encò!"

5. Vol. iii., p. 382-3. Edition of 1722.

6. The parrots of Martinique he describes as having been green, with slate-colored plumage on the top of the head, mixed with a little red, and as having a few red feathers in the wings, throat, and tail.

7. The creole word *moudongue* is said to be a corruption of *Mondongue*, the name of an African coast tribe who had the reputation of being cannibals. A Mondongue slave on the plantations was generally feared by his fellow-blacks of other tribes; and the name of the cannibal race became transformed into an adjective to denote anything formidable or terrible. A blow with a stick made of the wood described being greatly dreaded, the term was applied first to the stick, and afterward to the wood itself.

8. Accounting for the origin of the trade-winds, he writes: "I say that the Trade-Winds do not exist in the Torrid Zone merely by chance; forasmuch as the cause which produces them is very necessary, very sure, and very continuous, since they result *either from the movement of the Earth around the Sun, or from the movement of the Sun around the Earth. Whether it be the one or the other of these two great bodies which moves...*"etc.

IV. La Guiablesse

I

NIGHT in all countries brings with it vaguenesses and illusions which terrify certain imaginations;—but in the tropics it produces effects peculiarly impressive and particularly sinister. Shapes of vegetation that startle even while the sun shines upon them assume, after his setting, a grimness,—a grotesquery,—a suggestiveness for which there is no name... In the North a tree is simply a tree;—here it is a personality that makes itself felt; it has a vague physiognomy, an indefinable *Me*: it is an Individual (with a capital I); it is a Being (with a capital B).

From the high woods, as the moon mounts, fantastic darknesses descend into the roads,—black distortions, mockeries, bad dreams,—an endless procession of goblins. Least startling are the shadows flung down by the various forms of palm, because instantly recognizable;—yet these take the semblance of giant fingers opening and closing over the way, or a black crawling of unutterable spiders...

Nevertheless, these phasma seldom alarm the solitary and belated Bitaco: the darknesses that creep stealthily along the path have no frightful signification for him, do not appeal to his imagination;—if he suddenly starts and stops and stares, it is not because of such shapes, but because he has perceived two specks of orange light, and is not yet sure whether they are only fire-flies, or the eyes of a trigonocephalus. The spectres of his fancy have nothing in common with those indistinct and monstrous umbrages: what he most fears, next to the deadly serpent, are human witchcrafts. A white rag, an old one lying in the path, might be a *maléfice* which, if trodden upon, would cause his leg to blacken and swell up to the size of the limb of an elephant;—an unopened bundle of plantain leaves or of bamboo strippings, dropped by the way-side, might contain the skin of a *Soucou-yan*. But the ghastly being who doffs or dons his skin at will— and the Zombi—and the *Moun-Mò*—may be quelled or exorcised by prayer; and the lights of shrines, the white gleaming of crosses, continually remind the traveller of his duty to the Powers that save. All along the way there are shrines at intervals, not very far apart: while standing in the radiance of one niche-lamp, you may perhaps discern the glow of the next, if the road be level and straight. They are almost everywhere,—shining along the skirts of the woods, at the entrance of ravines, by the verges of precipices;—there is a cross even upon the summit of the loftiest peak in the island. And the night-walker removes his hat each time his bare feet touch the soft stream of yellow light outpoured from the illuminated shrine of a white Virgin or a white Christ. These are good ghostly company for him;—he salutes them, talks to them, tells them his pains or fears: their blanched faces seem to him full of sympathy;—they appear to cheer him voicelessly as he strides from gloom to gloom, under the goblinry of those woods which tower ebony under the stars... And he has other companionship. One of the greatest terrors of darkness does not exist here after the setting of the sun,—the terror of *Silence...* Tropical night is full of voices;—extraordinary populations of crickets are trilling; nations of tree-frogs are chanting; the *Cabri-des-bois* [1], or *cra-cra,* almost deafens you with the wheezy bleating sound by which it earned its creole name; birds pipe: everything that bells, ululates, drones, clacks, guggles, joins the enormous chorus; and you fancy you see all the shadows vibrating to the force of this vocal storm. The true life of Nature in the tropics begins with the darkness, ends with the light.

And it is partly, perhaps, because of these conditions that the coming of the dawn does not dissipate all fears of the supernatural. *I ni pè zombi mênm gran'-jou* (he is afraid of ghosts even in broad daylight) is a phrase which does not sound exaggerated in these latitudes,—not, at least, to any one knowing something of the conditions that nourish or inspire weird beliefs. In the awful peace of tropical day, in the hush of the woods, the solemn silence of the hills (broken only by torrent voices that cannot make themselves heard at night), even in the amazing luminosity, there is a something apparitional and weird,—something that seems to weigh upon the world like a measureless haunting. So still all Nature's chambers are that a loud utterance jars upon the ear brutally, like a burst of laughter in a sanctuary. With all its luxuriance of color, with all its violence of light, this tropical day has its ghostliness and its ghosts. Among the people of color there are many who believe that even at noon—when the boulevards behind the city are most deserted—the zombis will show themselves to solitary loiterers.

II

HERE a doubt occurs to me,—a doubt regarding the precise nature of a word, which I call upon Adou to explain. Adou is the daughter of the kind old capresse from whom I rent my room in this little mountain cottage. The mother is almost precisely the color of cinnamon; the daughter's complexion is brighter,—the ripe tint of an orange... Adou tells me creole stories and *tim-tim*. Adou knows all about ghosts, and believes in them. So does Adou's extraordinarily tall brother, Yébé,—my guide among the mountains.

—"Adou," I ask, "what is a zombi?"

The smile that showed Adou's beautiful white teeth has instantly disappeared; and she answers, very seriously, that she has never seen a zombi, and does not want to see one.

—"*Moin pa té janmain ouè zombi,—pa' lè ouè ça, moin!*"

—"But, Adou, child, I did not ask you whether you ever saw It;—I asked you only to tell me what It is like?"...

Adou hesitates a little, and answers:

—"*Zombi? Mais ça fai désòde lanuitt, zombi!*"

Ah! it is Something which "makes disorder at night." Still, that is not a satisfactory explanation. "Is it the spectre of a dead person, Adou? Is it *one who comes back?*"

—"*Non, Missié,—non; cé pa ça.*"

—"Not that?... Then what was it you said the other night when you were afraid to pass the cemetery on an errand,—*ça ou té ka di,* Adou?"

—"Moin té ka di: 'Moin pa lé k'allé bò cimétiè-là pa ouappò moun-mò;—moun-mò ké barré moin: moin pa sé pè vini enco.'" (*I said, "I do not want to go by that cemetery because of the dead folk;—the dead folk will bar the way, and I cannot get back again."*)

—"And you believe that, Adou?"

—"Yes, that is what they say... And if you go into the cemetery at night you cannot come out again: the dead folk will stop you—*moun-mò ké barré ou.*"...

—"But are the dead folk zombis, Adou?"

—"No; the moun-mò are not zombis. The zombis go everywhere: the dead folk remain in the graveyard... Except on the Night of All Souls: then they go to the houses of their people everywhere."

—"Adou, if after the doors and windows were locked and barred you were to see entering your room in the middle of the night, a Woman fourteen feet high?"...

—"*Ah! pa pàlé ça!!*"...

—"No! tell me, Adou?"

—"Why, yes: that would be a zombi. It is the zombis who make all those noises at night one cannot understand... Or, again, if I were to see a dog that high [she holds her hand about five feet above the floor] coming into our house at night, I would scream: *Mi Zombi!*"

...Then it suddenly occurs to Adou that her mother knows something about zombis.

—"*Ou! Manman!*"

—"*Eti!*" answers old Théréza's voice from the little out-building where the evening meal is being prepared, over a charcoal furnace, in an earthen canari.

—"*Missié-là ka mandé save ça ça yé yonne zombi;—vini ti bouin!*"... The mother laughs, abandons her canari, and comes in to tell me all she knows about the weird word.

"*I ni pè Zombi*"—I find from old Théréza's explanations—is a phrase indefinite as our own vague expressions, "afraid of ghosts," "afraid of the dark." But the word "Zombi" also has special strange meanings... "Ou passé nans grand chimin lanuitt, épi ou ka ouè gouôs difé, épi plis ou ka vini assou difé-à pli ou ka ouè difé-à ka màché: cé zombi ka fai ça... Encò, chouval ka passé,—chouval ka ni anni toua patt: ça zombi." (You pass along the high-road at night, and you see a great fire, and the more you walk to get to it the more it moves away: it is the zombi makes that... Or a horse *with only three legs* passes you: that is a zombi.)

—"How big is the fire that the zombi makes?" I ask.

—"It fills the whole road," answers Théréza: "*li ka rempli toutt chimin-là*. Folk call those fires the Evil Fires,—*mauvai difé*; —and if you follow them they will lead you into chasms,—*ou ké tombé adans labîme*."...

And then she tells me this:

—"Baidaux was a mad man of color who used to live at St. Pierre, in the Street of the Precipice. He was not dangerous,—never did any harm;—his sister used to take care of him. And what I am going to relate is true,—*çe zhistouè veritabe!*

"One day Baidaux said to his sister: 'Moin ni yonne yche,va!—ou pa connaitt li!' [I have a child, ah!—you never saw it!] His sister paid no attention to what he said that day; but the next day he said it again, and the next, and the next, and every day after,—so that his sister at last became much annoyed by it, and used to cry out: Ah! mais pé guiole ou, Baidaux! Ou fou pou embêté moin conm ça!—ou bien fou!'... But he tormented her that way for months and for years.

"One evening he went out, and only came home at midnight leading a child by the hand,—a black child he had found in the street; and he said to his sister:—

"'Mi yche-là moin mené ba ou! Tou léjou moin té ka di ou moin tini yonne yche: ou pa té 'lè couè,—eh ben! MI Y' [Look at the child I have brought you! Everyday I have been telling you I had a child: you would not believe me,—very well, LOOK AT HIM!]

"The sister gave one look, and cried out: 'Baidaux, otí ou pouend yche-là?'... For the child was growing taller and taller every moment... And Baidaux,—because he was mad,—kept saying: 'Çé yche-moin! çé yche moin!'[It is my child!]

"And the sister threw open the shutters and screamed to all the neighbours,—'Sécou, sécou, sécou! Vini oué ça Baidaux mené ba moin!" [Help! Help! Come see what Baidaux has brought here!] And the child said to Baidaux: 'Ou ni bonhè ou fou! [You are lucky that you are mad!]...Then all the neighbours came running in; but they could not see anything: the Zombi was gone."...

III

...AS I was saying, the hours of vastest light have their weirdness here;—and it is of a Something which walketh abroad under the eye of the sun, even at high noontide, that I desire to speak, while the impressions of a morning journey to the scene of Its last alleged apparition yet remains vivid in my recollection.

You follow the mountain road leading from Calebasse over long meadowed levels two thousand feet above the ocean, into the woods of La Couresse, where it begins to descend slowly, through deep green shadowing, by great zigzags. Then, at a turn, you find yourself unexpectedly looking down upon a planted valley, through plumy fronds of arborescent fern. The surface below seems almost like a lake of gold-green water,—especially when long breaths of mountain-wind set the miles of ripening cane a-ripple from verge to verge: the illusion is marred only by the road, fringed with young cocoa-palms, which serpentines across the luminous plain. East, west, and north the horizon is almost wholly hidden by surging of hills: those nearest are softly shaped and exquisitely green; above them loftier undulations take hazier verdancy and darker shadows; farther yet rise silhouettes of blue or violet tone, with one beautiful breast-shaped peak thrusting up in the midst;—while, westward, over all, topping even the Piton, is a vapory huddling of prodigious shapes—wrinkled, fissured, horned, fantastically tall... Such at least are the tints of the morning... Here and there, between gaps in the volcanic chain, the land hollows into gorges, slopes down into ravines;—and the sea's vast disk of turquoise flames up through the interval. Southwardly those deep woods, through which the way winds down, shut in the view... You do not see the plantation buildings till you have advanced some distance into the valley;—they are hidden by a fold of the land, and stand in a little hollow where the road turns: a great quadrangle of low gray antiquated edifices, heavily walled and buttressed, and roofed with red tiles. The court they form opens upon the main route by an immense archway. Farther along ajoupas begin to line the way,—the dwellings of the field hands,—tiny cottages built with trunks of the arborescent fern or with stems of bamboo, and thatched with cane-straw: each in a little garden planted with bananas, yams, couscous, camanioc, choux-caraïbes, or other things,—and hedged about with roseaux d'Inde and various flowering shrubs.

Thereafter, only the high whispering wildernesses of cane on either hand,—the white silent road winding between its swaying cocoa-trees,—and the tips of hills that seem to glide on before you as you walk, and that take, with the deepening of the afternoon light, such amethystine color as if they were going to become transparent.

IV

...It is a breezeless and cloudless noon. Under the dazzling downpour of light the hills seem to smoke blue: something like a thin yellow fog haloes the leagues of ripening cane,—a vast reflection. There is no stir in all the green mysterious front of the vine-veiled woods. The palms of the roads keep their heads quite still, as if listening. The canes do not utter a single susurration. Rarely is there such absolute stillness among them: upon the calmest days there are usually rustlings audible, thin cracklings, feint creepings: sounds that betray the passing of some little animal or reptile—a rat or a manicou, or a zanoli or couresse,—more often, however, no harmless lizard or snake, but the deadly *fer-de-lance*. Today, all these seem to sleep; and there are no workers among the cane to clear away the weeds,—to uproot the *pié-treffe, pié-poule, pié-balai, zhèbe-en-mè*: it is the hour of rest.

A woman is coming along the road,—young, very swarthy, very tall, and barefooted, and black-robed: she wears a high white turban with dark stripes, and a white foulard is thrown about her fine shoulders; she bears no burden, and walks very swiftly and noiselessly… Soundless as shadow the motion of all these naked-footed people is. On any quiet mountain-way, full of curves, where you fancy yourself alone, you may often be startled by something you *feel* rather than hear, behind you,—surd steps, the springy movement of a long lithe body, dumb oscillations of raiment;—and ere you can turn to look, the haunter swiftly passes with creole greeting of "bonjou" or "bonsouè, Missié." This sudden "becoming aware" in broad daylight of a living presence unseen is even more disquieting than that sensation which, in absolute darkness, makes one halt all breathlessly before great solid objects, whose proximity has been revealed by some mute blind emanation of force alone. But it is very seldom, indeed, that the negro or half-breed is thus surprised: he seems to divine an advent by some specialized sense,—like an animal,—and to become conscious of a look directed upon him from any distance or from behind any covert;—to pass within the range of his keen vision unnoticed is almost impossible… And the approach of this woman has been already observed by the habitants of the ajoupas;—dark faces peer out from windows and door-ways;—one half-nude laborer even strolls out to the road-side under the sun to watch her coming. He looks a moment, turns to the hut again, and calls:—

—"Ou-ou! Fafa!"

—"Étí! Gabou!"

—"Vini ti bouin!—mi bel négresse!"

Out rushes Fafa, with his huge straw hat in his hand: "Otí, Gabou?"

—"Mi!"

—"Ah! quimbé moin!" cries black Fafa, enthusiastically; "fouinq! li bel!—Jésis-Maïa! li doux!"… Neither ever saw that woman before; and both feel as if they could watch her forever.

There is something superb in the port of a tall young mountain-griffone, or negress, who is comely and knows that she is comely: it is a black poem of artless dignity, primitive grace, savage exultation of movement… "Ou marché tête enlai conm couresse qui ka passé lariviè" (*You walk with your head in the air, like the couresse-serpent swimming a river*) is a creole comparison which pictures perfectly the poise of her neck and chin. And in her walk there is also a serpentine elegance, a sinuous charm: the shoulders do not swing; the cambered torso seems immobile—but alternately from waist to heel, and from heel to waist, with each long full stride, an indescribable undulation seems to pass; while the folds of her loose robe oscillate to right and left behind her, in perfect libration, with the free swaying of the hips. With us, only a finely trained dancer could attempt such a walk;—with the Martinique woman of color it is natural as the tint of her skin; and this allurement of motion unrestrained is most marked in those who have never worn shoes, and are clad lightly as the women of antiquity,—in two very thin and simple garments;—chemise and *robe-d'indienne*... But whence is she?—of what canton? Not from Vauclin, nor from Lamentin, nor from Marigot,—from Case-Pilote or from Case-Navire: Fafa knows all the people there. Never of Sainte-Anne, nor of Sainte-Luce, nor of Sainte-Marie, nor of Diamant, nor of Gros-Morne, nor of Carbet,—the birthplace of Gabou. Neither is she of the village of the Abysms, which is in the Parish of the Preacher,—nor yet of Ducos nor of François, which are in the Commune of the Holy Ghost...

V

...SHE approaches the ajoupa: both men remove their big straw hats; and both salute her with a simultaneous "Bonjou', Manzell."

—"Bonjou', Missié," she responds, in a sonorous alto, without appearing to notice Gabou,—but smiling upon Fafa as she passes, with her great eyes turned full upon his face... All the libertine blood of the man flames under that look;—he feels as if momentarily wrapped in a blaze of black lightning.

—"Ça ka fai moin pè," exclaims Gabou, turning his face towards the ajoupa. Something indefinable in the gaze of the stranger has terrified him.

—"*Pa ka fai moin pè—fouinq!*" (She does not make me afraid) laughs Fafa, boldly following her with a smiling swagger.

—"Fafa!" cries Gabou, in alarm. "*Fafa, pa fai ça!*"

But Fafa does not heed. The strange woman has slackened her pace, as if inviting pursuit;—another moment and he is at her side.

—"Oti ou ka rété, chè?" he demands, with the boldness of one who knows himself a fine specimen of his race.

—"Zaffai cabritt pa zaffai lapin," she answers, mockingly.

—"Mais pouki ou rhabillé toutt nouè comn ça."

—"Moin pòté deil pou name moin mò."

—"Aïe ya yaïe!... Non, vouè!—ça ou kallé atouèlement?"

—"Lanmou pàti: moin pàti deïé lanmou."

—"Ho!—ou ni guêpe, anh?"

—"Zanoli bail yon bal; épi maboya rentré ladans."

—"Di moin oti ou kallé, doudoux?"

—"Jouq lariviè Lezà."

—"Fouinq!—ni plis passé trente kilomett!"

—"Eh ben?—ess ou 'lè vini épi moin?"[2]

And as she puts the question she stands still and gazes at him;—her voice is no longer mocking: it has taken another tone,—a tone soft as the long golden note of the little brown bird they call the *siffleur-de-montagne*, the mountain-whistler… Yet Fafa hesitates. He hears the clear clang of the plantation bell recalling him to duty—he sees far down the road—(*Ouill!* how fast they have been walking!)—a white and black speck in the sun: Gabou, uttering through his joined hollowed hands, as through a horn, the *ouklé*, the rally call. For an instant he thinks of the overseer's anger,—of the distance,—of the white road glaring in the dead heat: then he looks again into the black eyes of the strange woman, and answers:

—"Oui;—moin ké vini épi ou."

With a burst of mischievous laughter, in which Fafa joins, she walks on,—Fafa striding at her side… And Gabou, far off, watches them go,—and wonders that, for the first time since ever they worked together, his comrade failed to answer his *ouklé*.

—"Coument yo ka crié ou, chè?" asks Fafa, curious to know her name.

—"Châché nom moin ou-menm, duviné."

But Fafa never was a good guesser,—never could guess the simplest of tim-tim.

—"Ess Cendrine?"

—"Non, çé pa ça."

—"Ess Vitaline?"

—"Non, çé pa ça."

—"Ess Aza?"

—"Non, çé pa ça."

—"Ess Nini?"

—"Châché encò."

—"Ess Tité?"

—"Ou pa save,—tant pis pou ou!"

—"Ess Youma?"

—"Pouki ou 'lé save nom moin?—ça ou ké fai épi y?"

—"Ess Yaiya?"

—"Non, çé pa y."

—"Ess Maiyotte?"

—"Non! ou pa ké janmain trouvé y!"

—"Ess Sounoune?—ess Loulouze?"

She does not answer, but quickens her pace and begins to sing,—not as the half-breed, but as the African sings,—commencing with a low long weird intonation that suddenly breaks into fractions of notes inexpressible, then rising all at once to a liquid purling bird-tone, and descending as abruptly again to the first deep quavering strain:—

> *"À té—*
> *moin ka dòmi toute longue;*
> *Yon paillasse sé fai moin bien,*
> *Doudoux!*
>
> *À té—*
> *moin ka dòmi toute longue;*
> *Yon robe biésé sé fai moin bien,*
> *Doudoux!*
>
> *À té—*
> *moin ka dòmi toute longue;*
> *Dè jolis foulà sé fai moin bien,*
> *Doudoux!*
>
> *À té—*
> *moin ka dòmi toute longue;*
> *Yon joli madras sé fai moin bien,*
> *Doudoux!*
>
> *À té—*
> *moin ka dòmi toute longue;*
> *Çé à té..."*

...Obliged from the first to lengthen his stride in order to keep up with her, Fafa has found his utmost powers of walking overtaxed, and has been left behind. Already his thin attire is saturated with sweat; his breathing is almost a panting;—yet the black bronze of his companion's skin shows no moisture; her rhythmic step, her silent respiration, reveal no effort: she laughs at his desperate straining to remain by her side.

—"Marché toujou' deïé moin,—anh, chè?—marché toujou' deïé!"...

And the involuntary laggard—utterly bewitched by the supple allurement of her motion, by the black flame of her gaze, by the savage melody of her chant—wonders more and more who she may be, while she waits for him with her mocking smile.

But Gabou—who has been following and watching from afar off, and sounding his fruitless ouklé betimes—suddenly starts, halts, turns, and hurries back, fearfully crossing himself at every step.

He has seen the sign by which She is known...

VI

...NONE ever saw her by night. Her hour is the fulness of the sun's flood-tide: she comes in the dead hush and white flame of windless noons,—when colors appear to take a very unearthliness of intensity,— when even the flash of some colibri, bosomed with living fire, shooting hither and thither among the grenadilla blossoms, seemeth a spectral happening because of the great green trance of the land...

Mostly she haunts the mountain roads, winding from plantation to plantation, from hamlet to hamlet,—sometimes dominating huge sweeps of azure sea, sometimes shadowed by mornes deep-wooded to the sky. But close to the great towns she sometimes walks: she has been seen at mid-day upon the highway which overlooks the Cemetery of the Anchorage, behind the cathedral of St. Pierre... A black Woman, simply clad, of lofty stature and strange beauty, silently standing in the light, *keeping her eyes fixed upon the Sun!*...

VII

DAY wanes. The further western altitudes shift their pearline gray to deep blue where the sky is yellowing up behind them; and in the darkening hollows of nearer mornes strange shadows gather with the changing of the light—dead indigoes, fuliginous purples, rubifications as of scoriae,—ancient volcanic colors momentarily resurrected by the illusive haze of evening. And the fallow of the canes takes a faint warm ruddy tinge. On certain far high slopes, as the sun lowers, they look like thin golden hairs against the glow,—blond down upon the skin of the living hills.

Still the Woman and her follower walk together,—chatting loudly, laughing, chanting snatches of song betimes. And now the valley is well behind them;—they climb the steep road crossing the eastern peaks,— through woods that seem to stifle under burdening of creepers. The shadow of the Woman and the shadow of the man,—broadening from their feet,—lengthening prodigiously,—sometimes, mixing, fill all the way; sometimes, at a turn, rise up to climb the trees. Huge masses of frondage, catching the failing light, take strange fiery color;—the sun's rim almost touches one violet hump in the western procession of volcanic silhouettes...

Sunset, in the tropics, is vaster than sunrise... The dawn, upflaming swiftly from the sea, has no heralding erubescence, no awful blossoming—as in the North: its fairest hues are fawn-colors, dove-tints, and yellows,—pale yellows as of old dead gold, in horizon and flood. But after the mighty heat of day has charged all the blue air with translucent vapor, colors become strangely changed, magnified, transcendentalized when the sun falls once more below the verge of visibility. Nearly an hour before his death, his light begins to turn tint; and all the horizon yellows to the color of a lemon. Then this hue deepens, through tones of magnificence unspeakable, into orange; and the sea becomes lilac. Orange is the light of the world for a little space; and as the orb sinks, the indigo darkness comes—not descending, but rising, as if from the ground—all within a few minutes. And during those brief minutes peaks and mornes, purpling into richest velvety blackness, appear outlined against passions of fire that rise half-way to the zenith,—enormous furies of vermilion.

...The Woman all at once leaves the main road,—begins to mount a steep narrow path leading up from it through the woods upon the left. But Fafa hesitates,—halts a moment to look back. He sees the sun's huge orange face sink down,—sees the weird procession of the peaks vesture themselves in blackness funereal,—sees the burning behind them crimson into awfulness; and a vague fear comes upon him as he looks again up the darkling path to the left. Whither is she now going?

—"Oti ou kallé là?" he cries.

—"Mais conm ça!—chimin tala plis cou't,—coument?"

It may be the shortest route, indeed;—but then, the fer-de-lance!...

—"Ni sèpent ciya,—en pile."

No: there is not a single one, she avers; she has taken that path too often not to know:

—"Pa ni sèpent piess! Moin ni coutime passé là;—pa ni piess!"

...She leads the way... Behind them the tremendous glow deepens;—before them the gloom. Enormous gnarled forms of ceiba, balata, acoma, stand dimly revealed as they pass; masses of viny drooping things take, by the failing light, a sanguine tone. For a little while Fafa can plainly discern the figure of the Woman before him;—then, as the path zigzags into shadow, he can descry only the white turban and the white foulard;—and then the boughs meet overhead: he can see her no more, and calls to her in alarm:—

—"Oti ou?—moin pa pè ouè arien!"

Forked pending ends of creepers trail cold across his face. Huge fire-flies sparkle by,—like atoms of kindled charcoal thinkling, blown by a wind.

—"Içitt!—quimbé lanmain-moin!"...

How cold the hand that guides him!... She walks swiftly, surely, as one knowing the path by heart. It zigzags once more; and the incandescent color flames again between the trees;—the high vaulting of foliage fissures overhead, revealing the first stars. A *cabritt-bois* begins its chant. They reach the summit of the morne under the clear sky.

The wood is below their feet now; the path curves eastward between a long swaying of ferns sable in the gloom,—as between a waving of prodigious black feathers. Through the further purpling, loftier altitudes dimly loom; and from some viewless depth, a dull vast rushing sound rises into the night... Is it the speech of hurrying waters, or only some tempest of insect voices from those ravines in which the night begins?

Her face is in the darkness as she stands;—Fafa's eyes are turned to the iron-crimson of the western sky. He still holds her hand, fondles it,—murmurs something to her in undertones.

—"Ess ou ainmein moin conm ça?" she asks, almost in a whisper.

Oh! yes, yes, yes!... more than any living being he loves her!... How much? Ever so much,—*gouôs conm caze!*... Yet she seems to doubt him,—repeating her question over and over:

—"Ess ou ainmein moin?"

And all the while,—gently, caressingly, imperceptibly,—she draws him a little nearer to the side of the path, nearer to the black waving of the ferns, nearer to the great dull rushing sound that rises from beyond them:

—"Ess ou ainmein moin?"

—"Oui, oui!" he responds,—"ou save ça!—oui, chè doudoux, ou save ça!"…

And she, suddenly,—turning at once to him and to the last red light, the goblin horror of her face transformed,—shrieks with a burst of hideous laughter:

—"*Atò, bô!*"[3]

For the fraction of a moment he knows her name:—then, smitten to the brain with the sight of her, reels, recoils, and, backward falling, crashes two thousand feet to his death upon the rocks of a mountain torrent.

NOTES

1. In creole, *cabritt-bois*,—("the Wood-Kid")—a colossal cricket. Precisely at half-past four in the morning it becomes silent; and for thousands of early risers too poor to own a clock, the cessation of its song is the signal to get up.

2. —"Where dost stay, dear?"
—"Affairs of the goat are not affairs of the rabbit."
—"But why art thou dressed all in black thus?"
—"I wear mourning for my dead soul."
—"*Aïe ya yaïe!*… No, true!… where art thou going now?"
—"Love is gone: I go after love."
—"Ho! thou hast a Wasp [lover]—eh?"
—"The zanoli gives a ball; the *maboya* enters unasked."
—"Tell me where thou art going, sweetheart?"
—"As far as the River of the Lizard."
—"*Fouinq!*—there are more than thirty kilometres!"
—"What of that?—dost thou want to come with me?"

3. "Kiss me now!"

V. La Vérette

I.

—St. Pierre, *1887*

ONE returning from the country to the city in the Carnival season is lucky to find any comfortable rooms for rent. I have been happy to secure one even in a rather retired street,—so steep that it is really dangerous to sneeze while descending it, lest one lose one's balance and tumble right across the town. It is not a fashionable street, the Rue du Morne Mirail; but, after all, there is no particularly fashionable street in this extraordinary city, and the poorer the neighborhood, the better one's chance to see something of its human nature.

One consolation is that I have Manm-Robert for a next-door neighbor, who keeps the best bouts in town (those long thin Martinique cigars of which a stranger soon becomes fond), and who can relate more queer stories and legends of old times in the island than anybody else I know of. Manm-Robert is *yon màchanne lapacotte*, a dealer in such cheap articles of food as the poor live upon: fruits and tropical vegetables, manioc-flour, "macadam" (a singular dish of rice stewed with salt fish - *diri épi coubouyon lamori*), akras, etc.; but her bouts probably bring her the largest profit—they are all bought up by the békés. Manm-Robert is also a sort of doctor: whenever any one in the neighborhood falls sick she is sent for, and always comes, and very often cures,—as she is skilled in the knowledge and use of medicinal herbs, which she gathers herself upon the mornes. But for these services she never accepts any remuneration: she is a sort of Mother of the poor in her immediate vicinity. She helps everybody, listens to everybody's troubles, gives everybody some sort of consolation, trusts everybody, and sees a great deal of the thankless side of human nature without seeming to feel any the worse for it. Poor as she must really be she appears to have everything that everybody wants; and will lend anything to her neighbors except a scissors or a broom, which it is thought bad-luck to lend. And, finally, if anybody is afraid of being bewitched (*quimboisè*) Manm-Robert can furnish him or her with something that will keep the bewitchment away...

II

February 15th

...ASH-WEDNESDAY. The last masquerade will appear this afternoon, notwithstanding; for the Carnival lasts in Martinique a day longer than elsewhere.

All through the country districts since the first week of January there have been wild festivities every Sunday—dancing on the public highways to the pattering of tamtams,—African dancing, too, such as is never seen in St Pierre. In the city, however, there has been less merriment than in previous years;—the natural gaiety of the population has been visibly affected by the advent of a terrible and unfamiliar visitor to the island,—*La Vérette*: she came by steamer from Colon.

...It was in September. Only two cases had been reported when every neighboring British colony quarantined against Martinique. Then other West Indian colonies did likewise. Only two cases of small-pox. "But there may be two thousand in another month," answered the governors and the consuls to many indignant protests. Among West Indian populations the malady has signification unknown in Europe or the United States: it means an exterminating plague.

Two months later the little capital of Fort-de-France was swept by the pestilence as by a wind of death. Then the evil began to spread. It entered St. Pierre in December, about Christmas time. Last week 173 cases were reported; and a serious epidemic is almost certain. There were only 8,500 inhabitants in Fort-de-France; there are 28,000 in the three quarters of St. Pierre proper, not including her suburbs; and there is no saying what ravages the disease may make here.

III

...THREE o'clock, hot and clear... In the distance there is a heavy sound of drums, always drawing nearer: *tam!—tam!—tamtamtam!* The Grande Rue is lined with expectant multitudes; and its tiny square,—the Batterie d'Esnotz,—thronged with békés. *Tam!—tam!—tamtamtam!*... In our own street the people are beginning to gather at door-ways, and peer out of windows,—prepared to descend to the main thoroughfare at the first glimpse of the procession.

—"*Oti masque-à?*" Where are the maskers?

It is little Mimi's voice: she is speaking for two besides herself, both quite as anxious as she to know where the maskers are,—Maurice, her little fair-haired and blue-eyed brother, three years old; and Gabrielle, her child-sister, aged four,—two years her junior.

Every day I have been observing the three, playing in the door-way of the house across the street. Mimi, with her brilliant white skin, black hair, and laughing black eyes, is the prettiest,—though all are unusually pretty children. Were it not for the fact that their mother's beautiful brown hair is usually covered with a violet foulard, you would certainly believe them white as any children in the world. Now there are children whom every one knows to be white, living not very far from here, but in a much more silent street, and in a rich house full of servants,—children who resemble these as one *fleur-d'amour* blossom resembles another;—there is actually another Mimi (though she is not so called at home) so like this Mimi that you could not possibly tell one from the other,—except by their dress. And yet the most unhappy experience of the Mimi who wears white satin slippers was certainly that punishment given her for having been once caught playing in the street with this Mimi, who wears no shoes at all. What mischance could have brought them thus together?—and the worst of it was they had fallen in love with each other at first sight!… It was not because the other Mimi must not talk to nice little colored girls, or that this one may not play with white children of her own age: it was because there are cases… It was not because the other children I speak of are prettier or sweeter or more intelligent than these now playing before me;—or because the finest microscopist in the world could not detect any imaginable race difference between those delicate satin skins. It was only because human nature has little changed since the day that Hagar knew the hate of Sarah, and the thing was grievous in Abraham's sight because of his son…

…The father of these children loved them very much: he had provided a home for them,—a house in the Quarter of the Fort, with an allowance of two hundred francs monthly; and he died in the belief their future was secured. But relatives fought the will with large means and shrewd lawyers, and won !… Yzore, the mother, found herself homeless and penniless with three children to care for. But she was brave; she abandoned the costume of the upper class forever, put on the douillette and the foulard,—the attire that is a confession of race,—and went to work. She is still comely, and so white that she seems only to be masquerading in that violet head-dress and long loose robe…

—"*Vini ouè!—vini ouè!*" cry the children to one another,—"come and see!" The drums are drawing near;—everybody is running to the Grande Rue...

IV

Tam!—tam!—tamtamtam!... The spectacle is interesting from the Batterie d'Esnotz. High up the Rue Peysette,—up all the precipitous streets that ascend the mornes,—a far gathering of showy color appears: the massing of maskers in rose and blue and sulphur-yellow attire... Then what a *dégringolade* begins!—what a tumbling, leaping, cascading of color as the troupes descend. Simultaneously from north and south, from the Mouillage and the Fort, two immense bands enter the Grande Rue;—the great dancing societies these,—the *Sans-souci* and the *Intrépides*. They are rivals; they are the composers and singers of those Carnival songs,—cruel satires most often, of which the local meaning is unintelligible to those unacquainted with the incident inspiring the improvisation,—of which the words are too often coarse or obscene,— whose burdens will be caught up and re-echoed through all the burghs of the island. Vile as may be the motive, the satire, the malice, these chants are preserved for generations by the singular beauty of the airs; and the victim of Carnival song need never hope that his failing or wrong will be forgotten: it will be sung of long after he is in his grave.

...Ten minutes more, and the entire length of the street is thronged with a shouting, shrieking, laughing, gesticulating host of maskers. Thicker and thicker the press becomes;—the drums are silent: all are waiting for the signal of the general dance. Jests and practical jokes are being everywhere perpetrated; there is a vast hubbub, made up of screams, cries, chattering, laughter. Here and there snatches of Carnival song are being sung:—"*Cambronne, Cambronne*," or "*Ti fenm-là doux, li doux, li doux!*"... "Sweeter than sirup the little woman is";—this burden will be remembered when the rest of the song passes out of fashion. Brown hands reach out from the crowd of masks, pulling the beards and patting the faces of white spectators... "*Moin connaitt ou, chè!—moin connaitt ou, doudoux! ba moin ti d'mi franc!*" It is well to refuse the half-franc,—though you do not know what these maskers might take a notion to do today... Then all the great drums suddenly boom together; all the bands strike up; the mad medley kaleidoscopes into some sort of order; and the immense processional dance begins.

Rue Victor Hugo (Formerly Grande Rue), St. Pierre

From the Mouillage to the Fort there is but one continuous torrent of sound and color: you are dazed by the tossing of peaked caps, the waving of hands, and twinkling of feet;—and all this passes with a huge swing,—a regular swaying to right and left... It will take at least an hour for all to pass; and it is an hour well worth passing. Band after band whirls by; the musicians all garbed as women or as monks in canary-colored habits;—before them the dancers are dancing backward, with a motion as of skaters, behind them all leap and wave hands as in pursuit. Most of the bands are playing creole airs,—but that of the *Sans-souci* strikes up the melody of the latest French song in vogue,—*Petits amoureux aux plumes* ("Little feathered lovers"[1]). Everybody now seems to know this song by heart; you hear children only five or six years old singing it: there are pretty lines in it, although two out of its four stanzas are commonplace enough, and it is certainly the air rather than the words which accounts for its sudden popularity.

V

EXTRAORDINARY things are happening in the streets through which the procession passes. Pest-smitten women rise from their beds to costume themselves,—to mask face already made unrecognizable by the hideous malady,—and stagger out to join the dancers... They do this in the Rue Longchamps, in the Rue St. Jean-de-Dieu, in the Rue Peysette, in the Rue de Petit Versailles. And in the Rue Ste.-Marthe there are three young girls sick with the disease, who hear the blowing of the horns and the pattering of feet and clapping of hands in chorus;—they get up to look through the slats of their windows on the masquerade,—and the creole passion of the dance comes upon them. "*Ah!*" cries one,—"*nou ké bien amieusé nou!—c'est zaffai si nou mò!*' [We will have our fill of fun: what matter if we die after!] And all mask, and join the rout, and dance down to the Savane, and over the river-bridge into the high streets of the Fort, carrying contagion with them!... No extraordinary example, this: the ranks of the dancers hold many and many a *verrettier*.

VI

THE costumes are rather disappointing,—though the mummery has some general characteristics that are not unpicturesque;—for example, the predominance of crimson and canary-yellow in choice of color, and a marked predilection for pointed hoods and high-peaked head-dresses. Mock religious costumes also form a striking element in the general tone of the display,—Franciscan, Dominican, or Penitent habits,—usually crimson or yellow, rarely sky-blue. There are no historical costumes, few eccentricities or monsters: only a few "vampire-bat" head-dresses abruptly break the effect of the peaked caps and the hoods… Still there are some decidedly local ideas in dress which deserve notice,—the *congo*, the *bébé* (or *ti-manmaille*) the *ti nègue gous-sirop* ("little molasses-negro"); and the *diablesse*.

The congo is merely the exact reproduction of the dress worn by workers on the plantations. For the women, a gray calico shirt and coarse petticoat of percaline; with two coarse handkerchiefs (*mouchoirs fatas*), one for her neck, and one for the head, over which is worn a monstrous straw hat—she walks either barefoot or shod with rude native sandals, and she carries a hoe. For the man the costume consists of a gray shirt of rough material, blue canvas pantaloons, a large mouchoir fatas to tie around his waist, and a *chapeau Bacoué*,—an enormous hat of Martinique palm-straw. He walks barefooted and carries a cutlass.

The sight of a troupe of young girls *en bébé*, in baby-dress, is really pretty. This costume comprises only a loose embroidered chemise, lace-edged pantalettes, and a child's cap; the whole being decorated with bright ribbons of various colors. As the dress is short and leaves much of the lower limbs exposed, there is ample opportunity for display of tinted stockings and elegant slippers.

The "molasses-negro" wears nothing but a cloth around his loins;—his whole body and face being smeared with an atrocious mixture of soot and molasses. He is supposed to represent the original African ancestor.

The *devilesses* (*diablesses*) are few in number; for it requires a very tall woman to play deviless. These are robed all in black, with a white turban and white foulard; they wear black masks. They also carry *boms* (large tin cans), which they allow to fall upon the pavement from time to time; and they walk barefoot… The deviless (in true Bitaco idiom, "*guiablesse*") represents a singular Martinique superstition. It is said that sometimes at noonday, a beautiful negress passes silently through some isolated plantation,—smiling at the workers in the cane-fields,—tempting men to follow her. But he who follows her never comes back again; and when a field hand mysteriously disappears, his fellows say "*Y té ka ouè la Guiablesse!*" … The tallest among the devilesses always walks first, chanting the question, "*Jou ouvè?*" (Is it yet daybreak?) And all the others reply in chorus, "*Jou pa'ncò ouvè*" (It is not yet day.)

—The masks worn by the multitude include very few grotesques: as a rule, they are simply white wire masks, having the form of an oval and regular human face;—and they disguise the wearer absolutely, although they can be seen through perfectly well from within. It struck me at once that this peculiar type of wire mask gave an indescribable tone of ghostliness to the whole exhibition. It is not in the least comical; it is neither comely nor ugly; it is colorless as mist,—expressionless, void, dead;—it lies on the face like a vapor, like a cloud,—creating the idea of a spectral vacuity behind it...

VII

NOW comes the band of the *Intrépides*, playing the *bouèné*. It is a dance melody,—also the name of a *mode* of dancing, peculiar and unrestrained;—the dancers advance and retreat face to face; they hug each other, press together, and separate to embrace again. A very old dance, this,—of African origin; perhaps the same of which Père Labat wrote in 1722:—

—"It is not modest. Nevertheless, it has not failed to become so popular with the Spanish Creoles of America, and so much in vogue among them, that it now forms the chief of their amusements, and that it enters even into their devotions. They dance it even in their Churches, and in their Processions; and the Nuns seldom fail to dance it Christmas Night, upon a stage erected in their Choir and immediately in front of their iron grating, which is left open, so that the People may share in the joy manifested by these good souls for the birth of the Saviour" [2]...

VIII

...EVERY year, on the last day of the Carnival, a droll ceremony used to take place called the "Burial of the Bois-bois",—the bois-bois being a dummy, a guy, caricaturing the most unpopular thing in city life or in politics. This bois-bois, after having been paraded with mock solemnity through all the ways of St. Pierre, was either interred or "drowned",—flung into the sea... And yesterday the dancing societies had announced their intention to bury a *bois-bois laverette*,—a manikin that was to represent the plague. But this bois-bois does not make its appearance. *La Vérette* is too terrible a visitor to be made fun of, my friends;—you will not laugh at her, because you dare not...

No: there is one who has the courage,—a yellow goblin crying from behind his wire mask, in imitation of the màchannes: *"Ça qui 'lè quatòze graines laverette pou yon sou?"* (Who wants to buy fourteen verette-spots for a sou?)

Not a single laugh follows that jest… And just one week from today, poor mocking goblin, you will have a great many more than *quatorze graines*, which will not cost you even a sou, and which will disguise you infinitely better than the mask you now wear;—and they will pour quick-lime over you, ere ever they let you pass through this street again—in a seven franc coffin!…

IX

AND the multicolored clamoring stream rushes by,—swerves off at last through the Rue des Ursulines to the Savane,—rolls over the new bridge of the Roxelane to the ancient quarter of the Fort.

All of a sudden there is a hush, a halt;—the drums stop beating, the songs cease. Then I see a sudden scattering of goblins and demons and devilesses in all directions: they run into houses, up alleys,—hide behind door-ways. And the crowd parts; and straight through it, walking very quickly, comes a priest in his vestments, preceded by an acolyte who rings a little bell. *C'est Bon-Dié ka passé!* ("It is the Good-God who goes by!") The father is bearing the "viaticum" to some victim of the pestilence: one must not appear masked as a devil or a deviless in the presence of the Bon-Dié.

He goes by. The flood of maskers recloses behind the ominous passage;—the drums boom again; the dance recommences; and all the fantastic mummery ebbs swiftly out of sight.

X

NIGHT falls;—the maskers crowd to the ball-rooms to dance strange tropical measures that will become wilder and wilder as the hours pass. And through the black streets, the Devil makes his last Carnival-round.

By the gleam of the old-fashioned oil lamps hung across the thoroughfares I can make out a few details of his costume. He is clad in red, wears a hideous blood-colored mask, and a cap of which the four sides are formed by four looking-glasses;—the whole head-dress being surmounted by a red lantern. He has a white wig made of horse-hair; to make him look weird and old,—since the Devil is older than the world!

Down the street he comes, leaping nearly his own height,—chanting words without human signification,—and followed by some three hundred boys, who form the chorus to his chant—all clapping hands together and giving tongue with a simultaneity that testifies how strongly the sense of rhythm enters into the natural musical feeling of the African,—a feeling powerful enough to impose itself upon all Spanish-America, and there create the unmistakable characteristics of all that is called "creole music."

—"Bimbolo!"
—"Zimabolo!"
—"Bimbolo!"
—"Zimabolo!"
—"Et zimbolo!"
—"Et bolo-po!"

—sing the Devil and his chorus. His chant is cavernous, abysmal,—booms from his chest like the sound of a drum beaten in the bottom of a well... *Ti manmaille-là, baill moin lavoix!* ("Give me voice, little folk,—give me voice!") And all chant after him, in a chanting like the rushing of many waters, and with triple clapping of hands:—" *Ti manmaille-là, baill moin lavoix!*"... Then he halts before a dwelling in the Rue Peysette, and thunders;—

Quarter of the Fort, St. Pierre (overlooking the Rivière Roxelane)

—"*Eh! Marie-sans-dent !—Mi! diabe-là derhò!*"

That is evidently a piece of spite-work: there is somebody living there against whom he has a grudge...

"*Hey! Marie-without-teeth! Look! The devil is outside!*"

And the chorus catch the clue.

DEVIL—"*Eh! Marie-sans-dent!*"...

CHORUS—"*Marie-sans-dent! mi!—diabe-là derhò!*"

D—"*Eh! Marie-sans-dent!*"...

C—"*Marie-sans-dent! mi!—diabe-là derhò!*"

D—"*Eh! Marie-sans-dent!*"...etc.

The Devil at last descends to the main street, always singing the same song;—I follow the chorus to the Savanna, where the rout makes for the new bridge over the Roxelane, to mount the high streets of the old quarter of the Fort; and the chant changes as they cross over:—

DEVIL—"*Oti ouè diabe-là passé lariviè?*" (Where did you see the Devil going over the river?) And all the boys repeat the words, falling into another rhythm with perfect regularity and ease:—"*Oti ouè diabe-là passé lariviè?*"

DEVIL—"*Oti ouè diabe?*" ...

CHORUS—"*Oti ouè diabe-là passé lariviè?*"

D—"*Oti ouè diabe?*"

C—"*Oti ouè diabe-là passé lariviè?*"

D—"*Oti ouè diabe?*" ... etc.

About midnight the return of the Devil and his following arouses me from sleep:—all are chanting a new refrain, "The Devil and the zombis sleep anywhere and everywhere!" (*Diabe épi zombi ka dòmi tout-pàtout.*) The voices of the boys are still clear, shrill, fresh,—clear as a chant of frogs;—they still clap hands with a precision of rhythm that is simply wonderful,—making each time a sound almost exactly like the bursting of a heavy wave:—

DEVIL—"*Diabe épi zombi.*"...

CHORUS—"*Diabe épi zombi ka dòmi tout-pàtout!*"

D—"*Diabe épi zombi.*"...

C—"*Diabe épi zombi ka dòmi tout-pàtout!*"

D—"*Diabe épi zombi.*"...etc.

...What is this after all but the old African method of chanting at labor. The practice of carrying the burden upon the head left the hands free for the rhythmic accompaniment of clapping. And you may still hear the women who load the transatlantic steamers with coal at Fort-de-France thus chanting and clapping...

Evidently the Devil is moving very fast; for all the boys are running;—the pattering of bare feet upon the pavement sounds like a heavy shower... Then the chanting grows fainter in distance; the Devil's immense basso becomes inaudible;—one only distinguishes at regular intervals the *crescendo* of the burden,—a wild swelling of many hundred boy-voices all rising together,—a retreating storm of rhythmic song, wafted to the ear in gusts, in *rafales* of contralto...

XI

February 17th

...YZORE is a *calendeuse*.

The calendeuses are the women who make up the beautiful Madras turbans and color them; for the amazingly brilliant yellow of these head-dresses is not the result of any dyeing process: they are all painted by hand. When purchased the Madras is simply a great oblong handkerchief, having a pale green or pale pink ground, and checkered or plaided by intersecting bands of dark blue, purple, crimson, or maroon. The calendeuse lays the Madras upon a broad board placed across her knees,— then, taking a camel's-hair brush, she begins to fill in the spaces between the bands with a sulphur-yellow paint, which is always mixed with gum-arabic. It requires a sure eye, very steady fingers, and long experience to do this well... After the Madras has been "calendered" (*calendé*) and has become quite stiff and dry, it is folded about the head of the purchaser after the comely Martinique fashion,—which varies considerably from the modes popular in Guadeloupe or Cayenne,—is fixed into the form thus obtained; and can thereafter be taken off or put on without arrangement or disarrangement, like a cap. The price for calendering a Madras is now two francs and fifteen sous;—and for making-up the turban, six sous additional, except in Carnival-time, or upon holiday occasions, when the price rises to twenty-five sous...The making-up of the Madras into a turban is called "tying a head" (*marré yon tête*); and a prettily folded turban is spoken of as "a head well tied" (*yon tête bien marré*)... However, the profession of calendeuse is far from being a lucrative one: it is two or three days' work to calender a single Madras well...

But Yzore does not depend upon calendering alone for a living: she earns much more by the manufacture of *moresques* and of *chinoises* than by painting Madras turbans… Everybody in Martinique who can afford it wears moresques and chinoises. The moresques are large loose comfortable pantaloons of thin printed calico (*indienne*),—having colored designs representing birds, frogs, leaves, lizards, flowers, butterflies, or kittens,—or perhaps representing nothing in particular, being simply arabesques. The chinoise is a loose body-garment, very much like the real Chinese blouse, but always of brightly colored calico with fantastic designs. These things are worn at home during siestas, after office-hours, and at night. To take a nap during the day with one's ordinary clothing on means always a terrible drenching from perspiration, and an after-feeling of exhaustion almost indescribable—best expressed, perhaps, by the local term: *corps écrasé*. Therefore, on entering one's room for the siesta, one strips, puts on the light moresques and the chinoise, and dozes in comfort. A suit of this sort is very neat, often quite pretty, and very cheap (costing only about six francs);—the colors do not fade out in washing, and two good suits will last a year… Yzore can make two pair of moresques and two chinoises in a single day upon her machine.

…I have observed there is a prejudice here against treadle machines;—the creole girls are persuaded they injure the health. Most of the sewing-machines I have seen among this people are operated by hand,—with a sort of little crank…

XII

February 22nd

…OLD physicians indeed predicted it; but who believed them?…

It is as though something sluggish and viewless, dormant and deadly, had been suddenly upstirred to furious life by the wind of robes and tread of myriad dancing feet,—by the crash of cymbals and heavy vibration of drums! Within a few days there has been a frightful increase of the visitation, an almost incredible expansion of the invisible poison: the number of new cases and of deaths has successively doubled, tripled, quadrupled…

Great caldrons of tar are kindled now at night in the more thickly peopled streets,—about one hundred paces apart, each being tended by an Indian laborer in the pay of the city: this is done with the idea of purifying the air. These sinister fires are never lighted but in times of pestilence and of tempest: on hurricane nights, when enormous waves roll in from the fathomless sea upon one of the most fearful coasts in the world, and great vessels are being driven ashore, such is the illumination by which the brave men of the coast make desperate efforts to save the lives of shipwrecked men, often at the cost of their own.[3]

XIII

February 23rd

A COFFIN passes, balanced on the heads of black men. It holds the body of Pascaline Z—, covered with quick lime.

She was the prettiest, assuredly, among the pretty shop-girls of the Grande Rue,—a rare type of *sang-mêlée*. So oddly pleasing, the young face, that once seen, you could never again dissociate the recollection of it from the memory of the street. But one who saw it last night before they poured quick-lime upon it could discern no features,—only a dark brown mass, like a fungus, too frightful to think about.

…And they are all going thus; the beautiful women of color. In the opinion of physicians, the whole generation is doomed…Yet a curious fact is that the young children of octoroons are suffering least: these women have their children vaccinated,—though they will not be vaccinated themselves. I see many brightly colored children, too, recovering from the disorder: the skin is not pitted, like that of the darker classes; and the rose-colored patches finally disappear altogether, leaving no trace.

…Here the sick are wrapped in banana leaves, after having been smeared with a certain unguent… There is an immense demand for banana leaves. In ordinary times these leaves—especially the younger ones, still unrolled, and tender and soft beyond any fabric possible for man to make—are used for poultices of all kinds, and sell from one to two sous each, according to size and quality.

XIV

February 29th

…THE whites remain exempt from the malady.

One might therefore hastily suppose that liability to contagion would be diminished in proportion to the excess of white blood over African; but such is far from being the case;—St. Pierre is losing its handsomest octoroons. Where the proportion of white to black blood is 116 to 8, as in type called *mamelouc*;—or 122 to 4, as in the *quarteronné* (not to be confounded with the *quarteron* or quadroon),—or even 127 to 1, as in the *sang-mêlé*, the liability to attack remains the same, while the chances of recovery are considerably less than in the case of the black. Some few striking instances of immunity appear to offer a different basis for argument; but these might be due to the social position of the individual rather than to any constitutional temper: wealth and comfort, it must be remembered, have no small prophylactic value in such times. Still,—although there is reason to doubt whether mixed races have a constitutional vigor comparable to that of the original parent races,—the liability to diseases of this class is decided less, perhaps, by race characteristics than by ancestral experience. The white peoples of the world have been practically inoculated, vaccinated, by experience of centuries;—while among these visibly mixed or black populations the seeds of the pest find absolutely fresh soil in which to germinate, and its ravages are therefore scarcely less terrible than those it made among the American-Indian or the Polynesian races in other times. Moreover, there is an unfortunate prejudice against vaccination here. People even now declare that those vaccinated die just as speedily of the plague as those who have never been;—and they can cite cases in proof. It is useless to talk to them about averages of immunity, percentage of liability, etc.;—they have seen with their own eyes persons who had been well vaccinated die of the verette, and that is enough to destroy their faith in the system… Even the priests, who pray their congregations to adopt the only known safeguard against the disease, can do little against this scepticism.

XV

March 5th

…THE streets are so narrow in this old-fashioned quarter that even a whisper is audible across them; and after dark I hear a great many things,—sometimes sounds of pain, sobbing, despairing cries as Death makes his nightly round,—sometimes, again, angry words, and laughter, and even song,—always one melancholy chant: the voice has that peculiar metallic timbre that reveals the young negress:—

> *"Pauv' ti Lélé*
> *Pauv' ti Lélé!*
> *Li gagnin doulè, doulè, doulè,—*
> *Li gagnin doulè*
> *Tout-pàtout!"*

I want to know who little Lélé was, and why she had pains "all over";—for however artless and childish these creole songs seem, they are invariably originated by some real incident. And at last somebody tells me that "poor little Lélé" had the reputation in other years of being the most unlucky girl in St. Pierre; whatever she tried to do resulted only in misfortune;—when it was morning she wished it were evening, that she might sleep and forget; but when the night came she could not sleep for thinking of the trouble she had had during the day, so that she wished it were morning…

More pleasant it is to hear the chatting of Yzore's children across the way, after the sun has set, and the stars come out… Gabrielle always wants to know what the stars are:—

—"*Ça qui ka clairé conm ça, manman?*" (What is it that shines like that?)

And Yzore answers:—

—"*Ça, mafi,—c'est ti limiè Bon-Dié.*" (Those are the little lights of the Good-God.)

—"It is so pretty,—eh, mamma? I want to count them."

—"You cannot count them, child."

—"One-two-three-four-five-six-seven." Gabrielle can only count up to seven. "*Moin peide!*—I am lost, mamma!"

The moon comes up;—she cries:—"*Mi manman!—gàdé gouôs difé qui adans ciel-à!* Look at the great fire in the sky."

—"It is the Moon, child!… Don't you see St. Joseph in it, carrying a bundle of wood?"

—"Yes, mamma! I see him!… A great big bundle of wood!"…

But Mimi is wiser in moon-lore: she borrows half a franc from her mother "to show to the Moon." And holding it up before the silver light, she sings:—

—"Pretty Moon, I show you my little money;—now let me always have money so long as you shine!"[4]

Then the mother takes them up to bed;—and in a little while there floats to me, through the open window, the murmur of the children's evening prayer:—

> "*Ange-gardien*
> *Veillez sur moi;*
> *Ayez pitié de ma faiblesse*
> *Couchez-vous sur mon petit lit;*
> *Suivez-moi sans cesse.*" [5]

I can only catch a line here and there... They do not sleep immediately;—they continue to chat in bed. Gabrielle wants to know what a guardian-angel is like. And I hear Mimi's voice replying in creole;—

—"*Zange-gàdien, c'est yon jeine fi, toutt bel.*" (The guardian-angel is a young girl, all beautiful.)

A little while, and there is silence; and I see Yzore come out, barefooted, upon the moonlit balcony of her little room,—looking up and down the hushed street, looking at the sea, looking up betimes at the high flickering of stars,—moving her lips as in prayer... And, standing there white-robed, with her rich dark hair loose-falling, there is a weird grace about her that recalls those long slim figures of guardian-angels in French religious prints...

XVI

March 6th

THIS morning Manm-Robert brings me something queer,—something hard tied up in a tiny piece of black cloth, with a string attached to hang it round my neck. I must wear it, she says.

—"*Ça ça yé, Manm-Robert?*"

—"*Pou empêché ou pouend laverette,*" she answers. It is to keep me from catching the *verette!*... And what is inside it?

—"*Toua graines maïs, épi dicamfre.*" (Three grains of corn, with a bit of camphor!)...

XVII

March 8th

...RICH households throughout the city are almost helpless for the want of servants. One can scarcely obtain help at any price: it is true that young country-girls keep coming into town to fill the places of the dead; but these new-comers fall a prey to the disease much more readily than those who preceded them. And such deaths often represent more than a mere derangement in the mechanism of domestic life. The creole *bonne* bears a relation to the family of an absolutely peculiar sort,—a relation of which the term "house-servant" does not convey the faintest idea. She is really a member of the household: her association with its life usually begins in childhood, when she is barely strong enough to carry a dobanne of water up-stairs;—and in many cases she has the additional claim of having been born in the house. As a child, she plays with the white children,—shares their pleasures and presents. She is very seldom harshly spoken to, or reminded of the fact that she is a servitor: she has a pet name;—she is allowed much familiarity,—is often permitted to join in conversation when there is no company present, and to express her opinion about domestic affairs. She costs very little to keep; four or five dollars a year will supply her with all necessary clothing;—she rarely wears shoes;—she sleeps on a little straw mattress (*paillasse*) on the floor, or perhaps upon a paillasse supported upon an "elephant" (*léfan*)—two thick square pieces of hard mattress placed together so as to form an oblong. She is only a nominal expense to the family; and she is the confidential messenger, the nurse, the chamber-maid, the water-carrier,—everything, in short, except cook and washer-woman. Families possessing a really good bonne would not part with her on any consideration. If she has been brought up in the household, she is regarded almost as a kind of adopted child. If she leave that household to make a home of her own, and have ill-fortune afterwards, she will not be afraid to return with her baby, which will perhaps be received and brought up as she herself was, under the old roof. The stranger may feel puzzled at first by this state of affairs; yet the cause is not obscure. It is traceable to the time of the formation of creole society—to the early period of slavery. Among the Latin races,—especially the French,—slavery preserved in modern times many of the least harsh features of slavery in the antique world,—where the domestic slave, entering the *familia*, actually became a member of it.

XVIII

March 10th

…YZORE and her little ones are all in Manm-Robert's shop;—she is recounting her troubles,—fresh troubles: forty-seven francs' worth of work delivered on time, and no money received… So much I hear as I enter the little *boutique* myself, to buy a package of "bouts."

—"*Assise!*" says Manm-Robert, handing me her own chair;—she is always pleased to see me, pleased to chat with me about creole folk-lore. Then observing a smile exchanged between myself and Mimi, she tells the children to bid me good-day:—"*Allé di bonjou' Missié-à!*"

One after another, each holds up a velvety cheek to kiss. And Mimi, who has been asking her mother the same question over and over again for at least five minutes without being able to obtain an answer, ventures to demand of me on the strength of this introduction;—

—"*Missié, oti masque-à?*"

—"*Y ben fou, pouloss!*" the mother cries out;—"Why, the child must be going out of her senses!... *Mimi pa 'mbêté moune conm ça!—pa ni piess masque: c'est la-vérette qui ni.*" (Don't annoy people like that!—there are no maskers now; there is nothing but the verette!)

[You are not annoying me at all, little Mimi; but I would not like to answer your question truthfully. I know where the maskers are,—most of them, child; and I do not think it would be well for you to know. They wear no masks now; but if you were to see them for even one moment, by some extraordinary accident, pretty Mimi, I think you would feel more frightened than you ever felt before.]

—"*Toutt lanuite y k'anni rêvé masque-à*" continues Yzore... I am curious to know what Mimi's dreams are like;—wonder if I can coax her to tell me...

XIX

...I HAVE written Mimi's last dream from the child's dictation:—[6]

—"I saw a ball," she says. "I was dreaming: I saw everybody dancing with masks on;—I was looking at them. And all at once I saw that the folks who were dancing were all made of pasteboard. And I saw a commandeur: he asked me what I was doing there. I answered him: 'Why, I saw a ball, and I came to look—what of it?' He answered me:—'Since you are so curious to come and look at other folks' business, you will have to stop here and dance too'. I said to him:—'No! I won't dance with people made of pasteboard;—I am afraid of them!'... And I ran and ran and ran,—I was so much afraid. And I ran into a big garden, where I saw a big cherry-tree that had only leaves upon it; and I saw a man sitting under the cherry-tree. He asked me:—'What are you doing here?' I said to him:—'I am trying to find my way out.' He said:—'You must stay here.' I said:—'No, no!'—and I said, in order to be able to get away:—'Go up there—you will see a fine ball: all pasteboard people dancing there, and a pasteboard commandeur commanding them!... And then I got so frightened that I awoke."...

..."And why were you so afraid of them, Mimi?" I ask.

—"*Pace yo té toutt vide endedans!*" answers Mimi, (*Because they were all hollow inside!*)

XX

March 19th

...THE death-rate in St. Pierre is now between three hundred and fifty and four hundred a month. Our street is being depopulated. Every day men come with immense stretchers,—covered with a sort of canvas awning,—to take somebody away to the *lazaretto*. At brief intervals, also, coffins are carried into houses empty, and carried out again followed by women who cry so loud that their sobbing can be heard a great way off.

...Before the visitation few quarters were so densely peopled: there were living often in one small house as many as fifty. The poorer classes had been accustomed from birth to live as simply as animals,—wearing scarcely any clothing, sleeping on bare floors, exposing themselves to all changes of weather, eating the cheapest and coarsest food. Yet, though living under such adverse conditions, no healthier people could be found, perhaps, in the world,—nor a more cleanly. Every yard having its fountain, almost everybody could bathe daily,—and with hundreds it was the custom to enter the river every morning at daybreak, or to take a swim in the bay (the young women here swim as well as the men)... But the pestilence, entering among so dense and unprotected a life, made extraordinarily rapid havoc; and bodily cleanliness availed little against the contagion. Now all the bathing resorts are deserted,—because the lazarettos infect the bay with refuse, and because the clothing of the sick is washed in the Roxelane.

...Guadeloupe, the sister colony, now sends aid;—the sum total is less than a single American merchant might give to a charitable undertaking; but it is a great deal for Guadeloupe to give. And far Cayenne sends money too; and the mother-country will send one hundred thousand francs.

XXI

March 20th

...THE infinite goodness of this colored population to one another is something which impresses with astonishment those accustomed to the selfishness of the world's great cities. No one is suffered to go to the pest-house who has a bed to lie upon, and a single relative or tried friend to administer remedies;—the multitude who pass through the lazarettos are strangers,—persons from the country who have no home of their own, or

servants who are not permitted to remain sick in houses of employers...
There are, however, many cases where a mistress will not suffer her bonne
to take the risks of the pest-house,—especially in families where there are
no children: the domestic is carefully nursed; a physician hired for her,
remedies purchased for her...

But among the colored people themselves the heroism displayed is
beautiful, is touching,—something which makes one doubt all accepted
theories about the natural egotism of mankind, and would compel the
most hardened pessimist to conceive a higher idea of humanity. There is
never a moment's hesitation in visiting a stricken individual: every relative,
and even the most intimate friends of every relative, may be seen hurrying
to the bedside. They take turns at nursing, sitting up all night, securing
medical attendance and medicines, without ever thought of the danger,—
nay, of the almost absolute certainty of contagion. If the patients have no
means, all contribute: what the sister or brother has not, the uncle or the
aunt, the godfather or godmother, the cousin, brother-in-law or sister-in-
law, may be able to give. No one dreams of refusing money or linen or
wine or anything possible to give, lend, or procure on credit. Women seem
to forget that they are beautiful, that they are young, that they are loved,—
to forget everything but the sense of that which they hold to be duty. You
see young girls of remarkably elegant presence,—young colored girls well
educated and *élevées-en-chapeau* [7] (that is to say, brought up like white
creole girls, dressed and accomplished like them), voluntarily leave rich
homes to nurse some poor mulatress or capresse in the indigent quarters
of the town, because the sick one happens to be a distant relative. They
will not trust others to perform this for them;—they feel bound to do it
in person. I heard such a one say, in reply to some earnest protest about
thus exposing herself (she had never been vaccinated):—"*Ah! quand il
s'agit du devoir, la vie ou la mort c'est pour moi la même chose.*"

...But without any sanitary law to check this self-immolation, and
with the conviction that in the presence of duty, or what is believed to be
duty, "life or death is the same thing," or ought to be so considered,—you
can readily imagine how soon the city must become one vast hospital.

XXII

...BY nine o'clock, as a general rule, St. Pierre becomes silent: every one
here retires early and rises with the sun. But sometimes, when the night
is exceptionally warm, people continue to sit at their doors and chat

until a far later hour; and on such a night one may hear and see curious things, in this period of plague…

It is certainly singular that while the howling of a dog at night has no ghastly signification here (nobody ever pays the least attention to the sound, however hideous), the moaning and screaming of cats is believed to bode death; and in these times folks never appear to feel too sleepy to rise at any hour and drive them away when they begin their cries… Tonight—a night so oppressive that all but the sick are sitting up—almost a panic is created in our street by a screaming of cats;—and long after the creatures have been hunted out of sight and hearing, everybody who has a relative ill with the prevailing malady continues to discuss the omen with terror.

…Then I observe a colored child standing barefooted in the moonlight, with her little round arms uplifted and hands joined above her head. A more graceful little figure it would be hard to find as she appears thus posed; but, all unconsciously, she is violating another superstition by this very attitude; and the angry mother shrieks;—

—"*Ti manmaille-là!—tiré lanmain-ou assous tête-ou, foute! pisse moin encò là!…Espéré moin allé lazarett avant metté lanmain conm ça!*" (Child, take down your hands from your head… because I am here yet! Wait till I go to the lazaretto before you put up your hands like that!)

For it was the savage, natural, primitive gesture of mourning,—of great despair.

…Then all begin to compare their misfortunes, to relate their miseries;—they say grotesque things,—even make jests about their troubles. One declares:—

—"*Si moin tè ka venne chapeau, à fôce moin ni malhè toutt manman sé fai yche yo sans tête.*" (I have that ill luck that if I were selling hats all the mothers would have children without heads!)

—Those who sit at their doors, I observe, do not sit, as a rule, upon the steps, even when these are of wood. There is a superstition which checks such a practice. "*Si ou assise assous pas- lapòte, ou ké pouend doulè toutt moune.*" (If you sit upon the door-step, you will take the pain of all who pass by.)

XXIII

March 30th

GOOD-FRIDAY…

The bells have ceased to ring,—even the bells for the dead; the hours are marked by cannon-shots. The ships in the harbor form crosses with their spars, turn their flags upside down. And the entire colored population put on mourning:—it is a custom among them centuries old.

You will not perceive a single gaudy robe today, a single calendered Madras: not a speck of showy color is visible through all the ways of St. Pierre. The costumes donned are all similar to those worn for the death of relatives: either full mourning,—a black robe with violet foulard, and dark violet-banded headkerchief; or half-mourning,—a dark violet robe with black foulard and turban—the half-mourning being worn only by those who cannot afford the more sombre costume. From my window I can see long processions climbing the mornes about the city, to visit the shrines and crucifixes, and to pray for the cessation of the pestilence.

...Three o'clock. Three cannon-shots shake the hills: it is the supposed hour of the Saviour's death. All believers—whether in the churches, on the highways, or in their homes—bow down and kiss the cross thrice, or, if there be no cross, press their lips three times to the ground or the pavement, and utter those three wishes which if expressed precisely at this traditional moment will surely, it is held, be fulfilled. Immense crowds are assembled before the crosses on the heights, and about the statue of Notre Dame de la Garde.

...There is no hubbub in the streets; there is not even the customary loud weeping to be heard as the coffins go by. One must not complain today, nor become angry, nor utter unkind words,— any fault committed on Good Friday is thought to obtain a special and awful magnitude in the sight of Heaven... There is a curious saying in vogue here. If a son or daughter grow up vicious,— become a shame to the family and a curse to the parents,—it is observed of such:—"*Ça, c'est yon péché Vendredi-Saint!*" (Must be a *Good-Friday sin!*)

There are two other strange beliefs connected with Good Friday. One is that it always rains on that day,—that the sky weeps for the death of the Saviour; and that this rain, if caught in a vessel, will never evaporate or spoil, and will cure all diseases.

The other is that only Jesus Christ died precisely at three o'clock. Nobody else ever died exactly at that hour;—they may die a second before or a second after three, but never exactly at three.

XXIV

March 31st

...HOLY SATURDAY morning;—nine o'clock. All the bells suddenly ring out; the humming of the *bourdon* blends with the thunder of a hundred guns: this is the *Gloria!*... At this signal it is a religious custom for the whole coast-population to enter the sea, and for those living too far from the beach to bathe in the rivers. But rivers and sea are now alike infected;—all the linen of the lazarettos has been washed therein; and today there are fewer bathers than usual.

But there are twenty-seven burials. Now they are burying the dead two together: the cemeteries are over-burdened...

XXV

...IN most of the old stone houses you will occasionally see spiders of terrifying size,—measuring across perhaps as much as six inches from the tip of one outstretched leg to the tip of its opposite fellow, as they cling to the wall. I never heard of any one being bitten by them; and among the poor it is deemed unlucky to injure or drive them away... But early this morning Yzore swept her house clean, and ejected through the door-way quite a host of these monster insects. Manm-Robert is quite dismayed:—

—"*Jesis-Maïa!—ou 'lè malhè encò pou fai ça, chè?*" (You want to have still more bad luck, that you do such a thing?)

And Yzore answers:—

—"*Toutt moune içitt pa ni yon soul!—gouôs conm ça fil zagrignin, et moin pa menm mangé! Epi laverette encò....Moin couè toutt ça ka pòté malhé!*" (No one here has a soul!—heaps of cobwebs like that, and nothing to eat yet, and the verette into the bargain... I think those things bring bad luck.)

—"Ah! you have not eaten yet!" cries Manm-Robert. "*Vini épi mom!*" (Come with me!)

And Yzore—already feeling a little remorse for her treatment of the spiders—murmurs apologetically as she crosses over to Manm-Robert's little shop:—"*Moin pa tchoué yo; moin chassé yo—ké vini encò.*" (I did not kill them; I only put them out;—they will come back again.)

But long afterwards, Manm-Robert remarked to me that they never went back...

XXVI

April 5th

—"*Toutt bel bois ka allé*," says Manm-Robert. (All the beautiful trees are going.)... I do not understand.

—"*Toutt bel bois—tout bel moune ka allé*," she adds, interpretatively. (All the "beautiful trees,"—all the handsome people,—are passing away.)... As in the speech of the world's primitive poets, so in the creole patois is a beautiful woman compared with a comely tree: nay, more than this, the name of the object is actually substituted for that of the living being. *Yon bel bois* may mean a fine tree: it more generally signifies a graceful woman: this is the very comparison made by Ulysses looking upon Nausicaa,—though more naïvely expressed.

...And now there comes to me the recollection of a creole ballad illustrating the use of the phrase,—a ballad about a youth of Fort-de-France sent to St. Pierre by his father to purchase a stock of dobannes,[8] who, falling in love with a handsome colored girl, spent all his father's money in buying her presents and a wedding outfit:—

> *"Moin descenne Saint-Piè*
> *Acheté dobannes*
> *Auliè ces dobannes*
> *C'est yon bel-bois moin mennein monté!"*

("I went down to Saint-Pierre to buy dobannes: instead of the dobannes, 'tis a pretty tree—a charming girl—that I bring back with me.")

—"Why, who is dead now, Manm-Robert?"

—"It is little Marie, the porteuse, who has got the vérette. She is gone to the lazaretto."

XXVII

April 7th

—*Toutt bel bois ka allé*... News has just come that Ti Marie died last night at the lazaretto of the Fort: she was attacked by what they call the *lavérette-pouff*,—a form of the disease which strangles its victim within a few hours.

Ti Marie was certainly the neatest little màchanne I ever knew. Without being actually pretty, her face had a childish charm which made it a pleasure to look at her;—and she had a clear chocolate-red skin, a light compact little figure, and a remarkably symmetrical pair of little feet which had never felt the pressure of a shoe. Every morning I used to hear her passing cry, just about daybreak: "*Qui 'lè café?—qui 'lè sirop?*" (Who wants coffee?—who wants syrup?) She looked about sixteen; but was a mother. "Where is her husband?" I ask. "*Nhomme-y mò laverette 'tou.*" (Her man died of the verette also.) "And the little one, her *yche?*" "*Y lazarett.*" (At the lazaretto.)... But only those without friends or relatives in the city are suffered to go to the lazaretto;—Ti Marie cannot have been of St. Pierre?

—"No: she was from Vauclin," answers Manm-Robert. "You do not often see pretty red girls who are natives of St. Pierre. St. Pierre has pretty *sang-mêlées.* The pretty red girls mostly come from Vauclin. The yellow ones, who are really *bel-bois,* are from Grande Anse: they are banana-colored people there. At Gros-Morne they are generally black."...

XXVIII

...IT appears that the red race here, the *race capresse,* is particularly liable to the disease. Every family employing capresses for house-servants loses them;—one family living at the next corner has lost four in succession...

The tint is a cinnamon or chocolate color;—the skin is naturally clear, smooth, glossy: it is of the capresse especially that the term "sapota-skin" (*peau-chapoti*) is used,—coupled with all curious creole adjectives to express what is comely,—*jojoll, beaujoll,*[9] etc. The hair is long, but bushy; the limbs light and strong, and admirably shaped... I am told that when transported to a colder climate, the capre or capresse partly loses this ruddy tint. Here, under the tropic sun, it has a beauty only possible to imitate in metal... And because photography cannot convey any idea of this singular color, the capresse hates a photograph.—"*Moin pas nouè,*" she says;—"*Moin ouôuge: ou fai moin nouè nans pòtrait-à.*" (I am not black: I am red:—you make me black in that portrait.) It is difficult to make her pose before the camera: she is red, as she avers, beautifully red; but the malicious instrument makes her gray or black—*nouè conm poule-zo-nouè* ("black as a black-boned hen!")

...And this red race is disappearing from St. Pierre—doubtless also from other plague-stricken centres.

XXIX

April 10th

...MANM-ROBERT is much annoyed and puzzled because the American steamer—the *bom-mangé*, as she calls it, does not come. It used to bring regularly so many barrels of potatoes and beans, so much lard and cheese and garlic and dried pease—everything, almost, of which she keeps a stock. It is now nearly eight weeks since the cannon of a New York steamer aroused the echoes of the harbor. Every morning Manm-Robert has been sending out her little servant Louis to see if there is any sign of the American packet:—"*Allé ouè Batterie d'Esnotz si bom-mangé-à pas vini.*" But Louis always returns with same rueful answer:—

—"*Manm-Robert, pa ni piess bom-mangé*" (there is not so much as a bit of a *bom-mangé*).

..."No more American steamers for Martinique:" that is the news received by telegraph! The disease has broken out among the shipping; the harbors have been declared infected. United States mail-packets drop their Martinique mails at St. Kitt's or Dominica, and pass us by. There will be suffering now among the *canotiers*, the *caboteurs*, all those who live by stowing or unloading cargo;—great warehouses are being closed up, and strong men discharged, because there will be nothing for them to do.

...They are burying twenty-five *verettiers* per day in the city.

But never was this tropic sky more beautiful;—never was this circling sea more marvellously blue;—never were the mornes more richly robed in luminous green, under a more golden day... And it seems strange that Nature should remain so lovely...

...Suddenly it occurs to me that I have not seen Yzore nor her children for some days; and I wonder if they have moved away... Towards evening, passing by Manm-Robert's, I ask about them. The old woman answers me very gravely:—

—"*Atò, mon chè, c'est Yzore qui ni lavérette!*"

The mother has been seized by the plague at last. But Manm-Robert will look after her; and Manm-Robert has taken charge of the three little ones, who are not now allowed to leave the house, for fear some one should tell them what it were best they should not know... *Pauv ti manmaille!*

XXX

April 13th

...STILL the vérette does not attack the native whites. But the whole air has become poisoned; the sanitary condition of the city becomes unprecedentedly bad; and a new epidemic makes its appearance,—typhoid fever. And now the békés begin to go, especially the young and strong; and the bells keep sounding for them, and the tolling bourdon fills the city with its enormous hum all day and far into the night. For these are rich; and the high solemnities of burial are theirs—the coffin of acajou, and the triple ringing, and the Cross of Gold to be carried before them as they pass to their long sleep under the palms,—saluted for the last time by all the population of St. Pierre, standing bareheaded in the sun...

...Is it in times like these, when all the conditions are febrile, that one is most apt to have queer dreams?

Last night it seemed to me that I saw that Carnival dance again,—the hooded musicians, the fantastic torrent of peaked caps, and the spectral masks, and the swaying of bodies and waving of arms,—but soundless as a passing of smoke. There were figures I thought I knew;—hands I had somewhere seen reached out and touched me in silence;—and then, all suddenly, a Viewless Something seemed to scatter the shapes as leaves are blown by a wind... And waking, I thought I heard again,—plainly as on that last Carnival afternoon,—the strange cry of fear;—"*C'est Bon-Dié ka passé!*" ...

XXXI

April 20th

...VERY early yesterday morning Yzore was carried away under a covering of quick-lime: the children do not know; Manm-Robert took heed they should not see. They have been told their mother has been taken to the country to get well,—that the doctor will bring her back soon... All the furniture is to be sold at auction to pay the debts;—the landlord was patient, he waited four months; the doctor was kindly: but now these must have their due. Everything will be bidden off, except the chapelle, with its Virgin and angels of porcelain: *yo pa ka pè venne*

Bon-Dié (the things of the Good-God must not be sold). And Manm-Robert will take care of the little ones.

The bed—a relic of former good-fortune,—a great Martinique bed of carved heavy native wood,—a *lit-à-bateau* (boat-bed), so called because shaped almost like a barge, perhaps—will surely bring three hundred francs;—the armoire, with its mirror doors, not less than two hundred and fifty. There is little else of value: the whole will not fetch enough to pay all the dead owes.

XXXII

April 28th

—*Tam-tam-tam!*—*Tam-tam-tam!*... It is the booming of the auction-drum from the Place: Yzore's furniture is about to change hands.

The children start at the sound, so vividly associated in their minds with the sights of Carnival days, with the fantastic mirth of the great processional dance: they run to the sunny street, calling to each other,—*Vini ouè!*—they look up and down. But there is a great quiet in the Rue du Morne Mirail;—the street is empty.

...Manm-Robert enters very weary: she has been at the sale, trying to save something for the children, but the prices were too high. In silence she takes her accustomed seat at the worn counter of her little shop; the young ones gather about her, caress her;—Mimi looks up laughing into the kind brown face, and wonders why Manm-Robert will not smile. Then Mimi becomes afraid to ask where the maskers are,—why they do not come. But little Maurice, bolder and less sensitive, cries out:—

—"*Manm-Robert, oti masque-à?*"

Manm-Robert does not answer;—she does not hear. She is gazing directly into the young faces clustered about her knee,—yet she does not see them: she sees far, far beyond them,—into the hidden years. And, suddenly, with a savage tenderness in her voice, she utters all the dark thought of her heart for them:—

—"*Toua ti blancs sans lesou!—quitté moin châché papa-ou qui adans cimétiè pou vini pouend ou tou!*" (Ye three little penniless white ones!—let me go call your father, who is in the cemetery, to come and take you also away!)

NOTES

1. "Petits amoureux aux plumes,
Enfants d'un brillant séjour,
Vous ignorez l'amertume,
Vous parlez souvent d'amour:...
Vous méprisez la dorure,
Les salons, et les bijoux;
Vous chérissez la Nature,
Petits oiseaux, becquetez-vous!

"Voyez làbas, dans cette église,
Auprès d'un confessional,
Le prêtre, qui veut faire croire à Lise,
Qu'un baiser est un grand mal;—
Pour prouver à la mignonne
Qu'un baiser bien fait, bien doux,
N'a jamais damné personne
Petits oiseaux, becquetez-vous!"

[*Translation*]

Little feathered lovers, cooing,
Children of the radiant air,
Sweet your speech,—the speech of wooing;
Ye have ne'er a grief to bear!
Gilded ease and jewelled fashion
Never own a charm for you;
Ye love Nature's truth with passion,
Pretty birdlings, bill and coo!

See that priest who, Lise confessing,
Wants to make the girl believe
That a kiss without a blessing
Is a fault for which to grieve!
Now to prove, to his vexation,
That no tender kiss and true
Ever caused a soul's damnation,
Pretty birdlings, bill and coo!

2. "...Cette danse est opposée à la pudeur. Avec tout cela, elle ne laisse pas d'être tellement du goût des Espagnols Créolles de l'Amérique, & si fort en usage parmi eux, qu'elle fait la meilleure partie de leurs divertissements, & qu'elle entre même dans leurs devotions. Ils la dansent même dans leurs Églises & à leurs processions; et les Religieuses ne manquent guère de la danser la Nuit de Noël, sur un théatre élevé dans leur Choeur, vis-à-vis de leur grille, qui est ouverte, afin que le Peuple aît

sa part dans la joye que ces bonnes âmes temoignent pour la naissance du Sauveur."

3. During a hurricane, several years ago, a West Indian steamer was disabled at a dangerously brief distance from the coast of the island by having her propeller fouled. Some broken and drifting rigging had become wrapped around it. One of the crew, a Martinique mulatto, tied a rope about his waist, took his knife between his teeth, dived overboard, and in that tremendous sea performed the difficult feat of disengaging the propeller, and thus saving the steamer from otherwise certain destruction... This brave fellow received the Cross of the Legion of Honor...

4. "*Bel laline, moin ka montré ou ti pièce moin!—ba moin làgent toutt temps ou ka clairé!*"... This little invocation is supposed to have most power when uttered on the first appearance of the new moon.

5. "Guardian-angel, watch over me;—have pity upon my weakness; lie down on my little bed with me; follow me whithersoever I go."... The prayers are always said in French. Metaphysical and theological terms cannot be rendered in the patois; and the authors of creole catechisms have always been obliged to borrow and explain French religious phrases in order to make their texts comprehensible.

6. —"Moin té ouè yon bal;—moin rêvé: moin té ka ouè toutt moune ka dansé masqué; moin té ka gàdé. Et toutt-à-coup moin ka ouè c'est bonhomme-càton ka dansé. Et moin ka ouè yon Commandè: y ka mandé moin ça moin ka fai là. Moin réponne y conm ça:—'Moin ouè yon bal, moin gàdé—coument!' Y ka réponne moin:—'Pisse ou si quirièse pou vini gàdé baggaïe moune, faut rété là pou dansé 'tou.' Moin réponne y:—'Non! moin pa dansé épi bonhomme-càton!—moin pè!'... Et moin ka couri, moin ka couri, moin ka couri à fòce moin té ni pè. Et moin rentré adans grand jàdin; et moin ouè gouôs pié-cirise qui té chàgé anni feuill; et moin ka ouè yon nhomme assise enba cirise-à. Y mandé moin:—'Ça ou ka fai là?' Moin di y:—'Moin ka chàché chimin pou moin allé.' Y di moin:—'Faut rété içitt.' Et moin di y:—'Non!'—et pou chappé cò moin, moin di y:—'Allé enhaut-là: ou ké ouè yon bel bal,—toutt bonhomme-càton ka dansé, épi yon Commandè-en-càton ka commandé yo'... Epi moin levé, à fòce moin té pè."...

7. Lit.,—"brought-up-in-a-hat." To wear the Madras is to acknowledge oneself of color;—to follow the European style of dressing the hair, and adopt the costume of the white creoles indicates a desire to affiliate with the white class.

8. Red earthen-ware jars for keeping drinking-water cool. The origin of the word is probably to be sought in the name of the town, near Marseilles, where they are made,—"Aubagne."

9. I may cite in this relation one stanza of a creole song—very popular in St. Pierre—celebrating the charms of a little capresse:—

Moin toutt jeine,

Gouôs, gouâs, vaillant,
Peau di chapoti
Ka fai plaisi;—
Lapeau moin
Li bien poli;
Et moin ka plai
Mênm toutt nhomme grave!"

—Which might he freely rendered thus:—

"I am dimpled, young,
Round-limbed, and strong,
With sapota-skin
That is good to see:
All glossy-smooth
Is this skin of mine;
And the gravest men
like to look at me!"

VI. Les Blanchisseuses

I

WHOEVER stops for a few months in St. Pierre is certain, sooner or later, to pass an idle half-hour in that charming place of Martinique idlers,—the beautiful Savane du Fort,—and, once there, is equally certain to lean a little while over the mossy parapet of the river-wall to watch the *blanchisseuses* at work. It has a curious interest, this spectacle of primitive toil: the deep channel of the Roxelane winding under the palm-crowned heights of the Fort; the blinding whiteness of linen laid out to bleach for miles upon the huge bowlders of porphyry and prismatic basalt; and the dark bronze-limbed women, with faces hidden under immense straw hats, and knees in the rushing torrent,—all form a scene that makes one think of the earliest civilizations. Even here, in this modern colony, it is nearly three centuries old; and it will probably continue thus at the Rivière des Blanchisseuses for fully another three hundred years. Quaint as certain weird Breton legends whereof it reminds you,—especially if you watch it before daybreak while the city still sleeps,—this fashion of washing is not likely to change. There is a local prejudice against new methods, new inventions, new ideas;—several efforts at introducing a less savage style of washing proved unsuccessful; and an attempt to establish a steam-laundry resulted in failure. The public were quite contented with the old ways of laundrying, and saw no benefits to be gained by forsaking them;—while the washers and ironers engaged by the laundry proprietor at higher rates than they had ever obtained before soon wearied of in-door work, abandoned their situations, and returned with a sense of relief to their ancient way of working out in the blue air and the wind of the hills, with their feet in the mountain-water and their heads in the awful sun.

…It is one of the sights of St. Pierre,—this daily scene at the River of the Washerwomen: everybody likes to watch it;—the men, because among the blanchisseuses there are not a few decidedly handsome girls; the women, probably because a woman feels always interested in woman's work. All the white bridges of the Roxelane are dotted with lookers-on during fine days, and particularly in the morning, when every bonne on her way to and from the market stops a moment to observe or to greet those blanchisseuses whom she knows. Then one hears such a calling and clamoring,—such an intercrossing of cries from the bridge to the river, and the river to the bridge.

...“Ouill! Noémi!”... “Comment ou yé, chè?”... “Eh! Pascaline!”... “Bonjou', Youtte!—Dédé!—Fifi!—Henrillia!”... “Comment ou kallé, Cyrillia?”... “Toutt douce, chè!—et Ti Mémé?”... “Y bien—oti Ninotte?”... “Bo ti manmaille pou moin, chè—ou tanne?”... But the bridge leading to the market of the Fort is the poorest point of view; for the better classes of blanchisseuses are not there: only the lazy, the weak, or non-professionals—house-servants, who do washing at the river two or three times a month as part of their family-service—are apt to get so far down. The experienced professionals and early risers secure the best places and choice of rocks; and among the hundreds at work you can discern something like a physical gradation. At the next bridge the women look better, stronger; more young faces appear; and the further you follow the river-course towards the Jardin des Plantes, the more the appearance of the blanchisseuses improves,—so that within the space of a mile you can see well exemplified one natural law of life's struggle,— the best chances to the best constitutions.

Rivière des Blanchisseuses

You might also observe, if you watch long enough, that among the blanchisseuses there are few sufficiently of color to be classed as bright mulatresses;—the majority are black or of that dark copper-red race which is perhaps superior to the black creole in strength and bulk; for it requires a skin insensible to sun as well as the toughest of constitutions to be a blanchisseuse. A porteuse can begin to make long trips at nine or ten years; but no girl is strong enough to learn the washing-trade until she is past twelve. The blanchisseuse is the hardest worker among the whole population;—her daily labor is rarely less than thirteen hours; and during the greater part of that time she is working in the sun, and standing up to her knees in water that descends quite cold from the mountain peaks. Her labor makes her perspire profusely; and she can never venture to cool herself by further immersion without serious danger of pleurisy. The trade is said to kill all who continue at it beyond a certain number of years:—"*Nou ka mò toutt dleau*" (we all die of the water), one told me, replying to a question. No feeble or light-skinned person can attempt to do a single day's work of this kind without danger; and a weak girl, driven by necessity to do her own washing, seldom ventures to go to the river. Yet I saw an instance of such rashness one day. A pretty sang-mêlée, perhaps about eighteen or nineteen years old,—whom I afterwards learned had just lost her mother and found herself thus absolutely destitute,—began to descend one of the flights of stone steps leading to the river, with a small bundle upon her head; and two or three of the blanchisseuses stopped their work to look at her. A tall capresse inquired mischievously;—

—"*Ou vini pou pouend yon bain?*" (Coming to take a bath?) For the river is a great bathing-place.

—"*Non; moin vini lavé.*" (No; I am coming to wash.)

—"*Aïe! aïe! aïe!—y vini lavé!*" ... And all within hearing laughed together. "Are you crazy, girl?—*ess ou fou?*" The tall capresse snatched the bundle from her, opened it, threw a garment to her nearest neighbor, another to the next one, dividing the work among a little circle of friends, and said to the stranger, "Non ké lavé toutt ça ba ou bien vite, chè,—va, amisé ou!" (We'll wash this for you very quickly, dear—go and amuse yourself!) These kind women even did more for the poor girl;— they subscribed to buy her a good breakfast, when the food-seller—the màchanne-mangé—made her regular round among them, with fried fish and eggs and manioc flour and bananas.

II

ALL of the multitude who wash clothing at the river are not professional blanchisseuses. Hundreds of women, too poor to pay for laundrying, do their own work at the Roxelane;—and numerous bonnes there wash the linen of their mistresses as a regular part of their domestic duty. But even if the professionals did not always occupy a certain well-known portion of the channel, they could easily be distinguished from others by their rapid and methodical manner of work, by the ease with which immense masses of linen are handled by them, and, above all, by their way of whipping it against the rocks. Furthermore, the greater number of professionals are likewise teachers, mistresses (*bou'geoises*), and have their apprentices beside them,— young girls from twelve to sixteen years of age. Among these *apprenti*, as they are called in the patois, there are many attractive types, such as idlers upon the bridges like to look at.

If after one year of instruction, the apprentice fails to prove a good washer, it is not likely she will ever become one; and there are some branches of the trade requiring a longer period of teaching and of practice. The young girl first learns simply to soap and wash the linen in the river, which operation is called "rubbing" (*frotté* in creole);—after she can do this pretty well, she is taught the curious art of whipping it (*fessé*). You can hear the sound of the fessé a great way off, echoing and re-echoing among the mornes: it is not a sharp smacking noise, as the name might seem to imply, but a heavy hollow sound exactly like that of an axe splitting dry timber. In fact, it so closely resembles the latter sound that you are apt on first hearing it to look up at the mornes with the expectation of seeing woodmen there at work. And it is not made by striking the linen with anything, but only by lashing it against the sides of the rocks... After a piece has been well rubbed and rinsed, it is folded up into a peculiar sheaf-shape, and seized by the closely gathered end for the fessé. Then the folding process is repeated on the reverse, and the other end whipped. This process expels suds that rinsing cannot remove: it must be done very dextrously to avoid tearing or damaging the material. By an experienced hand the linen is never torn; and even pearl and bone buttons are much less often broken than might be supposed. The singular echo is altogether due to the manner of folding the article for the fessé.

After this, all the pieces are spread out upon the rocks, in the sun, for the "first bleaching" (*pouèmié lablanie*). In the evening they are gathered into large wooden trays or baskets, and carried to what is called the "lye-house" (*lacaïe lessive*)—overlooking the river from a point on the Fort bank opposite to the higher end of the Savane. Here each blanchisseuse hires a small or a large vat, or even several,—according to the quantity of work done,—at two, three, or ten sous, and leaves her washing to steep in lye (*coulé* is the creole word used) during the night. There are watchmen to guard it. Before daybreak it is rinsed in warm water; then it is taken back to the river,—is rinsed again, bleached again, blued and starched. Then it is ready for ironing. To press and iron well is the most difficult part of the trade. When an apprentice is able to iron a gentleman's shirt nicely, and a pair of white pantaloons, she is considered to have finished her time;—she becomes a journey-woman (*ouvouïyé*).

Even in a country where wages are almost incredibly low, the blanchisseuse earns considerable money. There is no fixed scale of prices: it is even customary to bargain with these women beforehand. Shirts and white pantaloons figure at six and eight cents in laundry bills; but other washing is much cheaper. I saw a lot of thirty-three pieces—including such large ones as sheets, bedcovers, and several douillettes (the long Martinique trailing robes of one piece from neck to feet)—for which only three francs was charged. Articles are frequently stolen or lost by house-servants sent to do washing at the river; but very seldom indeed by the regular blanchisseuses. Few of them can read or write or understand owners' marks on wearing apparel; and when you see at the river the wilderness of scattered linen, the seemingly enormous confusion, you cannot understand how these women manage to separate and classify it all. Yet they do this admirably,—and for that reason perhaps more than any other, are able to charge fair rates;—it is false economy to have your washing done by the house-servant;—with the professionals your property is safe. And cheap as her rates are, a good professional can make from twenty-five to thirty francs a week; averaging fully a hundred francs a month,—as much as many a white clerk can earn in the stores of St. Pierre, and quite as much (considering local differences in the purchasing power of money) as $60 per month would represent in the United States.

Probably the ability to earn large wages often tempts the blanchisseuse to continue at her trade until it kills her. The "water-disease," as she calls it (*maladie-dleau*), makes its appearance after middle-life: the feet, lower limbs, and abdomen swell enormously, while the face becomes almost fleshless;—then, gradually tissues give way, muscles yield, and the whole physical structure crumbles.

Nevertheless, the blanchisseuse is essentially a sober liver,—never a drunkard. In fact, she is sober from rigid necessity: she would not dare to swallow one mouthful of spirits while at work with her feet in the water; everybody else in Martinique, even the little children, can drink rum; the blanchisseuse cannot, unless she wishes to die of a congestion. Her strongest refreshment is *mabi*,—a mild, effervescent, and, I think, rather disagreeable, beer made from molasses.

III

ALWAYS before daybreak they rise to work, while the vapors of the mornes fill the air with scent of mouldering vegetation,—clayey odors,—grassy smells: there is only a faint gray light, and the water of the river is very chill. One by one they arrive, barefooted, under their burdens built up tower-shape on their trays;—silently as ghosts they descend the steps to the river-bed, and begin to unfold and immerse their washing. They greet each other as they come, then become silent again; there is scarcely any talking; the hearts of all are heavy with the heaviness of the hour. But the gray light turns yellow; the sun climbs over the peaks: light changes the dark water to living crystal, and all begin to chatter a little. Then the city awakens; the currents of its daily life circulate again,—thinly and slowly at first, then swiftly and strongly up and down every yellow street, and through the Savane, and over the bridges of the river. Passers-by pause to look down, and cry "*bonjou', chè!*" Idle men stare at some pretty washer, till she points at them and cries:—"*Gadé Missié-à ka guetté nou!—anh!—anh!—anh!*" And all the others look up and repeat the groan—"*anh!—anh!—anh!*" till the starers beat a retreat. The air grows warmer; the sky blue takes fire: the great light makes joy for the washers; they shout to each other from distance to distance, jest, laugh, sing. Gusty of speech these women are: long habit of calling to one another through the roar of the torrent has given their voices a singular sonority and force: it is well worth while to hear them sing. One starts the song,—the next joins her; then another and another, till the channel rings with the melody from the bridge of the Jardin des Plantes to the Pont-bois:—

> *"C'est moin qui té ka lavé,*
> *Passé, raccommodé:*
> *Y té néf hè disouè*
> *Ou metté moin derhò,—*
> *Yche moin assous bouas moin;—*
> *Laplie té ka tombé—*
> *Léfan moin assous tête moin!*
> *Doudoux, ou m'abandonne!*
> *Moin pa ni pèsonne pou soigné moin"* [1]

...A melancholy chant—originally a Carnival improvisation made to bring public shame upon the perpetrator of a cruel act;—but it contains the story of many of these lives—the story of industrious affectionate women temporarily united to brutal and worthless men in a country where legal marriages are rare. Half of the creole songs I was able to collect during a residence of nearly two years in the island touch upon the same sad theme. Of these, "Chè Manman Moin," a great favourite still with the older blanchisseuses, has a simple pathos unrivalled, I believe, in the oral literature of these people. Here is an attempt to translate its three rhymeless stanzas into prose; but the childish sweetness of the patois original is lost;—

CHÈ MANMAN MOIN.

I

"Dear mamma, once you were young like I;—dear papa, you have also been young;—dear great elder brother, you too have been young. Ah! let me cherish this sweet friendship!—so sick my heart is—yes, 'tis very, very ill, this heart of mine: love, only love can make it well again."...

II

"O cursed eyes he praised that led me to him! O cursed lips of mine which ever repeated his name! O cursed moment in which I gave up my heart to the ingrate who no longer knows how to love."...

III

"Doudoux, you swore to me by Heaven!—doudoux, you swore to me by your faith!... And now you cannot come to me?... Oh! my heart is withering with pain!... I was passing by the cemetery;—I saw my name upon a stone—all by itself. I saw two white roses; and in a moment one faded and fell before me… So my forgotten heart will be!"…

The air is not so charming, however, as that of a little song which every creole knows, and which may be often heard still at the river: I think it is the prettiest of all creole melodies. "To-to-to" (patois for the French *toc*) is an onomatope for the sound of knocking at a door.

> "*To-to-to!*—'ça qui là?'
> —'C'est moin-mênme, lanmou;—
> Ouvé lapott ba moin!'

> "*To-to-to!*—'ça qui là?'
> —'C'est moin-mênme, lanmou;—
> Qui ka ba ou khè moin!'

> "*To-to-to!*—'ça qui là?'
> —'C'est moin-mênme, lanmou;—
> Laplie ka mouillé moin!'"

[*To-to-to*… "Who taps there?"—"'Tis mine own self Love: open the door for me."
To-to-to… "Who taps there?"—"'Tis mine own self Love, who give my heart to thee."
To-to-to… "Who taps there?"—"'Tis mine own self Love: open thy door to me;—the rain is wetting me!"…]

…But it is more common to hear the blanchisseuses singing merry, jaunty, sarcastic ditties,—Carnival compositions,—in which the African sense of rhythmic melody is more marked;—"Marie-Clémence maudi," "Loéma tombé," "Quand ou ni ti mari jojoll." [2]

—At midday the màchanne-mangé comes, with her girls,—carrying trays of fried fish, and *akras,* and cooked beans, and bottles of mabi. The blanchisseuses buy, and eat with their feet in the water, using rocks for tables. Each has her little tin cup to drink her mabi in… Then the washing and the chanting and the booming of the fessé begin again. Afternoon wanes;—school-hours close; and children of many beautiful colors come to the river, and leap down the steps crying, "*Eti! manman!*" —"*Sésé!*" —"*Nenneine!*" calling their elder sisters, mothers, and godmothers: the little boys strip naked to play in the water a while… Towards sunset the more rapid and active workers begin to gather in their linen, and pile it on trays. Large patches of bald rock appear again… By six o'clock almost the whole bed of the river is bare;—the women are nearly all gone. A few linger a while on the Savane, to watch the last-comer. There is always a great laugh at the last to leave the channel: they ask her if she has not forgotten "to lock up the river."

—"*Ou fèmé lapòte larivié, chè—anh?*"

—"*Ah! oui, chè!—moin fèmé y, ou tanne?—moin ni laclé-à!*" (Oh yes, dear. I locked it up,—you hear? I've got the key!)

But there are days and weeks when they do not sing,—times of want or of plague, when the silence of the valley is broken only by the sound of linen beaten upon the rocks, and the great voice of the Roxelane, which will sing on when the city itself shall have ceased to be, just as it sang one hundred thousand years ago… "Why do they not sing today?" I once asked during the summer of 1887,—a year of pestilence. "*Yo ka pensé toutt lanmizè yo—toutt lapeine yo,*" I was answered. (They are thinking of all their trouble, all their misery.) Yet in all seasons, while youth and strength stay with them, they work on in wind and sun, mist and rain, washing the linen of the living and the dead,—white wraps for the newly born, white robes for the bride, white shrouds for them that pass into the Great Silence. And the torrent that wears away the ribs of the perpetual hills wears away their lives,—sometimes slowly, slowly as black basalt is worn,—sometimes suddenly,—in the twinkling of an eye.

For a strange danger ever menaces the blanchisseuse,—the treachery of the stream!… Watch them working, and observe how often they turn their eyes to the high north-east, to look at Pelée. Pelée gives them warning betimes. When all is sunny in St.Pierre, and the harbor lies blue as lapis-lazuli, there may be mighty rains in the regions of the great woods and the valleys of the higher peaks; and thin streams swell to raging floods which burst suddenly from the altitudes, rolling down rocks and trees and wreck of forests, uplifting crags, devastating slopes. And sometimes, down the ravine of the Roxelane, there comes a roar as of eruption, with a rush of foaming water like a moving mountain-wall; and bridges and buildings vanish with its passing. In 1865 the Savane, high as it lies above the river-bed was flooded;—and all the bridges were swept into the sea.

So the older and wiser blanchisseuses keep watch upon Pelée; and if a blackness gather over it, with lightnings breaking through, then—

however fair the sun shine on St. Pierre—the alarm is given, the miles of bleaching linen vanish from the rocks in a few minutes, and every one leaves the channel. But it has occasionally happened that Pelée gave no such friendly signal before the river rose: thus lives have been lost. Most of the blanchisseuses are swimmers, and good ones,—I have seen one of these girls swim almost out of sight in the harbor, during an idle hour;— but no swimmer has any chances in a rising of the Roxelane: all overtaken by it are stricken by rocks and drift;—*yo crazé*, as a creole term expresses it,—a term signifying to crush, to bray, to dash to pieces.

...Sometimes it happens that one who has been absent at home for a brief while returns to the river only to meet her comrades fleeing from it,—many leaving their linen behind them. But she will not abandon the linen entrusted to her: she makes a run for it,—in spite of warning screams,—in spite of the vain clutching of kind rough fingers. She gains the river-bed;—the flood has already reached her waist, but she is strong; she reaches her linen,—snatches it up, piece by piece, scattered as it is—"one!—two!—five!—seven!";—there is a roaring in her ears— "eleven!—thirteen!" she has it all... but now the rocks are moving! For one instant she strives to reach the steps, only a few yards off;—another, and the thunder of the deluge is upon her,—and the crashing crags,— and the spinning trees...

Perhaps before sundown some canotier may find her floating far in the bay,—drifting upon her face in a thousand feet of water,—with faithful dead hands still holding fast the property of her employer.

NOTES

1. It was I who washed and ironed and mended; at nine o'clock at night thou didst put me out-of-doors, with my child in my arms,—the rain was falling,—with my poor straw mattress upon my head! Doudoux! thou dost abandon me!... I have none to care for me.

2. See Appendix for specimens of creole music.

VII. La Pelée

I

THE first attempt made to colonize Martinique was abandoned almost as soon as begun, because the leaders of the expedition found the country "too rugged and too mountainous," and were "terrified by the prodigious number of serpents which covered its soil." Landing on June 25, 1635, Olive and Duplessis left the island after a few hours' exploration, or, rather, observation, and made sail for Guadeloupe,—according to the quaint and most veracious history of Père Dutertre, of the Order of Friars-Preachers.

A single glance at the topographical map of Martinique would suffice to confirm the father's assertion that the country was found to be *trop haché et trop montueux:* more than two-thirds of it is peak and mountain;—even today only 42,445 of its supposed 98,782 hectares have been cultivated; and on page 426 of the last "Annuaire" (1887) I find the statement that in the interior there are extensive Government lands of which the area is "not exactly known." Yet mountainous as a country must be which—although scarcely forty-nine miles long and twenty miles in average breadth—remains partly unfamiliar to its own inhabitants after nearly three centuries of civilization (there are not half a dozen creoles who have travelled all over it), only two elevations in Martinique bear the name *montagne*. These are La Montagne Pelée, in the north, and La Montagne du Vauclin, in the south. The term *morne*, used throughout the French West Indian colonies to designate certain altitudes of volcanic origin, a term rather unsatisfactorily translated in certain dictionaries as "a small mountain," is justly applied to the majority of Martinique hills, and unjustly sometimes even to its mightiest elevation,—called Morne Pelé, or Montagne Pelée, or simply "La Montagne," according, perhaps, to the varying degree of respect it inspires in different minds. But even in the popular nomenclature one finds the orography of Martinique, as well as of other West Indian islands, regularly classified by *pitons, mornes,* and *monts* or *montagnes*. Mornes usually have those beautiful and curious forms which bespeak volcanic origin even to the unscientific observer:

they are most often pyramidal or conoid up to a certain height; but have summits either rounded or truncated;—their sides, green with the richest vegetation, rise from valley-levels and coast-lines with remarkable abruptness, and are apt to be curiously ribbed or wrinkled. The pitons, far fewer in number, are much more fantastic in form;—volcanic cones, or volcanic upheavals of splintered strata almost at right angles,—sometimes sharp of line as spires, and mostly too steep for habitation. They are occasionally mammiform, and so symmetrical that one might imagine them artificial creations,—particularly when they occur in pairs. Only a very important mass is dignified by the name *montagne*: there are, as I have already observed, but two thus called in all Martinique,—Pelée, the head and summit of the island; and La Montagne du Vauclin, in the south-east. Vauclin is inferior in height and bulk to several mornes and pitons of the north and north-west,—and owes its distinction probably to its position as centre of a system of ranges: but in altitude and mass and majesty, Pelée far outranks everything in the island, and well deserves its special appellation, "La Montagne."

No description could give the reader a just idea of what Martinique is, configuratively, so well as the simple statement that, although less than fifty miles in extreme length, and less than twenty in average breadth, there are upwards of *four hundred mountains* in this little island, or of what at least might be termed mountains elsewhere. These again are divided and interpeaked, and bear hillocks on their slopes;—and the lowest hillock in Martinique is fifty metres high. Some of the peaks are said to be totally inaccessible: many mornes are so on one or two or even three sides. Ninety-one only of the principal mountains have been named; and among these several bear similar appellations: for example, there are two Mornes-Rouges, one in the north and one in the south; and there are four or five Gros-Mornes. All the elevations belong to six great groups, clustering about or radiating from six ancient volcanic centres,— 1. La Pelée; 2. Pitons du Carbet; 3. Roches Carrées;[1] 4. Vauclin; 5. Marin; 6. Morne de la Plaine. Forty-two distinct mountain-masses belong to the Carbet system alone,—that of Pelée including but thirteen; and the whole Carbet area has a circumference of 120,000 metres,—much more considerable than that of Pelée. But its centre is not one enormous pyramidal mass like that of "La Montagne": it is marked only by a group of five remarkable porphyritic cones,—the Pitons of Carbet;—while Pelée, dominating everything, and filling the north, presents an aspect and occupies an area scarcely inferior to those of Aetna.

—Sometimes, while looking at La Pelée, I have wondered if the enterprise of the great Japanese painter who made the Hundred Views of Fusiyama could not be imitated by some creole artist equally proud of his native hills, and fearless of the heat of the plains or the snakes of the slopes. A hundred views of Pelée might certainly be made; for the enormous mass is omnipresent to dwellers in the northern part of the island, and can be seen from the heights of the most southern mornes. It is visible from almost any part of St. Pierre,—which nestles in a fold of its rocky skirts. It overlooks all the island ranges, and overtops the mighty Pitons of Carbet by a thousand feet;—you can only lose sight of it by entering gorges, or journeying into the valleys of the south... But the peaked character of the whole country, and the hot moist climate, oppose any artistic undertaking of the sort suggested: even photographers never dream of taking views in the further interior, nor on the east coast. Travel, moreover, is no less costly than difficult: there are no inns or places of rest for tourists; there are, almost daily, sudden and violent rains, which are much dreaded (since a thorough wetting, with the pores all distended by heat, may produce pleurisy); and there are serpents! The artist willing to devote a few weeks of travel and study to Pelée, in spite of these annoyances and risks, has not yet made his appearance in Martinique.[2]

Huge as the mountain looks from St. Pierre, the eye under-estimates its bulk; and when you climb the mornes about the town, Labelle, d'Orange, or the much grander Parnasse, you are surprised to find how much vaster Pelée appears from these summits. Volcanic hills often seem higher, by reason of their steepness, than they really are; but Pelée deludes in another manner. From surrounding valleys it appears lower, and from adjacent mornes higher than it really is: the illusion in the former case being due to the singular slope of its contours, and the remarkable breadth of its base, occupying nearly all the northern end of the island; in the latter, to misconception of the comparative height of the eminence you have reached, which deceives by the precipitous pitch of its sides. Pelée is not very remarkable in point of altitude, however: its height was estimated by Moreau de Jonnés at 1,600 metres; and by others at between 4,400 and 4,500 feet. The sum of the various imperfect estimates made justify the opinion of Dr. Cornilliac that the extreme summit is over 5,000 feet above the sea—perhaps 5,200.[3] The clouds of the summit afford no indication to eyes accustomed to mountain scenery in northern countries; for in these hot moist latitudes

Foot of La Pelée, behind the Quarter of the Fort

clouds hang very low, even in fair weather. But in bulk Pelée is grandiose: it spurs out across the island from the Caribbean to the Atlantic: the great chains of mornes about it are merely counter-forts; the Piton Pierreux and the Piton Pain-à-Sucre (*Sugar-loaf Peak*), and other elevations varying from 800 to 2,100 feet, are its volcanic children. Nearly thirty rivers have their birth in its flanks,—besides many thermal springs, variously mineralized. As the culminant point of the island, Pelée is also the ruler of its meteorologic life,—cloud-herder, lightning-forger, and rain-maker. During clear weather you can see it drawing to itself all the white vapors of the land,—robbing lesser eminences of their shoulder-wraps and head-coverings;—though the Pitons of Carbet (3,700 feet) usually manage to retain about their middle a cloud-clout,—a *lantchô*. You will also see that the clouds run in a circle about Pelée,—gathering bulk as they turn by continual accessions from other points. If the crater be totally bare in the morning, and shows the broken edges very sharply against the blue, it is a sign of foul rather than of fair weather to come.[4]

Even in bulk, perhaps, Pelée might not impress those who know the stupendous scenery of the American ranges; but none could deny it special attractions appealing to the senses of form and color. There is an imposing fantasticality in its configuration worth months of artistic study: one does not easily tire of watching its slopes undulating against the north sky,—and the strange jagging of its ridges,—and the succession of its terraces crumbling down to other terraces, which again break into ravines here and there bridged by enormous buttresses of basalt: an extravaganza of lava-shapes overpitching and cascading into sea and plain. All this is verdant wherever surfaces catch the sun: you can divine what the frame is only by examining the dark and ponderous rocks of the torrents. And the hundred tints of this verdure do not form the only colorific charms of the landscape. Lovely as the long upreaching slopes of cane are,—and the loftier bands of forest-growths, so far off that they look like belts of moss,—and the more tender-colored masses above, wrinkling and folding together up to the frost-white clouds of the summit,—you will be still more delighted by the shadow-colors,— opulent, diaphanous. The umbrages lining the wrinkles, collecting in the hollows, slanting from sudden projections, may become before your eyes almost as unreally beautiful as the landscape colors of a Japanese fan;— they shift most generally during the day from indigo-blue through violets and paler blues to final lilacs and purples; and even the shadows of passing clouds have a faint blue tinge when they fall on Pelée.

Is the great volcano dead?... Nobody knows. Less than forty years ago it rained ashes over all the roofs of St. Pierre;—within twenty years it has uttered mutterings. For the moment, it appears to sleep; and the clouds have dripped into the cup of its highest crater till it has become a lake, several hundred yards in circumference. The crater occupied by this lake—called L'Étang, or "The Pool"—has never been active within human memory. There are others,—difficult and dangerous to visit because opening on the side of a tremendous gorge; and it was one of these, no doubt, which has always been called *La Souffrière*, that rained ashes over the city in 1851.

The explosion was almost concomitant with the last of a series of earthquake shocks, which began in the middle of May and ended in the first week of August,—all much more severe in Guadeloupe than in Martinique. In the village of Au Prêcheur, lying at the foot of the western slope of Pelée, the people had been for some time complaining of an oppressive stench of sulphur,—or, as chemists declared it, sulphuretted hydrogen,—when, on the 4th of August, much trepidation was caused by a long and appalling noise from the mountain,—a noise compared by planters on the neighboring slopes to the hollow roaring made by a packet blowing off steam, but infinitely louder. These sounds continued through intervals until the following night, sometimes deepening into a rumble like thunder. The mountain guides declared: "*C'est la Souffrière qui bout!*" (the Souffrière is boiling); and a panic seized the negroes of the neighboring plantations. At 11 P.M. the noise was terrible enough to fill all St. Pierre with alarm; and on the morning of the 6th the city presented an unwonted aspect, compared by creoles who had lived abroad to the effect of a great hoar-frost. All the roofs, trees, balconies, awnings, pavements, were covered with a white layer of ashes. The same shower blanched the roofs of Morne Rouge, and all the villages about the chief city,—Carbet, Fond-Corré, and Au Prêcheur; also whitening the neighboring country: the mountain was sending up columns of smoke or vapor; and it was noticed that the Rivière Blanche, usually of a glaucous color, ran black into the sea like an outpouring of ink, staining its azure for a mile. A committee appointed to make an investigation, and prepare an official report, found that a number of rents had had either been newly formed, or suddenly become active, in the flank of the mountain: these were all situated in the immense gorge sloping westward from that point now known as the Morne de la Croix. Several were visited with much difficulty,—members of the commission being obliged to lower themselves down a succession of precipices with cords of lianas; and it is noteworthy that their researches were prosecuted in spite of the momentary panic created by another outburst. It was satisfactorily ascertained that the main force of the explosion had been exerted within a perimeter of about one thousand yards; that various hot springs had suddenly gushed out,—the temperature of the least warm being about 37° Réaumur (116°F.);—that there was no change in the configuration of the mountain;—and that the terrific sounds had been produced only be the violent outrush of vapor and ashes from some of the rents. In hope of allying the general alarm, a creole priest climbed the summit of the volcano, and there planted the great cross that gives the height its name and still remains to commemorate the event.

There was an extraordinary emigration of serpents from the high woods, and from the higher to the lower plantations,—where they were killed by thousands. For a long time Pelée continued to send up an immense column of white vapor; but there were no more showers of ashes; and the mountain gradually settled down to its present state of quiescence.

II

FROM St. Pierre, trips can be made by several routes;—the most popular is that by way of Morne Rouge and the Calebasse; but the summit can be reached in much less time by making the ascent from different points along the coast-road to Au Prêcheur,—such as the Morne St. Martin, or a well-known path further north, passing near the celebrated hot springs (*Fontaines Chaudes*). You drive towards Au Prêcheur, and begin the ascent on foot, through cane-plantations... The road by which you follow the north-west coast round the skirts of Pelée is very picturesque;—you cross the Roxelane, the Rivière des Pères, the Rivière Sèche (whose bed is now occupied only by a motionless torrent of rocks);—passing first by the suburb of Fond-Corré, with its cocoa groves, and broad beach of iron-gray sand,—a bathing resort;—then Pointe Prince, and the Fond de Canonville, somnolent villages that occupy wrinkles in the hem of Pelée's lava robe. The drive ultimately rises and lowers over the undulations of the cliff, and is well shadowed along the greater part of its course: you will admire many huge *fromagers*, or silk-cotton trees, various heavy lines of tamarinds, and groups of *flamboyants* with thick dark feathery foliage, and cassia-trees with long pods pending and blackening from every branch, and hedges of *campêche*, or logwood, and calabash-trees, and multitudes of the pretty shrubs bearing the fruit called in creole *raisins-bò-lanmè* or "seaside grapes." Then you reach Au Prêcheur: a very antiquated village, which boasts a stone church and a little public square with a fountain in it. If you have time to cross the Rivière du Prêcheur, a little further on, you can obtain a fine view of the coast, which, rising suddenly to a grand altitude, sweeps round in a semicircle over the Village of the Abysses (*Aux Abymes*),—whose name was doubtless suggested by the immense depth of the sea at that point...

It was under the shadow of those cliffs that the Confederate cruiser *Alabama* once hid herself, as a fish hides in the shadow of a rock, and escaped from her pursuer, the *Iroquois*. She had long been blockaded in the harbor of St Pierre by the Northern man-of-war,—anxiously awaiting a chance to pounce upon her the instant she should leave French waters;—and various Yankee vessels in port were to send up rocket-signals should the *Alabama* attempt to escape under cover of darkness. But one night the privateer took a creole pilot on board, and steamed southward, with all her lights masked, and her chimneys so arranged that neither smoke nor sparks could betray her to the enemy in the offing. However, some Yankee vessels near enough to discern her movements through the darkness at once shot rockets south; and the *Iroquois* gave chase. The *Alabama* hugged the high shore as far as Carbet, remaining quite invisible in the shadow of it: then she suddenly turned and recrossed the harbor. Again Yankee rockets betrayed her manoeuvre to the *Iroquois*; but she gained Aux Abymes, laid herself close to the enormous black cliff, and there remained indistinguishable; the *Iroquois* steamed by north without seeing her. Once the Confederate cruiser found her enemy well out of sight, she put her pilot ashore and escaped into the Dominica channel. The pilot was a poor mulatto, who thought himself well paid with five hundred francs!

...The more popular route to Pelée by way of Morne Rouge is otherwise interesting... Anybody not too much afraid of the tropic sun must find it a delightful experience to follow the mountain roads leading to the interior from the city, as all the mornes traversed by them command landscapes of extraordinary beauty. According to the zigzags of the way, the scenery shifts panoramically. At one moment you are looking down into valleys a thousand feet below; at another, over luminous leagues of meadow or cane-field, you see some far crowding of cones and cratered shapes—sharp as the teeth of a saw, and blue as sapphire,—with further eminences ranging away through pearline color to high-peaked re-motenesses of vapory gold. As you follow the windings of such a way as the road of the Morne Labelle, or the Morne d'Orange, the city disappears and reappears many times,—always diminishing, till at last it looks no bigger than a chess-board. Simultaneously distant mountain shapes appear to unfold and lengthen;—and always, always the sea rises with your rising. Viewed at first from the bulwark (*boulevard*) commanding the roofs of the town, its horizon-line seemed straight and keen as a knife-edge;—but as you mount higher, it elongates, begins to curve; and gradually the whole azure expanse of water broadens out roundly like a disk. From certain very lofty summits further inland you behold the immense blue circle touching the sky all round you,—except where a still greater altitude, like that of Pelée or the Pitons, breaks the ring; and this high vision of the sea has a phantasmal effect hard to describe, and due to vapory conditions of the atmosphere. There are bright cloudless days when, even as seen from the city, the ocean-verge has a spectral vagueness; but on any day, in any season, that you ascend to a point dominating the sea by a thousand feet, the rim of the visible world takes a ghostliness that startles,—because the prodigious light gives to all near shapes such intense sharpness of outline and vividness of color.

Yet wonderful as are the perspective beauties of those mountain routes from which one can keep St. Pierre in view, the road to Morne Rouge surpasses them, notwithstanding that it almost immediately leaves the city behind, and out of sight. Excepting only *La Trace*,—the long route winding over mountain ridges and between primitive forests south to Fort-de-France,—there is probably no section of national highway in the island more remarkable than the Morne Rouge road. Leaving the Grande Rue by the public conveyance, you drive out through the Savane du Fort, with its immense mango and tamarind trees, skirting the Roxelane. Then reaching the boulevard, you pass high Morne Labelle,— and then the Jardin des Plantes on the right, where white-stemmed palms are lifting their heads two hundred feet,—and beautiful Parnasse, heavily timbered to the top;—while on your left the valley of the Roxelane shallows up, and Pelée shows less and less of its tremendous base. Then you pass through the sleepy, palmy, pretty Village of the Three Bridges (*Trois Ponts*),—where a Fahrenheit thermometer shows already three degree of temperature lower than at St. Pierre;—and the national road, making a sharp turn to the right, become all at once very steep—so steep that the horses can mount only at a walk. Around and between the wooded hills it ascends by zigzags,—occasionally overlooking the sea,—sometimes following the verges of ravines. Now and then you catch glimpses of the road over which you passed half an hour before undulating far below, looking narrow as a tape-line,—and of the gorge of the Roxelane,—and of Pelée, always higher, now thrusting out long spurs of green and purple land into the sea. You drive under cool shadowing of mountain woods— under waving bamboos like enormous ostrich feathers dyed green,—and exquisite tree-ferns thirty to forty feet high,—and imposing ceibas, with strangely buttressed trunks,—and all sorts of broad-leaved forms: cachibous, balisiers, bananiers... Then you reach a plateau covered with cane, whose yellow expanse is bounded on the right by a demilune of hills sharply angled as crystals;—on the left it dips seaward; and before you Pelée's head towers over the shoulders of intervening mornes. A strong cool wind is blowing; and the horses can trot a while. Twenty minutes, and the road, leaving the plateau, becomes steep again;—you are approaching the volcano over the ridge of a colossal spur. The way turns in a semicircle,—zigzags,—once more touches the edge of a valley,—where the clear fall might be nearly fifteen hundred feet. But narrowing more and more, the valley becomes an ascending gorge; and across its chasm, upon the brow of the opposite cliff, you catch sight of houses and a spire seemingly perched on the verge, like so many birds'-nests,—the village of Morne Rouge. It is two thousand feet above the sea; and Pelée although looming high over it, looks a trifle less lofty now.

One's first impression of Morne Rouge is that of a straggling street

Village of Morne Rouge, Martinique

of gray-painted cottages and shops (or rather booths), dominated by a plain church, with four pursy-bodied palmistes facing the main porch. Nevertheless, Morne Rouge is not a small place, considering its situation;—there are nearly five thousand inhabitants; but in order to find out where they live, you must leave the public road, which is on a ridge, and explore the high-hedged lanes leading down from it on either side. Then you will find a veritable city of little garden cottages,—each screened about with banana-trees, Indian-reeds, and *pommiers-roses*. You will also see a number of handsome private residences—country houses of wealthy merchants; and you will find that the church, though uninteresting exteriorly, is rich and impressive within: it is a famous shrine, where miracles are alleged to have been wrought. Immense processions periodically wend their way to it from St. Pierre,—starting at three or four o'clock in the morning, so as to arrive before the sun is well up... But there are no woods here,—only fields. An odd tone is given to the lanes by a local custom of planting hedges of what are termed *roseaux d'Inde*, having a dark-red foliage; and there is a visible fondness for ornamental plants with crimson leaves. Otherwise the mountain summit is somewhat bare; trees have a scrubby aspect. You must have noticed while ascending that the palmistes became smaller as they were situated higher: at Morne Rouge they are dwarfed,—having a short stature, and very thick trunks.

In spite of the fine views of the sea, the mountain-heights, and the valley reaches, obtainable from Morne Rouge, the place has a somewhat bleak look. Perhaps this is largely owing to the universal slate-gray tint of the buildings,—very melancholy by comparison with the apricot and banana yellows tinting the walls of St. Pierre. But this cheerless gray is the only color which can resist the climate of Morne Rouge, where people are literally dwelling in the clouds. Rolling down like white smoke from Pelée, these often create a dismal fog; and Morne Rouge is certainly one of the rainiest places in the world. When it is dry everywhere else, it rains at Morne Rouge. It rains at least three hundred and sixty days and three hundred and sixty nights of the year. It rains almost invariably once in every twenty-four hours; but oftener five or six times. The dampness is phenomenal. All mirrors become patchy; linen moulds in one day; leather turns white; woollen goods feel as if saturated with moisture; new brass becomes green; steel crumbles into red powder: wood-work rots with astonishing rapidity; salt is quickly transformed into brine; and matches, unless kept in a very warm place, refuse to light. Everything moulders and peels and decomposes; even the frescos of the church-interior lump out in immense blisters; and a microscopic vegetation, green or brown, attacks all exposed surfaces of timber or stone. At night it is often really cold;—and it is hard to understand how, with all this dampness and coolness and mouldiness, Morne Rouge can be a healthy place. But it is so, beyond any question: it is the great Martinique resort for invalids; strangers debilitated by the climate of Trinidad or Cayenne come to it for recuperation.

Leaving the village by the still uprising road, you will be surprised, after a walk of twenty minutes northward by a magnificent view,—the vast valley of the Champ-Flore, watered by many torrents, and bounded south and west by double, triple, and quadruple surging of mountains,—mountains broken, peaked, tormented-looking and tinted (*irisées*, as the creoles say) with all those gemstones distance gives in a West Indian atmosphere. Particularly impressive is the beauty of one purple cone in the midst of this many-colored chain: the Piton Gélé. All the valley-expanse of rich land is checkered with alternations of meadow and cane and cacao,—except north-westwardly, where woods billow out of sight beyond a curve. Facing this landscape, on your left, are mornes of various heights,—among which you will notice La Calebasse, overtopping everything but Pelée shadowing behind it;—and a grass-grown road leads up westward from the national highway towards the volcano. This is the Calebasse route to Pelée.

III

ONE must be very sure of the weather before undertaking the ascent of Pelée; for if one merely selects some particular leisure day in advance, one's chances of seeing anything from the summit are considerably less than an astronomer's chances of being able to make a satisfactory observation of the next transit of Venus. Moreover, if the heights remain even partly clouded, it may not be safe to ascend the Morne de la Croix,—a cone-point above the crater itself, and ordinarily invisible from below. And a cloudless afternoon can never be predicated from the aspect of deceitful Pelée: when the crater edges are quite clearly cut against the sky at dawn, you may be tolerably certain there will be bad weather during the day; and when they are all bare at sundown, you have no good reason to believe they will not be hidden next morning. Hundreds of tourists, deluded by such appearances, have made the weary trip in vain,—found themselves obliged to return without having seen anything but a thick white cold fog. The sky may remain perfectly blue for weeks in every other direction, and Pelée's head remain always hidden. In order to make a successful ascent one must not wait for a period of dry weather,—one might thus wait for years! What one must look for is a certain periodicity in the diurnal rains,—a regular alternation of sun and cloud; such as characterizes a certain portion of the *hivernage* or rainy summer season, when mornings and evenings are perfectly limpid, with very heavy sudden rains in the middle of the day. It is of no use to rely on the prospect of a dry spell. There is no really dry weather, notwithstanding there recurs—in books—a *Saison de la Sécheresse*. In fact, there are no distinctly marked seasons in Martinique:—a little less heat and rain from October to July, a little more rain and heat from July to October: that is about all the notable difference! Perhaps the official notification by cannon-shot that the hivernage, the season of heavy rains and hurricanes, begins on July 15th, is no more trustworthy than the contradictory declarations of Martinique authors who have attempted to define the vague and illusive limits of the tropic seasons. Still, the Government report on the subject is more satisfactory than any: according to the "Annuaire," there are these seasons:—

1. *Saison fraîche.* December to March. Rainfall, about 475 millimetres.
2. *Saison chaude et sèche.* April to July. Rainfall, about 140 millimetres.

3. *Saison chaude et pluvieuse.* July to November. Rainfall average, 1121 millimetres.

Other authorities divide the *saison chaude et sèche* into two periods, of which the latter, beginning about May, is called the *Renouveau*; and it is at least true that at the time indicated there is a great burst of vegetal luxuriance. But there is always rain, there are almost always clouds, there is no possibility of marking and dating the beginnings and the endings of weather in this country where the barometer is almost useless, and the thermometer mounts in the sun to twice the figure it reaches in the shade. Long and patient observation has, however, established the fact that during the hivernage, if the heavy showers have a certain fixed periodicity,—falling at midday or in the heated part of the afternoon,—Pelée, is likely to be clear early in the morning; and by starting before daylight one can then have good chances of a fine view from the summit.

IV

AT five o'clock of a September morning, warm and starry, I leave St. Pierre in a carriage with several friends, to make the ascent by the shortest route of all,—that of the Morne St. Martin, one of Pelée's west counterforts. We drive north along the shore for about half an hour; then, leaving the coast behind, pursue a winding mountain road, leading to the upper plantations, between leagues of cane. The sky begins to brighten as we ascend, and a steely glow announces that day has begun on the other side of the island. Miles up, the crest of the volcano cuts sharp as a saw-edge against the growing light: there is not a cloud visible. Then the light slowly yellows behind the vast cone; and one of the most beautiful dawns I ever saw reveals on our right an immense valley through which three rivers flow. This deepens very quickly as we drive; the mornes about St. Pierre, beginning to catch the light, sink below us in distance; and above them, southwardly, an amazing silhouette begins to rise,—all blue,—a mountain wall capped with cusps and cones, seeming high as Pelée itself in the middle, but sinking down to the sea-level westward. There are a number of extraordinary acuminations; but the most impressive shape is the nearest,—a tremendous conoidal mass crowned with a group of peaks, of which two, taller than the rest, tell their name at once by the beauty of their forms,—the Pitons of Carbet. They wear their girdles of cloud, though Pelée is naked today. All this is blue: the growing light only deepens the color, does not dissipate it;—but in the nearer valleys gleams of tender yellowish green begin to appear. Still the sun has not been able to show himself;—it will take him some time yet to climb Pelée.

Reaching the last plantation, we draw rein in a village of small wooden cottages, the quarters of the field hands,—and receive from the proprietor, a personal friend of my friends, the kindest welcome. At his house we change clothing and prepare for the journey;—he provides for our horses, and secures experienced guides for us,—two young colored men belonging to the plantation. Then we begin the ascent. The guides walk before, barefoot, each carrying a cutlass in his hand and a package on his head—our provisions, photographic instruments, etc.

The mountain is cultivated in spots up to twenty-five hundred feet; and for three-quarters of an hour after leaving the planter's residence we still traverse fields of cane and of manioc. The light is now strong in the valley; but we are in the shadow of Pelée. Cultivated fields end at last; the ascending path is through wild cane, wild guavas, guinea-grass run mad, and other tough growths, some bearing pretty pink blossoms. The forest is before us. Startled by our approach, a tiny fer-de-lance glides out from a bunch of dead wild-cane, almost under the bare feet of our foremost guide, who as instantly decapitates it with a touch of his cutlass. It is not quite fifteen inches long, and almost the color of the yellowish leaves under which it had been hiding... The conversation turns on snakes as we make our first halt at the verge of the woods.

Hundreds may he hiding around us; but a snake never shows himself by daylight except under the pressure of sudden alarm. We are not likely, in the opinion of all present, to meet with another. Every one in the party, except myself, has some curious experience to relate. I hear for the first time about the alleged inability of the trigonocephalus to wound except at a distance from his enemy of not less than one-third of his length;—about M. A—, a former director of the Jardin des Plantes, who used to boldly thrust his arm into holes where he knew snakes were, and pull them out,—catching them just behind the head and wrapping the tail round his arm,—and place them alive in a cage without ever getting bitten;—about M. B—, who, while hunting one day, tripped in the coils of an immense trigonocephalus, and ran so fast in his fright that the serpent, entangled round his leg, could not bite him;—about M. C—, who could catch a fer-de-lance by the tail, and "crack it like a whip" until the head would fly off;—about an old white man living in the Champ-

Flore, whose diet was snake meat, and who always kept in his ajoupa "a keg of salted serpents" (*yon ka sèpent-salè*);—about a monster eight feet long which killed, near Morne Rouge, M. Charles Fabre's white cat, but was also killed by the cat after she had been caught in the folds of the reptile;—about the value of snakes as protectors of the sugar-cane and cocoa-shrub against rats;—about an unsuccessful effort made, during a plague of rats in Guadeloupe, to introduce the fer-de-lance there;—about the alleged power of a monstrous toad, the *crapud-ladre*, to cause the death of the snake that swallows it;—and, finally, about the total absence of the idyllic and pastoral elements in Martinique literature, as due to the presence of reptiles everywhere. "Even the flora and fauna of the country remain to a large extent unknown,"—adds the last speaker, an amiable old physician of St. Pierre,—"because the existence of the fer-de-lance renders all serious research dangerous in the extreme."

My own experiences do not justify my taking part in such a conversation;—I never saw alive but two small specimens of the trigonocephalus. People who have passed even a considerable time in Martinique may have never seen a fer-de-lance except in a jar of alcohol, or as exhibited by negro snake-catchers, tied fast to a bamboo. But this is only because strangers rarely travel much in the interior of the country, or find themselves on country roads after sundown. It is not correct to suppose that snakes are uncommon even in the neighborhood of St. Pierre: they are often killed on the bulwarks behind the city and on the verge of the Savane; they have been often washed into the streets by heavy rains; and many washer-women at the Roxelane have been bitten by them. It is considered very dangerous to walk about the bulwarks after dark;—the snakes, which travel only at night, then descend from the mornes towards the river. The Jardin des Plantes shelters great numbers of the reptiles; and only a few days prior to the writing of these lines a colored laborer in the garden was stricken and killed by a fer-de-lance measuring one metre and sixty-seven centimetres in length. In the interior much larger reptiles are sometimes seen: I saw one freshly killed measuring six feet five inches, and thick as a man's leg in the middle. There are few planters in the island who have not some of their hands bitten during the cane-cutting and cocoa-gathering seasons;—the average annual mortality among the class of *travailleurs* from serpent bite alone is probably fifty[5],—always fine young men or women in the prime of life. Even among the wealthy whites deaths from this cause are less rare than might be supposed: I know one gentleman, a rich citizen of St.

Pierre, who in ten years lost three relatives by the trigonocephalus,—the wound having in each case been received in the neighbourhood of a vein. When the vein has been pierced, cure is impossible.

V

...WE look back over the upreaching yellow fan-spread of cane-fields, and winding of tortuous valleys, and the sea expanding beyond an opening in the west. It has already broadened surprisingly, the sea,— appears to have risen up, not as a horizontal plane, but like an immeasurable azure precipice: what will it look like when we shall have reached the top? Far down we can distinguish a line of field-hands—the whole *atelier*, as it is called, of a plantation—slowly descending a slope, hewing the canes as they go. There is a woman to every two men, a binder (*amarreuse*): she gathers the canes as they are cut down, binds them with their own tough long leaves into a sort of sheaf, and carries them away on her head;—the men wield their cutlasses so beautifully that it is a delight to watch them. One cannot often enjoy such a spectacle nowadays; for the introduction of the piece-work system has destroyed the picturesqueness of plantation labor throughout the island, with rare exceptions. Formerly the work of cane-cutting resembled the march of an army;—first advanced the cutlassers in line, naked to the waist; then the amarreuses, the women who tied and carried; and behind these the *ka*, the drum,—with a paid *crieur* or *crieuse* to lead the song;— and lastly the black Commandeur, for general. And in the old days, too, it was not infrequent that the sudden descent of an English corsair on the coast converted this soldiery of labor into veritable military: more than one attack was repelled by the cutlasses of a plantation atelier.

At this height the chatting and chanting can be heard, though not distinctly enough to catch the words. Suddenly a voice, powerful as a bugle, rings out,—the voice of the Commandeur: he walks along the line, looking, with his cutlass under his arm. I ask one of the guides what the cry is:—

—"*Y ka coumandé yo pouend gàde pou sèpent,*" he replies. (He is telling them to keep watch for serpents.) The nearer the cutlassers approach the end of their task, the greater the danger: for the reptiles, retreating before them to the last clump of cane, become massed there and will fight desperately. Regularly as the ripening-time, Death gathers his toll of human lives from among the workers. But when one falls, another steps into the vacant place,—perhaps the Commandeur himself: these dark swordsmen never retreat; all the blades swing swiftly as before; there is hardly any emotion; the travailleur is a fatalist...[6]

VI

...WE enter the *grands-bois*,—the primitive forest,—the "high woods."

As seen with a field-glass from St. Pierre, these woods present only the appearance of a band of moss belting the volcano, and following all its corrugations,—so densely do the leafy crests intermingle. But on actually entering them, you find yourself at once in green twilight, among lofty trunks uprising everywhere like huge pillars wrapped with vines;—and the interspaces between these bulks are all occupied by lianas and parasitic creepers,—some monstrous,—veritable parasite-trees,— ascending at all angles, or dropping straight down from the tallest crests to take root again. The effect in the dim light is that of innumerable black ropes and cables of varying thickness stretched taut from the soil to the tree-tops, and also from branch to branch, like rigging. There are rare and remarkable trees here,—acomats, courbarils, balatas, ceibas or fromagers, acajous, gommiers;—hundreds have been cut down by charcoal-makers; but the forest is still grand. It is to be regretted that the Government has placed no restriction upon the barbarous destruction of trees by the *charbonniers*, which is going on throughout the island. Many valuable woods are rapidly disappearing. The courbaril, yielding a fine-grained, heavy, chocolate-coloured timber; the balata, giving a wood even heavier, denser, and darker; the acajou, producing a rich red wood, with a strong scent of cedar; the bois-de-fer; the bois d'Inde; the superb acomat,—all used to flourish by tens of thousands upon these volcanic slopes, whose productiveness is eighteen times greater than that of European soil. All Martinique furniture used to be made of native woods; and the colored cabinet-makers still produce work which would probably astonish New York or London manufacturers. But today the island exports no more hard woods: it has even been found necessary to import much from neighboring islands;—and yet the destruction of the forests still goes on. The domestic fabrication of charcoal from forest areas has been estimated at 1,400,000 hectolitres per annum. Primitive forest still covers the island to the extent of 21.37 per cent; but to find precious woods now, one must climb heights like those of Pelée and Carbet, or penetrate into the mountains of the interior.

La Montaigne Pelée, as seen from Grande Anse

Most common formerly on these slopes were the gommiers, from which canoes of a single piece, forty-five feet long by seven wide, used to be made. There are plenty of gommiers still; but the difficulty of transporting them to the shore has latterly caused a demand for the gommiers of Dominica. The dimensions of canoes now made from these trees rarely exceed fifteen feet in length by eighteen inches in width: the art of making them is an inheritance from the ancient Caribs. First the trunk is shaped to the form of the canoe, and pointed at both ends; it is then hollowed out. The width of the hollow does not exceed six inches at the widest part; but the cavity is then filled with wet sand, which in the course of some weeks widens the excavation by its weight, and gives the boat perfect form. Finally gunwales of plank are fastened on; seats are put in—generally four;—and no boat is more durable nor more swift.

…We climb. There is a trace rather than a footpath;—no visible soil, only vegetable detritus, with roots woven over it in every direction. The foot never rests on a flat surface,—only upon surfaces of roots; and these are covered, like every protruding branch along the route, with a slimy green moss, slippery as ice. Unless accustomed to walking in tropical woods, one will fall at every step. In a little while I find it impossible to advance. Our nearest guide, observing my predicament, turns, and without moving the bundle upon his head, cuts and trims me an excellent staff with a few strokes of his cutlass. This staff not only saves me from dangerous slips, but serves at times to probe the way; for the further we proceed, the vaguer the path becomes. It was made by the *chasseurs-de-choux* (cabbage-hunters),—the negro mountaineers who live by furnishing heads of young cabbage-palm to the city markets; and these men also keep it open,—otherwise the woods would grow over it in a month. Two chasseurs-de-choux stride past us as we advance, with their freshly gathered palm-salad upon their heads, wrapped in cachibou or balisier leaves, and tied with lianas. The palmiste-franc easily reaches a stature of one hundred feet; but the young trees are so eagerly sought for by the chasseurs-de-choux that in these woods few reach a height of even twelve feet before being cut.

...Walking becomes more difficult;—there seems no termination to the grands-bois: always the same faint green light, the same rude natural stair-way of slippery roots,—half the time hidden by fern leaves and vines. Sharp ammoniacal scents are in the air; a dew, cold as ice-water, drenches our clothing. Unfamiliar insects make trilling noises in dark places; and now and then soft clear notes ring out, almost like a thrush's whistle: the chant of a little tree-frog. The path becomes more and more overgrown; and but for the constant excursions of the cabbage-hunters, we should certainly have to cutlass every foot of the way through creepers and brambles. More and more amazing also is the interminable interweaving of roots: the whole forest is thus spun together—not underground so much as overground. These tropical trees do not strike deep, although able to climb steep slopes of porphyry and basalt: they send out great far-reaching webs of roots,—each such web interknotting with others all round it, and these in turn with further ones; while between their reticulations lianas ascend and descend: and a nameless multitude of shrubs as tough as india-rubber push up, together with mosses, grasses, and ferns. Square miles upon square miles of woods are thus interlocked and interbound into one mass solid enough to resist the pressure of a hurricane; and where there is no path already made, entrance into them can only be effected by the most dexterous cutlassing.

An inexperienced stranger might be puzzled to understand how this cutlassing is done. It is no easy feat to sever with one blow a liana thick as a man's arm; the trained cutlasser does it without apparent difficulty: moreover, he cuts horizontally, so as to prevent the severed top presenting a sharp angle and proving afterwards dangerous. He never appears to strike hard,—only to give light taps with his blade, which flickers continually about him as he moves. Our own guides in cutlassing are not at all inconvenienced by their loads; they walk perfectly upright, never stumble, never slip, never hesitate, and do not even seem to perspire: their bare feet are prehensile. Some creoles in our party, habituated to the woods, walk nearly as well in their shoes; but they carry no loads.

...At last we are rejoiced to observe that the trees are becoming smaller;—there are no more colossal trunks;—there are frequent glimpses of sky: the sun has risen well above the peaks, and sends occasional beams down through the leaves. Ten minutes, and we reach a clear space,—a wild savane, very steep, above which looms a higher belt of woods. Here we take another short rest.

Northward the view is cut off by a ridge covered with herbaceous vegetation;—but to the south-west it is open, over a gorge of which both sides are shrouded in sombre-green—crests of trees forming a solid curtain against the sun. Beyond the outer and lower cliff valley-surfaces appear miles away, flinging up broad gleams of cane-gold; further off greens disappear into blues, and the fantastic masses of Carbet loom up far higher than before. St. Pierre, in a curve of the coast, is a little red-and-yellow semicircular streak, less than two inches long. The interspaces between far mountain chains,—masses of pyramids, cones, single and double humps, queer blue angles as of raised knees under coverings,—resemble misty lakes: they are filled with brume;—the sea-line has vanished altogether. Only the horizon, enormously heightened, can be discerned as a circling band of faint yellowish light,—auroral, ghostly,—almost on a level with the tips of the Pitons. Between this vague horizon and the shore, the sea no longer looks like a second hollow sky reversed. All the landscape has unreal beauty:—there are no keen lines; no definite beginnings or endings; the tints are half-colors only;—peaks rise suddenly from mysteries of bluish fog as from a flood; land melts into sea the same hue. It gives one the idea of some great aquarelle unfinished,—abandoned before tones were deepened and details brought out.

VII

...WE are overlooking from this height the birthplaces of several rivers; and the rivers of Pelée are the clearest and the coolest of the island.

From whatever direction the trip be undertaken, the ascent of the volcano must be made over some one of those many immense ridges sloping from the summit to the sea west, north, and east,—like buttresses eight to ten miles long,—formed by ancient lava-torrents. Down the deep gorges between them the cloud-fed rivers run,—receiving as they descend the waters of countless smaller streams gushing from either side of the ridge. There are also cold springs,—one of which furnishes St. Pierre with her *Eau-de-Gouyave* (guava-water), which is always sweet, clear, and cool in the very hottest weather. But the water of almost every one of the seventy-five principal rivers of Martinique is cool and clear and sweet. And these rivers are curious in their way. Their average fall has been estimated at nine inches to every six feet;—many are cataracts;—the Rivière de Case-Navire has a fall of nearly 150 feet to every fifty yards of its upper course. Naturally these streams cut for themselves channels of immense depth. Where they flow through forests and between mornes, their banks vary from 1,200 to 1,600 feet high,—so as to render their beds inaccessible; and many enter the sea through a channel of rock with perpendicular walls from 150 to 200 feet high. Their waters are necessarily shallow in normal weather; but during rain-storms they become torrents thunderous and terrific beyond description. In order to comprehend their sudden swelling, one must know what tropical rain is. Col. Boyer Peyreleau, in 1823, estimated the annual rainfall in these colonies at 150 inches on the coast, to 350 on the mountains,—while the annual fall at Paris was only eighteen inches. The character of such rain is totally different from that of rain in the temperate zone: the drops are enormous, heavy like hailstones,—one will spatter over the circumference of a saucer!—and the shower roars so that people cannot hear each other speak without shouting. When there is a true storm, no roofing seems able to shut out the cataract; the best-built houses leak in all directions; and objects but a short distance off become invisible behind the heavy curtain of water. The ravages of such rain may be imagined! Roads are cut away in an hour; trees are overthrown as if blown down;—for there are few West Indian trees which plunge their roots even as low as two feet; they merely extend them over a large diameter; and isolated trees will actually slide under rain. The swelling of rivers is so sudden that washerwomen at work in the Roxelane and other streams have been swept away and drowned without the least warning of their danger; the shower occurring seven or eight miles off.

Most of these rivers are well stocked with fish, of which the *tétart*, *banane*, *loche*, and *dormeur* are the principal varieties. The tétart (best of all) and the loche climb the torrents to the height of 2500 and even

3000 feet: they have a kind of pneumatic sucker, which enables them to cling to rocks. Under stones in the lower basins crawfish of the most extraordinary size are taken; some will measure thirty-six inches from claw to tail. And at all the river-mouths, during July and August, are caught vast numbers of *titiri* [7],—tiny white fish, of which a thousand might be put into one teacup. They are delicious when served in oil,—infinitely more delicate than the sardine. Some regard them as particular species: others believe them to be only the fry of larger fish,—as their periodical appearance and disappearance would seem to indicate. They are often swept by millions into the city of St. Pierre, with the flow of mountain water which purifies the streets: then you will see them swarming in the gutters, fountains, and bathing-basins;—and on Saturdays, when the water is temporarily shut off to allow of the pipes being cleansed, the titiri may die in the gutters in such numbers as to make the air offensive.

The mountain-crab, celebrated for its periodical migrations, is also found at considerable heights. Its numbers appear to have been diminished extraordinarily by its consumption as an article of negro diet; but in certain islands those armies of crabs described by the old writers are still occasionally to be seen. The Père Dutertre relates that in 1640, at St. Christophe, thirty sick emigrants, temporarily left on the beach, were attacked and devoured alive during the night by a similar species of crab. "They descended from the mountains in such multitude," he tells us, "that they were higher than houses over the bodies of the poor wretches... whose bones were picked so clean that not one speck of flesh could be found upon them."...

VIII

...WE enter the upper belt of woods—green twilight again. There are as many lianas as ever: but they are less massive in stem;—the trees, which are stunted, stand close together; and the web-work of roots is finer and more thickly spun. These are called the *petits-bois* (little woods), in contradistinction to the grand-bois, or high woods. Multitudes of balisiers, dwarf-palms, arborescent ferns, wild guavas, mingle with the lower growths on either side of the path, which is narrowed to the breadth of a wheel-rut, and is nearly concealed by protruding grasses and fern leaves. Never does the sole of the foot press upon a surface large as itself,—always the slippery backs of roots crossing at all angles, like

Arborescent Ferns on a Mountain Road

loop-traps, over sharp fragments of volcanic rock or pumice-stone. There are abrupt descents, sudden acclivities, mud-holes, and fissures;— one grasps at the ferns on both sides to keep from falling; and some ferns are spiked sometimes on the under surface, and tear the hands. But the barefooted guides stride on rapidly, erect as ever under their loads,— chopping off with their cutlasses any branches that hang too low. There are beautiful flowers here,—various unfamiliar species of lobelia;— pretty red and yellow blossoms belonging to plants which the creole physician calls *Bromeliaceae*; and a plant like the *Guy Lussacia* of Brazil, with violet-red petals. There is an indescribable multitude of ferns,—a very museum of ferns! The doctor, who is a great woodsman, says that he never makes a trip to the hills without finding some new kind of fern; and he had already a collection of several hundred.

The route is continually growing steeper, and makes a number of turns and windings: we reach another bit of savane, where we have to walk over black-pointed stones that resemble slag;—then more petits-bois, still more dwarfed, then another opening. The naked crest of the volcano appears like a peaked precipice, dark-red, with streaks of green, over a narrow but terrific chasm on the left: we are almost on a level with the crater, but must make a long circuit to reach it, through a wilderness of stunted timber and bush. The creoles call this undergrowth *razié*: — it is really only a prolongation of the low jungle which carpets the high forests below, with this difference, that there are fewer creepers and much more fern... Suddenly we reach a black gap in the path about thirty inches wide—half hidden by the tangle of leaves,—*La Fente*. It is a volcanic fissure which divides the whole ridge, and is said to have no bottom: for fear of a possible slip the guides insist upon holding our hands while we cross it. Happily there are no more such clefts; but there are mud-holes, snags, roots, and loose rocks beyond counting. Least disagreeable are the *bourbiers*, in which you sink to your knees in black or gray slime. Then the path descends into open light again;—and we find ourselves at the Étang,—in the dead Crater of the Three Palmistes.

An immense pool, completely encircled by high green walls of rock, which shut out all further view, and shoot up, here and there, into cones, or rise into queer lofty bumps and knobs. One of these elevations at the opposite side has almost the shape of a blunt horn: it is the Morne de la Croix. The scenery is at once imposing and sinister: the shapes towering above the lake and reflected in its still surface have the weirdness of things seen in photographs of the moon. Clouds are circling above them and between them;—one descends to the water, haunts us a moment, blurring everything; then rises again. We have travelled too slow; the clouds have had time to gather.

I look in vain for the Three Palmistes which gave the crater a name: they were destroyed long ago. But there are numbers of young ones scattered through the dense ferny covering of the lake-slopes,—just showing their heads like bunches of great dark-green feathers.

—The estimate of Dr. Rufz, made in 1851, and the estimate of the last "Annuaire" regarding the circumference of the lake, are evidently both at fault. That of the "Annuaire," 150 metres, is a gross error: the writer must have meant the diameter,—following Rufz, who estimated the circumference at something over 300 paces. As we find it, the Étang, which is nearly circular, must measure 200 yards across;—perhaps it has been greatly swollen by the extraordinary rains of this summer. Our guides say that the little iron cross projecting from the water about two yards off was high and dry on the shore last season. At present there is only one narrow patch of grassy bank on which we can rest, between the water and the walls of the crater.

The lake is perfectly clear, with a bottom of yellowish shallow mud, which rests—according to investigations made in 1851—upon a mass of pumice-stone mixed in places with ferruginous sand; and the yellow mud itself is a detritus of pumice-stone. We strip for a swim.

Though at an elevation of nearly 5,000 feet, this water is not so cold as that of the Roxelane, nor of other rivers of the north-west and north-east coasts. It has an agreeable fresh taste, like dew. Looking down into it, I see many larvae of the *maringouin*, or large mosquito: no fish. The maringouins themselves are troublesome,—whirring around us and stinging. On striking out for the middle, one is surprised to feel the water growing slightly warmer. The committee of investigation in 1851 found the temperature of the lake, in spite of a north wind, 20.5° Centigrade, while that of the air was but 19° (about 69°F for the water, and 66.2° for the air). The depth in the centre is over six feet; the average is scarcely four.

Regaining the bank, we prepare to ascend the Morne de la Croix. The circular path by which it is commonly reached is now under water; and we have to wade up to our waists. All the while clouds keep passing over us in great slow whirls. Some are white and half-transparent; others opaque and dark gray;—a dark cloud passing through a white one looks like a goblin. Gaining the opposite shore, we find a very rough path over splintered stone, ascending between the thickest fern-growths possible to imagine. The general tone of this fern is dark green; but there are paler cloudings of yellow and pink,—due to the varying age of the leaves, which are pressed into a cushion three or four feet high, and almost solid enough to sit upon. About two hundred and fifty yards from the crater edge, the path rises above this tangle, and zigzags up the morne, which now appears twice as lofty as from the lake, where we had a curiously foreshortened view of it. It then looked scarcely a hundred feet high; it is more than double that. The cone is green to the top with moss, low grasses, small fern, and creeping pretty plants, like violets, with big carmine flowers. The path is a black line: the rock laid bare by it looks as if burned to the core. We have now to use our hands in climbing; but the low thick ferns give a good hold. Out of breath, and drenched in perspiration, we reach the apex,—the highest point of the island. But we are curtained about with clouds,—moving in dense white and gray masses: we cannot see fifty feet away.

The top of the peak has a slightly slanting surface of perhaps twenty square yards, very irregular in outline;—southwardly the morne pitches sheer into a frightful chasm, between the converging of two of those long corrugated ridges already described as buttressing the volcano on all sides. Through a cloud-rift we can see another crater-lake twelve hundred feet below—said to be five times larger than the Étang we have just left: it is also of more irregular outline. This is called the *Étang Sec*, or "Dry Pool," because dry in less rainy seasons. It occupies a more ancient crater, and is very rarely visited: the path leading to it is difficult and dangerous,—a natural ladder of roots and lianas over a series of precipices. Behind us the Crater of the Three Palmistes now looks no larger than the surface on which we stand;—over its further boundary we can see the wall of another gorge, in which there is a third crater-lake. West and north are green peakings, ridges, and high lava walls steep as fortifications. All this we can only note in the intervals between passing of clouds. As yet there is no landscape visible southward;—we sit down and wait.

IX

...Two crosses are planted nearly at the verge of the precipice; a small one of iron; and a large one of wood—probably the same put up by the Abbé Lespinasse during the panic of 1851, after the eruption. This has been splintered to pieces by a flash of lightning; and the fragments are clumsily united with cord. There is also a little tin plate let into a slit in a black post: it bears a date,—*8 Avril,* 1867... The volcanic vents, which were active in 1851, are not visible from the peak: they are in the gorge descending from it, at a point nearly on a level with the Étang Sec.

The ground gives out a peculiar hollow sound when tapped, and is covered with a singular lichen,—all composed of round overlapping leaves about one-eighth of an inch in diameter, pale green, and tough as fish-scales. Here and there one sees a beautiful branching growth, like a mass of green coral: it is a gigantic moss. *Cabane-Jésus* ("bed of-Jesus") the patois name is: at Christmas-time, in all the churches, those decorated cribs in which the image of the Child-Saviour is laid are filled with it. The creeping crimson violet is also here. Fire-flies with bronze-green bodies are crawling about;—I notice also small frogs, large gray crickets, and a species of snail with a black shell. A solitary humming-bird passes, with a beautiful blue head, flaming like sapphire.

All at once the peak vibrates to a tremendous sound from somewhere below... It is only a peal of thunder; but it startled at first, because the mountain rumbles and grumbles occasionally... From the wilderness of ferns about the lake a sweet long low whistle comes—three times;—a *siffleur-de-montagne* has its nest there.

There is a rain-storm over the woods beneath us: clouds now hide everything but the point on which we rest; the crater of the Palmistes becomes invisible. But it is only for a little while that we are thus befogged: a wind comes, blows the clouds over us, lifts them up and folds them like a drapery, and slowly whirls them away northward. And for the first time the view is clear over the intervening gorge,—now spanned by the rocket-leap of a perfect rainbow.

...Valleys and mornes, peaks and ravines,—succeeding each other swiftly as surge succeeds surge in a storm,—a weirdly tossed world, but beautiful as it weird: all green the foreground, with all tints of green, shadowing off to billowy distances of purest blue. The sea-line remains invisible as ever: you know where it is only by the zone of pale light ringing the double sphericity of sky and ocean. And in this double blue void the island seems to hang suspended: far peaks seem to come up from nowhere, to rest on nothing—like forms of mirage. Useless to attempt photography:—distances take the same color as the sea. Vauclin's truncated mass is recognizable only by the shape of indigo shadows. All is vague, vertiginous;—the land still seems to quiver with the prodigious forces that up-heaved it.

High over all this billowing and peaking tower the Pitons of Carbet, gem-violet through the vapored miles,—the tallest one filleted with a single soft white band of cloud. Through all the wonderful chain of the Antilles you might seek in vain for other peaks exquisite of form as these. Their beauty no less surprises the traveller today than it did Columbus three hundred and eighty-six years ago, when—on the thirteenth day of June, 1502—his caravel first sailed into sight of them, and he asked his Indian guide the name of the unknown land, and the names of those marvellous shapes. Then, according to Pedro Martyr de Anghiera, the Indian answered that the name of the island was Madiana; that those peaks had been venerated from immemorial time by the ancient peoples of the archipelago as the birthplace of the human race; and that the first brown habitants of Madiana, having been driven from their natural heritage by the man-eating pirates of the south—the cannibal Caribs,— remembered and mourned for their sacred mountains, and gave the names of them, for a memory, to the loftiest summits of their new home,—Hayti... Surely never was fairer spot hallowed by the legend of man's nursing-place than the valley blue-shadowed by those peaks,— worthy, for their gracious femininity of shape, to seem the visible breasts of the All-nourishing Mother,—dreaming under this tropic sun.

Touching the zone of pale light north-east, appears a beautiful peaked silhouette,—Dominica. We had hoped to perceive Saint Lucia; but the atmosphere is too heavily charged with vapor today. How magnificent must be the view on certain extraordinary days, when it reaches from Antigua to the Grenadines—over a range of three hundred miles! But the atmospheric conditions which allow of such a spectacle are rare indeed. As a general rule, even in the most unclouded West Indian weather, the loftiest peaks fade into the light at a distance of one hundred miles.

A sharp ridge covered with fern cuts off the view of the northern slopes: one must climb it to look down upon Macouba. Macouba occupies the steepest slope of Pelée, and the grimmest part of the coast: its little *chef-lieu* is industrially famous for the manufacture of native tobacco, and historically for the ministrations of Père Labat, who rebuilt its church. Little change has taken place in the parish since his time. "Do you know Macouba?" asks a native writer;—"it is not Pelion upon Ossa, but ten or twelve Pelions side by side with ten or twelve Ossae, interseparated by prodigious ravines. Men can speak to each other from places whence, by rapid walking, it would require hours to meet;—to travel there is to experience on dry land the sensation of the sea."

With the diminution of the warmth provoked by the exertion of climbing, you begin to notice how cool it feels;—you could almost doubt the testimony of your latitude. Directly east is Senegambia: we are well south of Timbuktoo and the Sahara,—on a line with southern India. The ocean has cooled the winds; at this altitude the rarity of the air is northern;—but in the valleys below the vegetation is African. The best alimentary plants, the best forage, the flowers of the gardens, are of Guinea;—the graceful date-palms are from the Atlas region: those tamarinds, whose thick shade stifles all other vegetal life beneath it, are from Senegal. Only, in the touch of the air, the vapory colors of distance, the shapes of the hills, there is a something not of Africa: that strange fascination which has given to the island its poetic creole name,—*Le Pays des Revenants*. And the charm is as puissant in our own day as it was more than two hundred years ago, when Père Dutertre wrote:—"I have never met one single man, nor one single woman, of all those who came back therefrom, in whom I have not remarked a most passionate desire to return thereunto."

Time and familiarity do not weaken the charm, either for those born among these scenes who never voyaged beyond their native island, or for those to whom the streets of Paris and the streets of St. Pierre are equally well known. Even at a time when Martinique had been forsaken by hundreds of her ruined planters, and the paradise-life of the old days had become only a memory to embitter exile,—a Creole writes:—

—"Let there suddenly open before you one of those vistas, or *anses*, with colonnades of cocoa-palm—at the end of which you see smoking the chimney of a sugar-mill, and catch a glimpse of the hamlet of negro cabins (*cases*);—or merely picture to yourself one of the ordinary, most trivial scenes: nets being hauled by two ranks of fishermen; a *canot* waiting for the *embellie* to make a dash for the beach; even a negro bending under the weight of a basket of fruit; and running along the shore to get to market;—and illuminate that with the light of our sun! What landscapes!—O Salvator Rosa! O Claude Lorrain,—if I had your pencil !... Well do I remember the day on which, after twenty years of absence, I found myself again in presence of these wonders;—I feel once more the thrill of delight that made all my body tremble, the tears that came to my eyes. It was my land, my own land, that appeared so beautiful."...[7]

X

AT the beginning, while gazing south, east, west, to the rim of the world, all laughed, shouted, interchanged the quick delight of new impressions: every face was radiant... Now all look serious;—none speak. The first physical joy of finding oneself on this point in violet air, exalted above the hills, soon yields to other emotions inspired by the mighty vision and the colossal peace of the heights. Dominating all, I think, is the consciousness of the awful antiquity of what one is looking upon,—such a sensation, perhaps, as of old found utterance in that tremendous question of the Book of Job:—" *Wast thou brought forth before the hills?*" ... And the blue multitude of the peaks, the perpetual congregation of the mornes, seem to chorus in the vast resplendence,— telling of Nature's eternal youth, and the passionless permanence of that about us and beyond us and beneath,—until something like the fulness of a great grief begins to weigh at the heart... For all this astonishment of beauty, all this majesty of light and form and color, will surely endure,—marvellous as now,—after we shall have lain down to sleep where no dreams come, and may never arise from the dust of our rest to look upon it.

NOTES

1. Also called *La Barre de l'Isle,*—a long high mountain-wall interlinking the northern and southern system of ranges,—and only two metres broad at the summit. The "Roches-Carrées" display a geological formation unlike anything discovered in the rest of the Antillesian system, excepting in Grenada,—columnar or prismatic basalts... In the plains of Marin curious petrifactions exist;—I saw a honey-comb so perfect that the eye alone could scarcely divine the transformation.

2. Thibault de Chanvallon, writing of Martinique in 1751, declared:—"All possible hinderances to study are encountered here *(tout s'oppose à l'étude)*: if the Americans [creoles] do not devote themselves to research, the fact must not be attributed solely to indifference or indolence. On the one hand, the overpowering and continual heat,—the perpetual succession of mornes and acclivities,—the difficulty of entering forests rendered almost inaccessible by the lianas interwoven across all openings, and the prickly plants which oppose a barrier to the naturalist,—the continual anxiety and fear inspired by serpents also;—on the other hand, the disheartening necessity of having to work alone, and the discouragement of being unable to communicate one's ideas or discoveries to persons having similar tastes.

And finally, it must be remembered that these discouragements and dangers are never mitigated by the least hope of personal consideration, or by the pleasure of emulation,—since such study is necessarily unaccompanied either by the one or the other in a country where nobody undertakes it." (*Voyage à la Martinique.*) ... The conditions have scarcely changed since De Chanvallon's day, despite the creation of Government roads, and the thinning of the high woods.

3. Humboldt believed the height to be not less than 800 *toises* (1 toise=6 ft. 4.73 inches), or about 5,115 feet.

4. There used to be a strange popular belief that however heavily veiled by clouds the mountain might be prior to an earthquake, these would always vanish with the first shock. But Thibault de Chanvallon took pains to examine into the truth of this alleged phenomenon; and found that during a number of earthquake shocks the clouds remained over the crater precisely as usual... There was more foundation, however, for another popular belief, which still exists,—that the absolute purity of the atmosphere about Pelée, and the perfect exposure of its summit for any considerable time, might be regarded as an omen of hurricane.

5. "De la piqûre du serpent de la Martinique," par Auguste Charriez, Médecin de la Marine. Paris: Moquet, 1875.

6. M. Francard Bayardelle, overseer of the Prèsbourg plantation at Grande Anse, tells me that the most successful treatment of snakebite consists in severe local cupping and bleeding; the immediate application of twenty to thirty leeches (when these can be obtained), and the administration of alkali as an internal medicine. He has saved several lives by these methods.

The negro *panseur's* method is much more elaborate and, to some extent, mysterious. He cups and bleeds, using a small *couï*, or half-calabash, in lieu of a glass; and then applies cataplasms of herbs,—orange-leaves, cinnamon-leaves, clove-leaves, *chardon-béni, charpentier,* perhaps twenty other things, all mingled together;—this poulticing being continued every day for a month. Meantime the patient is given all sorts of absurd things to drink, in tafia and sour-orange juice—such as old clay pipes ground to powder, or *the head of the fer-de-lance itself,* roasted dry and pounded...The plantation negro has no faith in any other system of cure but that of the panseur;—he refuses to let the physician try to save him, and will scarcely submit to be treated even by an experienced white overseer.

7. Dr. E. Rufz: "Études historiques," vol. i., p. 189.

VIII. 'Ti Canotié

I

ONE might almost say that commercial time in St. Pierre is measured by cannon-shots,—by the signal-guns of steamers. Every such report announces an event of extreme importance to the whole population. To the merchant it is a notification that mails, money, and goods have arrived;—to consuls and Government officials it gives notice of fees and dues to be collected;—for the host of lightermen, longshoremen, port laborers of all classes, it promises work and pay;—for all it signifies the arrival of food. The island does not feed itself: cattle, salt, meats, hams, lard, flour, cheese, dried fish, all come from abroad,—particularly from America. And in the minds of the colored population the American steamer is so intimately associated with the idea of those great tin cans in which food-stuffs are brought from the United States, that the onomatope applied to the can, because of the sound outgiven by it when tapped,—*bom!*—is also applied to the ship itself. The English or French or Belgian steamer, however large, is only known as *packett-à, batiment-là*; but the American steamer is always the "bom-ship"—*batiment-bom-à*; or, the "food-ship"—*batiment-mangé-à*... You hear women and men asking each other, as the shock of the gun flaps through all the town, "*Mi! gadé ça qui là, chè?*" And if the answer be, "*Mais c'est bom-là, chè—bom-mangé-à ka rivé*" (Why, it is the bom, dear,—the food-bom that has come), great is the exultation.

Again, because of the sound of her whistle, we find a steamer called in this same picturesque idiom, *batiment-cône,*—"the horn-ship." There is even a song, of which the refrain is:—

> *"Bom-là rivé, chè,—*
> *Batiment-cône-là rivé."*

...But of all the various classes of citizens, those most joyously excited by the coming of a great steamer, whether she he a "bom" or not,—are the *'ti canotié*, who swarm out immediately in little canoes of their own manufacture to dive for coins which passengers gladly throw into the water for the pleasure of witnessing the graceful spectacle. No sooner does a steamer drop anchor—unless the water be very rough indeed—than she is surrounded by a fleet of the funniest little boats imaginable, full of naked urchins screaming creole.

These *'ti canotié*—these little canoe-boys and professional divers—are, for the most part, sons of boatmen of color, the real *canotiers*. I cannot find who first invented the *'ti canot*: the shape and dimensions of the little canoe are fixed according to a tradition several generations old; and no improvements upon the original model seem to have ever been attempted, with the sole exception of a tiny water-tight box contrived sometimes at one end, in which the *palettes*, or miniature paddles, and various other trifles may be stowed away. The actual cost of material for a canoe of this kind seldom exceeds twenty-five or thirty cents; and, nevertheless, the number of canoes is not very large—I doubt if there be more than fifteen in the harbor;—as the families of Martinique boatmen are all so poor that twenty-five sous are difficult to spare in spite of the certainty that the little son can earn fifty times the amount within a month after owning a canoe.

For the manufacture of a canoe an American lard-box or kerosene-oil box is preferred by reason of its shape; but any well-constructed shipping-case of small size would serve the purpose. The top is removed; the sides and the corners of the bottom are sawn out at certain angles; and the pieces removed are utilized for the sides of the bow and stern,—sometimes also in making the little box for the paddles, or palettes, which are simply thin pieces of tough wood about the form and size of a cigar box lid. Then the little boat is tarred and varnished: it cannot sink,—though it is quite easily upset. There are no seats. The boys (there

'Ti Canot (A, stern; B, little box for palettes, etc.; C, prow)

are usually two to each canoe) simply squat down in the bottom,—facing each other. They can paddle with surprising swiftness over a smooth sea; and it is a very pretty sight to witness one of their prize contests in racing,—which take place every 14th of July…

II

…IT was five o'clock in the afternoon: the horizon beyond the harbor was turning lemon-color;—and a thin warm wind began to come in weak puffs from the south-west,—the first breaths to break the immobility of the tropical air. Sails of vessels becalmed at the entrance of the bay commenced to flap lazily: they might belly after sundown.

The *La Guayra* was in port, lying well out:—her mountainous iron mass rising high above the modest sailing craft moored in her vicinity,—barks and brigantines and brigs and schooners and barkentines. She had lain before the town the whole afternoon, surrounded by the entire squadron of *'ti canots*; and the boys were still circling about her flanks, although she had got up steam and was lifting her anchor. They had been very lucky, indeed, that afternoon,—all the little canotiers;—and even many yellow lads, not fortunate enough to own canoes, had swum out to her in hope of sharing the silver shower falling from her saloon-deck. Some of these, tired out, were resting themselves by sitting on the slanting cables of neighboring ships. Perched naked thus,—balancing in the sun, against the blue of sky or water, their slender bodies took such orange from the mellowing light as to seem made of some self-luminous substance,—flesh of sea-fairies.

Suddenly the *La Guayra* opened her steam-throat and uttered such a moo that all the mornes cried out for at least a minute after;—and the little fellows perched on the cables of the sailing craft tumbled into the sea at the sound and struck out for shore. Then the water all at once burst backward in immense frothing swirls from beneath the stern of the steamer; and there arose such a heaving as made all the little canoes dance. The *La Guayra* was moving. She moved slowly at first, making a great fuss as she turned round: then she began to settle down to her journey very majestically,—just making the water pitch a little behind her, as the hem of a woman's robe tosses lightly at her heels while she walks.

And, contrary to custom, some of the canoes followed after her. A dark handsome man, wearing an immense Panama hat, and jewelled rings upon his hands, was still throwing money; and still the boys dived for it. But only one of each crew now plunged; for, though the *La Guayra* was yet moving slowly, it was a severe strain to follow her, and there was no time to be lost.

The captain of the little band—black Maximilien, ten years old, and his comrade Stéphane—nicknamed *Ti Chabin*, because of his bright hair,—a slim little yellow boy of eleven—led the pursuit, crying always, "*Encò, Missié,—encò!*"

The *La Guayra* had gained fully two hundred yards when the handsome passenger made his final largess,—proving himself quite an expert in flinging coin. The piece fell far short of the boys, but near enough to distinctly betray a yellow shimmer as it twirled to the water. That was gold!

In another minute the leading canoe had reached the spot, the other canotiers voluntarily abandoning the quest,—for it was little use to contend against Maximilien and Stéphane, who had won all the canoe contests last 14th of July. Stéphane, who was the better diver, plunged.

He was much longer below than usual, came up at quite a distance, panted as he regained the canoe, and rested his arms upon it. The water was so deep then he could not reach the coin the first time, though he could see it: he was going to try again,—it was gold sure enough.

—"*Fouinq! ça fond içitt!*" he gasped.

Maximilien felt all at once uneasy. Very deep water, and perhaps sharks. And sunset not far off! The *La Guayra* was diminishing in the offing.

—"*Boug-là lé fai nou néyé!—laissé y, Stéphane!*" he cried. (The fellow wants to drown us. *Laissé*—leave it alone.)

But Stéphane had recovered breath, and was evidently resolved to try again. It was gold!

—"*Mais ça c'est lò!*"

—"*Assez, non!*" screamed Maximilien. "*Pa plongé 'ncò, moin ka di ou! Ah! foute!*"…

Stéphane had dived again!

…And where were the others? "*Bon-Dié, gadé oti yo yé!*" They were almost out of sight,—tiny specks moving shoreward… The *La Guayra* now seemed no bigger than the little packet running between St. Pierre and Fort-de-France.

Up came Stéphane again, at a still greater distance than before,— holding high the yellow coin in one hand. He made for the canoe, and

Maximilien paddled towards him and helped him in. Blood was streaming from the little diver's nostrils, and blood colored the water he spat from his mouth.

—*"Ah! moin té ka di ou laissé y!"* cried Maximilien, in anger and alarm... *"Gàdé, gàdé sang-à ka coulé nans nez ou,—nans bouche ou!... Mi oti lézautt!"*

Lézautt, the rest, were no longer visible.

—*"Et mi oti nou yé!"* cried Maximilien again. They had never ventured so far from shore.

But Stéphane answered only, *"C'est lò!"* For the first time in his life he held a piece of gold in his fingers. He tied it up in a little rag attached to the string fastened about his waist,—a purse of his own invention,— and took up his paddles, coughing the while and spitting crimson.

—*"Mi! mi!—mi oti nou yé!"* reiterated Maximilien. *"Bon-Dié!* look where we are!"

The Place had become indistinct;—the light-house, directly behind half an hour earlier, now lay well south: the red light had just been kindled. Seaward, in advance of the sinking orange disk of the sun, was the *La Guayra*, passing to the horizon. There was no sound from the shore: about them a great silence had gathered, the Silence of seas, which is a fear. Panic seized them: they began to paddle furiously.

But St. Pierre did not appear to draw any nearer. Was it only an effect of the dying light, or were they actually moving towards the semicircular cliffs of Fond-Corré?... Maximilien began to cry. The little chabin paddled on,—though the blood was still trickling over his breast.

Maximilien screamed out to him:—

—*"Ou pa ka pagayé,—anh?—ou ni bousoin dòmi?"* (Thou dost not paddle, eh?—thou wouldst go to sleep?)

—*"Si! moin ka pagayé,—epi fò!"* (I am paddling and hard, too!) responded Stéphane.

—*"Ou ka pagayé!—ou ka menti!"* (Thou art paddling!—thou liest!) vociferated Maximilien... "And the fault is all thine. I cannot, all by myself, make the canoe to go in water like this! The fault is all thine: I told thee not to dive, thou stupid!"

—*"Ou fou!"* cried Stéphane, becoming angry. *"Moin ka pagayé!"* (I am paddling.)

—"Beast! never may we get home so! Paddle, thou lazy;—paddle, thou nasty!"

—*"Macaque* thou!—monkey!"

—"*Chabin!*—must be chabin, for to be stupid so!"

—"Thou black monkey—thou species of *ouistiti!*"

—"Thou tortoise-of-the-land!—thou slothful more than *molocoye!*"

—"Why, thou cursed monkey, if thou sayest I do not paddle, thou dost not know how to paddle!"…

… But Maximilien's whole expression changed: he suddenly stopped paddling, and stared before him and behind him at a great violet band broadening across the sea northward out of sight; and his eyes were big with terror as he cried out:—

—"*Mais ni qui chose qui douôle içitt!*… There is something queer, Stéphane; there is something queer."…

—"Ah! you begin to see now, Maximilien!—it is the current!"

—"A devil-current, Stéphane…We are drifting: we will go to the horizon!"…

To the horizon—"*nou kallé lhorizon!*"—a phrase of terrible picturesqueness… In the creole tongue, "to the horizon" signifies to the Great Open—into the measureless sea.

—"*C'est pa lapeine pagayé atouèlement*" (It is no use to paddle now), sobbed Maximilien, laying down his palettes.

—"*Si! si!*" said Stéphane, reversing the motion: "paddle with the current."

—"With the current! It runs to La Dominique!"

—"*Pouloss,*" phlegmatically returned Stéphane, "*en-nou!* Let us make for La Dominique!"

—"Thou fool!—it is more than past forty kilometres… *Stéphane, mi! gadé!—mi qui gouôs requ'em!*"

A long black fin cut the water almost beside them, passed, and vanished,—a *requin* indeed! But, in his patois, the boy almost re-echoed the name as uttered by quaint Père Dutertre, who, writing of strange fishes more than two hundred years ago, says it is called REQUIEM, because for the man who findeth himself alone with it in the midst of the sea, surely a requiem must be sung.

—"Do not paddle, Stéphane!—do not put thy hand in the water again!"

III

…THE *La Guayra* was a point on the sky-verge;—the sun's face had vanished. The silence and the darkness were deepening together.

—"*Si lanmè ka vini plis fò, ça nou ké fai?*" (If the sea roughens, what are we to do?) asked Maximilien.

—"Maybe we will meet a steamer," answered Stéphane: "the *Orinoco* was due today."

—"And if she passes in the night?"

—"They can see us."…

—"No, they will not be able to see us at all. There is no moon."

—"They have lights ahead."

—"I tell thee, they will not see us at all,—*pièss! pièss! pièss!*"

—"Then they will hear us cry out."

—"No,—we cannot cry so loud. One can hear nothing but a steam-whistle or a cannon, with the noise of the wind and the water and the machine… Even on the Fort-de-France packet one cannot hear for the machine. And the machine of the *Orinoco* is more big than the church of the 'Centre.'"

—"Then we must try to get to La Dominique."

…They could now feel the sweep of the mighty current;—it even seemed to them that they could hear it,—a deep low whispering. At long intervals they saw lights,—the lights of houses in Pointe-Prince, in Fond-Canonville,—in Au Prêcheur. Under them the depth was unfathomed;—hydrographic charts mark it *sans-fond*. And they passed the great cliffs of Aux Abymes, under which lies the Village of the Abysms.

The red glare in the west disappeared suddenly as if blown out;—the rim of the sea vanished into the void of the gloom;—the night narrowed about them, thickening like a black fog. And the invisible, irresistible power of the sea was now bearing them away from the tall coast,—over profundities unknown,—over the *sans-fond*,—out "to the horizon."

IV

…BEHIND the canoe a long thread of pale light quivered and twisted: bright points from time to time mounted up, glowered like eyes, and vanished again;—glimmerings of faint flame wormed away on either side as they floated on. And the little craft no longer rocked as before;—they felt another and a larger motion,—long slow ascents and descents enduring for minutes at a time;—they were riding the great swells,—*riding the horizon!*

Twice they were capsized. But happily the heaving was a smooth one, and their little canoe could not sink: they groped for it, found it, righted it, and climbed in, and baled out the water with their hands.

From time to time they both cried out together as loud as they could,—"*Sucou!—sucou!—sucou!* "—hoping that someone might be looking for them... The alarm had indeed been given; and one of the little steam-packets had been sent out to look for them,—with torch fires blazing at her bows; but she had taken the wrong direction.

—"Maximilien," said Stéphane, while the great heaving seemed to grow vaster,—"*fau nou ka prié Bon-Dié.*"...

Maximilien answered nothing.

—"*Fau prié Bon-Dié*" (we must prey to the Bon-Dié) repeated Stéphane.

—"*Pa lapeine, li pas pè ouè nou atò!*" (It is not worth while: He cannot see us now) answered the little black... In the immense darkness even the loom of the island was no longer visible.

—"O Maximilien!—*Bon-Dié ka ouè toutt, ka connaitt toutt*" (He sees all; He knows all) cried Stéphane.

—"*Y pa pè ouè non pièss atouèelement, moin ben sur!*" (He cannot see us at all,—I am quite sure) irreverently responded Maximilien.

—"Thou thinkest the Bon-Dié like thyself!—He has not eyes like thou," protested Stephane. "*Li pas ka tini coulè; li pas ka tini ziè*" (He has not color, He has not eyes), continued the boy, repeating the text of his catechism,—the curious creole catechism of old Perè Goux, of Carbet. [Quaint priest and quaint catechism have both passed away.]

—"*Moin pa save si li pa ka tini coulè*" (I know not if He has not color), answered Maximilien. "But what I well know is that if He has not eyes, He cannot see... *Fouinq!*—how idiot!"

—"Why, it is in the Catechism," cried Stéphane...—'*Bon-Dié, li conm vent: vent tout-patout, et nou pa save ouè li;—li ka touché nou,—li ka boulvésé lanmè.*' (The Good-God is like the Wind: the Wind is everywhere, and we cannot see It;—It touches us,—It tosses the sea.)

—"If the Bon-Dié is the Wind," responded Maximilien, "then pray thou the Wind to stay quiet."

—"The Bon-Dié is not the Wind," cried Stéphane: "He is *like* the Wind, but He is not the Wind."...

—"*Ah! soc-soc!—fouinq!*... More better past praying to care we be not upset again and eaten by sharks."

***

...Whether the little chabin prayed either to the Wind or to the Bon-Dié, I do not know. But the Wind remained very quiet all that night,—seemed to hold breath for fear of ruffling the sea. And in the Mouillage of St. Pierre furious American captains swore at the Wind because it would not fill their sails.

V

PERHAPS, if there had been a breeze, neither Stéphane nor Maximilien would have seen the sun again. But they saw him rise.

Light pearled in the east, over the edge of the ocean, ran around the rim of the sky and yellowed: then the sun's brow appeared;—a current of gold gushed rippling across the sea before him;—and all the heaven at once caught blue fire from horizon to zenith. Violet from flood to cloud the vast recumbent form of Pelée loomed far behind,—with long reaches of mountaining: pale grays o'ertopping misty blues. And in the north another lofty shape was towering,—strangely jagged and peaked and beautiful,—the silhouette of Dominica: a sapphire saw!... No wandering clouds:—over far Pelée only shadowy piling of nimbi... Under them the sea swayed dark as purple ink—a token of tremendous depth... Still a dead calm, and no sail in sight.

—"*Ça c'est la Dominique,*" said Maximilien,—"*Ennou pou ouivage-à!*"

They had lost their little palettes during the night;—they used their naked hands, and moved swiftly. But Dominica was many and many a mile away. Which was the nearer island, it was yet difficult to say;—in the morning sea haze, both were vapory,—difference of color was largely due to position...

Sough!—Sough!—Sough!—A bird with a white breast passed overhead; and they stopped paddling to look at it,—a gull. Sign of fair weather!—it was making for Dominica.

—"*Moin ni ben faim,*" murmured Maximilien. Neither had eaten since the morning of the previous day,—most of which they had passed sitting in their canoe.

—"*Moin ni anni soif,*" said Stéphane. And besides his thirst he complained of a burning pain in his head, always growing worse. He still coughed, and spat out pink threads after each burst of coughing.

...The heightening sun flamed whiter and whiter: the flashing of waters before his face began to dazzle like a play of lightning... Now the islands began to show sharper lines, stronger colors; and Dominica was evidently the nearer;—for bright streaks of green were breaking at various angles through its vapor-colored silhouette, and Martinique still remained all blue.

...Hotter and hotter the sun burned; more and more blinding became his reverberation. Maximilien's black skin suffered least; but both lads, accustomed as they were to remaining naked in the sun, found the heat difficult to bear. They would gladly have plunged into the deep water to cool themselves, but for fear of sharks;—all they could do was to moisten their heads, and rinse their mouths with sea-water.

Each from his end of the canoe continually watched the horizon. Neither hoped for a sail, there was no wind; but they looked for the coming of steamers,—the *Orinoco* might pass, or the English packet, or some one of the small Martinique steamboats might be sent out find them.

Yet hours went by; and there still appeared no smoke in the ring of the sky,—never a sign in all the round of the sea, broken only by the two huge silhouettes... But Dominica was certainly nearing;—the green lights were spreading through the luminous blue of her hills.

...Their long immobility in the squatting posture began to tell upon the endurance of both boys,—producing dull throbbing aches in thighs, hips, and loins...Then, about midday, Stéphane declared he could not paddle any more;—it seemed to him as if his head must soon burst open with the pain which filled it: even the sound of his own voice hurt him,—he did not want to talk.

VI

...AND another oppression came upon them,—in spite of all the pains, and the blinding dazzle of waters, and the biting of the sun: the oppression of drowsiness. They began to doze at intervals,—keeping their canoe balanced in some automatic way,—as cavalry soldiers, overweary, ride asleep in the saddle.

But at last, Stéphane, awaking suddenly with a paroxysm of coughing, so swayed himself to one side as to overturn the canoe; and both found themselves in themselves in the sea.

Maximilien righted the craft, and got in again; but the little chabin twice fell back in trying to raise himself upon his arms. He had had become almost helplessly feeble. Maximilien, attempting to aid him, again overturned the unsteady little boat; and this time it required all his skill and his utmost strength to get Stéphane out of the water. Evidently Stéphane could be of no more assistance;—the boy was so weak he could not even sit up straight.

—"*Aïe! Ou ké jété nou encò,*" panted Maximilien,—"*metté ou toutt longue.*"

Stéphane slowly let himself down, so as to lie nearly all his length in the canoe,—one foot on either side of Maximilien's hips. Then he lay very still for a long time,—so still that Maximilien became uneasy.

—"*Ou ben malade?*" he asked... Stéphane did not seem to hear: his eyes remained closed.

—"Stéphane!" cried Maximilien, in alarm,—"Stéphane!"

—"*C'est lò, papoute,*" murmured Stéphane, without lifting his eyelids,—"*ça c'est lò!—ou pa janmain ouè yon bel pièce conm ça?*" (It is gold, little father... Didst thou ever see a pretty piece like that?... No, thou wilt not beat me, little father?—no, *papoute!*)

—"*Ou ka dòmi, Stéphane?*" —queried Maximilien, wondering,— "art asleep?"

But Stéphane opened his eyes and looked at him so strangely! Never had he seen Stéphane look that way before.

—"*Ça ou ni, Stéphane?*" —what ails thee?—*aie! Bon-Dié, Bon-Dié!*"

—"*Bon-Dié!*" —muttered Stéphane, closing his eyes again at the sound of the great Name,—"He has no color;—He is like the Wind."....

—"Stéphane!"

—"He feels in the dark;—He has not eyes."...

—"*Stéphane, pa pàlé ça!!*"

—"He tosses the sea... He has no face;—He lifts up the dead... and the leaves."...

—"*Ou fou!*" cried Maximilien, bursting into a wild fit of sobbing,— "Stéphane, thou art mad!"

And all at once he became afraid of Stéphane,—afraid of all he said,—afraid of his touch,—afraid of his eyes,... he was growing like a *zombi!*

But Stéphane's eyes remained closed;—he ceased to speak.

About them deepened the enormous silence of the sea;—low swung the sun again. The horizon was yellowing: day had begun to fade. Tall Dominica was now half green; but there yet appeared no smoke, no sail, no sign of life.

And the tints of the two vast Shapes that shattered the rim of the light shifted as if evanescing,—shifted like tones of West Indian fishes,—of *pisquette* and *congre,*—of *caringue* and *gouôs-zié* and *balaou.* Lower sank the sun;—cloud-fleeces of orange pushed up over the edge of the west;—a thin warm breath caressed the sea,—sent long lilac shudderings over the flanks of the swells. Then colors changed again: violet richened to purple;—greens blackened softly;—grays smouldered into smoky gold.

And the sun went down.

VII

AND they floated into the fear of the night together. Again the ghostly fires began to wimple about them: naught else was visible but the high stars.

Black hours passed. From minute to minute Maximilien cried out:—"*Sucou! sucou!* " Stéphane lay motionless and dumb: his feet, touching Maximilien's naked hips, felt singularly cold.

Something knocked suddenly against the bottom of the canoe,—knocked heavily—making a hollow loud sound. It was not Stéphane;—Stéphane lay still as a stone: it was from the depth below. Perhaps a great fish passing.

It came again,—twice,—shaking the canoe like a great blow. Then Stéphane suddenly moved,—drew up his feet a little,—made as if to speak:—"*Ou...*"; but the speech failed at his lips,—ending in a sound like the moan of one trying to call out in sleep;—and Maximilien's heart almost stopped beating... Then Stéphane's limbs straightened again; he made no more movement;—Maximilien could not even hear him breathe... All the sea had begun to whisper.

A breeze was rising;—Maximilien felt it blowing upon him. All at once it seemed to him that he had ceased to be afraid,—that he did not care what might happen. He thought about a cricket he had one day watched in the harbor,—drifting out with the tide, on an atom of dead bark,—and he wondered what had become of it. Then he understood that he himself was the cricket,—still alive. But some boy had found him and pulled off his legs. There they were,—his own legs, pressing against him: he could still feel the aching where they had been pulled off; and they had been dead so long they were now quite cold... It was certainly Stéphane who had pulled them off...

The water was talking to him. It was saying the same thing over and over again,—louder each time, as if it thought he could not hear. But he heard it very well:—"*Bon-Dié, li conm vent... li ka touché nou... nou pa save ouè li.*" (But why had the Bon-Dié shaken the wind?) "*Li pa ka tini zié*," answered the water... *Ouille!*—He might all the same care not to upset folks in the sea!... *Mi!*...

But even as he thought these things, Maximilien became aware that a white, strange, bearded face was looking at him: the Bon-Dié was there,—bending over him with a lantern,—talking to him in a language he did not understand. And the Bon-Dié certainly had eyes,—great gray eyes that did not look wicked at all. He tried to tell the Bon-Dié how sorry he was for what he had been saying about him;—but found he could not utter a word. He felt great hands lift him up to the stars, and lay him down very near them,—just under them. They burned blue-white, and hurt his eyes like lightning:—he felt afraid of them... About him he heard voices,—always speaking the same language, which he could not understand..."*Poor little devils!—poor little devils!*" Then he heard a bell ring; and the Bon-Dié made him swallow something nice and warm;—everything became black again. The stars went out...

...Maximilien was lying under an electric-light on board the great steamer *Rio de Janeiro*, and dead Stéphane beside him... It was four o'clock in the morning.

IX. La Fille de Couleur

I

NOTHING else in the picturesque life of the French colonies of the Occident impresses the traveller on his first arrival more than the costumes of the women of color. They surprise the aesthetic sense agreeably;—they are local and special: you will see nothing resembling them among the populations of the British West Indies; they belong to Martinique, Guadeloupe, Désirade, Marie-Galante, and Cayenne,—in each place differing sufficiently to make the difference interesting, especially in regard to the head-dress. That of Martinique is quite Oriental;—more attractive, although less fantastic than the Cayenne coiffure, or the pretty drooping mouchoir of Guadeloupe.

These costumes are gradually disappearing, for various reasons,—the chief reason being of course the changes in the social condition of the colonies during the last forty years. Probably the question of health had also something to do with the almost universal abandonment in Martinique of the primitive slave-dress,—*chemise* and *jupe*,—which exposed its wearer to serious risks of pneumonia; for as far as economical reasons are concerned, there was no fault to find with it: six francs could purchase it when money was worth more than it is now. The douillette, a long trailing dress, one piece from neck to feet, has taken its place.[1] But there was a luxurious variety of the jupe costume which is disappearing because of its cost; there is no money in the colonies now for such display:—I refer to the celebrated attire of the pet slaves and *belles affranchies* of the old colonial days. A full costume,—including violet or crimson "petticoat" of silk or satin; chemise with half-sleeves, and much embroidery and lace; "trembling-pins" of gold (*zépingue tremblant*) to attach the folds of the brilliant Madras turban; the great necklace of three or four strings of gold beads bigger than peas (*collier-choux*); the ear-rings, immense but light as egg-shells (*zanneaux-à-clous* or *zanneaux-chenilles*); the bracelets (*portes-bonheur*); the studs (*boutons-à-clous*); the brooches, not only for the turban, but for the chemise, below the folds of the showy silken foulard or shoulder-scarf,—would

The Martinique Turban, or "Madras Calendé"

sometimes represent over five thousand francs expenditure. This gorgeous attire is becoming less visible every year: it is now rarely worn except on very solemn occasions,—weddings, baptisms, first communions, confirmations. The *da* (nurse) or "porteuse-de-baptême" who bears the baby to church, holds it at the baptismal font, and afterwards carries it from house to house in order that all the friends of the family may kiss it, is thus attired; but nowadays, unless she be a professional (for there are professional *das*, hired only for such occasions), she usually borrows the jewellery. If tall, young, graceful, with a rich gold tone of skin, the effect of her costume is dazzling as that of a Byzantine Virgin. I saw one young da who, thus garbed, scarcely seemed of the earth and earthly;—there was an Oriental something in her appearance difficult to describe,—something that made you think of the Queen of Sheba going to visit Solomon. She had brought a merchant's baby, just christened, to receive the caresses of the family at whose house I was visiting; and when it came to my turn to kiss it, I confess I could not notice the child: I saw only the beautiful dark face, coiffed with orange and purple, bending over it, in an illumination of antique gold... What a *da!*... She represented really the type of that *belle affranchie* of other days, against whose fascination special sumptuary laws were made: romantically she imaged for me the supernatural godmothers and Cinderellas of the creole fairy-tales. For these become transformed in the West Indian folklore,—adapted to the environment, and to local idealism: Cinderella, for example, is changed to a beautiful métisse wearing a quadruple *collier-choux, zéphingues tremblants*, and all the ornaments of a da.[2] Recalling the impression of that dazzling *da*, I can even now feel the picturesque justice of the fabulist's description of Cinderella's creole costume: *Ça té ka baille ou mal ziè!*—(it would have given you a pain in your eyes to look at her!)

Even the every-day Martinique costume is slowly changing. Year by year the "calendeuses"—the women who paint and fold the turbans—have less work to do;—the colors of the *douillette* are becoming less vivid;—while more and more young colored girls are being *élevées en chapeau* ("brought up in a hat")—*i.e.*, dressed and educated like the daughters of the whites. These, it must be confessed, look far less attractive in the latest Paris fashion, unless white as the whites themselves: on the other hand, few white girls could look well in *douillette* and *mouchoir*; —not merely because of color contrast, but because they have not that amplitude of limb and particular cambering of the torso peculiar to the half-breed race, with its large bulk and stature. Attractive as certain coolie women are, I observed that all who have adopted the Martinique costume look badly in it: they are too slender of body to wear it to advantage.

Slavery introduced these costumes, even though it probably did not invent them; and they were necessarily doomed to pass away with the peculiar social conditions to which they belonged. If the population clings still to its *douillettes, mouchoirs*, and *foulards*, the fact is largely due to the cheapness of such attire. A girl can dress very showily indeed for about twenty francs,—shoes excepted;—and thousands never wear shoes. But the fashion will no doubt have become cheaper and uglier within another decade.

The Guadeloupe Head-dress

At the present time, however, the stranger might be sufficiently impressed by the oddity and brilliancy of these dresses to ask about their origin,—in which case it is not likely that he will obtain any satisfactory answer. After long research I found myself obliged to give up all hope of being able to outline the history of Martinique costume,—partly because books and histories are scanty or defective, and partly because such an undertaking would require a knowledge possible only to a specialist. I found good reason, nevertheless, to suppose that these costumes were in the beginning adopted from certain fashions of provincial France,—that the respective fashions of Guadeloupe, Martinique, and Cayenne were patterned after modes still worn in parts of the mother-country. The old-time garb of the *affranchie*—that still worn by the *da*—somewhat recalls dresses worn by the women of Southern France, more particularly about Montpellier. Perhaps a specialist might also trace back the evolution of the various creole coiffures to old forms of head-dresses which still survive among the French country fashions of the south and south-west provinces;—but local taste has so much modified the original style as to leave it unrecognizable to those who have never studied the subject. The Martinique fashion of folding and tying the Madras, and of calendering it, are probably local; and I am assured that the designs of the curious semi-barbaric jewellery were all invented in the colony, where the *collier-choux* is still manufactured by local goldsmiths. Purchasers buy one, two, or three *grains*, or beads, at a time, and string them only on obtaining the requisite number... This is the sum of all that I was able to learn on the matter; but in the course of searching various West Indian authors and historians for information, I found something far more important than the origin of the *douillette* or the *collier-choux*: the facts of that strange struggle between nature and interest, between love and law, between prejudice and passion, which forms the evolutional history of the mixed race.

II

CONSIDERING only the French peasant colonist and the West African slave as the original factors of that physical evolution visible in the modern *fille-de-couleur*, it would seem incredible;—for the intercrossing alone could not adequately explain all the physical results.

To understand them fully, it will be necessary to bear in mind that both of the original races became modified in their lineage to a surprising degree by conditions of climate and environment.

The precise time of the first introduction of slaves into Martinique is not now possible to ascertain,—no record exists on the subject; but it is probable that the establishment of slavery was coincident with the settlement of the island. Most likely the first hundred colonists from St. Christophe, who landed, in 1635, near the bay whereon the city of St. Pierre is now situated, either brought slaves with them, or else were furnished with negroes very soon after their arrival. In the time of Père Dutertre (who visited the colonies in 1640, and printed his history of

Young Mulatress

the French Antilles at Paris in 1667) slavery was already a flourishing institution,—the foundation of the whole social structure. According to the Dominican missionary, the Africans then in the colony were decidedly repulsive; he describes the women as "hideous" (*hideuses*). There is no good reason to charge Dutertre with prejudice in his pictures of them. No writer of the century was more keenly sensitive to natural beauty than the author of that "Voyage aux Antilles" which inspired Chateaubriand, and which still, after two hundred and fifty years, delights even those perfectly familiar with the nature of the places and things spoken of. No other writer and traveller of the period possessed to a more marked degree that sense of generous pity which makes the unfortunate appear to us in an illusive, almost ideal aspect. Nevertheless, he asserts that the negresses were, as a general rule, revoltingly ugly,—and, although he had seen many strange sides of human nature (having been a soldier before becoming a monk), was astonished to find that miscegenation had already begun. Doubtless the first black women thus favored, or afflicted, as the case might be, were of the finer types of negresses; for he notes remarkable differences among the slaves procured from different coasts and various tribes. Still, these were rather differences of ugliness than aught else: they were all repulsive;—only some were more repulsive than others.[3] Granting that the first mothers of mulattoes in the colony were the superior rather than the inferior physical types,—which would be a perfectly natural supposition,—still we find their offspring worthy in his eyes of no higher sentiment than pity. He writes in his chapter entitled "*De la naissance honteuse des mulastres*":—

—"They have something of their Father and something of their Mother,—in the same wise that Mules partake of the qualities of the creatures that engendered them: for they are neither all white, like the French; nor all black, like the Negroes, but have a livid tint, which comes of both."...

Today, however, the traveller would look in vain for a *livid* tint among the descendants of those thus described: in less than two centuries and a half the physical characteristics of the race have been totally changed. What most surprises is the rapidity of the transformation. After the time of Père Labat, Europeans never could "have mistaken little negro children for monkeys." Nature had begun to remodel the white, the black, and half-breed according to environment and climate: the descendant, of the early colonists ceased to resemble

Plantation Coolie Woman in Martinique Costume

Coolie Half-breed

his fathers; the creole negro improved upon his progenitors,[4] the mulatto began to give evidence of those qualities of physical and mental power which were afterwards to render him dangerous to the integrity of the colony itself. In a temperate climate such a change would have been so gradual as to escape observation for a long period; — in the tropics it was effected with a quickness that astounds by its revelation of the natural forces at work.

– "Under the sun of the tropics," writes Dr. Rufz, of Martinique, "the African race, as well as the European, becomes greatly modified in its reproduction. Either race gives birth to a totally new being. The Creole African came into existence as did the Creole white. And just as the offspring of Europeans who emigrated to the tropics from different parts of France displayed characteristics so identical that it was impossible to divine the original race-source,—so likewise the Creole negro — whether brought into being by the heavy thick-set Congo or the long slender black of Senegambia, or the suppler and more active Mandingo,— appeared so remodelled, homogeneous, and adapted in such wise to his environment that it was utterly impossible to discern in his features anything of his parentage, his original kindred, his original source. The transformation is absolute. All that can be asserted is: 'This is a white Creole; this is a black creole; this is a black Creole';—or, 'this is a European white; this is an African black';—and furthermore, after a certain number of years passed in the tropics, the enervated and discolored aspect of the European may create uncertainty as to his origin. But with very few exceptions the primitive African, or, as he is termed here, the "Coast-black" (*le noir de la Côte*), can be recognized at once...

..."The Creole negro is gracefully shaped, finely proportioned: his limbs are lithe, his neck long;—his features are more delicate, his lips less thick, his nose less flattened, than those of the African;—he has the Carib's large and melancholy eye, better adapted to express the emotions... Rarely can you discover in him the sombre fury of the

African, rarely a surly and savage mien: he is brave, chatty, boastful. His skin has not the same tint as his father's,—it has become more satiny; his hair remains woolly, but it is a finer wool;... all his outlines are more rounded;—one may perceive that the cellular tissue predominates, as in cultivated plants, of which the ligneous and savage fibre has become transformed.".…[5]

This new and comelier black race naturally won from its masters a more sympathetic attention than could have been vouchsafed to its progenitors; and the consequences in Martinique and elsewhere seemed to have evoked the curious Article 9 of the *Code Noir* of 1665,—enacting, first, that free men who should have one or two children by slave women, as well as the slave-owners permitting the same, should be each condemned to pay two thousand pounds of sugar; secondly, that if the violator of the ordinance should be himself the owner of the mother and father of her children, the mother and the children should be confiscated for the profit of the Hospital, and deprived for their lives of the right to enfranchisement. An exception, however, was made to the effect that if the father were unmarried at the period of his concubinage, he could escape the provisions of the penalty by marrying, "according to the rites of Church," the female slave, who would thereby be enfranchised, and her children "rendered free and legitimate." Probably the legislators did not imagine that the first portion of the article could prove inefficacious, or that any violator of the ordinance would seek to escape the penalty by those means offered in the provision. The facts, however, proved the reverse. Miscegenation continued; and Labat notices two cases of marriage between whites and blacks,—describing the offspring of one union as "very handsome little mulattoes." These legitimate unions were certainly exceptional,—one of them was dissolved by the ridicule cast upon the father;—but illegitimate unions would seem to have become common within a very brief time after the passage of the law. At a later day they were to become customary. The Article 9

Country-girl — Pure Negro Race

was evidently at fault; and in March, 1724, the Black Code was reinforced by a new ordinance, of which the sixth provision prohibited marriage as well as concubinage between the races.

It appears to have had no more effect than the previous law, even in Martinique, where the state of public morals was better than in Santo Domingo. The slave race had begun to exercise an influence never anticipated by legislators. Scarcely a century had elapsed since the colonization of the island; but in that time climate and civilization had transfigured the black woman. "After one or two generations," writes the historian Rufz, "the *Africaine* reformed, refined, beautified in her descendants, transformed into the creole negress, commenced to exert a fascination irresistible, capable of winning anything (*capable de tout obtenir*)."[6] Travellers of the eighteenth century were confounded by the luxury of dress and of jewellery displayed by swarthy beauties in St. Pierre. It was a public scandal to European eyes. But the creole negress or mulattress, beginning to understand her power, sought for higher favors and privileges than silken robes and necklaces of gold beads: she sought to obtain, not merely liberty for herself, but for her parents, brothers, sisters,—even friends. What successes she achieved in this regard may be imagined from the serious statement of creole historians that if human nature had been left untrammelled to follow its better impulses, slavery would have ceased to exist a century before the actual period of emancipation! By 1738, when the white population had reached its maximum (15,000),[7] and colonial luxury had arrived at is greatest height, the question of voluntary enfranchisement was becoming very grave. So omnipotent the charm of half-breed beauty that masters were becoming the slaves of their slaves. It was not only the creole *negress* who had appeared to play a part in this strange drama which was the triumph of nature over interest and judgment: her daughters, far more beautiful, had grown up to aid her, and to form a special class. These women, whose tints of skin rivalled the colors of ripe fruit, and whose gracefulness—peculiar, exotic, and irresistible— made them formidable rivals to the daughters of the dominant race, were no doubt physically superior to the modern *filles-de-couleur*. They were results of a natural selection which could have taken place in no community otherwise constituted;—the offspring of the union between the finer types of both races. But that which only slavery could have rendered possible began to endanger the integrity of slavery itself: the institutions upon which the whole social structure rested were being steadily sapped by the influence of half-breed girls. Some new, severe, extreme policy was evidently necessary to avert the already visible peril. Special laws were passed by the Home-Government to check enfranchisement, to limit its reasons or motives; and the power of the slave woman was so well comprehended by the Métropole that an extraordinary enactment was made against it. It was decreed that whosoever should free a woman of color would have to pay to the Government *three times her value as a slave!*

Thus heavily weighted, emancipation advanced much more slowly than before, but it still continued to a considerable extent. The poorer creole planter or merchant might find it impossible to obey the impulse of his conscience or of his affection, but among the richer classes pecuniary considerations could scarcely affect enfranchisement. The country had grown wealthy; and although the acquisition of wealth may not evoke generosity in particular natures, the enrichment of a whole class develops pre-existing tendencies to kindness, and opens new ways for its exercise. Later in the eighteenth century, when hospitality had been cultivated as a gentleman's duty to fantastical extremes,—when liberality was the rule throughout society,—when a notary summoned to draw up a deed, or a priest invited to celebrate a marriage, might receive for fee five thousand francs in gold,—there were certainly many emancipations... "Even though interest and public opinion in the colonies," says a historian,[8] "were adverse to enfranchisement, the private feeling of each man combated that opinion;—Nature resumed her sway in the secret places of hearts;— and as local custom permitted a sort of polygamy, the rich man naturally felt himself bound in honor to secure the freedom of his own blood... It was not a rare thing to see legitimate wives taking care of the natural children of their husbands,—becoming their godmothers (*s'en faire les marraines*)."... Nature seemed to laugh all these laws to scorn, and the prejudices of race! In vain did the wisdom of legislators attempt to render the condition of the enfranchised more humble,— enacting extravagant penalties for the blow by which a mulatto might avenge the insult of a white,—prohibiting the freed from wearing the same dress as their former masters or mistresses wore;—"the *belles affranchies* found, in a costume whereof the negligence seemed a very inspiration of voluptuousness, means of evading that social inferiority which the law sought to impose upon them:—they began to inspire the most violent jealousies."[9]

III

WHAT the legislators of 1685 and 1724 endeavored to correct did not greatly improve with the abolition of slavery, nor yet with those political troubles which socially deranged colonial life. The *fille-de-couleur*, inheriting the charm of the *belle affranchie*, continued to exert a similar influence, and to fulfil an almost similar destiny. The latitude of morals persisted,—though with less ostentation: it has latterly contracted under the pressure of necessity rather than through any other influences. Certain ethical principles thought essential to social integrity elsewhere have always been largely relaxed in the tropics; and—excepting, perhaps, Santo Domingo—the moral standard in Martinique was not higher than in the other French colonies. Outward decorum might be to some degree maintained; but there was no great restraint of any sort upon private lives: it was not uncommon for a rich man to have many "natural" families; and almost every individual of means had children of color. The superficial character of race prejudices was everywhere manifested by unions, which although never mentioned in polite converse, were none the less universally known; and the "irresistible fascination" of the half-breed gave the open lie to pretended hate. Nature, in the guise of the *belle affranchie*, had mocked at slave codes;— in the *fille-de-couleur* she still laughed at race pretensions, and ridiculed the fable of physical degradation. Today the situation has not greatly changed; and with such examples on the part of the cultivated race, what could be expected from the other? Marriages are rare;—it has been officially stated that the illegitimate births are sixty per cent; but seventy-five to eighty per cent would probably be nearer the truth. It is very common to see in the local papers such announcements as: *Enfants légitimes*, I (one birth announced); *enfants naturels*, 25.

In speaking of the *fille-de-couleur* it is necessary also to speak of the extraordinary social stratification of the community to which she belongs. The official statement of 20,000 "colored" to the total population of between 173,000 and 174,000 (in which the number of pure whites is said to have fallen as low as 5,000) does not at all indicate the real proportion of mixed blood. Only a small element of unmixed African descent really exists; yet when a white creole speaks of the *gens-de-couleur* he certainly means nothing darker than a mulatto skin. Race classifications have been locally made by sentiments of political origin: at least four or five shades of visible color are classed as negro. There is, however, some natural truth at the bottom of this classification: where African blood predominates, the sympathies are likely to be African; and the turning-point is reached only in the true mulatto, where, allowing the proportions of mixed blood to be nearly equal, the white would have the dominant influence in situations more natural than existing politics. And in speaking of the *filles-de-couleur*, the local reference is always to women in whom the predominant element is white: a white creole, as a general rule, deigns only thus to distinguish those who are nearly white,—more usually he refers to the whole class as mulattresses. Those women whom wealth and education have placed in social position parallel with that of the daughters of creole whites are in some cases allowed to pass for white,—or at the very worst, are only referred to in a whisper as being *de couleur*. (Needless to say, these are totally beyond the range of the present considerations: there is nothing to be further said of them except that they can be classed with the most attractive and refined women of the entire tropical world.) As there is an almost infinite gradation from the true black up to the brightest *sang-mêlé*, it is impossible to establish any color-classification recognizable by the eye alone; and whatever line of demarcation can be drawn between castes must be social rather than ethnical. In this sense we may accept the local Creole definition of *fille-de-couleur* as signifying, not so much a daughter of the race of visible color, as the half-breed girl destined from her birth to a career like that of the *belle affranchie* of the old régime;—for the moral cruelties of slavery have survived emancipation.

Physically, the typical *fille-de-couleur* may certainly be classed, as white creole writers have not hesitated to class her, with the "most beautiful women of the human race."[10] She has inherited not only the finer bodily characteristics of either parent race, but a something else belonging originally to neither, and created by special climatic and physical conditions,—a grace, a suppleness of form, a delicacy of extremities (so that all the lines described by the bending of limbs or fingers are parts of clean curves), a satiny smoothness and fruit-tint of skin,—solely West Indian... Morally, of course, it is much more difficult to describe her; and whatever may safely be said refers rather to the fille-de-couleur of the past than of the present half-century. The race is now in a period of transition: public education and political changes are modifying the type, and it is impossible to guess the ultimate consequence, because it is impossible to safely predict what new influences may yet be brought to affect its social development. Before the present era of colonial decadence, the character of the fille-de-couleur was not what it is now. Even when totally uneducated, she had a peculiar charm,—that charm of childishness which has power to win sympathy from the rudest natures. One could not but feel attracted towards this *naïf* being, docile as an infant, and as easily pleased or as easily pained,—artless in her goodnesses as in her faults, to all outward appearance;—willing to give her youth, her beauty, her caresses to some one in exchange for the promise to love her,—perhaps also to care for a mother, or a younger brother. Her astonishing capacity for being delighted with trifles, her pretty vanities and pretty follies, her sudden veerings of mood from laughter to tears,—like the sudden rainbursts and sunbursts of her own passionate climate: these touched, drew, won, and tyrannized. Yet such easily created joys and pains did not really indicate any deep reserve of feeling: rather a superficial sensitiveness only,—like the *zhèbe-m'amisé*, or *zhèbe-manmzelle*, whose leaves close at the touch of a hair. Such human manifestations, nevertheless, are apt to attract more in proportion as they are more visible,—in proportion as the soul-current, being less profound, flows more audibly. But no hasty observation could have revealed the whole character of the fille-de-couleur to the stranger, equally charmed and surprised: the creole comprehended her better, and probably treated her with even more real kindness. The truth was that centuries of deprivation of natural rights and hopes had given to her race—itself fathered by passion unrestrained and mothered by subjection unlimited—an inherent scepticism in the duration of love, and a marvellous capacity for accepting the destiny of abandonment as one accepts the natural and the inevitable. And that desire to please — which in the fille-de-couleur seemed to prevail above all other motives of action (maternal affection excepted) — could have appeared absolutely natural only to those who never reflected that even sentiment had been artificially cultivated by slavery.

She asked for so little,—accepted a gift with such childish pleasure,—submitted so unresistingly to the will of the man who promised to love her. She bore him children—such beautiful children!—whom he rarely acknowledged, and was never asked to legitimatize;—and she did not ask perpetual affection notwithstanding, — regarded the relation as a necessarily temporary one, to be sooner or later dissolved by the marriage of her children's father. If deceived in all things,—if absolutely ill-treated and left destitute, she did not lose faith in human nature: she seemed a born optimist, believing most men good;—she would make a home for another and serve him better than any slave... "*Née de l'amour,*" says a creole writer, "*la fille-de-couleur vit d'amour, de rires, et d'oublis.*"[11]

Capresse

Then came the general colonial crash!... You cannot see its results without feeling touched by them. Everywhere the weird beauty, the immense melancholy of tropic ruin. Magnificent terraces, once golden with cane, now abandoned to weeds and serpents;—deserted plantation-homes, with trees rooted in the apartments and pushing up through the place of the roofs;—grass-grown alleys ravined by rains;—fruit-trees strangled by lianas;—here and there the stem of some splendid palmiste, brutally decapitated, naked as a mast;—petty frail growths of banana-trees or of bamboo slowly taking the place of century-old forest giants destroyed to make charcoal. But beauty enough remains to tell what the sensual paradise of the old days must have been, when sugar was selling at 52.

And the fille-de-couleur has also changed. She is much less humble and submissive,—somewhat more exacting: she comprehends better the moral injustice of her position. The almost extreme physical refinement and delicacy, bequeathed to her by the freedwomen of the old régime, are passing away: like a conservatory plant deprived of its shelter, she is returning to a more primitive condition,—hardening and growing perhaps less comely as well as less helpless. She perceives also in a vague way the peril of her race: the creole white, her lover and protector, is emigrating;—the domination of the black becomes more and more probable. Furthermore, with the continual increase of the difficulty of living, and the growing pressure of population, social cruelties and hatreds have been developed such as her ancestors never knew. She is still loved; but it is alleged that she rarely loves the white, no matter how large the sacrifices made for her sake, and she no longer enjoys that reputation of fidelity accorded to her class in other years. Probably the truth is that the fille-de-couleur never had at any time capacity to bestow that quality of affection imagined or exacted as a right. Her moral side is still half savage: her feelings are still those of a child. If she does not love the white man according to his unreasonable desire, it is certain at least that she loves him as well as he deserves. Her alleged demoralization is more apparent than real;—she is changing from an artificial to a very natural being, and revealing more and more in her sufferings the true character of the luxurious social condition that brought her into existence. As a general rule, even while questioning her fidelity, the creole freely confesses her kindness of heart, and grants her capable of extreme generosity and devotedness to strangers or to children whom she has an opportunity to care for.

Indeed, her natural kindness is so strikingly in contrast with the harder and subtler character of the men of color that one might almost feel tempted to doubt if she belong to the same race. Said a creole once, in my hearing:—"The gens-de-couleur are just like the *tourlouroux*: [12] one must pick out the females and leave the males alone." Although perhaps capable of a double meaning, his words were not lightly uttered;—he referred to the curious but indubitable fact that character of the colored woman appears in many respects far superior to that of the colored man. In order to understand this, one must bear in mind the difference in the colonial history of both sexes; and a citation from General Romanet, [13] who visited Martinique at the end of the last century, offers a clue to the mystery. Speaking of the tax upon enfranchisement, he writes: —

—"The governor appointed by the sovereign delivers the certificates of liberty,—on payment by the master of a sum usually equivalent to the value of the subject. Public interest frequently justifies him in making the price of the slave proportionate to the desire or the interest manifested by the master. It can be readily understood that the tax upon the liberty of the women ought to be higher than that of the men: the latter unfortunates having no greater advantage than that of being useful;—the former know how to please: they have those rights and privileges which the whole world allows to their sex; they know how to make even the fetters of slavery serve them for adornments. They may be seen placing upon their proud tyrants the same chains worn by themselves, and making them kiss the marks left thereby: the master becomes the slave, and purchases another's liberty only to lose his own."

Long before the time of General Romanet, the colored male slave might win liberty as the guerdon of bravery in fighting against foreign invasion, or might purchase it by extraordinary economy, while working as a mechanic on extra time for his own account (he always refused to labor with negroes); but in either case his success depended upon the possession and exercise of qualities the reverse of amiable. On the other hand, the bondwoman won manumission chiefly through her power to excite affection. In the survival and perpetuation of the fittest of both sexes these widely different characteristics would obtain more and more definition with successive generations.

I find in the "Bulletin des Actes Administratifs de la Martinique" for 1831 (No. 41) a list of slaves to whom liberty was accorded *pour services rendus à leurs maîtres.* Out of sixty-nine enfranchisements recorded under this head, there are only two names of male adults to be found,—one an old man of sixty;—the other, called Laurencin, the betrayer of a conspiracy. The rest are young girls, or young mothers and children;—plenty of those singular and pretty names in vogue among the creole population,—Acélie, Avrillette, Mélie, Robertine, Célianne, Francillette, Adée, Catharinette, Sidollie, Céline, Coraline;—and the ages given are from sixteen to twenty-one, with few exceptions. Yet these liberties were asked for and granted at a time when Louis Philippe had abolished the tax on manumissions... The same "Bulletin" contains a list of liberties granted to colored men, *pour service accompli dans la milice*, only!

Most of the French West Indian writers whose works I was able to obtain and examine speak severely of the *hommes-de-couleur* as a class,—in some instances the historian writes with a very violence of hatred. As far back as the commencement of the eighteenth century, Labat, who, with all his personal oddities, was undoubtedly a fine judge of men, declared:—"The mulattoes are as general rule well made, of good stature, vigorous, strong, adroit, industrious, and daring (*hardis*) beyond all conception. They have much vivacity, but are given to their pleasures, fickle, proud, deceitful (*cachés*), wicked and capable of the greatest crimes." A San Domingo historian, far more prejudiced than Père Labat, speaks of them "as physically superior, though morally inferior to the whites": he wrote at a time when the race had given to the world the two best swordsmen it has yet perhaps seen,—Saint-Georges and Jean-Louis.

Commenting on the judgement of Père Labat, the historian Borde observes:—"The wickedness spoken of by Père Labat doubtless relates to their political passions only; for the women of color are, beyond any question, the best and sweetest persons in the world—*à coup sûr, les meilleures et les plus douces personnes qu'il y ait au monde*"– ("Histoire de l'Ile de la Trinidad," par M. Pierre Gustave Louis Borde, vol. i., p.222.) The same author, speaking of their goodness of heart, generosity to strangers and the sick, says "they are born Sisters of Charity";—and he is not the only historian who has expressed such admiration of their moral qualities. What I myself saw during the epidemic of 1887-88 at Martinique convinced me that these eulogies of the women of color are not extravagant. On the other hand, the existing creole opinion of the men of color is much less favorable than even that expressed by Père Labat. Political events and passions have, perhaps, rendered a just estimate of their qualities difficult. The history of the *hommes-de-couleur* in all the French colonies has been the same;—distrusted by the whites, who feared their aspirations to social equality, distrusted even more by the blacks (who still hate them secretly, although ruled by them), the mulattoes became an Ishmaelitish clan, inimical to both races, and dreaded of both. In Martinique it was attempted, with some success, to manage them by according freedom to all who would serve in the militia for a certain period with credit. At no time was it found possible to compel them to work with blacks; and they formed the whole class of skilled city workmen and mechanics for a century prior to emancipation.

...Today it cannot be truly said of the *fille-de-couleur* that her existence is made up of "love, laughter, and forgettings." She has aims in life,—the bettering of her condition, the higher education of her children, whom she hopes to free from the curse of prejudice. She still clings to the white, because through him she may hope to improve her position. Under other conditions she might even hope to effect some sort of reconciliation between the races. But the gulf has become so much widened within the last forty years, that no *rapprochement* now appears possible; and it is perhaps too late even to restore the lost prosperity of the colony by any legislative or commercial reforms. The universal creole belief is summed up in the daily-repeated cry: *"C'est un pays perdu!"* Yearly the number of failures increase; and more whites emigrate; — and with every bankruptcy or departure some fille-de-couleur is left almost destitute, to begin life over again. Many a one has been rich and poor several times in succession; — one day her property is seized for debt; — perhaps on the morrow she finds some one able and willing to give her a home again... Whatever comes, she does not die for grief, this daughter of the sun: she pours out her pain in song, like a bird. Here is one of her little improvisations,—a song very popular in both Martinique and Guadeloupe, though originally composed in the latter colony: —

— "Good-bye Madras!	— "Adiéu Madras!
Good-bye foulard!	Adiéu foulard!
Good-bye pretty calicoes!	Adiéu dézinde!
Good-bye collier-choux!	Adiéu collier-choux!
That ship	Batiment-là
Which is there on the buoy,	Qui sou labouè-là,
It is taking	Li ka mennen
My doudoux away	Doudoux-à-moin allé.

— "Very good-day,
Monsieur the Consignee.
I come
To make one little petition.
My doudoux
Is going away.
Alas! I pray you
Delay his going."

— "Bien le-bonjou'
Missié le Consignataire.
Moin ka vini
Fai yon ti petition;
Doudoux-à-moin
Y ka pati, —
T'enprie, hélas!
Rétàdé li."

[He answers kindly in French: the *békés* are always kind to these gentle children.]

— "My dear child,
It is too late.
The bills of lading
Are already signed;
The ship
Is already on the buoy.
In an hour from now
They will be getting her under way."

— "Ma chère enfant
Il est trop tard,
Les connaissements
Sont déjà signés,
Le batiment
Est déjà sur la bouée
Dans une heure d'ici
Ils vont appareiller."

— "When the foulards came…
I always had some;
When the Madras-kerchiefs came,
I always had some;
When the printed calicoes came,
I always had some.
…That second officer
Is such a kind man!

— "Foulard rivé,
Moin té toujou tini;
Madras rivé
Moin té toujou tini.
Dézindes rivé,
Moin té toujou tini.
— Capitaine sougonde
C'est yon bon gàçon!

— "Everybody has
Somebody to love;
Everybody has
Somebody to pet;
Everybody has
A sweetheart of her own.
I am the only one
Who cannot have that, — I!"

"Toutt moune tini
Yon moune yo aimé;
Toutt moune tini
Yon moune yo chéri;
Toutt moune tini
Yon doudoux à yo.
Jusse moin tou sèle
Pa tini ça, — moin!"

On the eve of the *Fête Dieu*, or Corpus Christi festival, in all these Catholic countries, the city streets are hung with banners and decorated with festoons and with palm branches; and great altars are erected at various points along the route of the procession, to serve as resting-places for the Host. These are called *reposoirs*; in creole patois, "*reposoùè Bon-Dié.*" Each wealthy man lends something to help to make them attractive, — rich plate, dainty crystal, bronzes, paintings, beautiful models of ships or steamers, curiosities from remote parts of the world... The procession over, the altar is stripped, the valuables are returned to their owners: all the splendor disappears... And the spectacle of that evanescent magnificence, repeated year by year, suggested to this proverb-loving people a similitude for the unstable fortune of the fille-de-couleur:—*Fortune milatresse c'est reposoùè Bon-Dié.* (The luck of the mulattress is the resting-place of the Good-God).

NOTES

1. The brightly colored douillettes are classified by the people according to the designs of the printed calico:—*robe-à-bambou,*—*robe-à-bouquet,*—*robe-arc-en-ciel,*—*robe-à-carreau,*—etc., according as the pattern is in stripes, flower-designs, "rainbow" bands of different tints, or plaidings. *Ronde-en-ronde* means a stuff printed with disk-patterns, or link-patterns of different colors,—each joined with the other. A robe of one color only is called a *robe-uni.*

The general laws of contrasts observed in the costume require the silk foulard, or shoulder-kerchief, to make a sharp relief with color of the robe, thus:—

Robe	*Foulard*
Yellow	Blue
Dark blue	Yellow
Pink	Green
Violet	Bright red
Red	Violet
Chocolate (cacoa)	Pale blue
Sky blue	Pale rose

These refer, of course, to dominant or ground colors, as there are usually several tints in the foulard as well as the robe. The painted Madras should always be bright yellow. According to popular ideas of good dressing, the different tints of skin should be relieved by special choice of color in the robe, as follows:—

Capresse (a clear red skin) should wear ....Pale yellow

Mulatresse (according to shade)...............Rose, blue, green

Négresse ....White, scarlet, or any violent color

2. ..."Vouèla Cendrillon evec yon bel ròbe velou grande lakhè. ...Ça té ka bail ou mal ziè. Li té tini bel zanneau dans zòreill li, quate-tou-chou, bouoche, bracelet, tremblant,—toutt sòte bel baggaïe conm ça."... [*Conte Cendrillon, — d'après Turiault.*] —"There was Cendrillon with a beautiful long trailing robe of velvet on her!... It was enough to hurt one's eyes to look at her! She had beautiful rings in her ears, and a collier-choux of four rows, brooches, *tremblants,* bracelets,—everything fine of that sort." [Story of Cinderella in Turiault's Creole Grammar]

3. It is quite possible, however, that the slaves of Dutertre's time belonged for the most part to the uglier African tribes; and that later supplies may have been procured from other parts of the slave coast. Writing half a century later, Père Labat declares having seen freshly disembarked blacks handsome enough to inspire an artist:—"*J'en ai vu des deux sexes faits à peindre, et beaux par merveille*" (vol. iv., chap. vii.). He adds that their skin was extremely fine, and of velvety softness;—"*le velours n'est pas plus doux.*"... Among the 30,000 blacks yearly shipped to the French colonies, there were doubtless many representatives of the finer African races.

4. Leur sueur n'est pas fétide comme celle des nègres de la Guinée," writes the traveller Dauxion-Lavaysse, in 1813.

5. Dr. E. Rufz: "Études historiques et statistiques sur la population de la Martinique." St. Pierre: 1850. Vol. i., pp. 148-50.

It has been generally imagined that the physical constitution of the black race was proof against the deadly climate of the West Indies. The truth is that the freshly imported Africans died of fever by thousands and tens-of-thousands;—the creole-negro race, now so prolific, represents only the fittest survivors in the long and terrible struggle of the slave element to adapt itself to the new environment. Thirty thousand negroes a year were long needed to supply the French colonies. Between 1700 and 1789 no less than 900,000 slaves were imported by San Domingo alone;—yet there were less than half that number left in 1789. (See Placide Justin's history of Santo Domingo, p.147.) The entire slave population of Barbadoes had to he renewed every sixteen years, according to estimates: the loss to planters by deaths of slaves (reckoning the value of a slave at only £20 sterling) during the same period was £1,600,000 ($8,000,000). (Burck's "History of European Colonies," vol. ii., p. 141; French edition of 1767.)

6. Rufz: "Études," vol. i., p. 236.

7. I am assured it has now fallen to a figure not exceeding 5,000.

8. Rufz: "Études," vol. ii., pp. 311, 312.

9. Rufz: "Études," vol. i., p.237.

10. *La race de sang-mêlé, issue des blancs et des noirs, est éminement civilizable. Comme types physiques, elle fournit dans beaucoup d'individus, dans ses femmes en*

général, les plus beaux specimens de la race humaine.—"Le Préjugé de Race aux Antilles Françaises." Par G. Souquet-Basiège. St. Pierre, Martinique: 1883. pp. 661-62.

11. Turiault: "Étude sur le langage Créole de la Martinique." Brest: 1874. On page 136 he cites the following pretty verses in speaking of the *fille-de-couleur:*—

> *L'Amour prit soin de la former*
> *Tendre, naïve, et caressante,*
> *Faite pour plaire, encore plus pour aimer,*
> *Portant tous les traits précieux*
> *Du caractère d'une amante,*
> *Le plaisir sur sa bouche et l'amour dans ses yeux.*

12. A sort of land-crab;—the female is selected for food, and, properly cooked, makes a delicious dish;—the male is almost worthless.

13. "Voyage à la Martinique." Par J. R., Général de Brigade. Paris: An. XII., 1804. Page 106.

X. Bête-Ni-Pié

I

ST. PIERRE is in one respect fortunate beyond many tropical cities;—she has scarcely any mosquitoes, although there are plenty of mosquitoes in other parts of Martinique, even in the higher mountain villages. The flood of bright water that pours perpetually through all her streets, renders her comparatively free from the pest;—nobody sleeps under a mosquito bar.

Nevertheless, St. Pierre is not exempt from other peculiar plagues of tropical life; and you cannot be too careful about examining your bed before venturing to lie down, and your clothing before you dress;—for various disagreeable things might be hiding in them: a spider large as a big crab, or a scorpion or a *mabouya* or a centipede,—or certain large ants whose bite burns like the pricking of a red-hot needle. No one who has lived in St. Pierre is likely to forget the ants... There are three or four kinds in every house;—the *fourmi fou* (mad ant), a little speckled yellowish creature whose movements are so rapid as to delude the vision; the great black ant which allows itself to be killed before it lets go what it has bitten; the venomous little red ant, which is almost too small to see; and the small black ant which does not bite at all,—are usually omnipresent, and appear to dwell together in harmony. They are pests in kitchens, cupboards, and safes; but they are scavengers. It is marvellous to see them carrying away the body of a great dead roach or centipede,—pulling and pushing together like trained laborers, and guiding the corpse over obstacles or around them with extraordinary skill... There was a time when ants almost destroyed the colony,—in 1751. The plantations devastated by them are described by historians as having looked as if destroyed by fire. Underneath the ground in certain places, layers of their eggs two inches deep were found extending over acres. Infants left unwatched in the cradle for a few hours were devoured alive by them. Immense balls of living ants were washed ashore at the same time on various parts of the coast (a phenomenon repeated within the memory of creoles now living in the north-east parishes). The Government vainly offered rewards for the best means of destroying the insects; but the plague gradually disappeared as it came.

None of these creatures can be prevented from entering a dwelling;—you may as well resign yourself to the certainty of meeting with them from time to time. The great spiders (with the exception of those which are hairy) need excite no alarm or disgust;—indeed they are suffered to live unmolested in many houses, partly owing to a belief that they bring good-luck, and partly because they destroy multitudes of those enormous and noisome roaches which spoil whatever they cannot eat. The scorpion is less common; but it has a detestable habit of lurking under beds; and its bite communicates a burning fever. With far less reason, the mabouya is almost equally feared. It is a little lizard about six inches long and ashen-colored;—it haunts only the interior of houses, while the bright-green lizards dwell only upon the roofs. Like other reptiles of the same order, the mabouya can run over or cling to polished surfaces; and there is a popular belief that if frightened, it will leap at one's face or hands and there fasten itself so tightly that it cannot be dislodged except by cutting it to pieces. Moreover, its feet are supposed to have the power of leaving certain livid and ineffaceable marks upon the skin of the person to whom it attaches itself—*ça ka ba ou lota*, say the colored people. Nevertheless, there is no creature more timid and harmless than the mabouya.

But the most dreaded and the most insolent invader of domestic peace is the centipede. The water system of the city banished the mosquito; but it introduced the centipede into almost every dwelling. St. Pierre has a plague of centipedes. All the covered drains, the gutters, the crevices of fountain-basins and bathing-basins, the spaces between floor and ground, shelter centipedes. And the *bête-à-mille-pattes* is the terror of the barefooted population:—scarcely a day passes that some child or bonne or workman is not bitten by the creature.

The sight of a full-grown centipede is enough to affect a strong set of nerves. Ten to eleven inches is the average length of adults; but extraordinary individuals much exceeding this dimension may be sometimes observed in the neighborhood of distilleries (*rhommeries*) and sugar-refineries. According to age, the color of the creature varies from yellowish to black;—the younger ones often have several different tints; the old ones are uniformly jet-black, and have a carapace of surprising toughness difficult to break. If you tread, by accident or design, upon the tail, the poisonous head will instantly curl back and bite the foot through any ordinary thickness of upper-leather.

As a general rule the centipede lurks about the courtyards, foundations, and drains by preference; but in the season of heavy rains he does not hesitate to move upstairs, and make himself at home in parlors and bedrooms. He has a provoking habit of nestling in your *moresques* or your *chinoises*,—those wide light garments you put on before taking your siesta or retiring for the night. He also likes to get into your umbrella,—an article indispensable in the tropics; and you had better never open it carelessly. He may even take a notion to curl himself up in your hat, suspended on the wall—(I have known a trigonocephalus to do the same thing in a country-house). He has also a singular custom of mounting upon the long trailing dresses (douillettes) worn by Martinique women,—and climbing up very swiftly and lightly to the wearer's neck, where the prickling of his feet first betrays his presence. Sometimes he will get into bed with you and bite you, because you have not resolution enough to lie perfectly still while he is tickling you... It is well to remember before dressing that merely shaking a garment may not dislodge him;—you must examine every part very patiently, particularly the sleeves of a coat and the legs of pantaloons.

The vitality of the creature is amazing. I kept one in a bottle without food or water for thirteen weeks, at the end of which time it remained active and dangerous as ever. Then I fed it with living insects, which it devoured ravenously;—beetles, roaches, earthworms, several *lepismae*, even one of the dangerous-looking millipedes, which have a great resemblance in outward structure to the centipede, but a thinner body, and more numerous limbs,—all seemed equally palatable to the prisoner... I knew an instance of one, nearly a foot long, remaining in a silk parasol for more than four months, and emerging unexpectedly one day, with aggressiveness undiminished, to bite the hand that had involuntarily given it deliverance.

In the city the centipede has but one natural enemy able to cope with him,—the hen! The hen attacks him with delight, and often swallows him, head first, without taking the trouble to kill him. The cat hunts him, but she is careful never to put her head near him;—she has a trick of whirling him round and round upon the floor so quickly as to stupefy him: then, when she sees a good chance, she strikes him dead with her claws. But if you are fond of your cat you will let her run no risks, as the bite of a large centipede might have very bad results for your pet. Its quickness of movement demands all the quickness of even the cat for self-defence... I know of men who have proved themselves able to seize a fer-de-lance by the tail, whirl it round and round, then flip it as you would crack a whip,—whereupon the terrible head flies off; but I never heard of anyone in Martinique daring to handle a living centipede.

There are superstitions concerning the creature which have a good effect in diminishing his tribe. If you kill a centipede, you are sure to receive money soon; and even if you dream of killing one it is good-luck. Consequently, people are glad of any chance to kill centipedes,—usually taking a heavy stone or some iron utensil for the work,—a wooden stick is not a good weapon. There is always a little excitement when a *bête-ni-pié* (as the centipede is termed in the patois) exposes itself to death; and you may often hear those who kill it uttering a sort of litany of abuse with every blow, as if addressing a human enemy:—
"*Quitté moin tchoué ou, maudi!—quitté moin tchoué ou, scelerat!—quitté moin tchoué ou, Satan!—quitté moin tchoué ou, abonocio!*" etc. (Let me kill you, accursed! scoundrel! Satan! abomination!)

The patois term for the centipede is not a mere corruption of the French *bête-à-mille-pattes*. Among a population of slaves, unable to read or write,[1] there were only the vaguest conceptions of numerical values; and the French term bête-à-mille-pattes was not one which could appeal to negro imagination. The slaves themselves invented an equally vivid name, *bête-anni-pié* (the Beast-which-is-all-feet); *anni* in creole signifying "only," and in such a sense "all." Abbreviated by subsequent usage *bête-'ni-pié*, the appellation has amphibology;—for there are two words *ni* in the patois, one signifying "to have," and the other "naked." So that the creole for a centipede may be translated in three ways,—"the Beast-which-is-all-feet"; or, "the Naked-footed-Beast"; or, with fine irony of affirmation, "the Beast-which-has-feet."

II

WHAT is the secret of that horror inspired by the centipede?... It is but very faintly related to our knowledge that the creature is venomous;—the results of the bite are only temporary swelling and a brief fever;—it is less to be feared than the bite of other tropical insects and reptiles which never inspire the same loathing by their aspect. And the shapes of venomous creatures are not always shapes of ugliness. The serpent has elegance of form as well as attractions of metallic tinting;—the tarantula, or the *matoutou-falaise*, have geometric beauty. Lapidaries have in all ages expended rare skill upon imitations of serpent grace in gold and gems;—a princess would not scorn to wear a diamond spider. But what art could utilize successfully the form of the centipede? It is a form of absolute repulsiveness,—a skeleton-shape half defined:—the suggestion of some old reptile-spine astir, crawling with its fragments of ribs.

No other living thing excites exactly the same feeling produced by the sight of the centipede,—the intense loathing and peculiar fear. The instant you see a centipede you feel it is absolutely necessary to kill it: you cannot find peace in your house while you know that such a life exists in it: perhaps the intrusion of a serpent would annoy and disgust you less. And it is not easy to explain the whole reason of this loathing. The form alone has, of course, something to do with it,—a form that seems almost a departure from natural laws. But the form alone does not produce the full effect, which is only experienced when you see the creature in motion. The true horror of the centipede, perhaps, must be due to the monstrosity of its movement,—multiple and complex, as of a chain of pursuing and inter-devouring lives: there is something about it that makes you recoil, as from a sudden corrupt swarming-out. It is confusing,—a series of contractings and lengthenings and undulations so rapid as to allow of being only half seen: it alarms also, because the thing seems perpetually about to disappear, and because you know that to lose sight of it for one moment involves the very unpleasant chance of finding it upon you the next,—perhaps between skin and clothing.

But this is not all:—the sensation produced by the centipede is still more complex—complex, in fact, as the visible organization of the creature. For, during pursuit,—whether retreating or attacking, in hiding or fleeing,—it displays a something which seems more than instinct: calculation and cunning,—a sort of malevolent intelligence. It knows how to delude, how to terrify;—it has marvellous skill in feinting;—it is an abominable juggler...

III

I AM about to leave my room after breakfast, when little Victoire who carries the meals up-stairs in a wooden tray, screams out:—"*Gadé, Missié! ni bête-ni-pié assous dos ou!*" There is a thousand-footed beast upon my back!

Off goes my coat, which I throw upon the floor;—the little servant, who has a nervous horror of centipedes, climbs upon a chair. I cannot see anything upon the coat, nevertheless;—I lift it by the collar, turn it about very cautiously—nothing! Suddenly the child screams again; and I perceive the head close to my hand;—the execrable thing had been hiding in a perpendicular fold of the coat, which I drop only just in time to escape getting bitten. Immediately the centipede becomes invisible. Then I take the coat by one flap, and turn it over very quickly: just as quickly does the centipede pass over it in the inverse direction, and disappear under it again. I have had my first good look at him: he seems nearly a foot long, has a greenish-yellow hue against the black cloth,—and pink legs, and a violet head;—he is evidently young... I turn the coat a second time: same disgusting manoeuvre. Undulations of livid color flow over him as he lengthens and shortens;—while running his shape is but half apparent; it is only as he makes a half pause in doubling round and under the coat that the panic of his legs becomes discernible. When he is fully exposed they move with invisible rapidity,—like a vibration;—you can see only a sort of pink haze extending about him,—something to which you would no more dare advance your finger than to the vapory halo edging a circular saw in motion. Twice more I turn and re-turn the coat with the same result;—I observe that the centipede always runs towards my hand until I withdraw it: he feints!

With a stick I uplift one portion of the coat after another; and suddenly perceive him curved under a sleeve,—looking quite small!—how could he have seemed so large a moment ago?... But before I can strike him he has flickered over the cloth again, and vanished; and I discover that he has the power of *magnifying himself*,—dilating the disgust of his shape at will: he invariably amplifies himself to face attack...

It seems very difficult to dislodge him; he displays astonishing activity and cunning at finding wrinkles and folds to hide in. Even at the risk of damaging various things in the pockets, I stamp upon the coat;—then lift it up with the expectation of finding the creature dead. But it suddenly rushes out from some part or other, looking larger and more wicked than ever;—drops to the floor, and charges at my feet: a sortie! I strike at him unsuccessfully with the stick: he retreats to the angle between wainscoting and floor, and runs along it fast as a railroad train,—dodges two or three pokes,—gains the door-frame,—glides behind a hinge, and commences to run over the wall of the stair-way. There the hand of a black servant slaps him dead.

—"Always strike at the head," the servant tells me; "never tread on the tail... This is a small one: the big fellows can make you afraid if you do not know how to kill them."

...I pick up the carcass with a pair of scissors. It does not look formidable now that it is all contracted;—it is scarcely eight inches long,—thin as card-board, and even less heavy. It has no substantiality, no weight;—it is a mere appearance, a mask, a delusion... But remembering the spectral, cunning, juggling something which magnified and moved it but a moment ago,—I feel almost tempted to believe, with certain savages, that there are animal shapes inhabited by goblins...

IV

—"Is there anything still living and lurking in old black drains of Thought,—any bigotry, any prejudice, anything in the moral world whereunto the centipede may be likened?"

—"Really, I do not know," replied the friend to whom I had put the question; "but you need only go as far as the vegetable world for a likeness. Did you ever see anything like this?" he added, opening a drawer and taking therefrom something revolting, which, as he pressed it in his hand, looked like a long thick bundle of dried centipedes.

—"Touch them," he said, holding out to me the mass of articulated flat bodies and bristling legs.

—"Not for anything!" I replied, in astonished disgust. He laughed, and opened his hand. As he did so, the mass expanded.

—"Now look!" he exclaimed.

Then I saw that all the bodies were united at the tails—grew together upon one thick flat annulated stalk... a plant!—"But here is the fruit," he continued, taking from the same drawer a beautifully embossed ovoid nut large as a duck's egg, ruddy-colored, and so exquisitely varnished by nature as to resemble a rose-wood carving fresh from the hands of the cabinet-maker. In its proper place among the leaves and branches, it had the appearance of something delicious being devoured by a multitude of centipedes. Inside was a kernel, hard and heavy as iron-wood; but this in time, I was told, falls into dust: though the beautiful shell remains always perfect.

Negroes call it the *coco-macaque*.

NOTES

1. According to the Martinique "Annuaire" for 1887, there were even then, out of a total population of 173,182, no less than 125,366 unable to read and write.

XI. Ma Bonne

I

I CANNOT teach Cyrillia the clock;—I have tried until both of us had our patience strained to the breaking-point. Cyrillia still believes she will learn how to tell the time some day or other;—I am certain that she never will. "*Missié,*" she says, "*lézhè pa aïen pou moin: c'est minitt ka fouté moin yon travail!*"—the hours do not give her any trouble; but the minutes are a frightful bore! And nevertheless, Cyrillia is punctual as the sun;—she always brings my coffee and a slice of corrossole at five in the morning precisely. Her clock is the *cabritt-bois*. The great cricket stops singing, she says, at half-past four: the cessation of its chant awakens her.

—"*Bonjou', Missié. Comment ou passé lanuitt?*"—"Thanks, my daughter, I slept well."—"The weather is beautiful: if Missié would like to go to the beach, his bathing-towels are ready."—"Good! Cyrillia; I will go."... Such is our regular morning conversation.

Nobody breakfasts before eleven o'clock or thereabout; but after an early sea-bath, one is apt to feel a little hollow during the morning, unless one take some sort of refreshment. Cyrillia always prepares something for me on my return from the beach,—either a little pot of fresh cocoa-water, or a *cocoyage*, or a *mabiyage*, or a *bavaroise*.

The *cocoyage* I like the best of all. Cyrillia takes green cocoa-nut, slices off one side of it so as to open a hole, then pours the opalescent water into a bowl, adds to it a fresh egg, a little Holland gin, and some grated nutmeg and plenty of sugar. Then she whips up the mixture into effervescence with her *baton-lélé*. The *baton-lélé* is an indispensable article in every creole home: it is a thin stick which is cut from a young tree so as to leave at one end a whorl of branch-stumps sticking out at right angles like spokes;—by twirling the stem between the hands, the stumps whip up the drink in a moment.

The *mabiyage* is less agreeable, but is a popular morning drink among the poorer classes. It is made with a little white rum and a bottle of the bitter native root-beer called *mabi*. The taste of *mabi* I can only describe as that of molasses and water flavored with a little cinchona bark.

The *bavaroise* is fresh milk, sugar, and a little Holland gin or rum,—mixed with the baton-lélé until a fine thick foam is formed. After the cocoyage, I think it is the best drink one can take in the morning; but very little spirit must be used for any of these mixtures. It is not until just before the midday meal that one can venture to take a serious stimulant,—*yon ti ponch*,—rum and water, sweetened with plenty of sugar or sugar syrup.

The word *sucre* is rarely used in Martinique,—considering that sugar is still the chief product;—the word *doux*, "sweet," is commonly substituted for it. *Doux* has, however, a larger range of meaning: it may signify syrup, or any sort of sweets,—duplicated into *doudoux*, it means the corrossole fruit as well as the sweetheart. *Ça qui lè doudoux?* is the cry of the corrossole-seller. If a negro asks at a grocery store (*graisserie*) for *sique* instead of for *doux*, it is only because he does not want it to be supposed that he means syrup;—as a general rule, he will only use the word *sique* when referring to quality of sugar wanted or to sugar in hogsheads. *Doux* enters into domestic consumption in quite remarkable ways. People put sugar into fresh milk, English porter, beer, and cheap wine;—they cook various vegetables with sugar, such as peas; they seem to be particularly fond of sugar-and-water and of *d'leau-pain*,—bread-and-water boiled, strained, mixed with sugar, and flavored with cinnamon. The stranger gets accustomed to all this sweetness without evil results. In a northern climate the sequence would probably be at least a bilious attack; but in the tropics, where salt fish and fruits are popularly preferred to meat, the prodigal use of sugar or sugar-syrups appears to be decidedly beneficial.

...After Cyrillia has prepared my *cocoyage*, and rinsed the bathing-towels in fresh-water, she is ready to go to market, and wants to know what I would like to eat for breakfast. "Anything creole, Cyrillia;—I want to know what people eat in this country." She always does her best to please me in this respect,—almost daily introduces me to some unfamiliar dishes, something odd in the way of fruit or fish.

II

Cyrillia has given me a good idea of the range and character of *mangé-Créole*; and I can venture to write something about it after a year's observation. By *mangé-Créole* I refer only to the food of the people proper, the colored population; for the *cuisine* of the small class of wealthy whites is chiefly European, and devoid of local interest:—I might observe, however, that the fashion of cooking is rather Provençal than Parisian;—rather of southern than of northern France.

Meat, whether fresh or salt, enters little into the nourishment of the poorer classes. This is partly, no doubt, because of the cost of all meats; but it is also due to natural preference for fruits and fish. When fresh meat is purchased, it is usually to make a stew or *daube*; —probably salt meats are more popular; and native vegetables and manioc flour are preferred to bread. There are only two popular soups which are peculiar to the creole cuisine,—*calalou*, a gombo soup, almost precisely similar to that of Louisiana; and the *soupe-d'habitant*, or "country soup." It is made of yams, carrots, bananas, turnips, *choux-caraïbes*, pumpkins, salt pork, and pimento, all boiled together;—the salt meat being left out of the composition on Fridays.

The great staple, the true meat of the population, is salt codfish, which is prepared in a great number of ways. The most popular and the rudest preparation of it is called "Ferocious" (*féroce*); and it is not at all unpalatable. The codfish is simply fried, and served with vinegar, oil, pimento;—manioc flour and avocados being considered indispensable adjuncts. As manioc flour forms a part of almost every creole meal, a word of information regarding it will not be out of place here.

Everybody who has heard the name probably knows that the manioc root is naturally poisonous, and that the toxic elements must be removed by pressure and desiccation before the flour can be made. Good manioc flour has an appearance like very coarse oatmeal; and is probably quite as nourishing. Even when dear as bread, it is preferred, and forms the flour of the population, by whom the word *farine* is only used to signify manioc flour: if wheat-flour be referred to it is always qualified as "French flour" (*farine-Fouance*). Although certain flours are regularly advertised as American in the local papers, they are still *farine-Fouance* for the population, who call everything foreign French. American beer is *bié-Fouance*; canned peas, *ti-pois-Fouance*; any white foreigner who can talk French is *yon béké-Fouance*.

Usually the manioc flour is eaten uncooked:[1] merely poured into a plate, with a little water and stirred with a spoon into a thick paste or mush,—the thicker the better;—*dleau passé farine* (more water than manioc flour) is a saying which describes the condition of a very destitute person. When not served with fish, the flour is occasionally mixed with water and refined molasses (*sirop-battrie*): this preparation, which is very nice, is called *cousscaye*. There is also a way of boiling it with molasses and into a kind of pudding. This is called *matêtê*; children are very fond of it. Both of these names, *cousscaye* and *matêtê*, are alleged to be of Carib origin: the art of preparing the flour itself from manioc root is certainly an inheritance from the Caribs, who bequeathed many singular words to the creole patois of the French West Indies.

Of all the preparations of codfish with which manioc flour is eaten, I preferred the *lamori-bouilli,*—the fish boiled plain, after having been steeped long enough to remove the excess of salt; and then served with plenty of olive-oil and pimento. The people who have no home of their own, or at least no place to cook, can buy their food already prepared from the *màchannes lapacotte,* who seem to make a speciality of *macadam* (codfish stewed with rice) and the other two dishes already referred to. But in every colored family there are occasional feasts of *lamori-au-laitt,* codfish stewed with milk and potatoes; *lamori-au-grattin,* codfish boned, pounded with toast crumbs, and boiled with butter, onions, and pepper into a mush;—*coubouyon-lamori,* codfish stewed with butter and oil;—*bachamelle,* codfish boned and stewed with potatoes, pimentos, oil, garlic, and butter.

Pimento is an essential accompaniment to all dishes, whether it be cooked or raw: everything is served with plenty of pimento,—*en pile, en pile piment.* Among the various kinds I can mention only the *piment-café,* or "coffee-pepper," larger but about the same shape as a grain of Liberian coffee, violet-red at one end; the *piment-zouèseau,* or bird-pepper, small and long and scarlet;—and the *piment-capresse,* very large, pointed at one end, and bag-shaped at the other. It takes a very deep red color when ripe, and is so strong that if you only break the pod in a room, the sharp perfume instantly fills the apartment. Unless you are as well trained as any Mexican to eat pimento, you will probably regret your first encounter with the *capresse.*

Cyrillia told me a story about this infernal vegetable.

III

ZHISTOUÈ PIMENT

Té ni yon manman qui té ni en pile, en pile yche; et yon jou y pa té ni aïen pou y té baill yche-là mangé. Y té ka lévé bon matin là sans yon sou: y pa sa ça y té douè fai,—là y té ké baill latête. Y allé lacaïe macoumè-y, raconté lapeine-y. Macoumè baill y toua chopine farine-manioc. Y allé

lacaill lautt macoumè, qui baill y yon grand trai piment. Macoumè-là di
y venne trai-piment-à, épi y té pè acheté lamori,—pisse y ja té ni farine.
Madame-là di: "Mèci, macoumè;"—y di y bon-jou'; épi y allé lacaïe-y.

Lhè y rivé àcaïe y limé difè: y metté canari épi dleau assous difé-à; épi
y cassé toutt piment-là et metté yo adans canari-à assous difé. Lhè y ouè
canari-à ka bouï, y pouend baton-lélé, épi y lélé piment-à: aloss y ka fai
yonne cala-lou-piment. Lhè calalou-piment là té tchouitt, y pouend
chaque zassiett yche-li; y metté calalou yo fouète dans zassiett-là; y metté
ta-mari fouète, assou, épi ta-y. Épi lhè calalou-là té bien fouète, y metté
farine nans chaque zassiett-là. Épi y crié toutt moune vini mangé. Toutt
moune vini metté yo à-tabe.

Pouèmiè bouchée mari-à pouend, y rété,—y crié: "Aïe! ouaill!
mafenm!" Fenm-là réponne mari-y: "Ouaill! monmari!" Cés ti
manmaille-là crié: "Ouaill! manman!" Manman-à réponne:—"Ouaill!
Yches-moin!"...Yo toutt pouend couri, quitté caïe-là sèle,—épi yo toutt
tombé larivè à touempé bouche yo. Cés ti manmaille-là bouè dleau sitelle-
ment jusse temps yo toutt néyé: té ka rété anni manman-là épi papa-là.
Yo té là, bò larivè, qui té ka pleiré. Moin té ka passé à lhè-à;—moin ka
mandé yo: "Ça zautt ni ?"

Nhomme-là lévé: y baill moin yon sèle coup d'piè, y voyé moin lautt
bò larivè—ou ouè moin vini pou conté ça ba ou.

PIMENTO STORY

There was once a mamma who had ever so many children; and one
day she had nothing to give those children to eat. She had got up
very early that morning, without a sou in the world: she did not know
what to do: she was so worried that her head was upset. She went to
the house of a woman-friend, and told her about her trouble. The
friend gave her three *chopines* [three pints] of manioc flour. Then she
went to the house of another female friend, who gave her a big tray-
ful of pimentos. The friend told her to sell that tray of pimentos: then
she could buy some codfish,—since she already had some manioc
flour. The good-wife said: "Thank you, *macoumè*,"—she bid her
good-day, and then went to her own house.

The moment she got home, she made a fire, and put her *canari*
[earthen pot] full of water on the fire to boil: then she broke up all the
pimentos and put them into the canari on the fire.

As soon as she saw the canari boiling, she took her *baton-lélé* and beat
up all those pimentos: then she made a *pimento-calalou*. When the

pimento-calalou was well cooked, she took each one of the children's plates, and poured their calalou into the plates to cool it; she also put her husband's out to cool, and her own. And when the calalou was quite cool, she put some manioc flour into each of the plates. Then she called to everybody to come and eat. They all came, and sat down to table.

The first mouthful that husband took he stopped and screamed:—"*Aïe! ouaill!* my wife!" The woman answered her husband: "*Ouaill!* my husband!" The little children all screamed "*Ouaill!* mamma!" Their mamma answered: "*Ouaill!* My children!"... They all ran out, left the house empty; and they tumbled into the river to steep their mouths. Those little children just drank water and drank water till they were all drowned: there was nobody left except the mama and the papa. They stayed there on the river-bank, and cried. I was passing that way just at that time;—I asked them: "What ails you people?"

That man got up and gave me just one kick that sent me right across the river; I came here at once, as you see, to tell you all about it...

IV

...IT is no use for me to attempt anything like a detailed description of the fish Cyrillia brings me day after day from the Place du Fort: the variety seems to be infinite. I have learned, however, one curious fact which is worth noting: that, as a general rule, the more beautifully colored fish are the least palatable, and are sought after only by the poor. The *perroquet*, black, with bright bands of red and yellow; the *cirurgien*, blue and black, the *patate*, yellow and black; the *moringue*, which looks like polished granite; the *souri*, pink and yellow; the vermilion *Gouôs-zie*, the rosy *sade*; the red *Bon-Dié-manié-moin* ("the-Good-God-handled-me")—it has two queer marks as of great fingers; and the various kinds of all-blue fish, *balaou, conliou*, etc., varying from steel-color to violet,—these are seldom seen at the tables of the rich. There are exceptions, of course, to this and all general rules: notably the *couronné*, pink spotted beautifully with black,—a sort of Redfish, which never sells less than fourteen cents a pound; and the *zorphi*, which has exquisite changing lights of nacreous green and purple. It is said, however, that the zorphi is sometimes poisonous, like the *bécunne*; there are many fish which, although not venomous by nature, have always been considered dangerous. In the time of Père Dutertre it was believed these fish ate the apples of the manchineel-tree, washed into the sea by rains;—today it is popularly supposed that they are rendered occasionally poisonous by eating the barnacles attached to copper-plating of ships. The *tazard*, the *lune*, the *capitaine*, the *dorade*, the *perroquet*, the *couliou*, the *congre*, various crabs, and even the *tonne*—all are dangerous unless perfectly fresh: the least decomposition seems to develop a mysterious poison. A singular phenomenon regarding the poisoning occasionally produced by the bécunne and dorade is that the skin peels from the hands and feet of those lucky enough to survive the terrible colics, burnings, itchings, and delirium, which are early symptoms. Happily these accidents are very rare, since the markets have been properly inspected: in the time of Dr. Rufz, they would seem to have been very common,—so common that he tells us he would not eat fresh fish without being perfectly certain where it was caught and how long it had been out of the water.

The poor buy the brightly colored fish only when the finer qualities are not obtainable at low rates; but often and often the catch is so enormous that half of it has to be thrown back into the sea. In the hot moist air, fish decomposes very rapidly; it is impossible to transport it to any distance into the interior; and only the inhabitants of the coast can indulge in fresh fish,—at least sea-fish.

Old Market-place of the Fort, St. Pierre (removed in 1888)

Naturally, among the laboring class the question of quality is less important than that of quantity and substance, unless the fish-market be extraordinarily stocked. Of all fresh fish, the most popular is *tonne*, a great blue-gray creature whose flesh is solid as beef; next come in order of preferment the flying-fish (*volants*), which often sell as low as four for a cent;—then the *lambi*, or sea-snail, which has a very dense nutritious flesh;—then the small whitish fish classed as *sàdines*;—then the blue-colored fishes according to price, *couliou*, *balaou*, etc.;—lastly, the shark, which sells commonly at two cents a pound. Large sharks are not edible; the flesh is too hard; but a young shark is very good eating indeed. Cyrillia cooked me a slice one morning: it was quite delicate, tasted almost like veal.

The quantity of very small fish sold is surprising. With ten sous the family of a laborer can have a good fish-dinner: a pound of *sàdines* is never dearer than two sous;—a pint of manioc flour can be had for same price; and a big avocado sells for a sou. This is more than enough food for any one person; and by doubling the expense one obtains a proportionately greater quantity—enough for four or five individuals. The *sàdines* are roasted over a charcoal fire, and flavored with a sauce of lemon, pimento, and garlic. When there are no *sàdines*, there are sure to be *coulious* in plenty,—small *coulious* about as long as your little finger: these are more delicate, and fetch double the price. With four sous' worth of *coulious* a family can have a superb *blaffe*. To make a *blaffe* the fish are cooked in water, and served with pimento, lemon, spices, onions, and garlic; but without oil or butter. Experience has demonstrated that *coulious* make the best *blaffe*; and a *blaffe* is seldom prepared with other fish.

V

THERE are four dishes which are the holiday luxuries of the poor:—*manicou*, *ver-palmiste*, *zandouille*, and *poule-épi-diri*.[2]

The *manicou* is a brave little marsupial, which might be called the opossum of Martinique: it fights, although overmatched, with the serpent, and is a great enemy to the field-rat. In the market a manicou sells for two francs and a half at cheapest: it is generally salted before being cooked.

The great worm, or caterpillar, called *ver-palmiste* is found in the heads of cabbage-palms,—especially after the cabbage has been cut out, and the tree has begun to perish. It is the grub of a curious beetle, which has a proboscis of such form as suggested the creole appellation, *léfant*: the "elephant." These worms are sold in the Place du Fort at two sous each: they are spitted and roasted alive, and are said to taste like almonds. I have never tried to find out whether this be fact or fancy; and I am glad to say that few white creoles confess a liking for this barbarous food.

The *zandouilles* are delicious sausages made with pig-buff,—and only seen in the market on Sundays. They cost a franc and a half each; and there are several women who have an established reputation throughout Martinique for their skill in making them. I have tasted some not less palatable than the famous London "pork-pies." Those of Lamentin are reputed the best in the island.

But *poule-épi-diri* is certainly the most popular dish of all: it is the dearest, as well, and poor people can rarely afford it. In Louisiana an almost similar dish is called *jimbalaya*: chicken cooked with rice. The Martiniquais think it such a delicacy that an over-exacting person, or one difficult to satisfy, is reproved with the simple question:—"*Ça ou lè 'ncò—poule-épi-diri?*" (What more do you want, great heavens!—chicken-and-rice?) Naughty children are bribed into absolute goodness by the promise of poule-épi-diri:—

—"*Aïe! chè, bò doudoux!*
Doudoux ba ou poule-épi-diri;
Aïe! chè, bò doudoux!"…

(*Aïe*, dear! kiss *doudoux!*—*doudoux* has rice-and-chicken for you!—*Aïe*, dear! kiss *doudoux!*)

How far rice enters into the success of the dish above mentioned I cannot say; but rice ranks in favor generally above all cereals; it is at least six times more in demand than maize. *Diri-doux*, rice boiled with sugar, is sold in prodigious quantities daily,—especially at the markets, where little heaps of it, rolled in pieces of bananas or *cachibou* leaves, are retailed at a cent each. *Diri-aulaitt*, a veritable rice-pudding, is also very popular; but it would weary the reader to mention one-tenth of the creole preparations into which rice enters.

VI

EVERYBODY eats *akras*;—they sell at a cent apiece. The akra is a small fritter or pancake, which may be made of fifty different things,—among others codfish, titiri, beans, brains, *choux-caraïbes*, little black peas (*poix-zié-nouè*, "black-eyed peas"), or of crawfish (*akra-cribîche*). When made of carrots, bananas, chicken, palm-cabbage, etc., and sweetened, they are called *marinades*. On first acquaintance they seem rather greasy for so hot a climate; but one learns on becoming accustomed to tropical conditions, that a certain amount of oily or greasy food is both healthy and needful.

First among popular vegetables are beans. Red beans are preferred; but boiled white beans, served cold with vinegar and plenty of oil, form a favorite salad. Next in order of preferment come the *choux-caraïbes*, *patates*, *zignames*, *camanioc*, and *cousscouche*: all immense roots,—the true potatoes of the tropics. The camanioc is finer than the choux-caraïbe, boils whiter and softer: in appearance it resembles the manioc root very closely, but has no toxic element. The cousscouche is the best of all: the finest Irish potato boiled into sparkling flour is not so good. Most of these roots can be cooked into a sort of mush, called *migan*: such as *migan-choux*, made with the choux-caraïbe; *migan-zignames*, made with yams; *migan-cousscouche*, etc.,—in which case crabs or shrimps are usually served with the *migan*. There is a particular fondness for the little rosy crab called *tourlouroux*, in patois *touloulou*. *Migan* is also made with bread-fruit. Very large bananas or plantains are boiled with cod-fish, with *daubes*, or meat stews, and with eggs. The bread-fruit is a fair substitute for vegetables. It must be cooked very thoroughly, and has a dry potato taste. What is called the *fleu-fouitt-à-pain* or "bread-fruit flower"—a long pod-shaped solid growth, covered exteriorly with tiny seeds closely set as pin-heads could be, and having an interior pith very elastic and resistant,—is candied into a delicious sweetmeat.

VII

THE consumption of bananas is enormous: more bananas are eaten than vegetables; and more banana-trees are yearly being cultivated. The negro seems to recognize instinctively that economical value of the banana to which attention was long since called by Humboldt, who estimated that while an acre planted in wheat would barely support three persons, an acre planted in banana-trees would nourish fifty.

Bananas and plantains hold the first place among fruits in popular esteem;—they are cooked in every way, and served with almost every sort of meat or fish. What we call bananas in the United States, however, are not called bananas in Martinique, but figs (*figues*). Plantains seem to be called *bananes*. One is often surprised at popular nomenclature: *choux* may mean either a sort of root (*choux-caraïbe*), or the top of the cabbage-palm; *Jacquot* may mean a fish; *cabane* never means a cabin, but a bed; *crickett* means not a cricket, but a frog; and least fifty other words have equally deceptive uses. If one desires to speak of real figs—dried figs—he must say *figues-Fouance* (French figs): otherwise nobody will understand him. There are many kinds of bananas here called *figues*,—the four most popular are the *figues-bananes*, which are plantains, I think; the *figues-makouenga*, which grow wild, and have a red skin; the *figues-pommes* (apple-bananas), which are large and yellow; and the *figues-dessè* (little-dessert-bananas), which are to be seen on all tables in St. Pierre. They are small, sweet, and always agreeable, even when one has no appetite for other fruits.

It requires some little time to become accustomed to many tropical fruits, or at least to find patience as well as inclination to eat them. A large number, in spite of delicious flavor, are provokingly stony: such as the ripe guavas, the cherries, the barbadines; even the corrossole and *pomme-cannelle* are little more than huge masses of very hard seeds buried in pulp of exquisite taste. The *sapota*, or *sapodilla*, is less characterized by stoniness, and one soon learns to like it. It has large flat seeds, which can be split into two with the finger-nail; and a fine white skin lies between these two halves. It requires some skill to remove entire this little skin, or pellicle, without breaking it: to do so is said to be a test of affection. Perhaps this bit of folk-lore was suggested by the shape of the pellicle, which is that of a heart. The pretty fille-de-couleur asks her doudoux: "*Ess ou ainmein moin?—pouloss tiré ti lapeau-là sans cassé-y.*" Woe to him if he breaks it... The most disagreeable fruit is, I think, the *pomme-d'Haïti*, or Haytian apple: it is very attractive exteriorly; but has a strong musky odor and taste which nauseates. Few white creoles ever eat it.

Of the oranges, nothing except praise can be said; but there are fruits that look like oranges, and are not oranges, that are far more noteworthy. There is the *chadèque*, which grows here to fully three feet in circumference, and has a sweet pink pulp; and there is the "forbidden-fruit" (*fouitt-défendu*), a sort of cross between the orange and the chadèque, and superior to both. The colored people declare that this monster fruit is the same which grew in Eden upon the fatal tree: *c'est la mênm qui fai moune ka fai yche conm ça atouèlement!* The fouitt-défendu is wonderful, indeed, in its way; but the fruit which most surprised me on my first acquaintance with it was the *zabricôt*.

—"*Ou lè yon zabricôt?*" (Would you like an apricot?) Cyrillia asked me one day. I replied that I liked apricots very much,—wanted more than one. Cyrillia looked astonished, but said nothing until she returned from market, and put on the table *two* apricots, with the observation:—

"*Ça ké fai ou malade mangé toutt ça!*" (You will get sick if you eat all that.) I could not eat even half of one of them. Imagine a plum larger than the largest turnip, with a skin like a russet apple, solid sweet flesh of a carrot-red color, and a nut in the middle bigger than a duck's egg

Bread-fruit Tree

and hard as a rock. These fruits are aromatic as well as sweet to the taste: the price varies from one to four cents each, according to size. The tree is indigenous to the West Indies; the aborigines of Hayti had a strange belief regarding it. They alleged that its fruits formed the nourishment of the dead; and however pressed by hunger, an Indian in the woods would rather remain without food than strip one of these trees, lest he should deprive the ghosts of their sustenance... No trace of this belief seems to exist among the colored people of Martinique.

Among the poor such fruits are luxuries: they eat more mangoes than any other fruits excepting bananas. It is rather slobbery work eating a common mango, in which every particle of pulp is threaded fast to the kernel: one prefers to gnaw it when alone. But there are cultivated mangoes with finer and thicker flesh which can be sliced off, so that the greater part of the fruit may be eaten without smearing and sucking. Among grafted varieties the *mangue* is quite as delicious as the orange. Perhaps there are nearly as many varieties of mangoes in Martinique as there are varieties of peaches with us: I am acquainted, however, with only a few,—such as the *mango-Bassignac*;—*mango-pêche* (or peach-mango);—*mango-vert* (green mango), very large and oblong;—*mango-greffe*;—*mangotine*, quite round and small;—*mango-quinette*, very small also, almost egg-shaped;—*mango-Zézé*, very sweet, rather small, and of flattened form;—*mango-d'or* (golden mango), worth half a franc each;—*mango-Lamentin*, a highly cultivated variety;—and the superb *Reine-Amélie* (or Queen Amelia), a great yellow fruit which retails even in Martinique at five cents apiece.

VIII

... "*Ou c'est bonhomme càton?—ou c'est zimage, non?*"

(Am I a pasteboard man, or an image, that I do not eat?) Cyrillia wants to know. The fact is that I am a little overfed; but the stranger in the tropics cannot eat like a native, and my abstemiousness is a surprise. In the North we eat a good deal for the sake of caloric; in the tropics, unless one be in the habit of taking much physical exercise, which is a very difficult thing to do, a generous appetite is out of the question. Cyrillia will not suffer me to live upon *mangé-Créole* altogether; she insists upon occasional beefsteaks and roasts, and tries to tempt me with all kinds of queer delicious desserts as well,—particularly those cakes made of grated cocoanut and sugar-syrup (*tablett-coco-rapé*) of which a stranger becomes very fond. But, nevertheless, I cannot eat enough to quiet Cyrillia's fears.

Not eating enough is not her only complaint against me. I am perpetually doing something or other which shocks her. The Creoles are the most cautious livers in the world, perhaps;—the stranger who walks in the sun without an umbrella, or stands in currents of air, is for them an object of wonder and compassion. Cyrillia's complaints about my recklessness in the matter of hygiene always terminate with the refrain: "*Yo pa fai ça içi*"—(People never do such things in Martinique.) Among such rash acts are washing one's face or hands while perspiring, taking off one's hat on coming in from a walk, going out immediately after a bath, and washing my face with soap. "Oh, Cyrillia! what foolishness!—why should I not wash my face with soap?" "Because it will blind you," Cyrillia answers: "*ça ké tchoué limiè zié ou*" (it will kill the light in your eyes). There is no cleaner person than Cyrillia; and, indeed among the city people, the daily bath is the rule in all weathers; but soap is never used on the face by thousands, who, like Cyrillia, believe it will "kill the light of the eyes."

One day I had been taking a long walk in the sun, and returned so thirsty that all the old stories about travellers suffering in waterless deserts returned to memory with new significance;—visions of simooms arose before me. What a delight to see and to grasp the heavy, red, thick-lipped *dobanne*, the water-jar, dewy and cool with the exudation of the *Eau-de-Gouyave* which filled it to the brim,—*toutt vivant*, as Cyrillia says, "all alive"! There was a sudden scream,—the water-pitcher was snatched from my hands by Cyrillia with the question: "*Ess ou lé tchoué cò-ou?—Saint Joseph!*" (Did I want to kill my body?)...The Creoles use the word "body" speaking of anything that can happen to one,—"hurt one's body," "tire one's body," "marry one's body", "bury one's body," etc.;—I wonder whether the expression originated in zealous desire to prove a profound faith in the soul... Then Cyrillia made me a little punch with sugar and rum, and told me I must never drink fresh-water after a walk unless I wanted to kill my body. In this matter her advice was good. The immediate result of a cold drink while heated is a profuse and icy perspiration, during which currents of air are really dangerous. A cold is not dreaded here, and colds are rare; but pleurisy is common, and may be the consequence of any imprudent exposure.

I do not often have the opportunity at home of committing even an unconscious imprudence; for Cyrillia is ubiquitous, and always on the watch lest something dreadful should happen to me. She is wonderful as a house-keeper as well as a cook: there is certainly much to do, and she has only a child to help her, but she always seems to have time. Her kitchen apparatus is of the simplest kind: a charcoal furnace constructed of bricks, a few earthenware pots (*canari*), and some gridirons;—yet with these she can certainly prepare as many dishes as there are days in the year. I have never known her to be busy with her *canari* for more than an hour; yet everything is kept in perfect order. When she is not working, she is quite happy in sitting at a window, and amusing herself by watching the life of the street,—or playing with a kitten, which she has trained so well that it seems to understand everything she says.

IX

WITH darkness all the population of the island retire to their homes;— the streets become silent, and the life of the day is done. By eight o'clock nearly all the windows are closed, and the lights put out;—by nine the people are asleep. There are no evening parties, no night amusements, except during rare theatrical seasons and times of Carnival; there are no evening visits: active existence is almost timed by the rising and setting of the sun... The only pleasure left for the stranger of evenings is a quiet smoke on his balcony or before his door: reading is out of the question, partly because books are rare, partly because lights are bad, partly because insects throng about every lamp or candle. I am lucky enough to have a balcony, broad enough for a rocking-chair: and sometimes Cyrillia and the kitten come to keep me company before bedtime. The kitten climbs on my knees; Cyrillia sits right down upon the balcony.

One bright evening, Cyrillia was amusing herself much by watching the clouds: they were floating high; the moonlight made them brilliant as frost. As they changed shape under the pressure of the trade-wind, Cyrillia seemed to discover wonderful things in them: sheep, ships with sails, cows, faces, perhaps even *zombis*.

—"*Travaill Bon-Dié joli,—anh?*" (Is not the work of the Good-God pretty?) she said at last... "There was Madame Rémy, who used to sell the finest *foulards* and Madrases in St. Pierre;—she used to study the clouds. She drew the patterns of the clouds for her *foulards*: whenever she saw a beautiful cloud or a beautiful rainbow, she would make a drawing of it in color at once and then she would send that to France to have *foulards* made just like it... Since she is dead, you do not see any more pretty *foulards* such as there used to be."

—"Would you like to look at the moon with my telescope, Cyrillia?" I asked. "Let me get it for you."

—"Oh no, no!" she answered, as if shocked.

—"Why?"

—"*Ah! faut pa gàdé baggaïe Bon-Dié conm ça!*" (It is not right to look at the things of the Good-God that way.)

I did not insist. After a little silence, Cyrillia resumed:—

—"But I saw the Sun and the Moon once fighting together: that was what people call an *eclipse*,—is not that the word?... They fought together a long time: I was looking at them. We put a *terrine* full of water on the ground, and looked into the water to see them. And the Moon is stronger than the Sun!—yes, the Sun was obliged to give way to the Moon... Why do they fight like that?"

—"They don't, Cyrillia."

—"Oh yes, they do. I saw them!... And the Moon is much stronger than the Sun!"

I did not attempt to contradict this testimony of the eyes. Cyrillia continued to watch the pretty clouds. Then she said:—

—"Would you not like to have a ladder long enough to let you climb up to those clouds, and see what they are made of?"

—"Why, Cyrillia, they are only vapor,—brume: I have been in clouds."

She looked at me in surprise, and, after a moment's silence, asked, with an irony of which I had not supposed her capable:—

—"Then you are the Good-God?"

—"Why, Cyrillia, it is not difficult to reach clouds. You see clouds always upon the top of the Montagne Pelée;—people go there. I have been there—in the clouds."

—"Ah! those are not the same clouds: those are not the clouds of the Good-God. You cannot touch the sky when you are on the Morne de la Croix."

—"My dear Cyrillia, there is no sky to touch. The sky is only an appearance."

—"*Anh, anh, anh!* No sky!—you say there is no sky?... Then what is that up there?"

—"That is air, Cyrillia, beautiful blue air."

—"And what are the stars fastened to?"

—"To nothing. They are suns, but so much further away than our sun that they look small."

—"No, they are not suns! They have not the same form as the sun…You must not say there is no sky: it is wicked! But you are not a Catholic!"

—"My dear Cyrillia, I don't see what that has to do with the sky."

—"Where does the Good-God stay, if there be no sky? And where is heaven?—and where is hell?"

—"Hell in the sky, Cyrillia?"

—"The Good-God made heaven in one part of the sky, and hell in another part, for bad people… Ah! you are a Protestant;—you do not know the things of the Good-God! That is why you talk like that."

—"What is a Protestant, Cyrillia?"

—"You are one. The Protestants do not believe in religion,—do not love the Good-God."

—"Well, I am neither a Protestant nor a Catholic, Cyrillia."

—"Oh! you do not mean that; you cannot be a *maudi*, an accursed. There are only the Protestants, the Catholics, and the accursed. You are not a *maudi*, I am sure. But you must not say there is no sky."…

—"But, Cyrillia"—

—"No: I will not listen to you:—you are a Protestant. Where does the rain come from, if there is no sky?"…

—"Why, Cyrillia,… the clouds"…

—"No, you are a Protestant… How can you say such things? There are the Three Kings and the Three Valets,—the beautiful stars that come at Christmas time,—there, over there—all beautiful, and big, big, big!… And you say there is no sky!"

—"Cyrillia, perhaps I am a *maudi*."

—"No, no! You are only a Protestant. But do not tell me there is no sky: it is wicked to say that!"

—"I won't say it any more, Cyrillia—there! But I will say there are no *zombis*."

—"I know you are not a *maudi*; —you have been baptized."

—"How do you know I have been baptized?"

—"Because, if you had not been baptized you would see *zombis* all the time, even in broad day. All children who are not baptized see *zombis*."

X

CYRILLIA'S solicitude for me extends beyond the commonplaces of hygiene and diet into the uncertain domain of matters ghostly. She fears much that something might happen to me through the agency of wizards, witches (*sociès*), or *zombis*. Especially zombis. Cyrillia's belief in zombis has a solidity that renders argument out of the question. This belief is part of her inner nature,—something hereditary, racial, ancient as Africa, as characteristic of her people as the love of rhythms and melodies totally different from our own musical conceptions, but possessing, even for the civilized, an inexplicable emotional charm.

Zombi!—the word is perhaps full of mystery even for those who made it. The explanations of those who utter it most often are never quite lucid: it seems to convey ideas darkly impossible to define,—fancies belonging to the mind of another race and another era,—unspeakably old. Perhaps the word in our own language which offers the best analogy is "goblin": yet the one is not fully translated by the other. Both have, however, one common ground on which they become indistinguishable,—that region of the supernatural which is most primitive and most vague; and the closest relation between the savage and the civilized fancy may be found in the fears which we call childish,—of darkness, shadows, and things dreamed. One form of the *zombi* belief—akin to certain ghostly superstitions held by various primitive races—would seem to have been suggested by nightmare,—that form of nightmare in which familiar persons become slowly and hideously transformed into malevolent beings. The *zombi* deludes under the appearance of a travelling companion, an old comrade—like the desert spirits of the Arabs—or even under the form of an animal. Consequently the creole negro fears everything living which he meets after dark upon a lonely road,—a stray horse, a cow, even a dog; and mothers quell the naughtiness of their children by the threat of summoning a zombi-cat or a zombi-creature of some kind. "*Zombi ké nana ou*" (the zombi will gobble thee up) is generally an effectual menace in the country parts, where it is believed zombis may be met with any time after sunset. In the city it is thought that their regular hours are between two and four o'clock in the morning. At least so Cyrillia says:—

—"Dèzhè, toua-zhè-matin: c'est lhè zombi. Yo ka sòti dèzhè, toua zhè: c'est lhè yo. A quattrhè yo ka rentré;—angelus ka sonné." (At four o'clock they go back where they came from, before the *Angelus* rings.) Why?

—"*C'est pou moune pas joinne yo dans larue.*" (So that people may not meet with them in the street), Cyrillia answers.

—"Are they afraid of the people, Cyrillia?" I asked.

—"No, they are not afraid; but they do not want people to know their business" (*pa lè moune ouè zaffai yo*).

Cyrillia also says one must not look out of the window when a dog howls at night. Such a dog may be a *mauvais vivant* (evil being): "If he sees me looking at him he will say, '*Ou tropp quirièse quitté cabane ou pou gàdé zaffai lezautt.*'" (You are too curious to leave your bed like that to look at other folks' business.)

—"And what then, Cyrillia?"

—"Then he will put out your eyes,—*y ké coqui zié ou*,—make you blind."

—"But, Cyrillia," I asked one day, "did you ever see any zombis?"

—"How? I often see them!... They walk about the room at night;—they walk like people. They sit in the rocking-chairs and rock themselves very softly, and look at me. I say to them:—'What do you want here?—I never did any harm to anybody. Go away!' Then they go away."

—"What do they look like?"

—"Like people,—sometimes like beautiful people (*bel moune*). I am afraid of them. I only see them when there is no light burning. While the lamp burns before the Virgin they do not come. But sometimes the oil fails, and the light dies."

In my own room there are dried palm leaves and some withered flowers fastened to the wall. Cyrillia put them there. They were taken from the *reposoirs* (temporary altars) erected for the last Corpus Christi procession: consequently they are blessed, and ought to keep the zombis away. That is why they are fastened to the wall, over my bed.

Nobody could be kinder to animals than Cyrillia usually shows herself to be: all the domestic animals in the neighborhood impose upon her;—various dogs and cats steal from her imprudently, without the least fear of being beaten. I was therefore very much surprised to see her one evening catch a flying beetle that approached the light, and deliberately put its head in the candle-flame. When I asked her how she could be so cruel, she replied:—

—"*Ah! ou pa connaitt choïe pays-ci.*" (You do not know Things in this country.)

The Things thus referred to I found to be supernatural Things. It is popularly believed that certain winged creatures which circle about candles at night may be *engagés* or *envoyés*—wicked people having the power of transformation or even zombis "sent" by witches or wizards to do harm. "There was a woman at Tricolore," Cyrillia says, "who used to sew a great deal at night; and a big beetle used to come into her room and fly about the candle, and bother her very much. One night she managed to get hold of it, and she singed its head in the candle. Next day, a woman who was her neighbor came to the house with her head all tied up. '*Ah! macoumè,*' asked the sewing-woman, '*ça ou ni dans guiôle-ou?*' And the other answered, very angrily, '*Ou ni toupet mandé moin ça moin ni dans guiôle moin!—et cété ou qui té brilé guiôle moin nans chandelle-ou hiè-souè.*'" (You have the impudence to ask what is the matter with my mouth! and you yourself burned my mouth in your candle last night.)

Early one morning, about five o'clock, Cyrillia, opening the front door, saw a huge crab walking down the street. Probably it had escaped from some barrel; for it is customary here to keep live crabs in barrels and fatten them,—feeding them with maize, mangoes, and, above all, green peppers: nobody likes to cook crabs as soon as caught; for they may have been eating manchineel apples at the river-mouths. Cyrillia uttered a cry of dismay on seeing that crab; then I heard her talking to herself:—"*I* touch it?—never! it can go about its business. How do I know it is not *an arranged crab (yon crabe rangè)*, or an *envoyé?*—since everybody knows I like crabs. For two sous I can buy a fine crab and know where it comes from." The crab went on down the street: everywhere the sight of it created consternation; nobody dared to touch it; women cried out at it, "*Miserabe!—envoyé Satan!—allez, maudi!*"—some threw holy water on the crab. Doubtless it reached the sea in safety. In the evening Cyrillia said: "I think that crab was a little zombi;— I am going to burn a light all night to keep it from coming back."

Another day, while I was out, a negro to whom I had lent two francs came to the house, and paid his debt. Cyrillia told me when I came back, and showed me the money carefully enveloped in a piece of brown paper; but said I must not touch it,—she would get rid of it for me at the market. I laughed at her fears; and she observed: "You do not know negroes, Missié!—negroes are wicked, negroes are jealous! I do not want you to touch that money because I have not a good opinion about this affair."

After I began learn more of the underside of Martinique life, I could understand the source and justification of many similar superstitions in simple and uneducated minds. The negro sorcerer is, at worst, only a poisoner; but he possesses a very curious art which long defied serious investigation, and in the beginning of the last century was attributed, even by whites, to diabolical influence. In 1721, 1723, and 1725, several negroes were burned alive at the stake as wizards in league with the devil. It was an era of comparative ignorance; but even now things are done which would astonish the most sceptical and practical physician. For example, a laborer discharged from a plantation vows vengeance; and the next morning the whole force of hands—the entire *atelier*—are totally disabled from work. Every man and woman on the place is unable to walk; everybody has one or both legs frightfully swollen. *Yo té ka pilé malifice:* they have trodden on a "malifice." What is the "malifice"? All that can be ascertained is that certain little prickly seeds have been scattered all over the ground, where the bare-footed workers are in the habit of passing. Ordinarily, treading on these seeds is of no consequence; but it is evident in such a case that they must have been prepared in a special way,—soaked in some poison, perhaps snake-venom. At all events, the physician deems it safest to treat the inflammations after the manner of snake wounds: and after many days the hands are perhaps able to resume duty.

XI

WHILE Cyrillia is busy with her *canari*, she talks to herself or sings. She has a low rich voice,—sings strange things, things that have been forgotten by this generation,—creole songs of the old days, having a weird rhythm and fractions of tones that are surely African. But more generally she talks to herself, as all the Martiniquaises do: it is a continual murmur as of a stream. At first I used to think she was talking to someone else, and would call out:—

—"*Épi quiless moune ça ou ka pàlé-à?*"

But she would always answer:—"*Moin ka pàlé anni cò moin*" (I am only talking to my own body), which is the creole expression for talking to oneself.

—"And what are you talking so much to your own body about, Cyrillia?"

—"I am talking about my own little affairs" (*ti zaffai-moin*)... That is all that I could ever draw from her.

But when not working, she will sit for hours looking out of the window. In this she resembles the kitten: both seem to find the same silent pleasure in watching the street, or the green heights that rise above its roofs:—the Morne d'Orange. Occasionally at such times she will break the silence in the strangest way, if she thinks I am not too busy with my papers to answer a question:—

—"*Missié?*" —timidly

—"Eh?"

—"*Di moin, chè, ti manmaille dans pays ou, toutt piti, piti,—ess ça pàlé Anglais?*" (Do the little children in my country—the very, very little children—talk English?)

—"Why, certainly, Cyrillia."

—"*Toutt piti, piti?*" —with growing surprise.

—"Why, of course!"

—"*C'est drôle, ça!*" (It is queer, that!) She cannot understand it.

—"And the little *manmaille* in Martinique, Cyrillia—*toutt piti, piti,* don't they talk creole?"

—"*Oui; mais toutt moune ka pâlé nègue: ça facile.*" (Yes; but anybody can talk negro—that is easy to learn.)

XII

CYRILLIA'S room has no furniture in it: the Martinique bonne lives as simply and as rudely as a domestic animal. One thin mattress covered with a sheet, and elevated from the floor only by a léfant, forms her bed. The *léfant* or "elephant," is composed of two thick square pieces of coarse hard mattress stuffed with shavings and placed end to end. Cyrillia has a good pillow, however,—*bourré épi flêches-canne,*—filled with the plumes of the sugar-cane. A cheap trunk with broken hinges contains her modest little wardrobe: a few *mouchoirs,* or kerchiefs, used for head-dresses, a spare *douillette,* or long robe, and some tattered linen. Still she is always clean, neat, fresh-looking. I see a pair of sandals in the corner,—such as the women of the country sometimes wear—wooden soles with a leather band for the instep, and two little straps; but she never puts them on. Fastened to the wall are two French prints— lithographs: one representing Victor Hugo's *Esmeralda* in prison with her pet goat; the other, Lamartine's *Laurence* with her fawn. Both are very old and stained and bitten by the *bête-à-ciseau,* a species of *lepisma,* which destroys books and papers, and everything it can find exposed. On a shelf are two bottles,—one filled with holy water; another with *tafia camphrée* (camphor dissolved in tafia), which is Cyrillia's sole remedy for colds, fevers, headaches—all maladies not of a very fatal description. There are also a little woollen monkey, about three inches high—the dusty plaything of a long-dead child;—an image of the Virgin, even smaller;—and a broken cup with fresh bright blossoms in it, the Virgin's flower-offering;—and the Virgin's invariable lamp—a night-light, a little wick floating on olive-oil in a tiny glass.

I know that Cyrillia must have bought these flowers—they are garden flowers—at the Marché du Fort. There are always old women sitting there who sell nothing else but bouquets for the Virgin,—and who cry out to passers-by:—"*Gagné ti bouquet pou Vièges-ou, chè!*... Buy a nosegay, dear, for your Virgin;—she is asking you for one;—give her a little one, *chè cocott*."... Cyrillia says you must not smell the flowers you give the Virgin: it would be stealing from her... The little lamp is always lighted at six o'clock. At six o'clock the Virgin is supposed to pass through all the streets of St. Pierre, and wherever a lamp burns before her image, she enters and blesses that house. "*Faut limé lampe ou pou fai la-Viège passé dans caïe-ou,*" says Cyrillia. (You must light the lamp to make the Virgin come into your house.)... Cyrillia often talks to her little image, exactly as if it were a baby,—calls it pet names,—asks if it is content with the flowers.

This image of the Virgin is broken: it is only half a Virgin,—the upper half. Cyrillia has arranged it so, nevertheless, that had I not been very inquisitive I should never have divined its mishap. She found a small broken powder-box without a lid,—probably thrown negligently out of a boudoir window by some wealthy beauty: she filled this little box with straw, and fixed the mutilated image upright within it, so that you could never suspect the loss of its feet. The Virgin looks very funny, thus peeping over the edge of her little box;—looks like a broken toy, which a child has been trying to mend. But this Virgin has offerings too: Cyrillia buys flowers for her, and sticks them all round her, between the edge of the powder-box and the straw. After all, Cyrillia's Virgin is quite as serious a fact as any image of silver or of ivory in the homes of the rich: probably the prayers said to her are more simply beautiful, and more direct from the heart, than many daily murmured before the *chapelles* of luxurious homes. And the more one looks at it, the more one feels that it were almost wicked to smile at this little broken toy of faith.

—"Cyrillia, *mafi,*" I asked her one day, after my discovery of the little Virgin,—"would you not like me to buy a *chapelle* for you?" The *chapelle* is the little bracket-altar, together with images and ornaments, to be found in every creole bedroom.

—"*Mais non, Missié,*" she answered, smiling, "*moin aimein ti Viège moin, pa lè gagnin dautt.* I love my little Virgin: do not want any other. I have seen much trouble:—she was with me in my trouble;—she heard my prayers. It would be wicked for me to throw her away. When I have a sou to spare, I buy flowers for her;—when I have no money, I climb the mornes, and pick pretty buds for her... But why should Missié want to buy me a *chapelle?*—Missié is a Protestant?"

—"I thought it might give you pleasure, Cyrillia."

—"No, Missié, I thank you; it would not give me pleasure. But Missié could give me something else which would make me very happy—I often thought of asking Missié… but—"

—"Tell me what it is, Cyrillia."

—"Missié makes photographs…"

—"You want a photograph of yourself, Cyrillia?"

—"Oh! no, Missié, I am too ugly and too old. But I have a daughter. She is beautiful—*yon bel bois*,—like a beautiful tree, as we say here. I would like so much to have her picture taken."

A photographic instrument belonging to a clumsy amateur suggested this request to Cyrillia. I could not attempt such work successfully; but I gave her a note to a photographer of much skill; and a few days later the portrait was sent to the house. Cyrillia's daughter was certainly a comely girl,—tall and almost gold-colored, with pleasing features; and the photograph looked very nice, though less nice than the original. Half the beauty of these people is a beauty of tint,—a tint so exquisite sometimes that I have even heard white creoles declare no white complexion compares with it: the greater part of the charm remaining is grace,—the grace of movement; and neither of these can be rendered by photography. I had the portrait framed for Cyrillia, to hang up beside her little pictures.

When it came, she was not in; I put it in her room and waited to see the effect. On returning, she entered there; and I did not see her for so long a time that I stole to the door of the chamber to observe her. She was standing before the portrait,—looking at it, talking to it as if it were alive. "*Yche moin, yche moin!… Oui! ou toutt bel!—yche moin bel.*" (My child, my child… Yes, thou art all beautiful: my child is beautiful.) All at once she turned—perhaps she noticed my shadow, or felt my presence in some way: her eyes were wet;—she started, flushed, then laughed.

—"Ah! Missié, you watch me;—*ou guetté moin…* But she is my child. Why should I not love her?… She looks so beautiful there."

—"She is beautiful, Cyrillia;—I love to see you love her."

She gazed at the picture a little longer in silence;—then turned to me again, and asked earnestly:—

—"*Pouki yo pa ka fai pòtrai pàlé—anh?… pisse yo ka tiré y toutt samm ou: c'est ou-menm!…Yo douè fai y palé 'tou.*" (Why do they not make a portrait talk,—tell me? For they draw it just all like you!—it is yourself: they ought to make it talk.)

—"Perhaps they will be able to do something like that one of these days, Cyrillia."

—"Ah! that would be so nice. Then I could talk to her. *C'est yon bel moune moin fai—y bel, joli moune!... Moin sé causé épi y."*...

...And I, watching her beautiful childish emotion, thought:—Cursed be the cruelty that would persuade itself that one soul may be like another,—that one affection may be replaced by another,—that individual goodness is not a thing apart, original, untwinned on earth, but only the general characteristic of a class or type, to be sought and found and utilized at will!... Self-curséd he who denies the divinity of love! Each heart, each brain in the billions of humanity,—even so surely as sorrow lives,—feels and thinks in some special way unlike any other; and goodness in each has its unlikeness to all other goodness,—and thus its own infinite preciousness; for however humble, however small, it is something all alone, and God never repeats his work. No heart-beat is cheap, no gentleness is despicable, no kindness is common; and Death, in removing a life—the simplest life ignored,—removes what never will reappear through the eternity of eternities,—since every being is the sum of a chain of experiences infinitely varied from all others... To some Cyrillia's happy tears might bring a smile: to me that smile would seem the unforgivable sin against the Giver of Life!...

NOTES

1. There is record of an attempt to manufacture bread with one part manioc flour to three of wheat flour. The result was excellent; but no serious effort was ever made to put the manioc bread on the market.

2. I must mention a surreptitious dish, *chatt*; —needless to say the cats are not sold, but stolen. It is true that only a small class of poor people eat cats; but they eat so many cats that cats have become quite rare in St. Pierre. The custom is purely superstitious: it is alleged that if you eat cat seven times, or if you eat seven cats, no witch, wizard or *quimboiseur* can ever do you any harm; and the cat ought to be eaten on Christmas Eve in order that the meal be perfectly efficacious... The mystic number "seven" enters into another and a better creole superstition;—if you kill a serpent, seven great sins are forgiven to you: *ou ké ni sept grands péchés effacé.*

XII. *"Pa Combiné, Chè!"*

I

...More finely than any term in our tongue does the French word *frisson* express that faint shiver—as of a ghostly touch thrilling from hair to feet—which intense pleasure sometimes gives, and which is felt most often and most strongly in childhood, when the imagination is still so sensitive and so powerful that one's whole being trembles to the vibration of a fancy. And this electric word best expresses, I think, that long thrill of amazed delight inspired by the first knowledge of the tropic world,—a sensation of weirdness in beauty, like the effect, in child-days, of fairy tales and stories of phantom isles.

For all unreal seems the vision of it. The transfiguration of all things by the stupendous light and the strange vapors of the West Indian sea,—the interorbing of flood and sky in blinding azure,—the sudden springs of gem-tinted coast from the ocean,—the iris-colors and astounding shapes of the hills,—the unimaginable magnificence of palms,—the high woods veiled and swathed in vines that blaze like emerald: all remind you in some queer way of things half forgotten,—the fables of enchantment. Enchantment it is indeed—but only the enchantment of that Great Wizard, the Sun, whose power you are scarcely beginning to know.

And into the life of the tropical city you enter as in dreams one enters into the life of a dead century. In all the quaint streets—over whose luminous yellow façades the beautiful burning violet of the sky appears as if but a few feet away—you see youth good to look upon as ripe fruit; and the speech of the people is soft as a coo; and eyes of brown girls caress you with a passing look... Love's world, you may have heard, has few restraints here, where Nature ever seems to cry out, like the swart seller of corrossoles:—*"Ça qui lè doudoux?"*

How often in some passing figure does one discern an ideal almost realized, and forbear to follow it with untired gaze only when another, another, and yet another, come to provoke the same aesthetic fancy,—to win the same unspoken praise! How often does one long for artist's power to fix the fleeting lines, to catch the color, to seize the whole exotic charm of some special type!... One finds a strange charm even in the timbre of these voices,—these half-breed voices, always with a tendency to contralto, and vibrant as ringing silver. What is that mysterious quality in a voice which has power to make the pulse beat faster, even when the singer is unseen?... do only the birds know?

...It seems to you that you could never weary of watching this picturesque life,—of studying the costumes, brilliant with butterfly colors,—and the statuesque semi-nudity of laboring hundreds,—and the untaught grace of attitudes,—and the simplicity of manners. Each day brings some new pleasure of surprise;—even from the window of your lodging you are ever noting something novel, something to delight the sense of oddity or beauty... Even in your room everything interests you, because of its queerness or quaintness: you become fond of the objects about you,—the great noiseless rocking-chairs that lull to sleep;—the immense bed (*lit-à-bateau*) of heavy polished wood, with its richly carven sides reaching down to the very floor;—and its invariable companion, the little couch or *sopha*, similarly shaped but much narrower, used only for the siesta; and the thick red earthen vessels (*dobannes*) which keep your drinking-water cool on the hottest days, but which are always filled thrice between sunrise and sunset with clear water from the mountain,— *dleau toutt vivant*, "all alive";—and the *verrines*, tall glass vases with stems of bronze in which your candle will burn steadily despite a draught;— and even those funny little angels and Virgins which look at you from their bracket in the corner, over the oil lamp you are presumed to kindle nightly in their honor, however great a heretic you may be...

You adopt at once, and without reservation, those creole home habits which are the result of centuries of experience with climate,—abstention from solid food before the middle of the day, repose after the noon meal;—and you find each repast an experience as curious as it is agreeable. It is not at all difficult to accustom oneself to green peas stewed with sugar, eggs mixed with tomatoes, salt fish stewed in milk, palmiste pith made into salad, grated cocoa formed into rich cakes, and dishes of titiri cooked in oil,—the minuscule fish, of which a thousand will scarcely fill a saucer. Above all, you are astonished by the endless variety of vegetables and fruits, of all conceivable shapes and inconceivable flavors.

And it does not seem possible that even the simplest little recurrences of this antiquated, gentle home-life could ever prove wearisome by daily repetition through the months and years. The musical greeting of the colored child, tapping at your door before sunrise,—"*Bonjou'*,

Missié" —as she brings your cup of black hot coffee and slice of corrossole;—the smile of the silent brown girl who carries your meals up-stairs in a tray poised upon her brightly coiffed head, and who stands by while you dine, watching every chance to serve, treading quite silently with her pretty bare feet;—the pleasant manners of the *màchanne* who brings your fruit, the *porteuse* who delivers your bread, the *blanchisseuse* who washes your linen at the river,—and all the kindly folk who circle about your existence, with their trays and turbans, their *foulards* and *douillettes*, their primitive grace and creole chatter: these can never cease to have a charm for you. You cannot fail to be touched also by the amusing solicitude of these good people for your health, because you are a stranger: their advice about hours to go out and hours to stay at home,—about roads to follow and paths to avoid on account of snakes,—about removing your hat and coat, or drinking while warm… Should you fall ill, this solicitude intensifies to devotion; you are tirelessly tended;—the good people will exhaust their wonderful knowledge of herbs to get you well,—will climb the mornes even at midnight, in spite of the risk of snakes and fear of zombis, to gather strange plants by the light of a lantern. Natural joyousness, natural kindliness, heart-felt desire to please, childish capacity of being delighted with trifles,—seem characteristic of all this colored population. It is turning its best side towards you, no doubt; but the side of the nature made visible appears none the less agreeable because you suspect there is another which you have not seen. What kindly inventiveness is displayed in contriving surprises for you, or in finding some queer thing to show you,—some fantastic plant, or grotesque fish, or singular bird! What apparent pleasure in taking trouble to gratify,— what innocent frankness of sympathy!…

Childishly beautiful seems the readiness of this tinted race to compassionate: you do not reflect that it is also a savage trait, while the charm of its novelty is yet upon you. No one is ashamed to shed tears for the death of a pet animal; any mishap to a child creates excitement, and evokes an immediate volunteering of services. And this compassionate sentiment is often extended, in a semi-poetical way, even to inanimate objects. One June morning, I remember, a three-masted schooner lying in the bay took fire, and had to be set adrift. An immense crowd gathered on the wharves, and I saw many curious manifestations of grief,—such grief, perhaps, as an infant feels for the misfortune of a toy it imagines to possess feeling, but not the less sincere because unreasoning. As the flames climbed the rigging, and the masts fell, the crowd moaned as though looking upon some human tragedy; and everywhere could hear such strange cries of pity as, "*Pauv' malhérè!*" (poor unfortunate), "*Pauv' diabe!*"... "*Toutt baggaïe-y pou allé, cassé!*"

(All its things-to-go-with are broken!) sobbed a girl, with tears streaming down her cheeks... She seemed to believe it was alive...

...And day by day the artlessness of this exotic humanity touches you more;—day by day this savage, somnolent, splendid Nature—delighting in furious color—bewitches you more. Already the anticipated necessity of having to leave it all some day—the far-seen pain of bidding it farewell—weighs upon you, even in dreams.

II

READER, if you be of those who have longed in vain for a glimpse of that tropic world,—tales of whose beauty charmed your childhood, and made stronger upon you that weird mesmerism of the sea which pulls at the heart of a boy,—one who had longed like you, and who, chance-led, beheld at last the fulfilment of the wish, can swear to you that the magnificence of the reality far excels the imagining. Those who know only the lands in which all processes for the satisfaction of human wants have been perfected under the terrible stimulus of necessity, can little guess the witchery of that Nature ruling the zones of color and of light. Within their primeval circles, the earth remains radiant and young as in that preglacial time whereof some transmitted memory may have created the hundred traditions of an Age of Gold. And the prediction of a paradise to come,—a phantom realm of rest and perpetual light: may this not have been but a sum of the remembrances and the yearnings of man first exiled from his heritage,—a dream born of the great nostalgia of races migrating to people the pallid North?

...But with the realization of the hope to know this magical Nature you learn that the actuality varies from the preconceived ideal otherwise than in surpassing it. Unless you enter the torrid world equipped with scientific knowledge extraordinary, your anticipations are likely to be at fault. Perhaps you had pictured to yourself the effect of perpetual summer as a physical delight;—something like an indefinite prolongation of the fairest summer weather ever enjoyed at home. Probably you had heard of fevers, risks of acclimatization, intense heat, and a swarming of venomous creatures; but you may nevertheless believe you know what precautions to take; and published statistics of climatic temperature may have persuaded you that the heat is not difficult to bear. By that enervation to which all white dwellers in the tropics are subject you may have understood a pleasant languor,—a painless disinclination to effort in a country where physical effort is less needed than elsewhere,—a soft temptation to idle away the hours in a hammock, under the shade of giant trees. Perhaps you have read, with eyes of faith, that torpor of the body is favorable to activity of the mind, and therefore believe that the intellectual powers can be stimulated and strengthened by tropical influences:—you suppose that enervation will reveal itself only as a beatific indolence which will leave the brain free to think with lucidity, or to revel in romantic dreams.

III

You are not at first undeceived;—the disillusion is long delayed. Doubtless you have read the delicious idyll of Bernardin de Saint-Pierre (this is not Mauritius, but the old life of Mauritius was wellnigh the same); and you look for idyllic personages among the beautiful humanity about you,—for idyllic scenes among the mornes shadowed by primeval forest, and the valleys threaded by a hundred brooks. I know not whether the faces and forms you seek will be revealed to you;—but you will not be able to complain for the lack of idyllic loveliness in the commonest landscape. Whatever artistic knowledge you possess will merely teach you the more to wonder at the luxuriant purple of the sea, the violet opulence of the sky, the violent beauty of foliage greens, the lilac tints of evening, and the color-enchantments distance gives in an atmosphere full of iridescent power,—the amethysts and agates, the pearls and ghostly golds, of far mountainings. Never, you imagine, never could one tire of wandering through those marvellous valleys,—of climbing silent roads under emeraldine shadow to heights from which the city seems but a few inches long, moored ships tinier than gnats that cling to a mirror,—or of swimming in that blue bay whose clear flood stays warm through all the year.[1] Or, standing alone, in some aisle of colossal palms, where humming-birds are flashing and shooting like a showering of jewel-fires, you feel how weak the skill of poet or painter to fix the sensation of that white-pillared imperial splendor;—and you think you know why creoles exiled by necessity to colder lands may sicken for love of their own,—die of home-yearning, as did many a one in far Louisiana, after the political tragedies of 1848...

...But you are not a creole, and must pay tribute of suffering to the climate of the tropics. You will have to learn that a temperature of 90° Fahr. in the tropics is by no means the same thing as 90° Fahr. in Europe or the United States;—that the mornes cannot be climbed with safety during the hotter hours of the afternoon;—that by taking a long walk you incur serious danger of catching a fever;—that to enter the high woods, a path must be hewn with the cutlass through the creepers and vines and undergrowth,—among snakes, venomous insects, venomous plants, and malarial exhalations;—that the finest blown dust is full of irritant and invisible enemies;—that it is folly to seek repose on a sward, or in the shade of trees,—particularly under tamarinds. Only after you have by experience become well convinced of these facts can you begin to comprehend something general in regard to West Indian conditions of life.

IV

...SLOWLY the knowledge comes... For months the vitality of a strong European (the American constitution bears the test even better) may resist the debilitating climate: perhaps the stranger will flatter himself that, like men habituated to heavy labor in stifling warmth,—those toiling in mines, in foundries, in engine rooms of ships, at iron furnaces,—so he too may become accustomed, without losing his strength, to the continuous draining of the pores, to the exhausting force of this strange motionless heat which compels change of clothing many times a day. But gradually he finds that it is not heat alone which is debilitating him, but the weight and septic nature of an atmosphere charged with vapor, with electricity, with unknown agents not less inimical to human existence than propitious to vegetal luxuriance. If he has learned those rules of careful living which served him well in a temperate climate, he will not be likely to abandon them among his new surroundings; and they will help him, no doubt,—particularly if he be prudent enough to avoid the sea-coast at night, and all exposure to dews or early morning mists, and all severe physical strain.

Nevertheless, he becomes slowly conscious of changes extraordinary going on within him,—in especial, a continual sensation of weight in the brain, daily growing, and compelling frequent repose;—also a curious heightening of nervous sensibility to atmospheric changes, to tastes and odors, to pleasure and pain. Total loss of appetite soon teaches him to follow the local custom of eating nothing solid before midday, and enables him to divine how large the necessity for caloric enters into the food-consumption of northern races. He becomes abstemious, eats sparingly, and discovers his palate to have become oddly exacting—finds that certain fruits and drinks are indeed as the creoles assert, appropriate only to particular physical conditions corresponding with particular hours of the day. Corrossole is only to be eaten in the morning, after black coffee;—vermouth is good to drink only between the hours of nine and half-past ten;—rum or other strong liquor only before meals or after fatigue;—claret or wine only during a repast, and then very sparingly,—for, strangely enough, wine is found to be injurious in a country where stronger liquors are considered among the prime necessaries of existence.

And he expected, at the worst, to feel lazy, to lose some physical energy! But this is no mere languor which now begins to oppress him;— it is a sense of vital exhaustion painful as the misery of convalescence: the least effort provokes a perspiration profuse enough to saturate clothing, and the limbs ache as from muscular overstrain;—the lightest attire feels almost insupportable;—the idea of sleeping even under a sheet is torture, for the weight of a silken handkerchief is discomfort. One wishes one could live as a savage,—naked in the heat. One burns with a thirst impossible to assuage—feels a desire for stimulants, a sense of difficulty breathing, occasional quickenings of the heart's action so violent as to alarm. Then comes at last the absolute dread of physical exertion. Some slight relief might be obtained, no doubt, by resigning oneself forthwith to adopt the gentle indolent manners of the white creoles, who do not walk when it is possible to ride, and never ride if it is equally convenient to drive;—but the northern nature generally refuses to accept this ultimate necessity without a protracted and painful struggle.

…Not even then has the stranger fully divined the evil power of this tropical climate, which remodels the characters of races within a couple of generations,—changing the shape of the skeleton,—deepening the cavities of the orbits to protect the eye from the flood of light,—transforming the blood,—darkening the skin. Following upon the nervous modifications of the first few months come modifications and changes of a yet graver kind;—with the loss of bodily energy ensues a more than corresponding loss of mental activity and strength. The whole range of thought diminishes, contracts,—shrinks to that narrowest of circles which surrounds the physical self, the inner ring of merely material sensation: the memory weakens appallingly;—the mind operates faintly, slowly, incoherently,—almost as in dreams. Serious reading, vigorous thinking, become impossible. You doze over the most important project;—you fall fast asleep over the most fascinating of books.

Then comes the vain revolt, the fruitless desperate striving with this occult power which numbs the memory and enchants the will. Against the set resolve to think, to act, to study, there is a hostile rush of unfamiliar pain to the temples, to the eyes, to the nerve centres of the brain; and a great weight is somewhere in the head, always growing heavier: then comes a drowsiness that overpowers and stupefies, like the effect of a narcotic. And this obligation to sleep, to sink into coma, will impose itself just so surely as you venture to attempt any mental work in leisure hours, after the noon repast, or during the heat of the afternoon. Yet at night you can scarcely sleep. Repose is made feverish by a still heat that keeps the skin drenched with thick sweat, or by a perpetual, unaccountable, tingling and prickling of the whole body-surface. With the approach of morning the air grows cooler, and slumber comes,—a slumber of exhaustion, dreamless and sickly; and perhaps when you would rise with the sun you feel such a dizziness, such a numbness, such a torpor, that only by the most intense effort can you keep your feet for the first five minutes. You experience a sensation that recalls the poet's fancy of death-in-life, or old stories of sudden rising from the grave: it is as though all the electricity of will had ebbed away,—all the vital force evaporated, in the heat of the night...

V

It might be stated, I think, with safety, that for a certain class of invalids the effect of the climate is like a powerful stimulant,—a tonic medicine which may produce astonishing results within a fixed time,—but which if taken beyond that time will prove dangerous. After a certain number of months, your first enthusiasm with your new surroundings dies out;—even Nature ceases to affect the senses in the same way: the *frisson* ceases to come to you. Meanwhile you may have striven to become as much as possible a part of the exotic life into which you have entered,—may have adopted its customs, learned its language. But you cannot mix with it mentally;—you circulate only as an oil-drop in its current. You still feel yourself alone.

The very longest West Indian day is but twelve hours fifty-six minutes;—perhaps your first dissatisfaction was evoked by the brevity of the days. There is no twilight whatever; and all activity ceases with sundown: there is no going outside of the city after dark, because of snakes;—club life here ends at the hour it only begins abroad;—there is no visiting of evenings; after the seven o'clock dinner, every one prepares to retire. And the foreigner, accustomed to make evening a time for social intercourse, finds no small difficulty in resigning himself to this habit of early retiring. The natural activity of a European or American mind requires some intellectual exercise,—at least some interchange of ideas with sympathetic natures; the hours during the suspension of business after noon, or those following the closing of offices at sunset, are the only ones in which busy men may find time for such relaxation; and these very hours have been always devoted to restorative sleep by the native population ever since the colony began. Naturally, therefore, the stranger dreads the coming of the darkness, the inevitable isolation of long sleepless hours. And if he seek those solaces for loneliness which he was wont to seek at home,—reading, study,—he is made to comprehend, as never before, what the absence of all libraries, lack of books, inaccessibility of all reading-matter, means for the man of the nineteenth century. One must send abroad to obtain even a review, and wait months for its coming. And this mental starvation gnaws at the brain more and more as one feels less inclination and less capacity for effort, and as that single enjoyment, which at first rendered a man indifferent to other pleasures,—the delight of being alone with tropical Nature,—becomes more difficult to indulge. When lethargy has totally mastered habit and purpose, and you must at last confess yourself resigned to view Nature from your chamber, or at best from a carriage window,—then, indeed, the want of all literature proves a positive torture. It is not a consolation to discover that you are an almost solitary sufferer,—from climate as well as from mental hunger. With amazement and envy you see young girls passing to walk right across the island and back before sunset, under burdens difficult for a strong man to lift to his shoulder;—the same journey on horseback would now weary you for days. You wonder of what flesh and blood can these people be made,—what wonderful vitality lies in those slender woman-bodies, which, under the terrible sun, and despite their astounding expenditure of force, remain cool to the sight and touch as bodies of lizards and serpents! And contrasting this savage strength with your own weakness, you begin to understand better how mighty the working of those powers which temper races and shape race habits in accordance with environment.

Ultimately, if destined for acclimatation, you will cease to suffer from these special conditions; but ere this can be, a long period of nervous irritability must be endured; and fevers must thin the blood, soften the muscles, transform the Northern tint of health to a dead brown. You will have to learn that intellectual pursuits can be persisted in only at risk of life;—that in this part of the world there is nothing to do but to plant cane and cocoa, and make rum, and cultivate tobacco,— or open a magazine for the sale of Madras handkerchiefs and foulards,— and eat, drink, sleep, perspire. You will understand why the tropics settled by European races produce no sciences, arts, or literature,—why the habits and the thoughts of other centuries still prevail where Time itself moves slowly as though enfeebled by the heat.

And with the compulsory indolence of your life, the long exasperation of the nervous system, will come the first pain of nostalgia,—the first weariness of the tropics. It is not that Nature can become ever less lovely to your sight; but that the tantalization of her dangerous beauty, which you may enjoy only at a safe distance, exasperates at last. The colors that at first bewitched will vex your eyes by their violence;—the creole life that appeared so simple, so gentle, will reveal dullnesses and discomforts undreamed of. You will ask yourself how much longer can you endure the prodigious light, and the furnace heat of blinding blue days, and the void misery of sleepless nights, and the curse of insects, and the sound of the mandibles of enormous roaches devouring the few books in your possession. You will grow weary of the grace of the palms, of the gemmy colors of the ever-clouded peaks, of the sight of the high woods made impenetrable by lianas and vines and serpents. You will weary even of the tepid sea, because to enjoy it as a swimmer you must rise and go out at hours while the morning air is still chill and heavy with miasma;—you will weary, above all, of tropic fruits, and feel that you would gladly pay a hundred francs for the momentary pleasure of biting into one rosy juicy Northern apple.

VI

...But if you believe this disillusion perpetual,—if you fancy the old bewitchment has spent all its force upon you,—you do not know this Nature. She is not done with you yet: she has only torpefied your energies a little. Of your willingness to obey her, she takes no cognizance;—she ignores human purposes, knows only molecules and their combinations; and the blind blood in your veins,—thick with Northern heat and habit,—is still in dumb desperate rebellion against her.

Perhaps she will quell this revolt forever,—thus:—

One day, in the second hour of the afternoon, a few moments after leaving home, there will come to you a sensation such as you have never known before: a sudden weird fear of the light.

It seems to you that the blue sky-fire is burning down into your brain,—that the flare of the white pavements and yellow walls is piercing somehow into your life,—creating an unfamiliar mental confusion,—blurring out thought... Is the whole world taking fire?... The flaming azure of the sea dazzles and pains like a crucible-glow;—the green of the mornes flickers and blazes in some amazing way... Then dizziness inexpressible: you grope with eyes shut fast—afraid to open them again in that stupefying torrefaction,—moving automatically,—vaguely knowing you must get out of the flaring and flashing,—somewhere, anywhere away from the white wrath of the sun, and the green fire of the hills, and the monstrous color of the sea... Then, remembering nothing, you find yourself in bed,—with an insupportable sense of weight at the back of the head,—a pulse beating furiously,—and a strange sharp pain at intervals stinging through your eyes... And the pain grows, expands,—fills all the skull,—forces you to cry out,—replaces all other sensations except a weak consciousness, vanishing and recurring, that you are very sick, more sick than ever before in all your life.

...And with the tedious ebbing of the long fierce fever, all the heat seems to pass from your veins. You can no longer imagine, as before, that it would be delicious to die of cold;—you shiver even with all the windows closed;—you feel currents of air,—imperceptible to nerves in a natural condition,—which shock like a dash of cold water, whenever doors are opened and closed; the very moisture upon your forehead is icy. What you now wish for are stimulants and warmth. Your blood has been changed;—tropic Nature has been good to you: she is preparing you to dwell with her.

...Gradually, under the kind nursing of those colored people,— among whom, as a stranger, your lot will probably be cast,—you recover strength; and perhaps it will seem to you that the pain of lying a while in the Shadow of Death is more than compensated by this rare and touching experience of human goodness. How tirelessly watchful,—how naïvely sympathetic,—how utterly self-sacrificing these women-natures are! Patiently, through weeks of stifling days and sleepless nights,—cruelly unnatural to them, for their life is in the open air,—they struggle to save without one murmur of fatigue, without heed of their most ordinary physical wants, without a thought of recompense;—trusting to their own skill when the physician abandons hope,—climbing to the woods for herbs when medicines prove without avail. The dream of angels holds nothing sweeter than this reality of woman's tenderness.

And simultaneously with the return of force, you may wonder whether this sickness has not sharpened your senses in some extraordinary way,—especially hearing, sight, and smell. Once well enough to be removed without danger, you will be taken up into the mountains somewhere,—for change of air; and there it will seem to you, perhaps, that never before did you feel so acutely the pleasure of perfumes,—of color-tones,—of the timbre of voices. You have simply been acclimated... And suddenly the old fascination of tropic Nature seizes you again,—more strongly than in the first days;—the *frisson* of delight returns; the joy of it thrills through all your blood,—making a great fulness at your heart as of unutterable desire to give thanks...

VII

...My friend Felicien had come to the colony fresh from the region of the Vosges, with the muscles and energies of a mountaineer, and cheeks pink as a French country-girl's;—he had never seemed to me physically adapted for acclimation; and I feared much for him on hearing of his first serious illness. Then the news of his convalescence came to me as a grateful surprise. But I did not feel reassured by his appearance the first evening I called at the little house to which he had been removed, on the brow of a green height overlooking the town. I found him seated in a *berceuse* on the veranda. How wan he was, and how spectral his smile of welcome,—as he held out to me a hand that seemed all of bone!

We chatted there a while. It had been one of those tropic days whose charm interpenetrates and blends with all the subtler life of sensation, and becomes a luminous part of it forever,—steeping all after-dreams of ideal peace in supernal glory of color,—transfiguring all fancies of the pure joy of being. Azure to the sea-line the sky had remained since morning; and the trade-wind, warm as a caress, never brought even one gauzy cloud to veil the naked beauty of the peaks.

And the sun was yellowing,—as only over the tropics he yellows to his death. Lilac tones slowly spread through sea and heaven from the west;—mornes facing the light began to take a wondrous glowing color,—a tone of green so fiery that it looked as though all the rich sap of their woods were phosphorescing. Shadows blued;—far peaks took tinting that scarcely seemed of earth,—iridescent violets and purples interchanging through vapor of gold… Such the colors of the *carangue*, when the beautiful tropic fish is turned in the light, and its gem-greens shift to rich azure and prism-purple.

Reclining in our chairs, we watched the strange splendor from the veranda of the little cottage,—saw the peaked land slowly steep itself in the aureate glow,—the changing color of the verdured mornes, and of the sweep of circling sea. Tiny birds, bosomed with fire, were shooting by in long curves, like embers flung by invisible hands. From far below, the murmur of the city rose to us,—a stormy hum. So motionless we remained that the green and gray lizards were putting out their heads from behind the columns of the veranda to stare at us,—as if wondering whether we were really alive. I turned my head suddenly to look at two queer butterflies; and all the lizards hid themselves again. *Papillon-lanmò*,—Death's butterflies,—these were called in the speech of the people: their broad wings were black like blackest velvet;—as they fluttered against the yellow light, they looked like silhouettes of butterflies. Always through my memory of that wondrous evening,—when I little thought I was seeing my friend's face for the last time,—there slowly passes the black palpitation of those wings…

…I had been chatting with Felicien about various things which I thought might have a cheerful interest for him; and more than once I had been happy to see him smile… But our converse waned. The ever-magnifying splendor before us had been mesmerizing our senses,—slowly overpowering our wills with the amazement of its beauty. Then, as the sun's disk—enormous,—blinding gold—touched the lilac flood, and the stupendous orange glow flamed up to the very zenith, we found ourselves awed at last into silence.

The orange in the west deepened into vermilion. Softly and very swiftly night rose like an indigo exhalation from the land,—filling the valleys, flooding the gorges, blackening the woods, leaving only the points of the peaks a while to catch the crimson glow. Forests and fields began to utter a rushing sound as of torrents, always deepening,—made up of the instrumentation and the voices of numberless little beings: clangings as of hammered iron, ringings as of dropping silver upon a stone, the dry bleatings of the *cabritt-bois*, and the chirruping of tree-frogs, and the *ki-i-i-i-i-i* of crickets. Immense trembling sparks began to rise and fall among the shadows,—twinkling out and disappearing all mysteriously: these were the fire-flies awakening. Then, about the branches of the *bois-canon* black shapes began to hover, which were not birds—shapes flitting processionally without any noise; each one in turn resting a moment as to nibble something at the end of a bough;—then yielding place to another, and circling away, to return again from the other side... the *guimbos*, the great bats.

But we were silent, with the emotion of sunset still upon us: that ghostly emotion which is the transmitted experience of a race,—the sum of ancestral experiences innumerable,—the mingled joy and pain of a million years... Suddenly a sweet voice pierced the stillness,— pleading:—

—"*Pa combiné, chè!—pa combiné conm ça!*" (Do not think, dear— do not think like that!)

...Only less beautiful than the sunset she seemed, this slender half-breed, who had come all unperceived behind us, treading soundlessly with her slim bare feet... "And you, Missié," she said to me, in a tone of gentle reproach;—"you are his friend! why do you let him think? It is thinking that will prevent him getting well."

Combiné in creole signifies to think intently, and therefore to be unhappy,—because, with this artless race, as with children, to think intensely about anything is possible only under great stress of suffering.

—"*Pa combiné,—non chè,*" she repeated, plaintively, stroking Felicien's hair. "It is thinking that makes us old... And it is time to bid your friend good-night."...

—"She is so good," said Felicien, smiling to make her pleased;—"I could never tell you how good. But she does not understand. She believes I suffer if I am silent. She is contented only when she sees me laugh; and so she will tell me creole stories by the hour to keep me amused as if I were a child."...

As he spoke she slipped an arm about his neck.

—"*Doudoux*," she persisted;—and her voice was a dove's coo,—" *Si ou ainmein moin, pa combiné—non!*"

And in her strange exotic beauty, her savage grace, her supple caress, the velvet witchery of her eyes,—it seemed to me that I beheld a something imaged, not of herself, nor of the moment only,—a something weirdly sensuous: the Spirit of tropic Nature made golden flesh, and murmuring to each lured wanderer:—"*If thou wouldst love me, do not think!*"...

NOTES

1. Rufz remarks that the first effect of this climate of the Antilles is a sort of general physical excitement, an exaltation, a sense of unaccustomed strength,—which begets the desire of immediate action to discharge the surplus of nervous force. "Then all distances seem brief;—the greatest fatigues are braved without hesitation."—*Études.*

XIII. Yé

I

ALMOST every night, just before bedtime, I hear some group of children in the street telling stories to each other. Stories, enigmas or *tim-tim*, and songs, and round games, are the joy of child-life here,—whether rich or poor. I am particularly fond of listening to the stories,—which seem to me the oddest stories I ever heard.

I succeeded in getting several dictated to me, so that I could write them;—others were written for me by creole friends, with better success. To obtain them in all their original simplicity and naïve humor of detail, one should be able to write them down in short-hand as fast as they are related: they lose greatly in the slow process of dictation. The simple mind of the native story-teller, child or adult, is seriously tried by the inevitable interruptions and restraints of the dictation method;—the reciter loses spirit, becomes soon weary, and purposely shortens the narrative to finish the task as soon as possible. It seems painful to such a one to repeat a phrase more than once,—at least in the same way; while frequent questioning may irritate the most good-natured in a degree that shows how painful to the untrained brain may be the exercise of memory and steady control of imagination required for continuous dictation. By patience, however, I succeeded in obtaining many curiosities of oral literature,—representing a group of stories which, whatever their primal origin, have been so changed by local thought and coloring as to form a distinctively Martinique folk-tale circle. Among them are several especially popular with the children of my neighborhood; and I notice that almost every narrator embellishes the original plot with details of his own, which he varies at pleasure.

I submit a free rendering of one of these tales,—the history of Yé and the Devil. The whole story of Yé would form a large book,—so numerous the list of his adventures; and this adventure seems to me the most characteristic of all. Yé is the most curious figure in Martinique folk-lore. Yé is the typical Bitaco, or mountain negro of the lazy kind,— the country black whom city blacks love to poke fun at. As for the Devil of Martinique folk-lore, he resembles the *travailleur* at a distance; but when you get dangerously near him, you find that he has red eyes and red hair, and two little horns under his *chapeau-Bacouè*, and feet like an ape, and fire in his throat. *Y ka sam yon gouôs, gouôs macaque...*

II

Ça qui pa té connaitt Yé?... Who is there in all Martinique who never heard of Yé? Everybody used to know the old rascal. He had every fault under the sun;—he was the laziest negro in the whole island; he was the biggest glutton in the whole world. He had an amazing number[1] of children; and they were most of the time all half dead for hunger.

Well, one day Yé went out to the woods to look for something to eat. And he walked through the woods all day, till he became ever so tired; but he could not find anything to eat. He was just going to give up the search, when he heard a queer crackling noise,—at no great distance. He went to see what it was,—hiding himself behind the big trees as he got nearer to it.

All at once he came to a little hollow in the woods, and saw a great fire burning there,—and he saw a Devil sitting beside the fire. The Devil was roasting a great heap of snails; and the sound Yé had heard was the crackling of the snail-shells. The Devil seemed to be very old;—he was sitting on the trunk of a bread-fruit tree; and Yé took a good long look at him. After Yé had watched him for a while, Yé found out that the old Devil was quite blind.

The Devil had a big calabash in his hand full of *féroce*,—that is to say, boiled salt codfish and manioc with ever so many pimentos (*épi en pile piment*),—just what negroes like Yé are most fond of. And the devil seemed to be very hungry; and the food was going so fast down his throat that it made Yé unhappy to see it disappearing. It made him so unhappy that he felt at last he could not resist the temptation to steal from the old blind Devil. He crept quite close up to the Devil without making any noise, and began to rob him. Every time the Devil would lift his hand to his mouth, Yé would slip his own fingers into the calabash, and snatch a piece. The old Devil did not even look puzzled;—he did not seem to know anything; and Yé thought to himself that the old Devil was a great fool. He began to get more and more courage;—he took bigger and bigger handfuls out of the calabash;—he ate even faster than the Devil could eat. At last there was only one little bit left in the calabash. Yé put out his hand to take it,—and all of a sudden the

Devil made a grab at Yé's hand and caught it! Yé was so frightened he could not even cry out, *Aïe-yaïe!* The Devil finished the last morsel, threw down the calabash, and said to Yé in a terrible voice:—"*Atò, saff!—ou c'est ta moin!*" (I've got you now, you glutton;—you belong to me!) Then he jumped on Yé's back, like a great ape, and twisted his legs round Yé's neck, and cried out:—

—"Carry me to your cabin,—and walk fast!"

***

...When Yé's poor children saw him coming, they wondered what their papa was carrying on his back. They thought it might be a sack of bread or vegetables or perhaps a *régime* of bananas,—for it was getting dark, and they could not see well. They laughed and showed their teeth and danced and screamed: "Here's papa coming with something to eat!—papa's coming with something to eat!" But when Yé had got near enough for them to see what he was carrying, they yelled and ran away to hide themselves. As for the poor mother, she could only hold up her two hands for horror.

When they got into the cabin the Devil pointed to a corner, and said to Yé:—"Put me down there!" Yé put him down. The Devil sat there in the corner and never moved or spoke all that evening and all that night. He seemed to be a very quiet Devil indeed. The children began to look at him.

But at breakfast-time, when the poor mother had managed to procure something for the children to eat,—just some bread-fruit and yams,—the old Devil suddenly rose up from his corner and muttered:—

—"*Manman mò!—papa mò!—toutt yche mò!* " (Mamma dead!—papa dead!—all the children dead!)

And he blew his breath on them, and they all fell down stiff as if they were dead—*raidi-cadave!* Then the Devil ate up everything there was on the table. When he was done, he filled the pots and dishes with dirt, and blew his breath again on Yé and all the family, and muttered:—

—"*Toutt moune lévé!*" (Everybody get up!)

Then they all got up. Then he pointed to all the plates and dishes full of dirt, and said to them:—[2]

—"*Gobe-moin ça!*"

And they had to gobble it all up, as he told them. After that it was no use trying to eat anything. Every time anything was cooked, the Devil would do the same thing. It was thus the next day, and the next, and the day after, and so every day for a long, long time.

***

Yé did not know what to do; but his wife said she did. If she was only a man, she would soon get rid of that Devil. "Yé," she insisted, "go and see the Bon-Dié [the Good-God], and ask him what to do. I would go myself if I could; but women are not strong enough to climb the great morne."

So Yé started off very, very early one morning, before the peep of day, and began to climb the Montagne Pelée. He climbed and walked, and walked and climbed until he got at last to the top of the Morne de la Croix.[3] Then he knocked at the sky as loud as he could till the Good-God put his head out of a cloud and asked him what he wanted:—

—"*Eh bien!—ça ou ni, Yé? ça ou lè?*"

When Yé had recounted his troubles, the Good-God said:—

—"*Pauv ma pauv!* I knew it all before you came, Yé. I can tell you what to do; but I am afraid it will be no use—you will never be able to do it! Your gluttony is going to be the ruin of you, poor Yé! Still, you can try. Now listen well to what I am going to tell you. First of all, you must not eat anything before you get home. Then when your wife has the children's dinner ready, and you see the Devil getting up, you must cry out:—"*Tam ni pou tam ni bé!*" Then the Devil will drop down dead. Don't forget not to eat anything—*ou tanne?*"…

Yé promised to remember all he was told, and not to eat anything on his way down;—then he said good-bye to the Bon-Dié (*bien conm y faut*), and started. All the way he kept repeating the words the Good-God had told him: "*Tam ni pou tam ni bé!—tam ni pou tam ni bé!*" — over and over again.

But before reaching home he had to cross a little stream; and on both banks he saw wild guava-bushes growing, with plenty of sour guavas upon them;—for it was not yet time for guavas to be ripe. Poor Yé was hungry! He did all he could to resist the temptation, but it proved too much for him. He broke all his promises to the Bon-Dié: he ate and ate and ate till there were no more guavas left,—and then he began to eat *zicaques* and green plums, and all sorts of nasty sour things, till he could not eat any more.

By the time he got to the cabin his teeth were so on edge that he could scarcely speak distinctly enough to tell his wife to get the supper ready.

And so while everybody was happy, thinking that they were going to be freed from their trouble, Yé was really in no condition to do anything. The moment the supper was ready, the Devil got up from his corner as usual, and approached the table. Then Yé tried to speak; but his teeth were so on edge that instead of saying,—"*Tam ni pou tam ni bé*," he could only stammer out:—

—"*Anni toqué Diabe-là cagnan.*"

This had no effect on the Devil at all: he seemed to be used to it! He blew his breath on them all, sent them to sleep, ate up all the supper, filled the empty dishes with filth, awoke Yé and his family, and ordered them as usual:—

—"*Gobe-moin ça!*" And they had to gobble it up,—every bit of it.

***

The family nearly died of hunger and disgust. Twice more Yé climbed the Montagne Pelée; twice more he climbed the Morne de La Croix; twice more he disturbed the poor Bon-Dié, all for nothing!—since each time on his way down he would fill his paunch with all sorts of nasty sour things, so that he could not speak right. The Devil remained in the house night and day;—the poor mother threw herself down on the ground, and pulled out her hair,—so unhappy she was!

But luckily for the poor woman, she had one child as cunning as a rat,—[4] a boy called Ti Fonté (little Impudent), who bore his name well. When he saw his mother crying so much, he said to her:—

—"Mamma, send papa just once more to see the Good-God: I know something to do!"

The mother knew how cunning her boy was: she felt sure he meant something by his words;—she sent old Yé for the last time to see the Bon-Dié.

Yé used always to wear one of those big long coats they call *lavalasses*;—whether it was hot or cool, wet or dry, he never went out without it. There were two very big pockets in it—one on each side. When Ti Fonté saw his father getting ready to go, he jumped *floup!* into one of the pockets and hid himself there. Yé climbed all the way to the top of the Morne de La Croix without suspecting anything. When he got there the little boy put one of his ears out of Yé's pocket,—so as to hear everything the Good-God would say.

This time he was very angry,—the Bon-Dié: he spoke very crossly; he scolded Yé a great deal. But he was so kind for all that,—he was so generous to good-for-nothing Yé, that he took the pains to repeat the words over and over again for him:—"*Tam ni pou tam ni bé*."... And this time the Bon-Dié was not talking to no purpose: there was somebody there well able to remember what he said. Ti Fonté made the most of his chance;—he sharpened that little tongue of his; he thought of his mamma and all his little brothers and sisters dying of hunger down below. As for his father, Yé did as he had done before—stuffed himself with all the green fruit he could find.

The moment Yé got home and took off his coat, Ti Fonté jumped out, *plapp!*—and ran to his mamma, and whispered:—

—"Mamma, get ready a really nice big dinner!—we are going to have it all to ourselves today: the Good-God didn't talk for nothing,—I heard every word he said!"

Then the mother got ready a nice *calalou-crabe*, a *tonton-banane*, a *matété-cirique*,—several calabashes of *cousscaye*, two *régimes-figues* (bunches of small bananas),—in short, a very fine dinner indeed, with a *chopine* of tafia to wash it all well down.

The Devil felt as sure of himself that day as he had always felt, and got up the moment everything was ready. But Ti Fonté got up too, and yelled out just as loud as he could:—

—"*Tam ni pou tam ni bé!*"

At once the Devil gave a scream so loud that it could be heard right down to the bottom of hell,—and he fell dead.

Meanwhile, Yé, like the old fool he was, kept trying to say what the Bon-Dié had told him, and could only mumble:—

—"*Anni toqué Diabe-là cagnan!*"

He would never have been able to do anything;—and his wife had a great mind to send him to bed at once, instead of letting him sit down to eat all those nice things. But she was a kind-hearted soul; and so she let Yé stay and eat with the children, though he did not deserve it. And they all ate and ate, and kept on filling themselves until daybreak—*pauv piti!*

But during this time the Devil had begun to smell badly, and he had become swollen so big that Yé found that he could not move him. Still, they knew they must get him out of the way somehow. The children had eaten so much that they were all full of strength—*yo té plein lafòce*; and Yé got a rope and tied one end round the Devil's foot; and then he and the children—all pulling together—managed to drag the Devil out of the cabin and into the bushes, where they left him just like a dead dog. They all felt themselves very happy to be rid of that old Devil.

***

But some days after old good-for-nothing Yé went off to hunt for birds. He had a whole lot of arrows with him. He suddenly remembered the Devil, and thought he would like to take one more look at him. And he did.

Fouinq! what a sight! The Devil's belly had swelled up like a morne: it was yellow and blue and green,—looked as if it was going to burst. And Yé, like the old fool he always was, shot an arrow up in the air, so that it fell down and stuck into the Devil's belly. Then he wanted to get the arrow, and he climbed up on the Devil, and pulled and pulled till he got the arrow out. Then he put the point of the arrow to his nose,—just to see what sort of a smell dead Devils had.

The moment he did that, his nose swelled up as big as the refinery-pot of a sugar plantation.

Yé could scarcely walk for the weight of his nose; but he had to go and see the Bon-Dié again. The Bon-Dié said to him:—

—"Ah! Yé, my poor Yé, you will live and die a fool!—you are certainly the biggest fool in the whole world!... Still, I must try to do something for you;—I'll help you anyhow to get rid of that nose!... I'll tell you how to do it. Tomorrow morning, very early, get up and take a big *taya* [whip], and beat all the bushes well, and drive all the birds to the Roche de la Caravelle. Then you must tell them that I, the Bon-Dié, want them to take off their bills and feathers, and take a good bath in the sea. While they are bathing, you can choose a nose for yourself out of the heap of bills there."

Poor Yé did just as the Good-God told him; and while the birds were bathing, he picked out a nose for himself from the heap of beaks,—and left his own refinery-pot in its place.

The nose he took was the nose of the *coulivicou*.[5] And that is why the *coulivicou* always looks so much ashamed of himself even to this day.

III

...POOR Yé!—you still live for me only too vividly outside of those strange folk-tales of eating and of drinking which so cruelly reveal the long slave-hunger of your race. For I have seen you cutting cane on peak slopes above the clouds;—I have seen you climbing from plantation to plantation with your cutlass in your hand, watching for snakes as you wander to look for work, when starvation forces you to obey a master, though born with the resentment of centuries against all masters;—I have seen you prefer to carry two hundred-weight of bananas twenty miles to market, rather than labor in the fields;—I have seen you ascending through serpent-swarming woods to some dead crater to find a cabbage-palm,—and always hungry,—and always shiftless! And you are still a great fool, poor Yé!—and you have still your swarm of children,—your *rafale yche*,—and they are famished; for you have taken into your *ajoupa* a Devil who devours even more than you can earn,— even your heart, and your splendid muscles, and your poor artless brain,—the Devil Tafia!... And there is no Bon-Dié to help you rid yourself of him now: for the only Bon-Dié you ever really had, your old creole master, cannot care for you any more, and you cannot care for yourself. Mercilessly moral, the will of this enlightened century has abolished forever that patriarchal power which brought you up strong and healthy on scanty fare, and scourged you into its own idea of righteousness, yet kept you innocent as a child of the law of the struggle for life. But you feel that law now;—you are a citizen of the Republic! you are free to vote, and free to work, and starve if you prefer it, and free to do evil and suffer for it;—and this new knowledge stupefies you so that you have almost forgotten how to laugh!

NOTES

1. In the patois, "*yon rafale yche*,"—a "whirlwind of children."

2. In the original:—"Y té ka monté assous tabe-là, épi y té ka fai caca adans toutt plats-à, adans toutt zassiett-là."

3. A peaklet rising above the verge of the ancient crater now filled with water.

4. The great field-rat of Martinique is, in Martinique folk-lore, the symbol of all cunning, and probably merits its reputation.

5. The *coulivicou*, or "Colin Vicou," is a Martinique bird with a long meagre body, and an enormous bill. It has a very tristful and taciturn expression... *Maig conm yon coulivicou*, "thin as a coulivicou," is a popular comparison for the appearance of anybody much reduced by sickness.

XIV. Lys

I

IT is only half-past four o'clock: there is the faintest blue light of beginning day,—and little Victoire already stands at the bedside with my wakening cup of hot black fragrant coffee. What! So early?... Then with a sudden heart-start I remember this is my last West Indian morning. And the child—her large timid eyes all gently luminous—is pressing something into my hand.

Two vanilla beans wrapped in a morsel of banana-leaf,—her poor little farewell gift!...

Other trifling souvenirs are already packed away. Almost everybody that knows me has given me something. Manm-Robert brought me a tiny packet of orange-seeds,—seeds of a "gift-orange": so long as I can keep these in my vest pocket I will never be without money. Cyrillia bought me a packet of *bouts*, and a pretty box of French matches, warranted inextinguishable by wind. Azaline, the blanchisseuse, sent me a little pocket looking-glass. Cerbonnie, the *màchanne*, left a little cup of guava jelly for me last night. Mimi—dear child!—brought me a little paper dog! It is her best toy; but those gentle black eyes would stream with tears if I dared to refuse it... Oh Mimi! what am I to do with a little paper dog? And what am I to do with the chocolate-sticks and the cocoanuts and all the sugar-cane and all the cinnamon-apples?...

II

...TWENTY minutes past five by the clock of the Bourse. The hill shadows are shrinking back from the shore;—the long wharves reach out yellow into the sun:—the tamarinds of the Place Bertin, and the pharos for half its height, and the red-tiled roofs along the bay are catching the glow. Then, over the light-house—on the outermost line depending from the southern yard-arm of the semaphore—a big black ball suddenly runs up like a spider climbing its own thread... *Steamer from the south!* The packet has been sighted. And I have not yet been able to pack away into a specially purchased wooden box all the fruits and vegetable curiosities and odd little presents sent to me. If Radice the boatman had not come to help me, I should never be able to get ready; for the work of packing is being continually interrupted by friends and acquaintances coming to say good-bye. Manm-Robert brings to see me a pretty young girl—very fair, with a violet foulard twisted about her blond head. It is little Basilique, who is going to make her *pouémiè communion.* So I kiss her, according to the old colonial custom, once on each downy cheek;—and she is to pray to *Notre Dame du Bon Port* that the ship shall bear me safely to far-away New York.

And even the steamer's cannon-call shakes over the town and into the hills behind us, which answer with all the thunder of their phantom artillery.

III

...THERE is a young white lady, accompanied by an aged negress, already waiting on the south wharf for the boat;—evidently she is to be one of my fellow passengers. Quite a pleasing presence: slight graceful figure,—a face not precisely pretty, but delicate and sensitive, with the odd charm of violet eyes under black eyebrows...

A friend who comes to see me off tells me all about her. Mademoiselle Lys is going to New York to be a governess,—to leave her native island forever. A story sad enough, though not more so than that of many a gentle creole girl. And she is going all alone; for I see her bidding good-bye to old Titine,—kissing her. "*Adié encò, chè:—Bon-Dié ké béni ou!*" sobs the poor servant, with tears streaming down her kind black face. She takes off her blue shoulder-kerchief, and waves it as the boat recedes from the wooden steps.

...Fifteen minutes later, Mademoiselle and I find ourselves under the awnings shading the saloon-deck of the *Guadeloupe.* There are at least fifty passengers,—many resting in chairs, lazy-looking Demerara chairs with arm-supports immensely lengthened so as to form rests for the lower limbs. Overhead, suspended from the awning-frames, are two tin cages containing parrots;—and I see two little greenish monkeys, no bigger than squirrels, tied to the wheel-hatch,—two *sakiwinkis.* These are from the forests of British Guiana. They keep up a continual thin sharp twittering, like birds,—all the while circling, ascending, descending, retreating or advancing to the limit of the little ropes attaching them to the hatch.

The *Guadeloupe* has seven hundred packages to deliver at St. Pierre: we have ample time,—Mademoiselle Violet-Eyes and I,—to take one last look at the "Pays des Revenants."

I wonder what her thoughts are, feeling a singular sympathy for her,—for I am in that sympathetic mood which the natural emotion of leaving places and persons one has become fond of, is apt to inspire. And now at the moment of my going,—when I seem to understand as never before the beauty of that tropic Nature, and the simple charm of the life to which I am bidding farewell,—the question comes to me: "Does she not love it all as I do,—nay, even much more, because of that in her own existence which belongs to it?" But as a child of the land, she has seen no other skies,—fancies, perhaps, there may be brighter ones...

...Nowhere on this earth, Violet-Eyes!—nowhere beneath this sun!... Oh! the dawnless glory of tropic morning!—the single sudden leap of the giant light over the purpling of a hundred peaks,—over the surging of the mornes! And the early breezes from the hills,—all cool out of the sleep of the forests, and heavy with vegetal odors thick, sappy, savage-sweet!—and the wild high winds that run ruffling and crumpling through the cane of the mountain slopes in storms of papery sound!—

And the mighty dreaming of the woods,—green-drenched with silent pouring of creepers,—dashed with the lilac and yellow and rosy foam of liana flowers!—

And the eternal azure apparition of the all-circling sea,—that as you mount the heights ever appears to rise perpendicularly behind you,—that seems, as you descend, to sink and flatten before you!—

And the violet velvet distances of evening;—and the swaying of palms against the orange-burning,—when all the heaven seems filled with vapors of a molten sun!...

IV

HOW beautiful the mornes and azure-shadowed hollows in the jewel-clearness of this perfect morning! Even Pelée wears only her very lightest head-dress of gauze; and all the wrinklings of her green robe take unfamiliar tenderness of tint from the early sun. All the quaint peaking of the colored town—sprinkling the sweep of blue bay with red and yellow and white-of-cream—takes a sharpness in this limpid light as if seen through a diamond lens; and there above the living green of the familiar hills I can see even the faces of the statues—the black Christ on his white cross, and the white lady of the Morne d'Orange—among upcurving palms.

…It is all as though the island were donning its utmost possible loveliness, exerting all its witchery,—seeking by supremest charm to win back and hold its wondering child,—Violet-Eyes over there!… She is looking too.

I wonder if she sees the great palms of the Voie du Parnasse,—curving far away as to bid us adieu, like beautiful bending women. I wonder if they are not trying to say something to her; and I try myself to fancy what that something is:—

—"Child, wilt thou indeed abandon all who love thee!… Listen!—'tis a grim grey land thou goest unto,—a land of bitter winds,—a land of strange gods,—a land of hardness and barrenness, where even Nature may not live through half the cycling of the year! Thou wilt never see us there… And there, when thou shalt sleep thy long sleep, child, that land will have no power to lift thee up;—vast weight of stone will press thee down forever;—until the heavens be no more thou shalt not awake!… But here, darling, our loving roots would seek for thee, would find thee: thou shouldst live again!—we lift, like Aztec priests, the blood of hearts to the Sun!"…

V

…It is very hot… I hold in my hand a Japanese paper-fan with a design upon it of the simplest sort: one jointed green bamboo, with a single spurt of sharp leaves, cutting across a pale blue murky double streak that means the horizon above a sea. That is all. Trivial to my Northern friends this design might seem; but to me it causes a pleasure bordering on pain… I know so well what the artist means; and they could not know, unless they had seen bamboos,—and bamboos particularly situated. As I look at this fan I know myself descending the Morne Parnasse by the steep winding road; I have the sense of windy heights behind me, and forest on either hand, and before me the blended azure of sky and sea with one bamboo-spray swaying across it at the level of my eyes. Nor is this all;—I have the every sensation of the very moment,—the vegetal odors, the mighty tropic light, the warmth, the intensity of irreproducible color… Beyond a doubt, the artist who dashed the design on this fan with his miraculous brush must have had a nearly similar experience to that of which the memory is thus aroused in me, but which I cannot communicate to others.

...And it seems to me now that all which I have tried to write about the *Pays des Revenants* can only be for others, who have never beheld it,—vague like the design upon this fan.

VI

Brrrrrrrrr!... The steam-winch is lifting the anchor; and the *Guadeloupe* trembles through every plank as the iron torrent of her chain-cable rumbles through the hawse-holes... At last the quivering ceases;—there is a moment's silence; and Violet-Eyes seems trying to catch a last glimpse of her faithful *bonne* among the ever-thickening crowd upon the quay... Ah! there she is—waving her foulard. Mademoiselle Lys is waving a handkerchief in reply...

Suddenly the shock of the farewell gun shakes heavily through our hearts, and over the bay,—where the tall mornes catch the flapping thunder, and buffet it through all their circle in tremendous mockery. Then there is a great whirling and whispering of whitened water behind the steamer—another,—another: and the whirl becomes a foaming stream: the mighty propeller is playing!... All the blue harbor swings slowly round;—and the green limbs of the land are pushed out further on the left, shrink back upon the right;—and the mountains are moving their shoulders. And then the many-tinted façades,—and the tamarinds of the Place Bertin,—and the light-house,—and the long wharves with

Basse-Terre, St. Kitt's

their throng of turbaned women,—and the cathedral towers,—and the fair palms,—and the statues of the hills,—all veer, change place, and begin to float away... steadily, very swiftly.

Farewell, fair city,—sun-kissed city,—many-fountained city!—dear yellow-glimmering streets,—white pavements learned by heart,—and faces ever looked for,—and voices ever loved! Farewell, white towers with your golden-throated bells!—farewell, green steeps, bathed in the light of summer everlasting!—craters with your coronets of forest!— bright mountain paths upwinding 'neath pomp of fern and angelin and feathery bamboo!—and gracious palms that drowse above the dead!

Farewell, soft-shadowing majesty of valleys unfolding to the sun,— green golden cane-fields ripening to the sea!...

...The town vanishes. The island slowly becomes a green silhouette. So might Columbus first have seen it from the deck of his caravel,—nearly four hundred years ago. At this distance there are no more signs of life upon it than when it first became visible to his eyes: yet there are cities there,—and toiling,—and suffering, and gentle hearts that knew me... Now it is turning blue,—the beautiful shape!—becoming a dream...

VII

AND Dominica draws nearer,—sharply massing her hills against the vast light in purple nodes and gibbosities and denticulations. Closer and closer it comes, until the green of its heights breaks through the purple here and there,—in flashings and ribbings of color. Then it remains as if motionless a while;—then the green lights go out again,—and all the shape begins to recede sideward towards the south.

...And what had appeared a pearl-gray cloud in the north slowly reveals itself as another island of mountains,—hunched and horned and mammiform: Guadeloupe begins to show her double profile. But Martinique is still visible;—Pelée still peers high over the rim of the south... Day wanes;— the shadow of the ship lengthens over the flower-blue water. Pelée changes aspect at last,—turns pale as a ghost,—but will not fade away...

...The sun begins to sink as he always sinks to his death in the tropics,—swiftly,—too swiftly!—and the glory of him makes golden all the hollow west,—and bronzes all the flickering wave-backs But still the gracious phantom of the island will not go,—softly haunting us through the splendid haze. And always the tropic wind blows soft and warm;—there is an indescribable caress in it! Perhaps some such breeze, blowing from Indian waters, might have inspired that prophecy of Islam concerning the Wind of the Last Day,—that "Yellow Wind, softer than silk, balmier than musk,"—which is to sweep the spirits of the just to God in the great Winnowing of Souls...

Then into the indigo night vanishes forever from my eyes the ghost of Pelée; and the moon swings up,—a young and lazy moon, drowsing upon her back, as in a hammock...Yet a few nights more, and we shall see this slim young moon erect,—gliding upright on her way,—coldly beautiful like a fair Northern girl.

VIII

AND ever through tepid nights and azure days the *Guadeloupe* rushes on,—her wake a river of snow beneath the sun, a torrent of fire beneath the stars,—steaming straight for the North.

Under the peaking of Montserrat we steam,—beautiful Montserrat, all softly wrinkled like a robe of greenest velvet fallen from the waist!—breaking the pretty sleep of Plymouth town behind its screen of palms... young palms, slender and full of grace as creole children are;—

And by tall Nevis, with her trinity of dead craters purpling through ocean-haze;—by clouded St. Christopher's mountain-giant;—past ghostly St. Martin's, far-floating in fog of gold, like some dream of the Saint's own Second Summer;—

Past low Antigua's vast blue harbor,—shark-haunted, bounded about by huddling of little hills, blue and green;—

Past Santa Cruz, the "Island of the Holy Cross,"—all radiant with verdure though wellnigh woodless,—nakedly beautiful in the tropic light as a perfect statue;—

Past the long cerulean reaching and heaping of Porto Rico on the left, and past hopeless St. Thomas on the right,—old St. Thomas, watching the going and the coming of the commerce that long since abandoned her port,—watching the ships once humbly solicitous for patronage now turning away to the Spanish rival, like ingrates forsaking a ruined patrician;—

And the vapory Vision of St. John;—and the grey ghost of Tortola,—and further, fainter; still more weirdly dim, the aureate phantom of Virgin Gorda.

IX

THEN only the enormous double-vision of sky and sea.

The sky: a cupola of blinding blue, shading down and paling into spectral green at the rim of the world,—and all fleckless, save at evening. Then, with sunset, comes a light gold-drift of little feathery cloudlets into the West,—stippling it as with a snow of fire.

The sea: no flower-tint may now make any comparison for the splendor of its lucent color. It has shifted its hue;—for we have entered into the Azure Stream: it has more than the magnificence of burning cyanogen...

But, at night, the Cross of the South appears no more. And other changes come, as day succeeds to day,—a lengthening of the hours of light, a longer lingering of the after-glow,—a cooling of the wind. Each morning the air seems a little cooler, a little rarer;—each noon the sky looks a little paler, a little further away,—always heightening, yet also more shadowy, as if its color, receding, were dimmed by distance,—were coming more faintly down from vaster altitudes.

...Mademoiselle is petted like a child by the lady passengers. And every man seems anxious to aid in making her voyage a pleasant one. For much of which, I think, she may thank her eyes!

X

A DIM morning and chill;—blank sky and sunless waters: the sombre heaven of the North with colorless horizon rounding in a blind gray sea... What a sudden weight comes to the heart with the touch of the cold mist, with the spectral melancholy of the dawn!—and then what foolish though irrepressible yearning for the vanished azure left behind!

...The little monkeys twitter plaintively, trembling in the chilly air. The parrots have nothing to say: they look benumbed, and sit on their perches with eyes closed.

...A vagueness begins to shape itself along the verge of the sea, far to port: that long heavy clouding which indicates the approach of land. And from it now floats to us something ghostly and frigid which makes the light filmy and the sea shadowy as a flood of dreams,—the fog of the Jersey coast.

At once the engines slacken their respiration. The *Guadeloupe* begins to utter her steam-cry of warning,—regularly at intervals of two minutes,—for she is now in the track of all the ocean vessels. And from far away we can hear a heavy knelling,—the booming of some great fog-bell.

...All in a white twilight. The place of the horizon has vanished;—we seem ringed in by a wall of smoke...Out of this vapory emptiness—very suddenly—an enormous steamer rushes, towering like a hill—passes so close that we can see faces, and disappears again, leaving the sea heaving and frothing behind her.

...As I lean over the rail to watch the swirling of the wake, I feel something pulling at my sleeve hand,—a tiny black hand,—the hand of a *sakiwinki*. One of the little monkeys, straining to the full length of his string, is making this dumb appeal for human sympathy;—the bird-black eyes of both are fixed upon me with the oddest look of pleading. Poor little tropical exiles! I stoop to caress them; but regret the impulse a moment later: they utter such beseeching cries when I find myself obliged to leave them again alone!...

...Hour after hour the *Guadeloupe* glides on through the white gloom,—cautiously, as if feeling her way; always sounding her whistle, ringing her bells, until at last some brown-winged bark comes flitting to us out of the mist, bearing a pilot... How strange it must all seem to Mademoiselle who stands so silent there at the rail!—how weird this veiled world must appear to her, after the sapphire light of her own West Indian sky, and the great lazulite splendor of her own tropic sea!

But a wind comes!—it strengthens,—begins to blow very cold. The mists thin before its blowing; and the wan blank sky is all revealed again with livid horizon around the heaving of the iron-gray sea.

...Thou dim and lofty heaven of the North,—gray sky of Odin,—bitter thy winds and spectral all thy colors!—they that dwell beneath thee know not the glory of Eternal Summer's green,—the azure splendor of southern day!—but thine are the lightnings of Thought illuminating for human eyes the interspaces between sun and sun. Thine the generations of might,—the strivers, the battlers,—the men who make Nature tame!—thine the domain of inspiration and achievement,—the larger heroisms, the vaster labors that endure, the higher knowledge, and all the witchcrafts of science!...

But in each one of us there lives a mysterious Something which is Self, yet also infinitely more than Self,—incomprehensibly multiple,—the complex total of sensations, impulses, timidities belonging to the unknown past. And the lips of the little stranger from the tropics have become all white, because that Something within her,—ghostly bequest from generations who loved the light and wondrous color of a more radiant world,—now shrinks all back about her girl's heart with fear of this pale grim North... And lo!—opening mile-wide in dream-gray majesty before us,—reaching away, through measureless mazes of masting, into remoteness all vapor-veiled,—the mighty perspective of New York harbor!...

Thou knowest it not, this gloom about us, little maiden;—'tis only a magical dusk we are entering,—only that mystic dimness in which miracles must be wrought!... See the marvellous shapes uprising,—the immensities, the astonishments! And other greater wonders thou wilt behold in a little while, when we shall have become lost to each other forever in the surging of the City's million-hearted life!... 'Tis all shadow here, thou sayest?—Ay, 'tis twilight, verily, by contrast with that glory out of which thou comest, Lys—twilight only,—but the Twilight of the Gods!... *Adié, chè!—Bon-Dié ké béni ou!*...

Appendix
Some Creole Melodies

MORE than a hundred years ago Thibault de Chanvallon expressed his astonishment at the charm and wonderful sense of musical rhythm characterizing the slave-songs and slave-dances of Martinique. The rhythmical sense of the negroes especially impressed him. "I have seen," he writes, "seven or eight hundred negroes accompanying a wedding-party to the sound of song: they would all leap up in the air and come down together;—the movement was so exact and general that the noise of their fall made but a single sound."

An almost similar phenomenon may be witnessed any Carnival season in St. Pierre,—while the Devil makes his nightly round, followed by many hundred boys clapping hands and leaping in chorus. It may also be observed in the popular malicious custom of the *pillard*, or, in creole, *piyà*. Some person whom it is deemed justifiable and safe to annoy, may suddenly find himself followed in street by a singing chorus of several hundred, all clapping hands and dancing or running in perfect time, so that all the bare feet strike the ground together. Or the *pillard-chorus* may even take up its position before the residence of the party disliked, and then proceed with its performance. An example of such a *pillard* is given further on, in the song entitled *Loéma tombé*. The improvisation by a single voice begins the *pillard*,—which in English might be rendered as follows:—

(*Single voice*)	You little children there!—you who were by the riverside!
	Tell me truly this:—Did you see Loéma fall?
	Tell me truly this:—
(*Chorus, opening*)	Did you see Loéma fall?
(*Single voice*)	Tell me truly this:—
(*Chorus*)	Did you see Loéma fall?
(*Single voice, more rapidly*)	Tell me truly this:—
(*Chorus, more quickly*)	Loéma fall?
(*Single voice*)	Tell me truly this:—

| (*Chorus*) | Loéma fall! |
| (*Single voice*) | Tell me truly this:— |

(*Chorus, always more quickly, and more loudly, all the hands clapping together like a fire of musketry*) Loéma fall! etc.

The same rhythmic element characterizes many of the games and round dances of Martinique children;—but, as a rule, I think it is perceptible that the sense of time is less developed in the colored children than in the black.

The other melodies which are given as specimens of Martinique show less of the African element,—the nearest approach to it being in *Tant sirop*; but all are probably creations of the mixed race. *Marie-Clémence* is a Carnival satire composed not more than four years ago. *To-to-to* is very old—dates back, perhaps, to the time of the *belles-affranchies*. It is seldom sung now except by survivors of the old régime: the sincerity and tenderness of the emotion that inspired it,—the old sweetness of heart and simplicity of thought,—are passing forever away.

To my friend, Henry Edward Krehbiel, the musical lecturer and critic,—at once historian and folklorist in the study of race-music,—and to Mr. Frank van der Stucken, the New York musical composer, I owe the preparation of these four melodies for voice and pianoforte. The arrangements of *To-to-to* and *Loéma tombé* are Mr. Van der Stucken's.

"TO-TO-TO."

(*Creole words.*)

MARIE–CLÉMENCE.

(Creole words.)

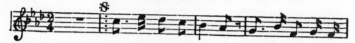

Ma - rie Clémence maudi,   La - mo-ri fritt li

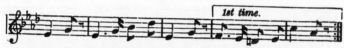

mau-di,   Collier-choux li mau-di,   Toutt baggaie li mau-di.

Toutt baggaie li mau-di.   Aie !...   La-gué moin, lagué moin,

la-gué moin! Moin ké né - yé cò moin, Moin ké né- yé

cò moin, En - ba gouôs pile ouôche là.

TANT SIROP EST DOUX.

(*Negro-French.*)

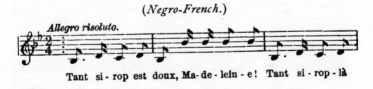

Tant si - rop est doux, Ma - de - lein - e! Tant si - rop - là

doux!   doux! Ne fai pas tant de bruit, Ma - de-leine, Ne

fai pas tant de bruit, Ma-de-leine, La mai - son n'est pas à

nous, Ma - de-leine, La mai - son n'est pas à   nous.

LOÉMA TOMBÉ.

(*Creole words.*)

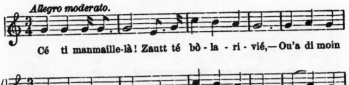

Cé ti manmaille-là! Zautt té bò - la - ri - vié,—Ou'a di moin

conm' ça: Si ouè Lo - é - ma tom - bé! Ou'a di moin conm' ça:

Ref. continued ad lib.

growing more and more rapid.

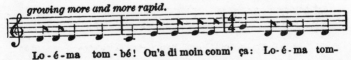

Lo - é - ma tom - bé! Ou'a di moin conm' ça: Lo - é - ma tom-

bé! Ou'a di moin conm' ça: Lo - é - ma tom - bé!